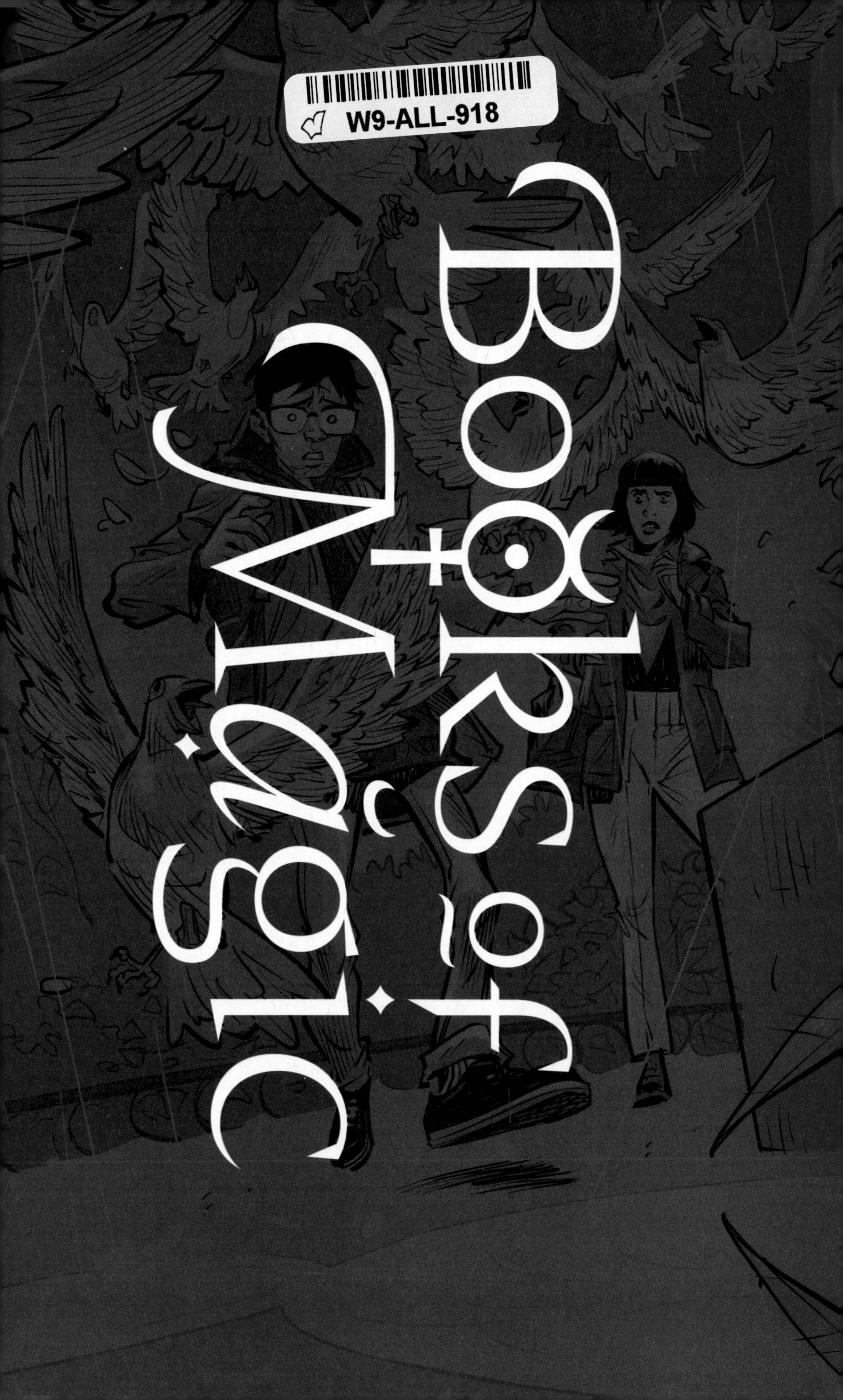
Books of Magic

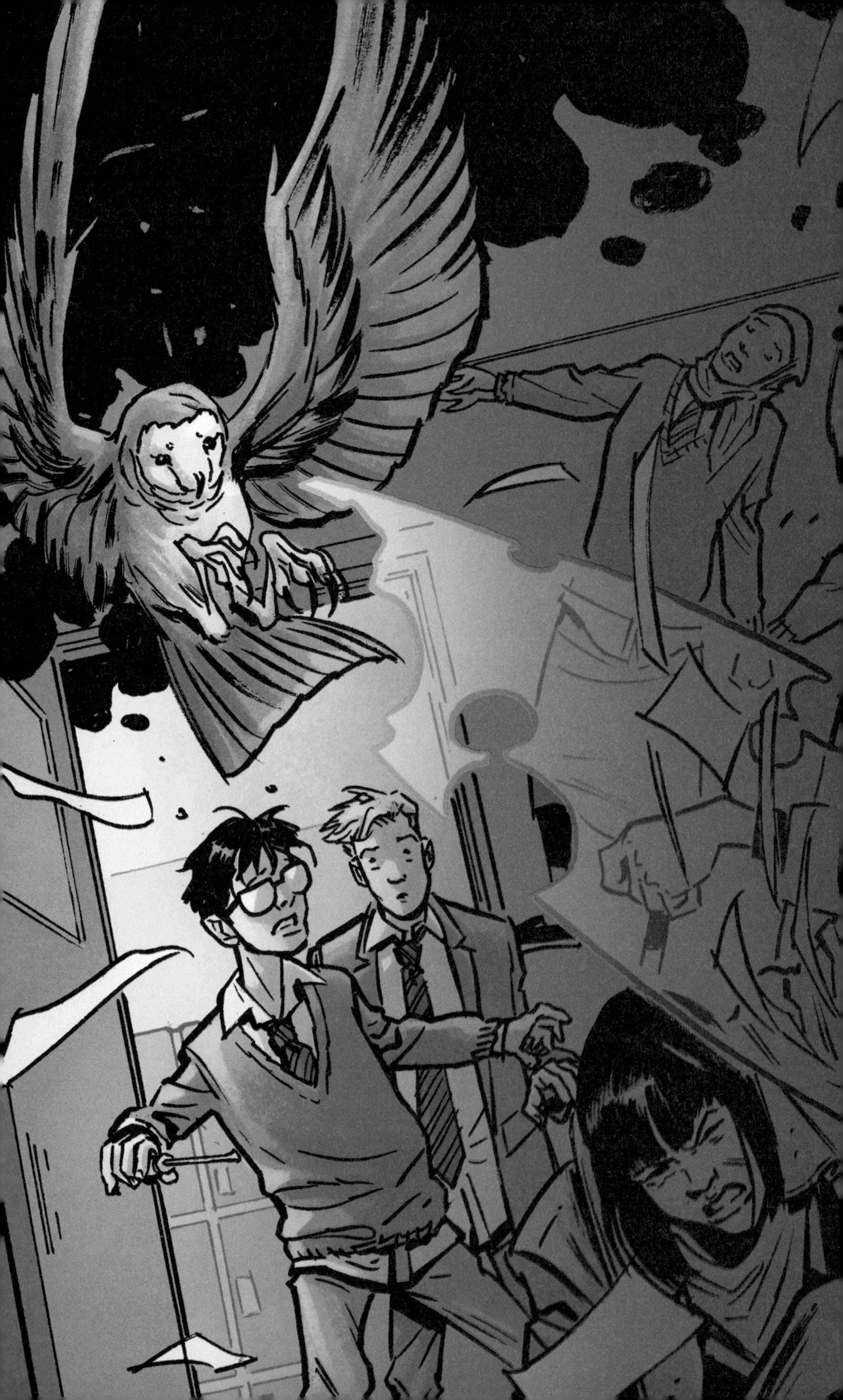

Books of Magic

VOLUME TWO

WRITTEN BY
Kat Howard

ART BY
*Tom Fowler
Brian Churilla
Craig Taillefer*

COLORS BY
*Jordan Boyd
Marissa Louise*

LETTERS BY
Todd Klein

COLLECTION
COVER ART AND
ORIGINAL SERIES
COVERS BY
Kai Carpenter

*Timothy Hunter and the Books of Magic
created by Neil Gaiman and John Bolton*

The Sandman Universe curated by Neil Gaiman

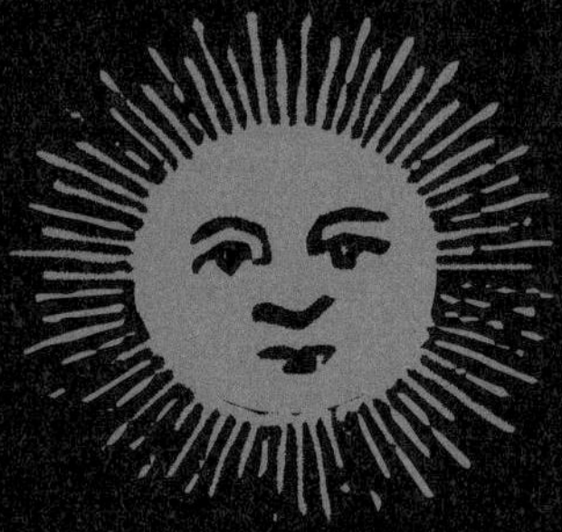

MOLLY MAHAN	
CHRIS CONROY	*Editors – Original Series*
AMEDEO TURTURRO	*Associate Editor – Original Series*
MAGGIE HOWELL	*Assistant Editor – Original Series*
JEB WOODARD	*Group Editor – Collected Editions*
SCOTT NYBAKKEN	*Editor – Collected Edition*
STEVE COOK	*Design Director – Books and Publication Design*
CHRISTY SAWYER	*Publication Production*
BOB HARRAS	*Senior VP – Editor-in-Chief, DC Comics*
MARK DOYLE	*Executive Editor, Vertigo & Black Label*
DAN DiDIO	*Publisher*
JIM LEE	*Publisher & Chief Creative Officer*
BOBBIE CHASE	*VP – New Publishing Initiatives & Talent Development*
DON FALLETTI	*VP – Manufacturing Operations & Workflow Management*
LAWRENCE GANEM	*VP – Talent Services*
ALISON GILL	*Senior VP – Manufacturing & Operations*
HANK KANALZ	*Senior VP – Publishing Strategy & Support Services*
DAN MIRON	*VP – Publishing Operations*
NICK J. NAPOLITANO	*VP – Manufacturing Administration & Design*
NANCY SPEARS	*VP – Sales*
MICHELE R. WELLS	*VP & Executive Editor, Young Reader*

BOOKS OF MAGIC VOL. 2: SECOND QUARTO

DC Comics, 2900 West Alameda Ave., Burbank, CA 91505
Printed by LSC Communications, Owensville, MO, USA. 1/3/20. First Printing.
ISBN: 978-1-4012-9904-0

Library of Congress Cataloging-in-Publication Data is available.

PEFC Certified
This product is from sustainably managed forests and controlled sources
PEFC
PEFC/29-31-337
www.pefc.org

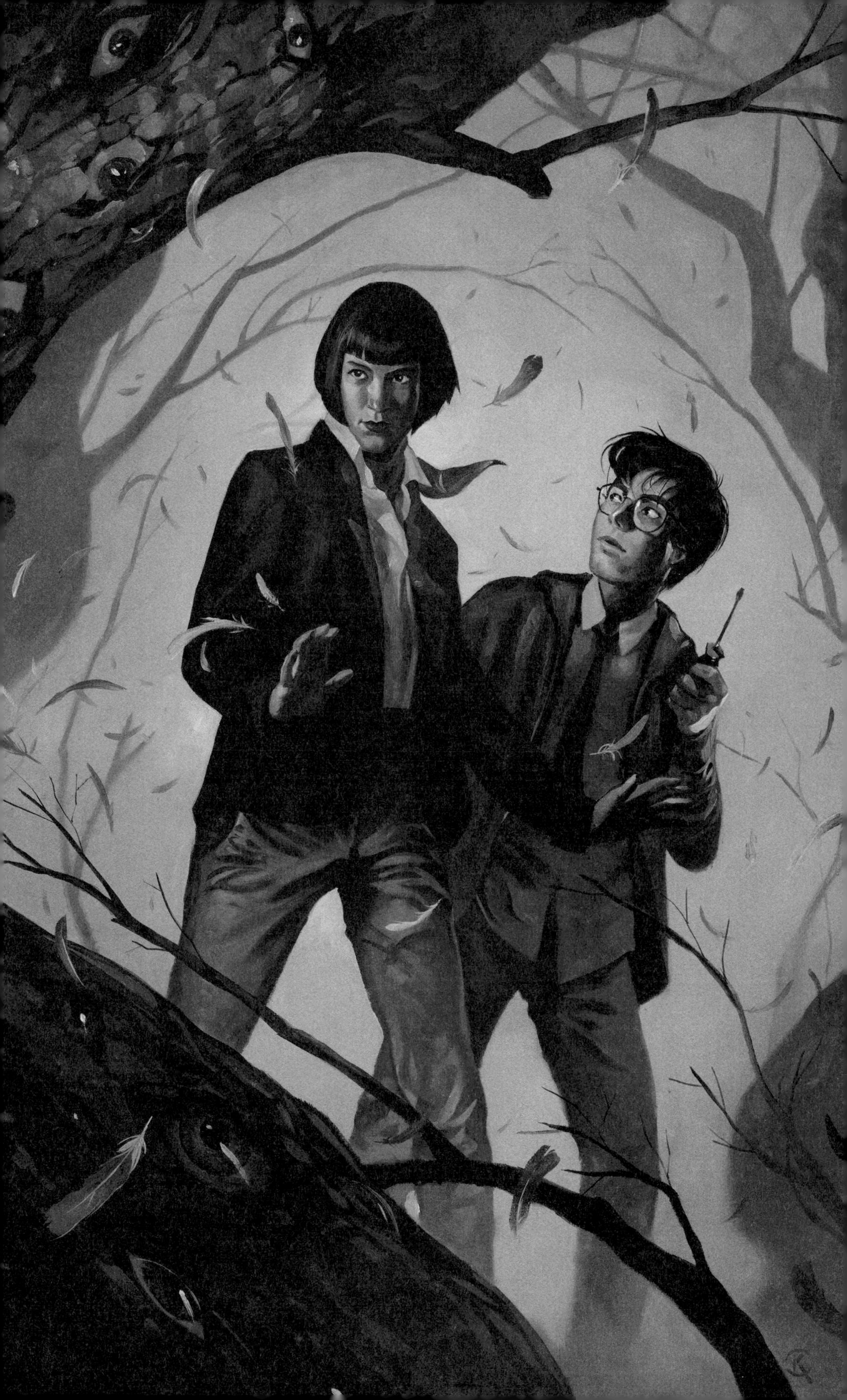

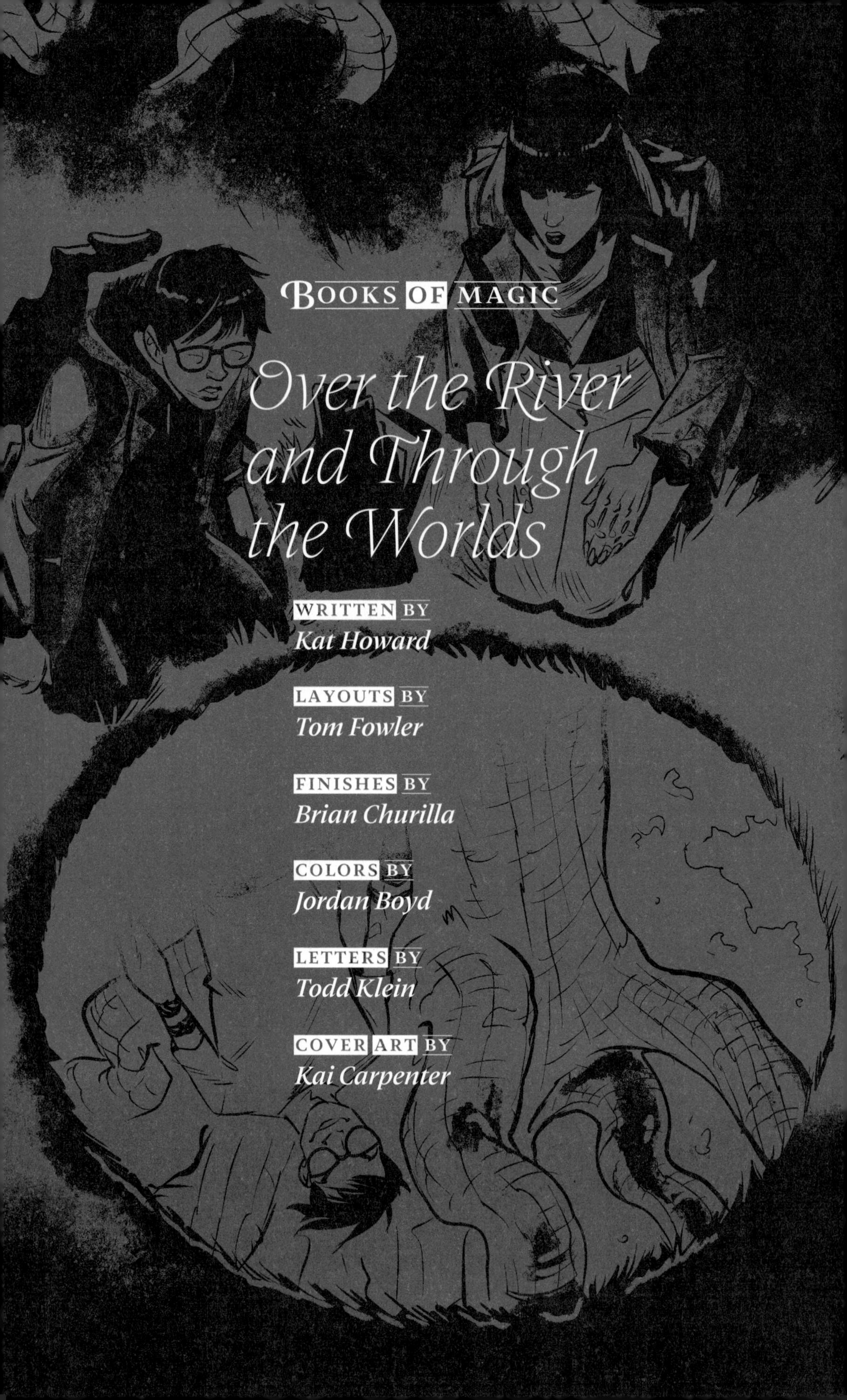

BOOKS OF MAGIC

Over the River and Through the Worlds

WRITTEN BY
Kat Howard

LAYOUTS BY
Tom Fowler

FINISHES BY
Brian Churilla

COLORS BY
Jordan Boyd

LETTERS BY
Todd Klein

COVER ART BY
Kai Carpenter

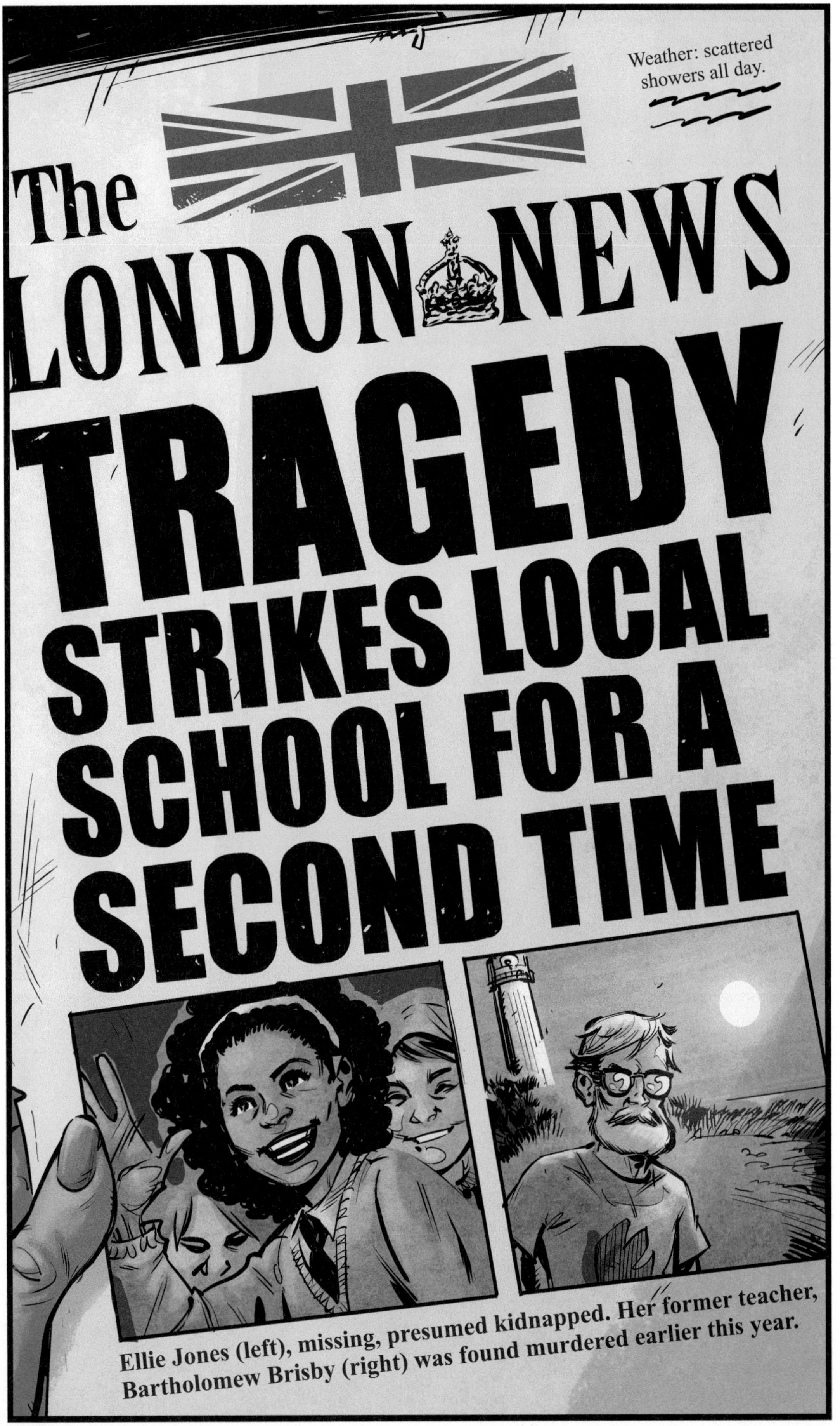
Weather: scattered showers all day.
The LONDON NEWS
TRAGEDY STRIKES LOCAL SCHOOL FOR A SECOND TIME
Ellie Jones (left), missing, presumed kidnapped. Her former teacher, Bartholomew Brisby (right) was found murdered earlier this year.

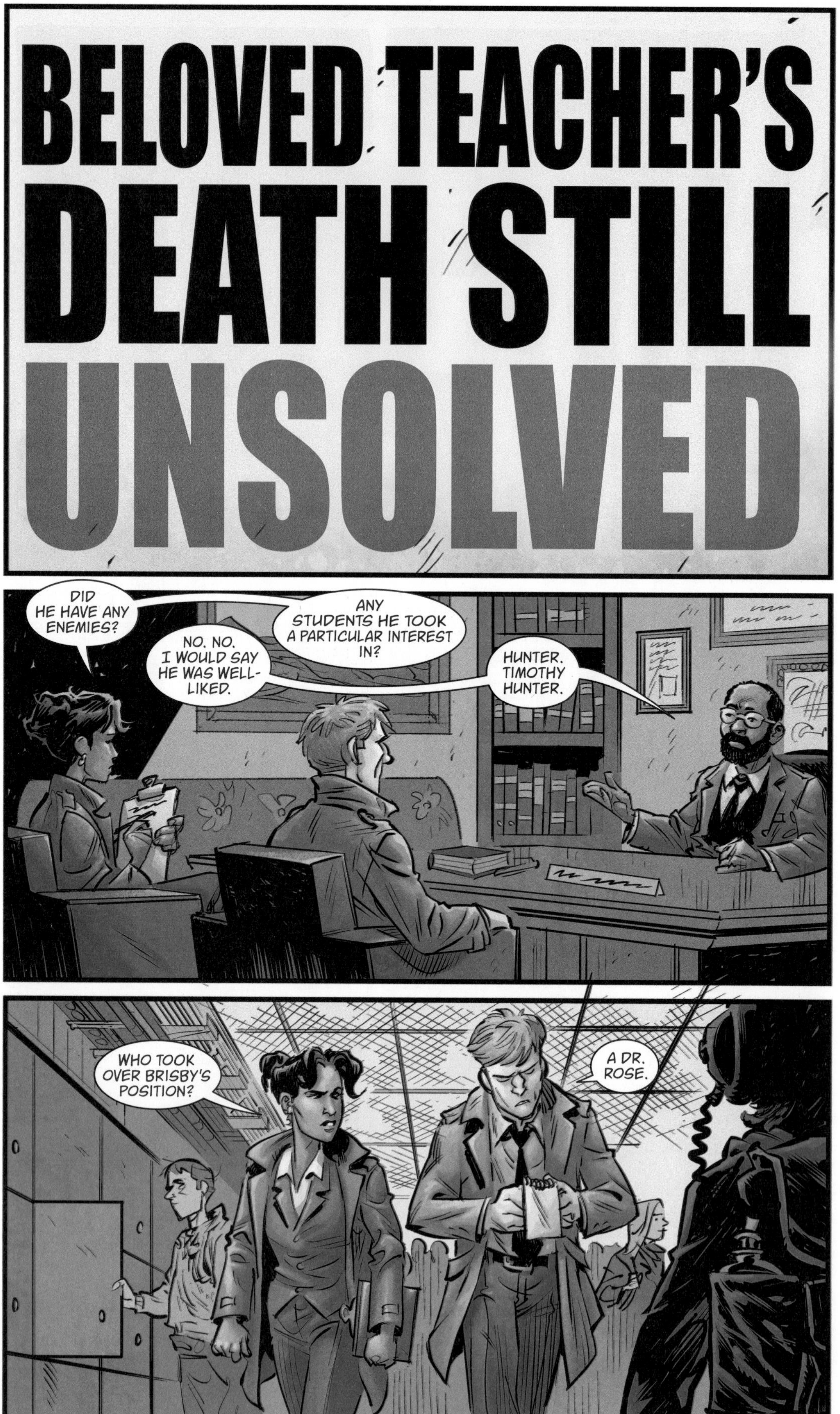
BELOVED TEACHER'S DEATH STILL UNSOLVED
DID HE HAVE ANY ENEMIES?
NO. NO. I WOULD SAY HE WAS WELL-LIKED.
ANY STUDENTS HE TOOK A PARTICULAR INTEREST IN?
HUNTER. TIMOTHY HUNTER.
WHO TOOK OVER BRISBY'S POSITION?
A DR. ROSE.

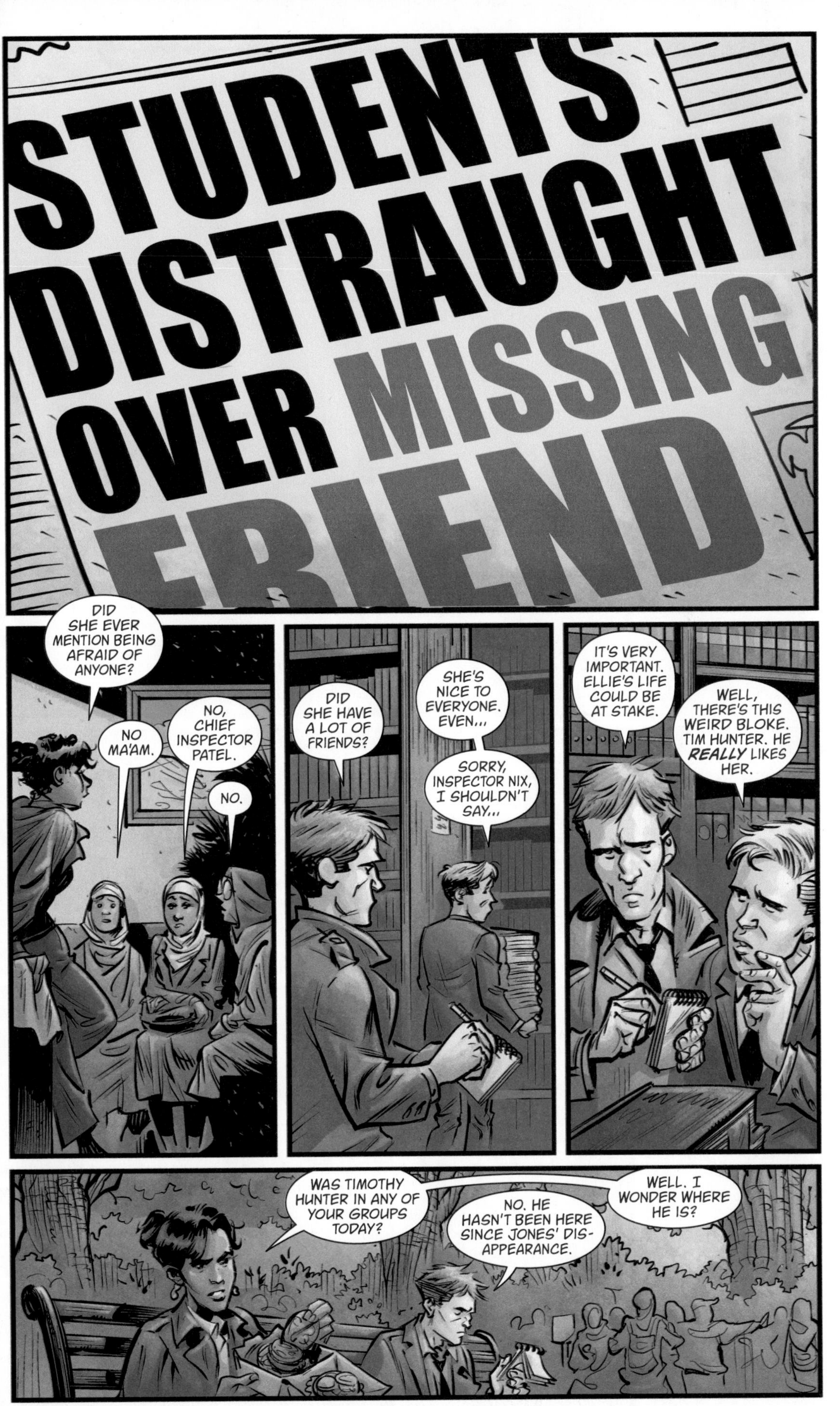
STUDENTS DISTRAUGHT OVER MISSING FRIEND
DID SHE EVER MENTION BEING AFRAID OF ANYONE?
NO MA'AM.
NO, CHIEF INSPECTOR PATEL.
NO.
DID SHE HAVE A LOT OF FRIENDS?
SHE'S NICE TO EVERYONE. EVEN...
SORRY, INSPECTOR NIX, I SHOULDN'T SAY...
IT'S VERY IMPORTANT. ELLIE'S LIFE COULD BE AT STAKE.
WELL, THERE'S THIS WEIRD BLOKE. TIM HUNTER. HE REALLY LIKES HER.
WAS TIMOTHY HUNTER IN ANY OF YOUR GROUPS TODAY?
NO. HE HASN'T BEEN HERE SINCE JONES' DIS-APPEARANCE.
WELL. I WONDER WHERE HE IS?

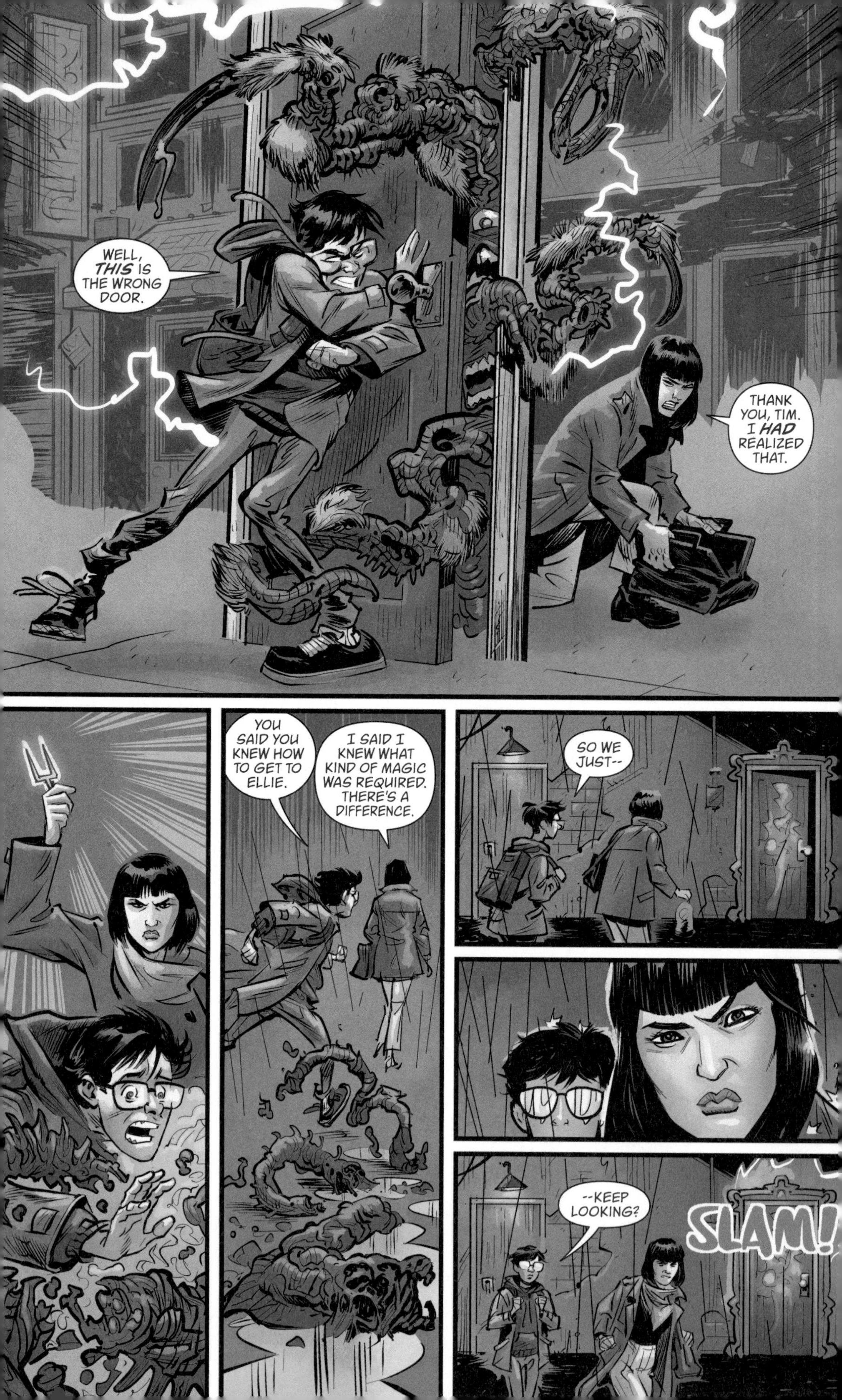
WELL, THIS IS THE WRONG DOOR.
THANK YOU, TIM. I HAD REALIZED THAT.
YOU SAID YOU KNEW HOW TO GET TO ELLIE.
I SAID I KNEW WHAT KIND OF MAGIC WAS REQUIRED. THERE'S A DIFFERENCE.
SO WE JUST--
--KEEP LOOKING?
SLAM!

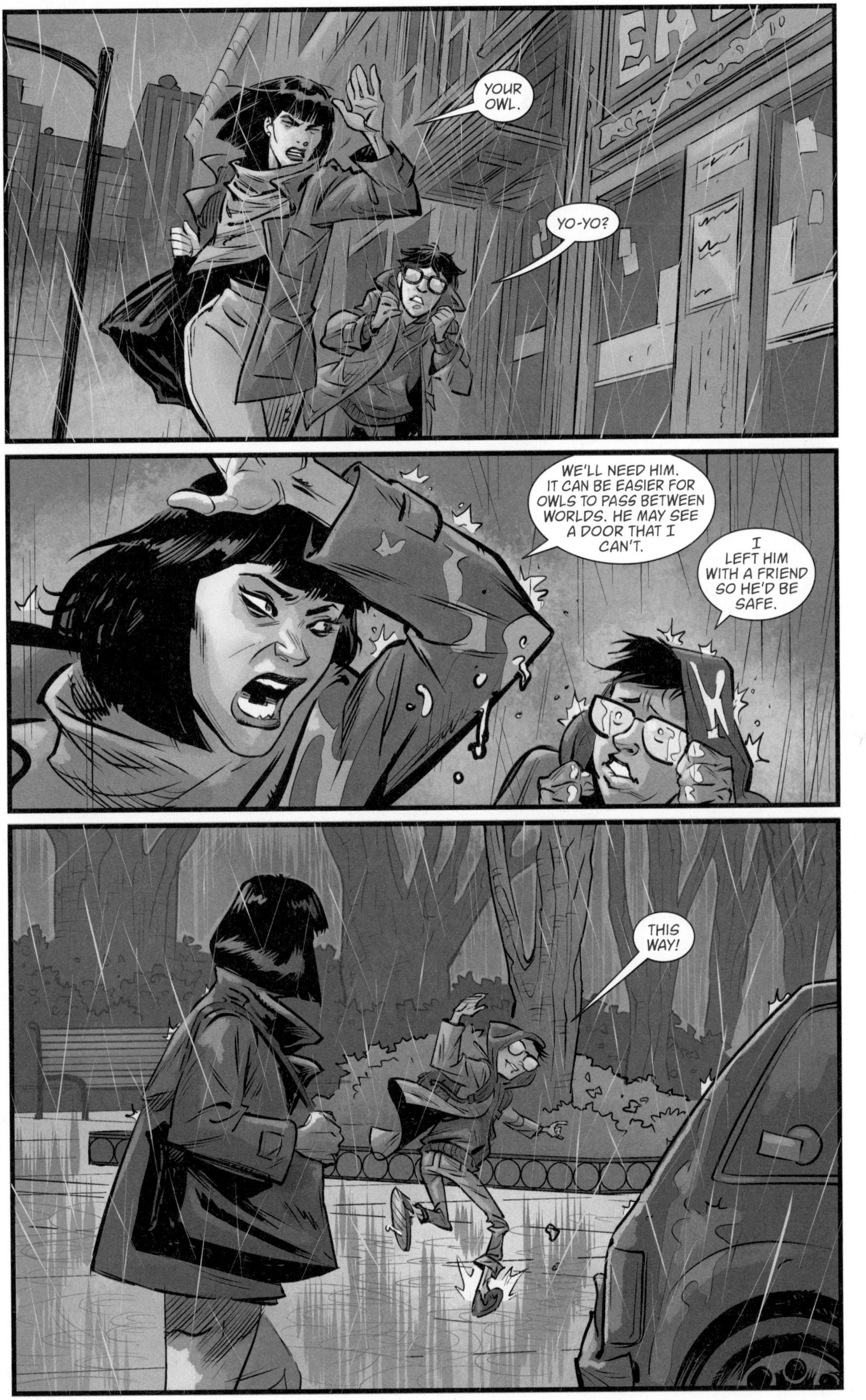
YOUR OWL.
YO-YO?
WE'LL NEED HIM. IT CAN BE EASIER FOR OWLS TO PASS BETWEEN WORLDS. HE MAY SEE A DOOR THAT I CAN'T.
I LEFT HIM WITH A FRIEND SO HE'D BE SAFE.
THIS WAY!

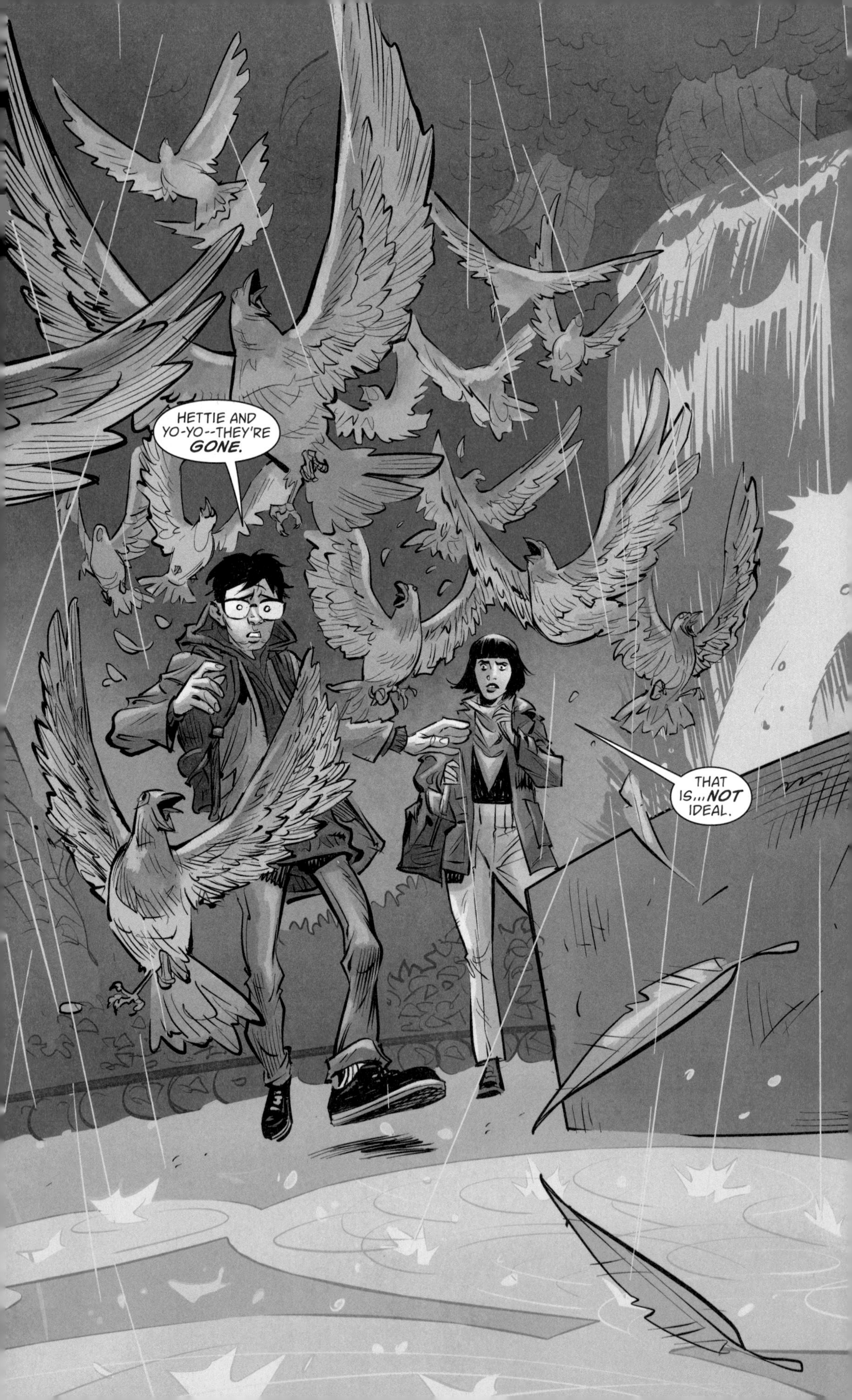
HETTIE AND YO-YO--THEY'RE ***GONE.***
THAT IS...***NOT*** IDEAL.

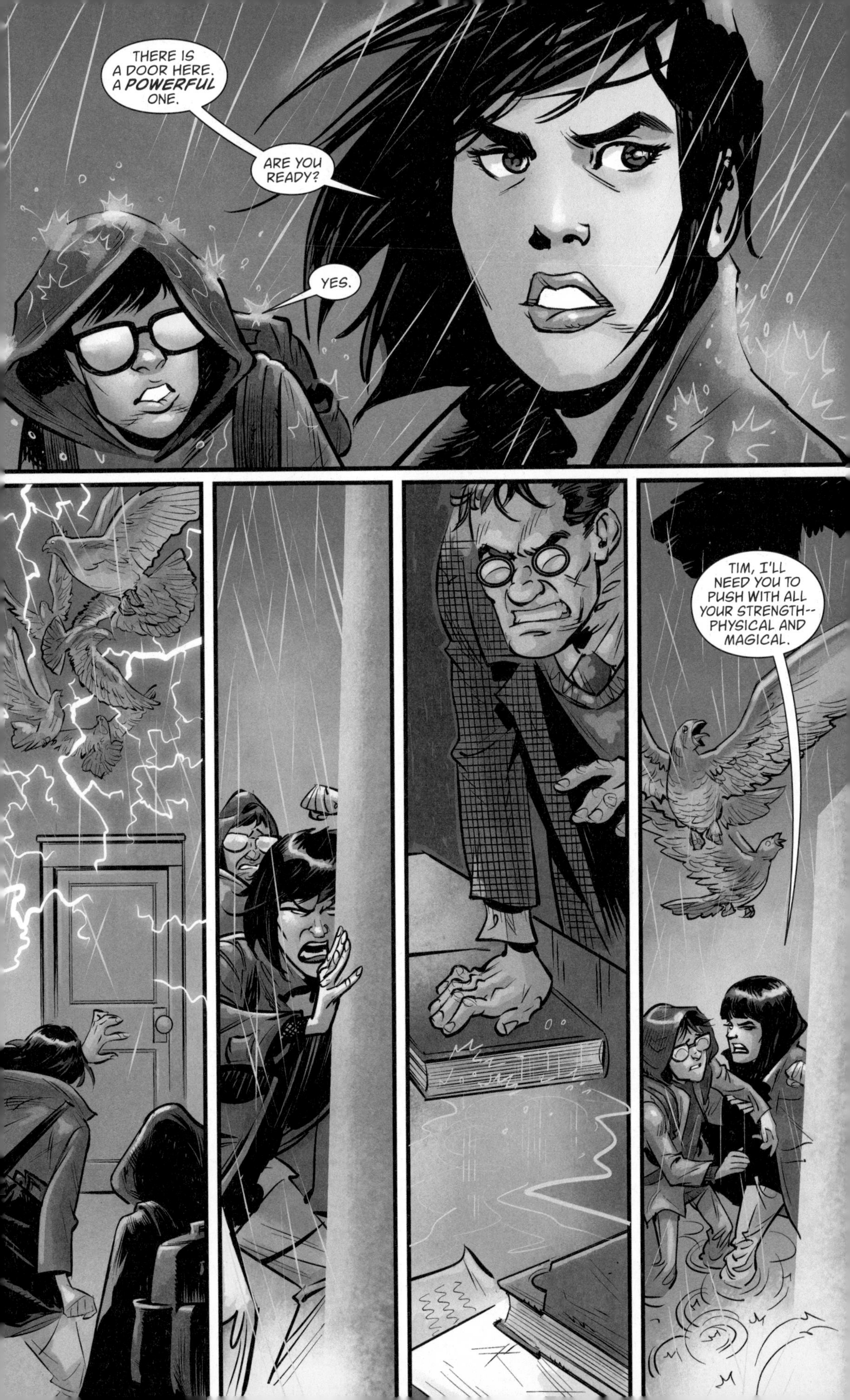
THERE IS A DOOR HERE. A **POWERFUL** ONE.
ARE YOU READY?
YES.
TIM, I'LL NEED YOU TO PUSH WITH ALL YOUR STRENGTH-- PHYSICAL AND MAGICAL.

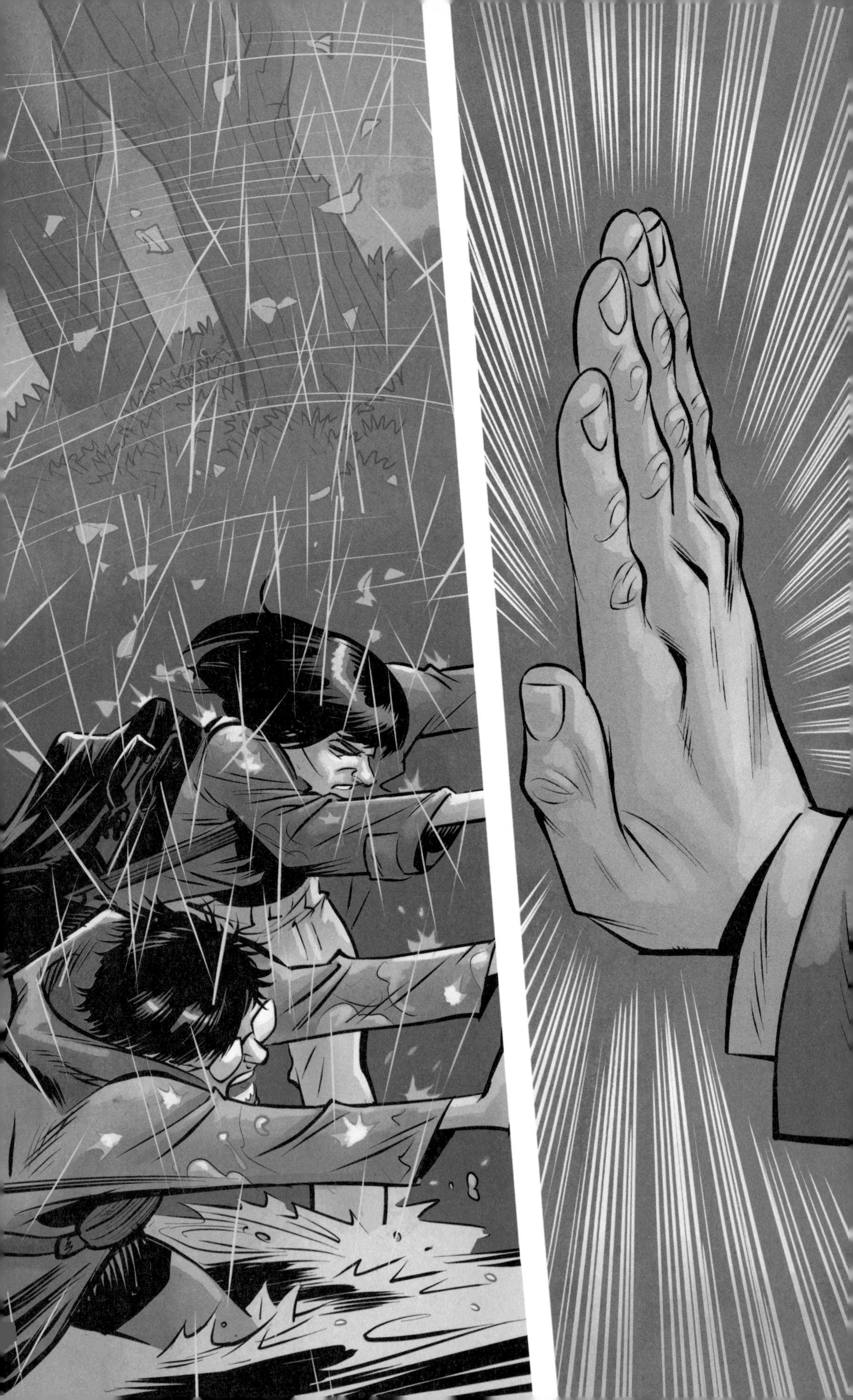

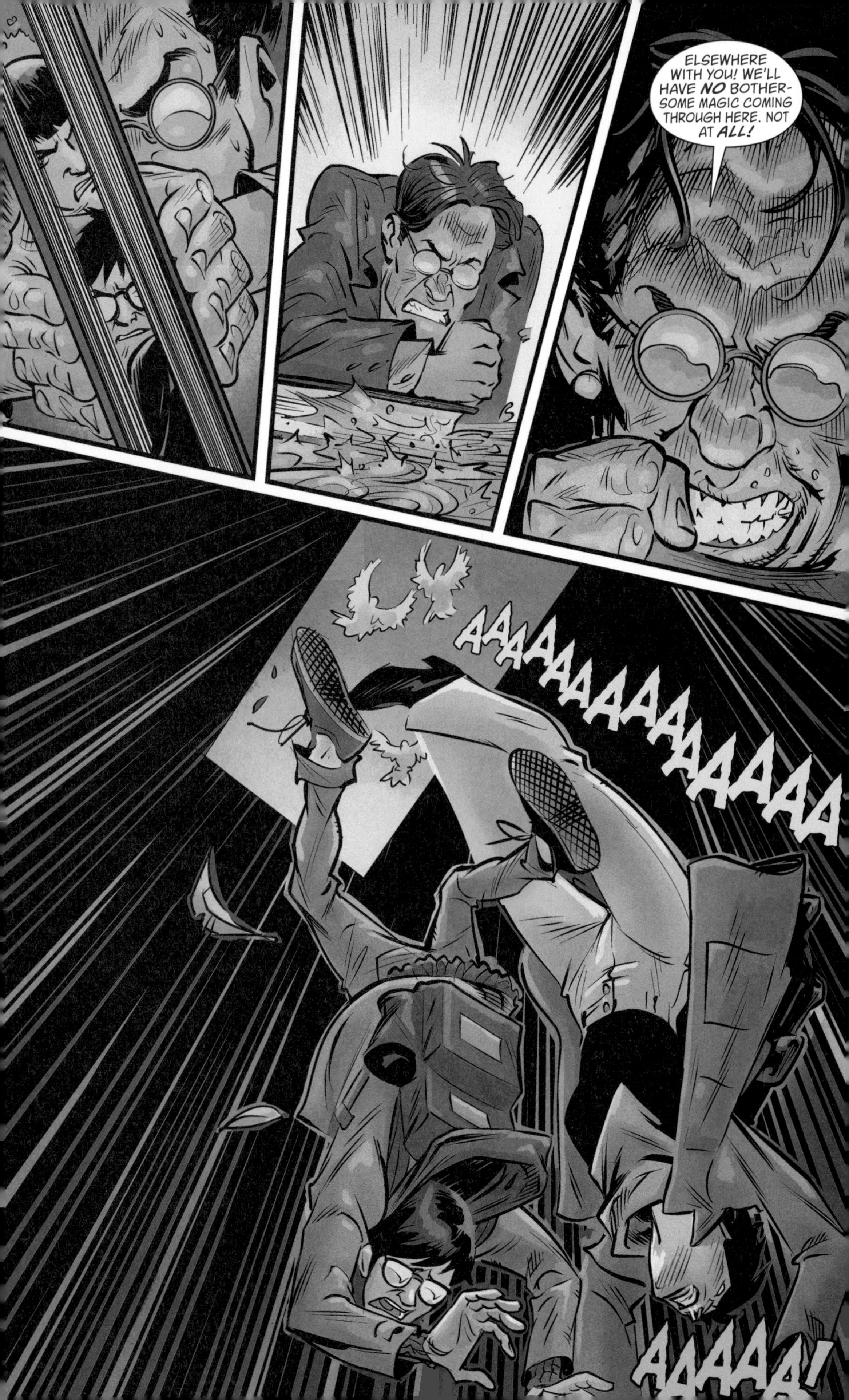
ELSEWHERE WITH YOU! WE'LL HAVE NO BOTHER-SOME MAGIC COMING THROUGH HERE. NOT AT ALL!
AAAAAAAAAAAAAAAAAA
AAAAA!

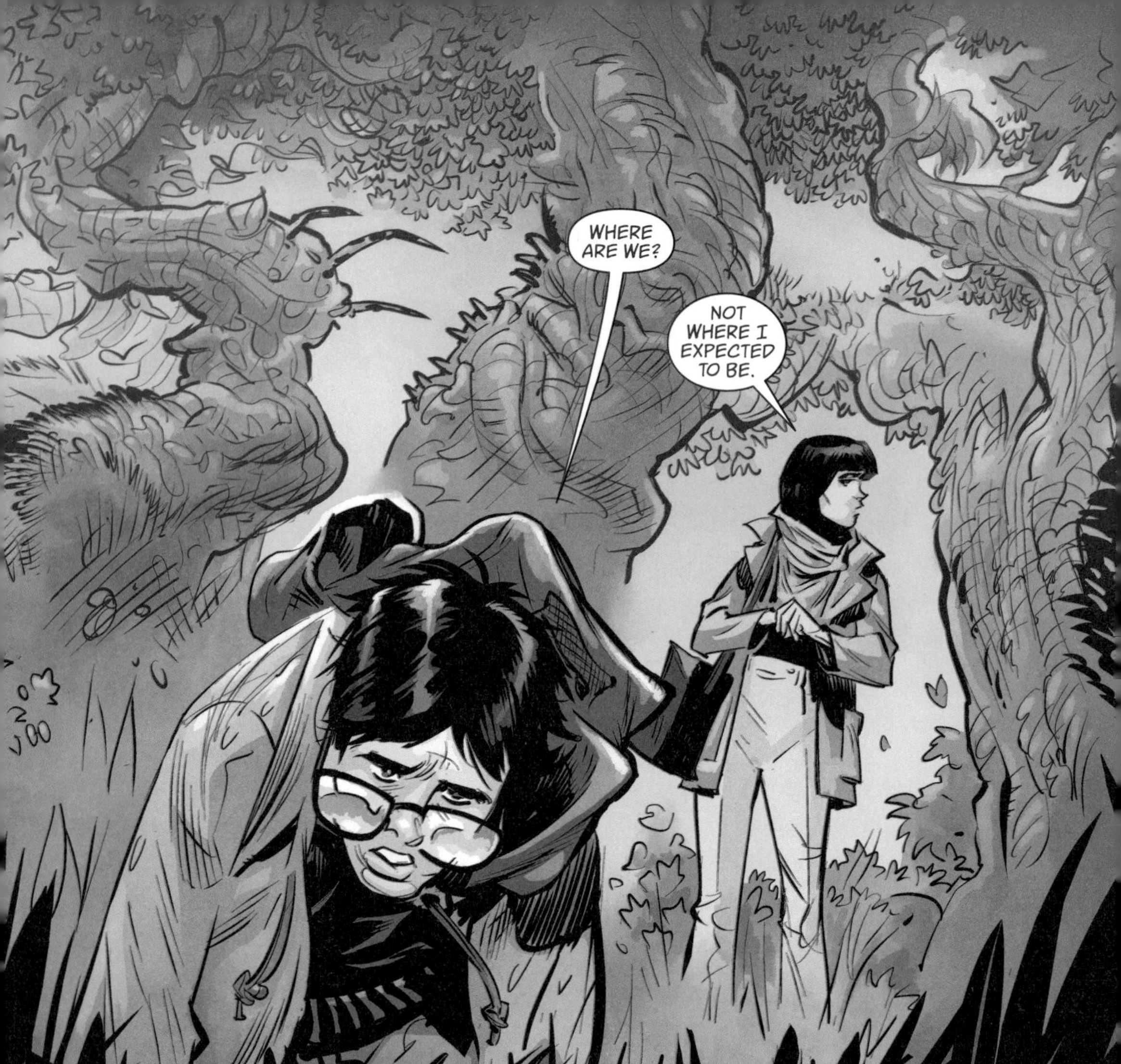
WHERE ARE WE?
NOT WHERE I EXPECTED TO BE.

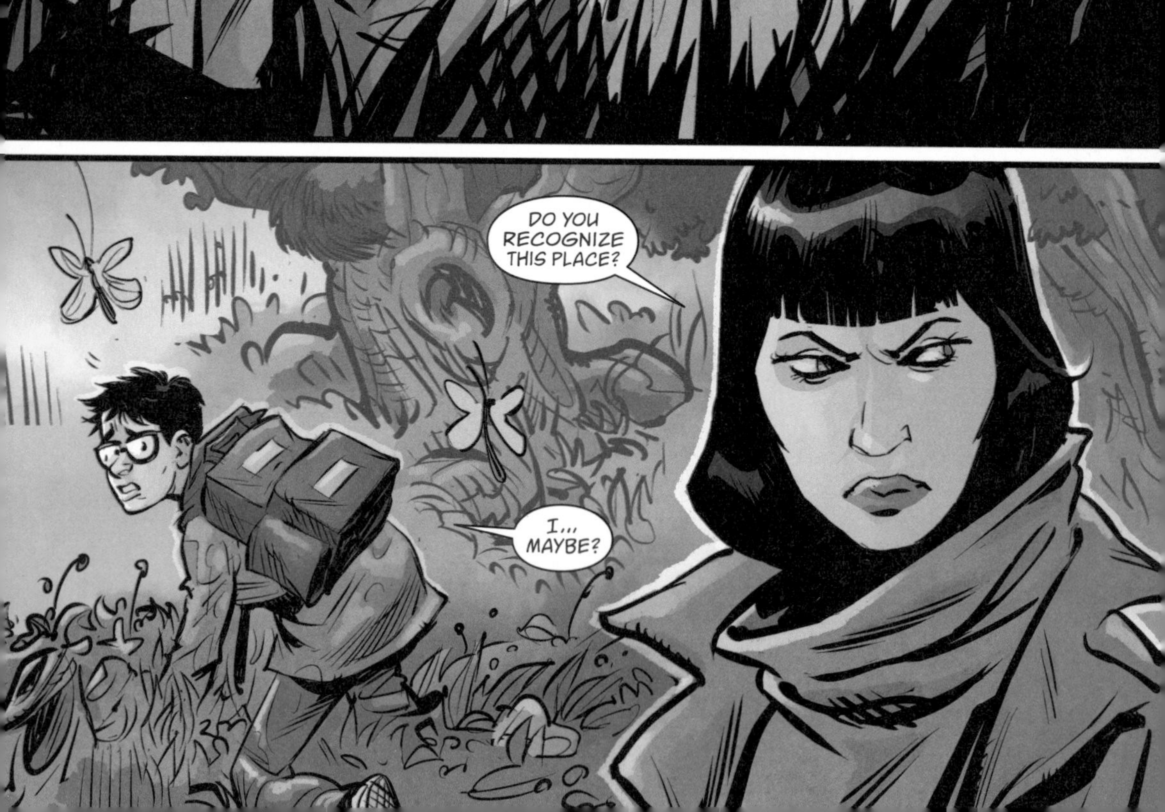
DO YOU RECOGNIZE THIS PLACE?
I... MAYBE?

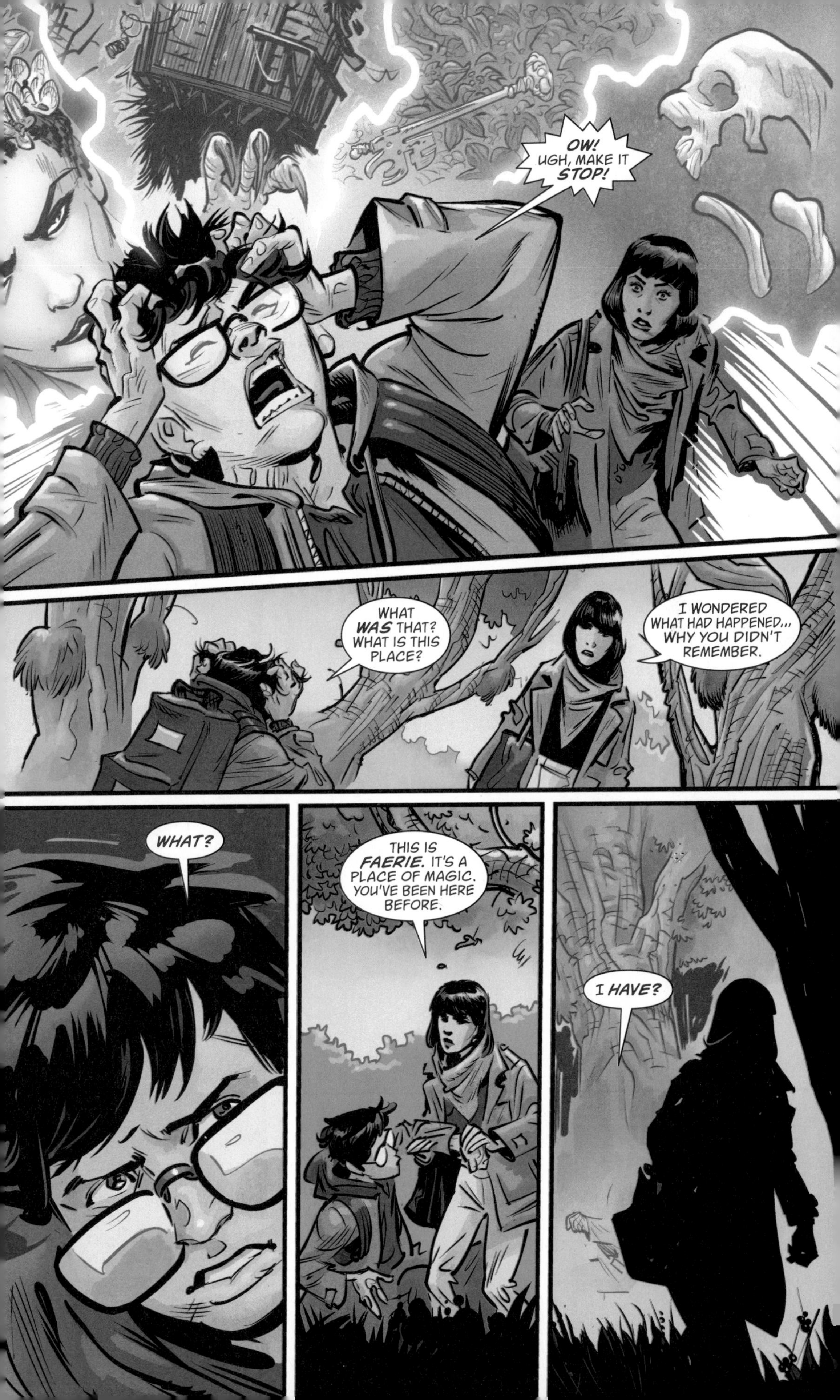
OW! UGH, MAKE IT STOP!
WHAT WAS THAT? WHAT IS THIS PLACE?
I WONDERED WHAT HAD HAPPENED... WHY YOU DIDN'T REMEMBER.
WHAT?
THIS IS FAERIE. IT'S A PLACE OF MAGIC. YOU'VE BEEN HERE BEFORE.
I HAVE?

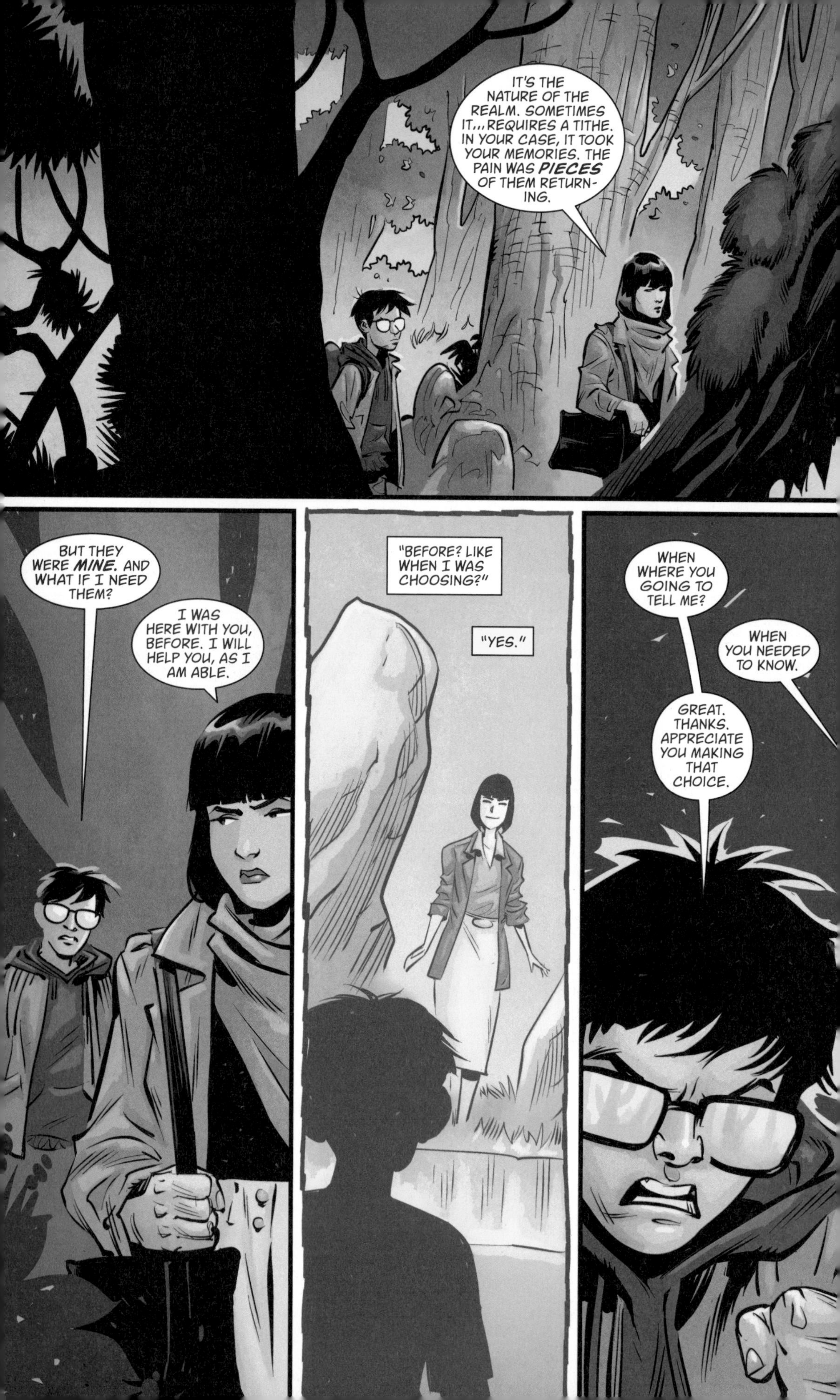
IT'S THE NATURE OF THE REALM. SOMETIMES IT...REQUIRES A TITHE. IN YOUR CASE, IT TOOK YOUR MEMORIES. THE PAIN WAS *PIECES* OF THEM RETURN-ING.
BUT THEY WERE *MINE.* AND WHAT IF I NEED THEM?
I WAS HERE WITH YOU, BEFORE. I WILL HELP YOU, AS I AM ABLE.
"BEFORE? LIKE WHEN I WAS CHOOSING?"
"YES."
WHEN WHERE YOU GOING TO TELL ME?
WHEN YOU NEEDED TO KNOW.
GREAT. THANKS. APPRECIATE YOU MAKING THAT CHOICE.

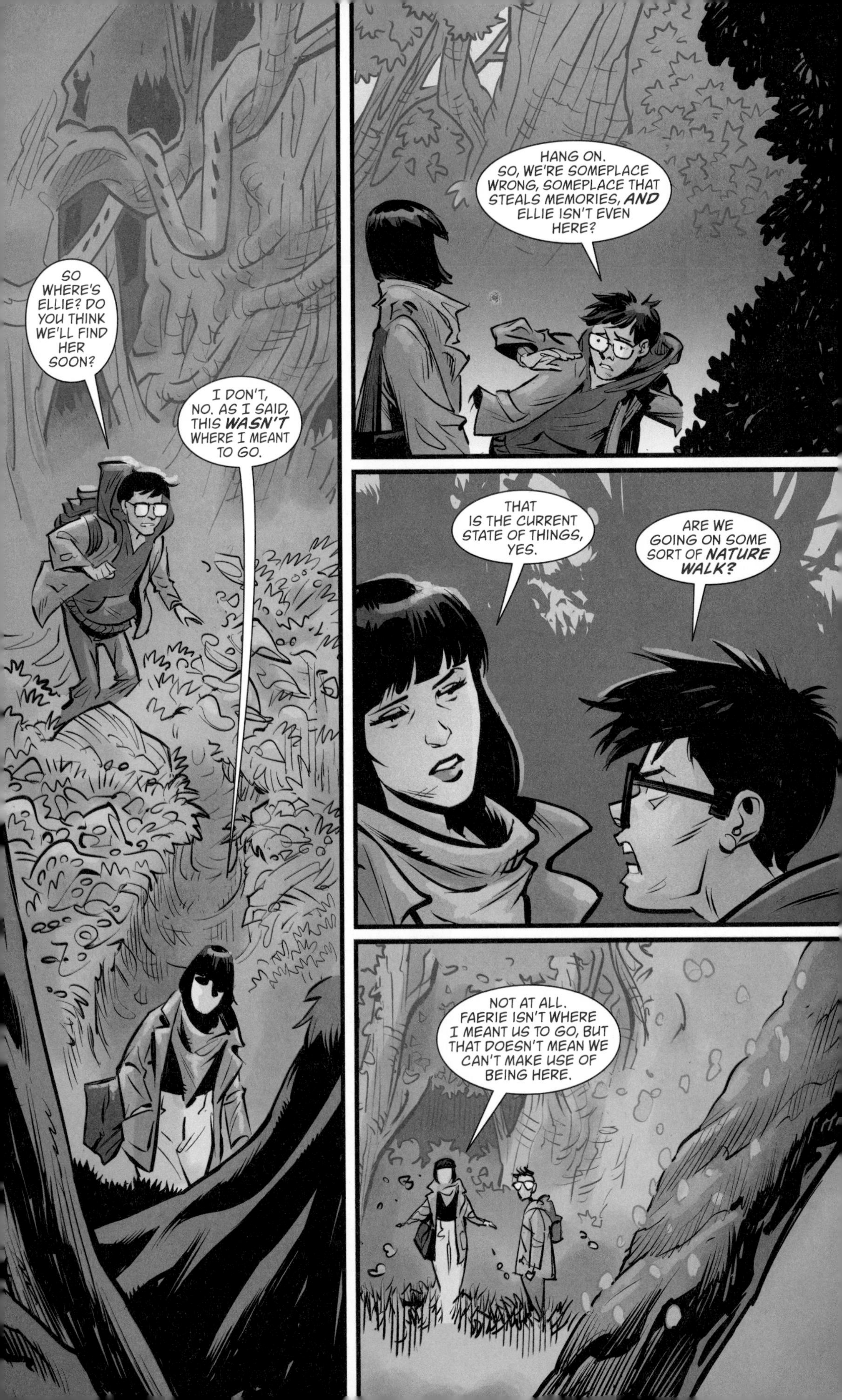
SO WHERE'S ELLIE? DO YOU THINK WE'LL FIND HER SOON?
I DON'T, NO. AS I SAID, THIS **WASN'T** WHERE I MEANT TO GO.
HANG ON. SO, WE'RE SOMEPLACE WRONG, SOMEPLACE THAT STEALS MEMORIES, **AND** ELLIE ISN'T EVEN HERE?
THAT IS THE CURRENT STATE OF THINGS, YES.
ARE WE GOING ON SOME SORT OF **NATURE WALK?**
NOT AT ALL. FAERIE ISN'T WHERE I MEANT US TO GO, BUT THAT DOESN'T MEAN WE CAN'T MAKE USE OF BEING HERE.

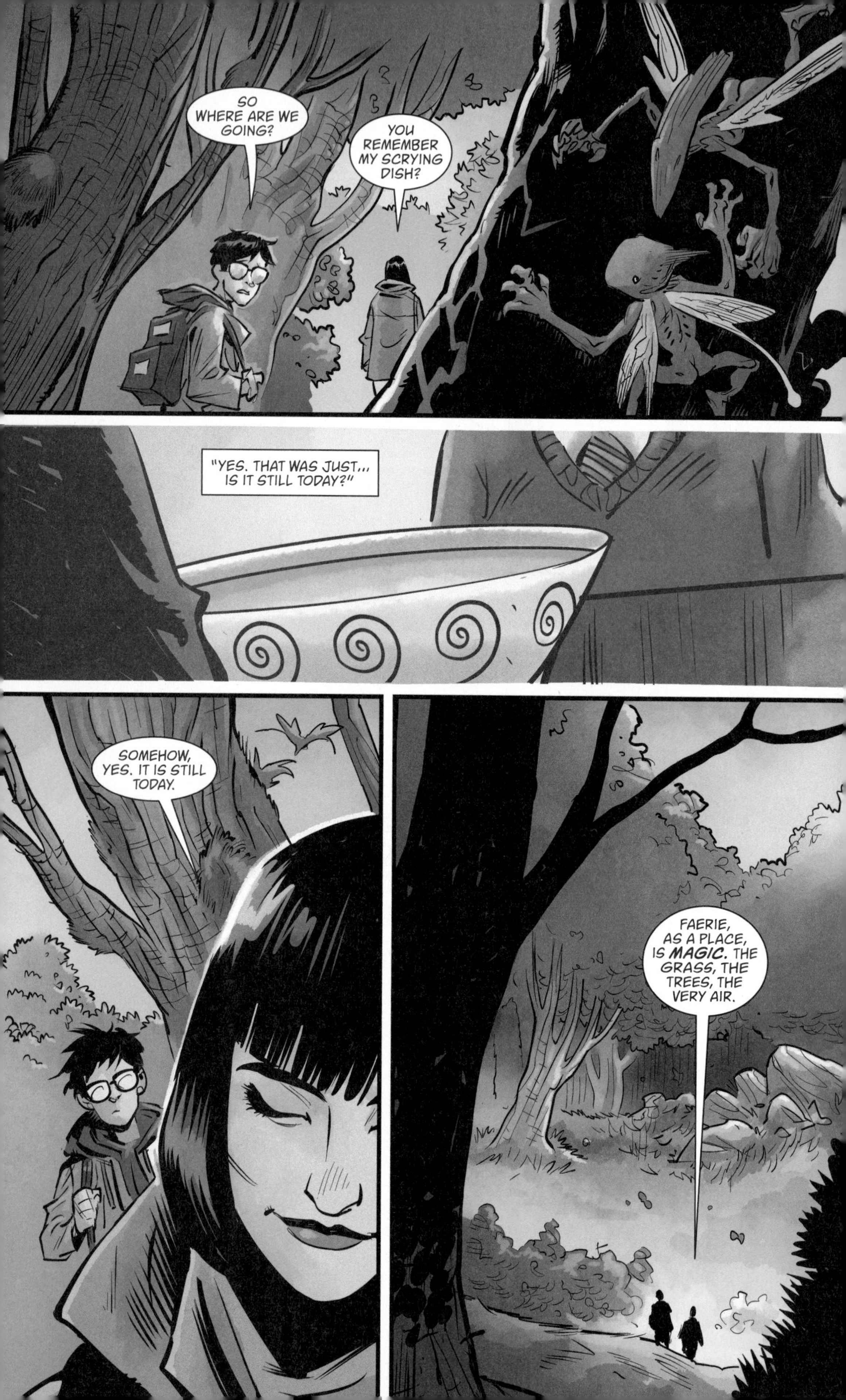
SO WHERE ARE WE GOING?
YOU REMEMBER MY SCRYING DISH?
"YES. THAT WAS JUST... IS IT STILL TODAY?"
SOMEHOW, YES. IT IS STILL TODAY.
FAERIE, AS A PLACE, IS MAGIC. THE GRASS, THE TREES, THE VERY AIR.

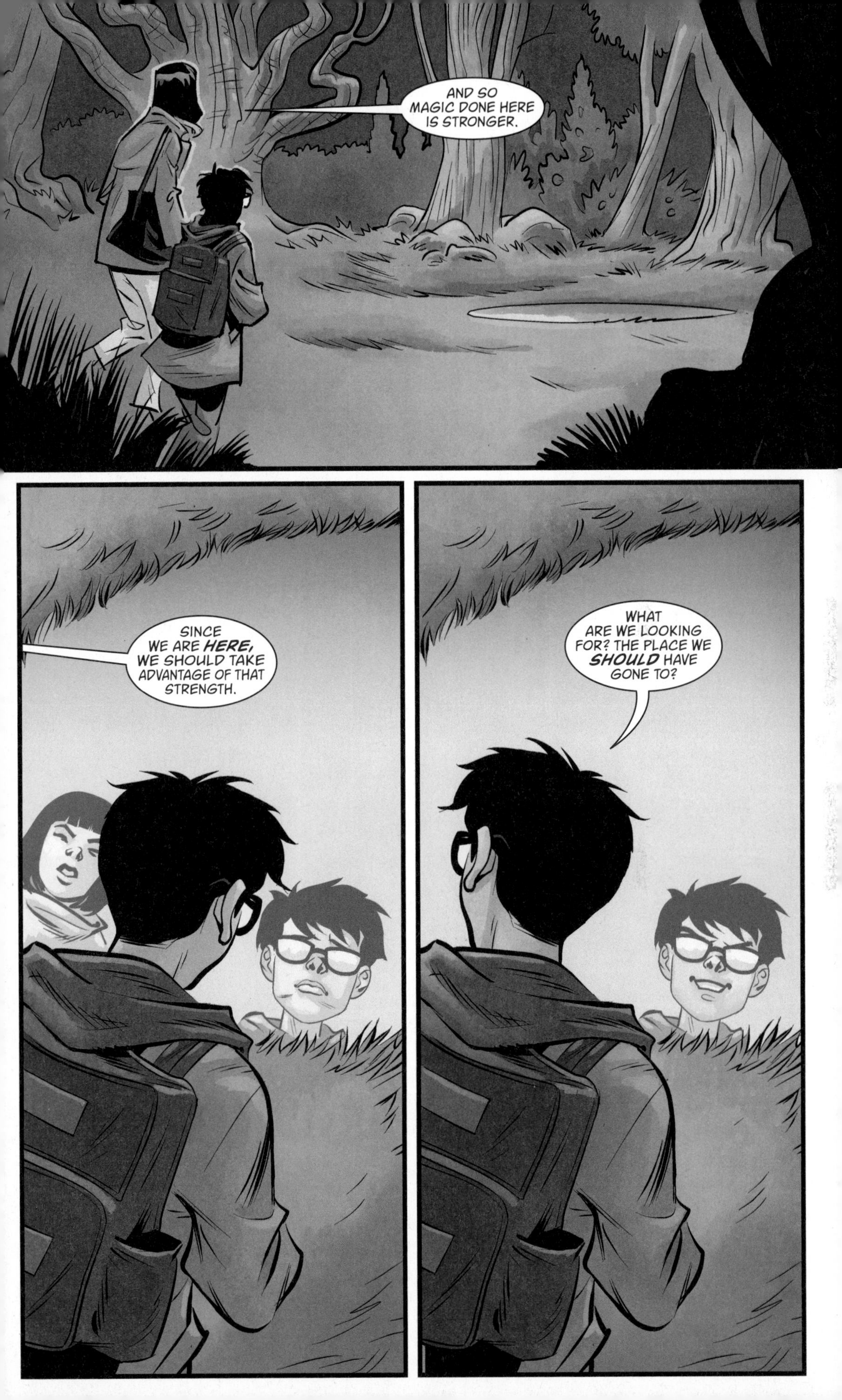
AND SO MAGIC DONE HERE IS STRONGER.
SINCE WE ARE HERE, WE SHOULD TAKE ADVANTAGE OF THAT STRENGTH.
WHAT ARE WE LOOKING FOR? THE PLACE WE SHOULD HAVE GONE TO?

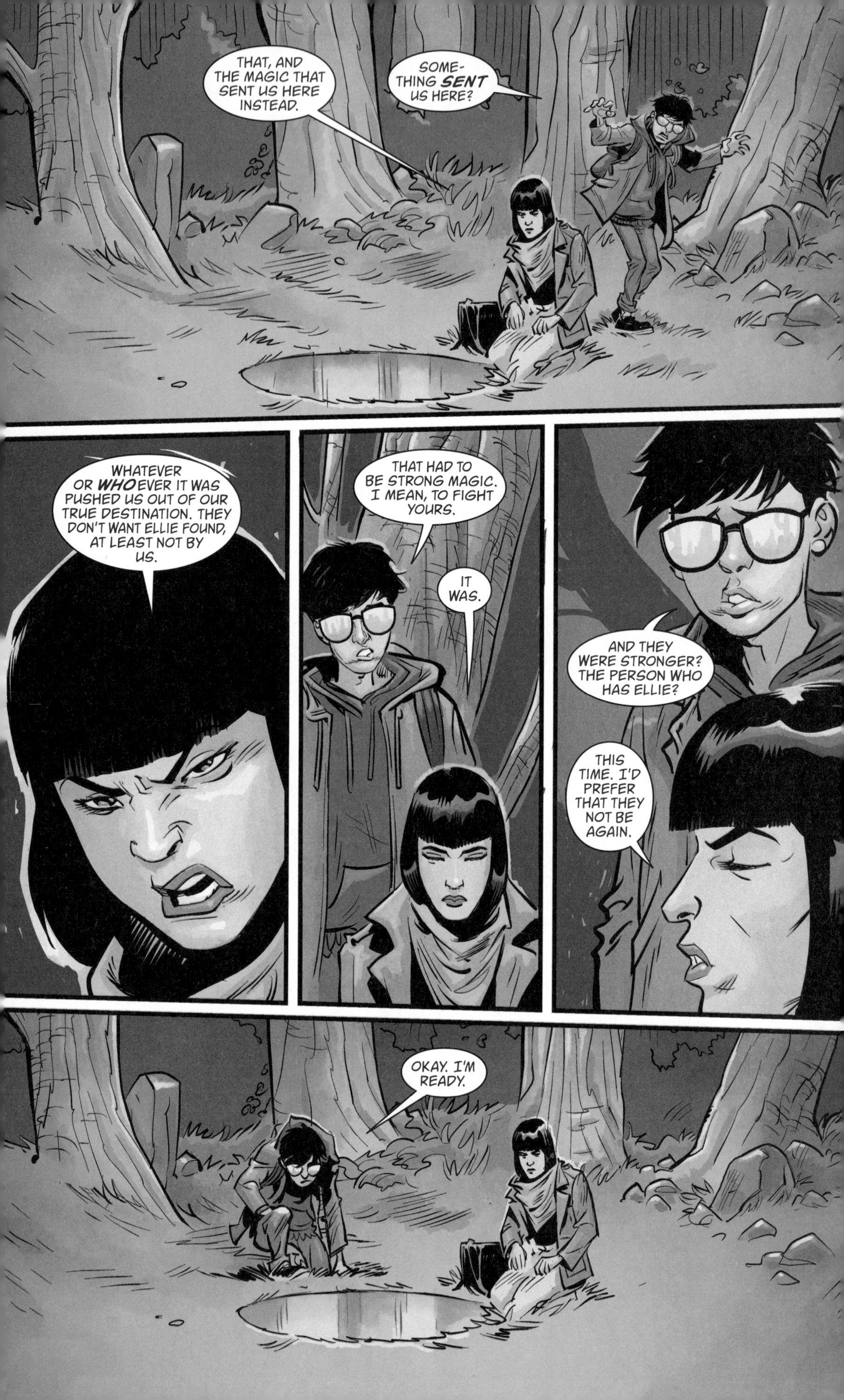
THAT, AND THE MAGIC THAT SENT US HERE INSTEAD.
SOME-THING SENT US HERE?
WHATEVER OR WHOEVER IT WAS PUSHED US OUT OF OUR TRUE DESTINATION. THEY DON'T WANT ELLIE FOUND, AT LEAST NOT BY US.
THAT HAD TO BE STRONG MAGIC. I MEAN, TO FIGHT YOURS.
IT WAS.
AND THEY WERE STRONGER? THE PERSON WHO HAS ELLIE?
THIS TIME. I'D PREFER THAT THEY NOT BE AGAIN.
OKAY. I'M READY.

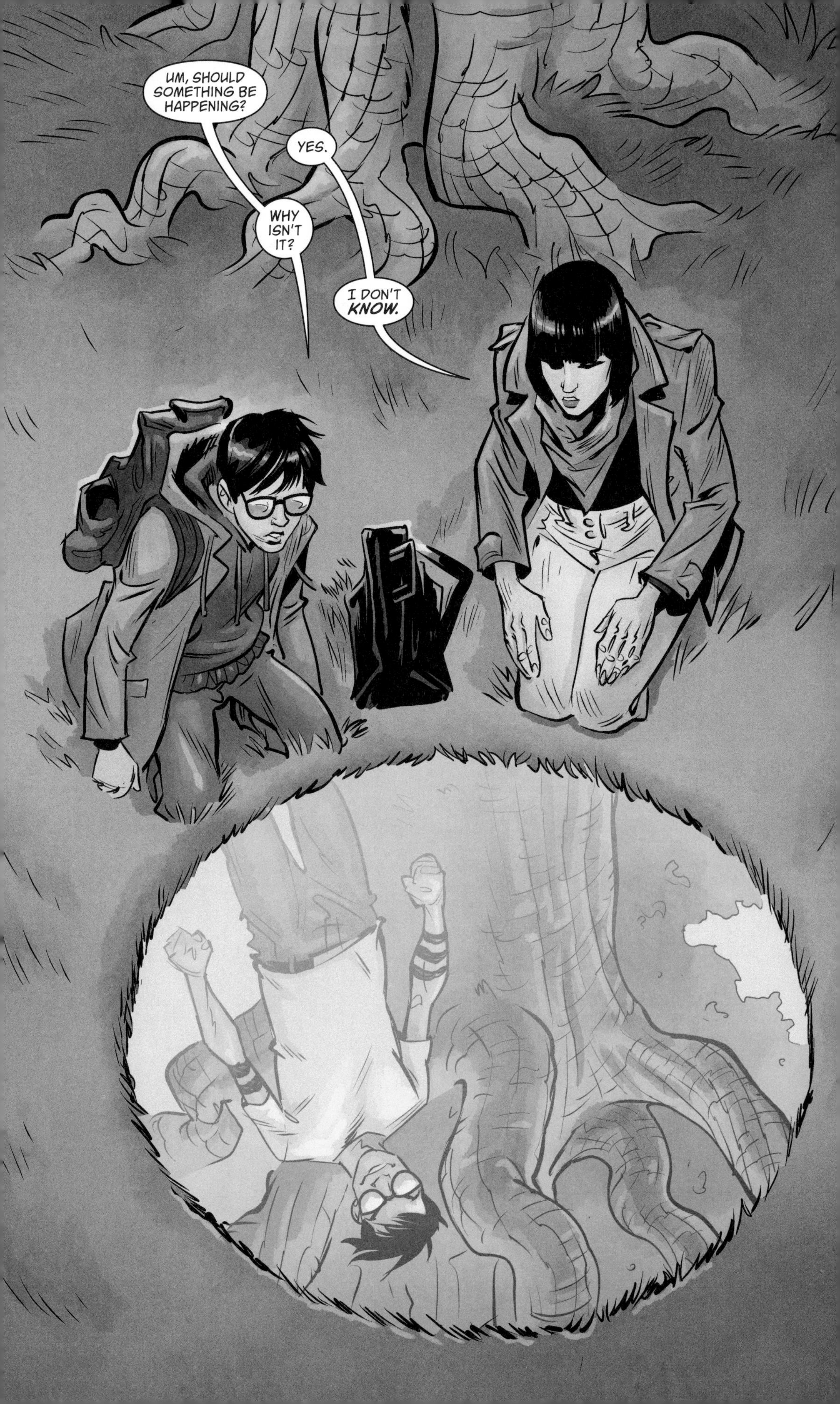
UM, SHOULD SOMETHING BE HAPPENING?
YES.
WHY ISN'T IT?
I DON'T *KNOW.*

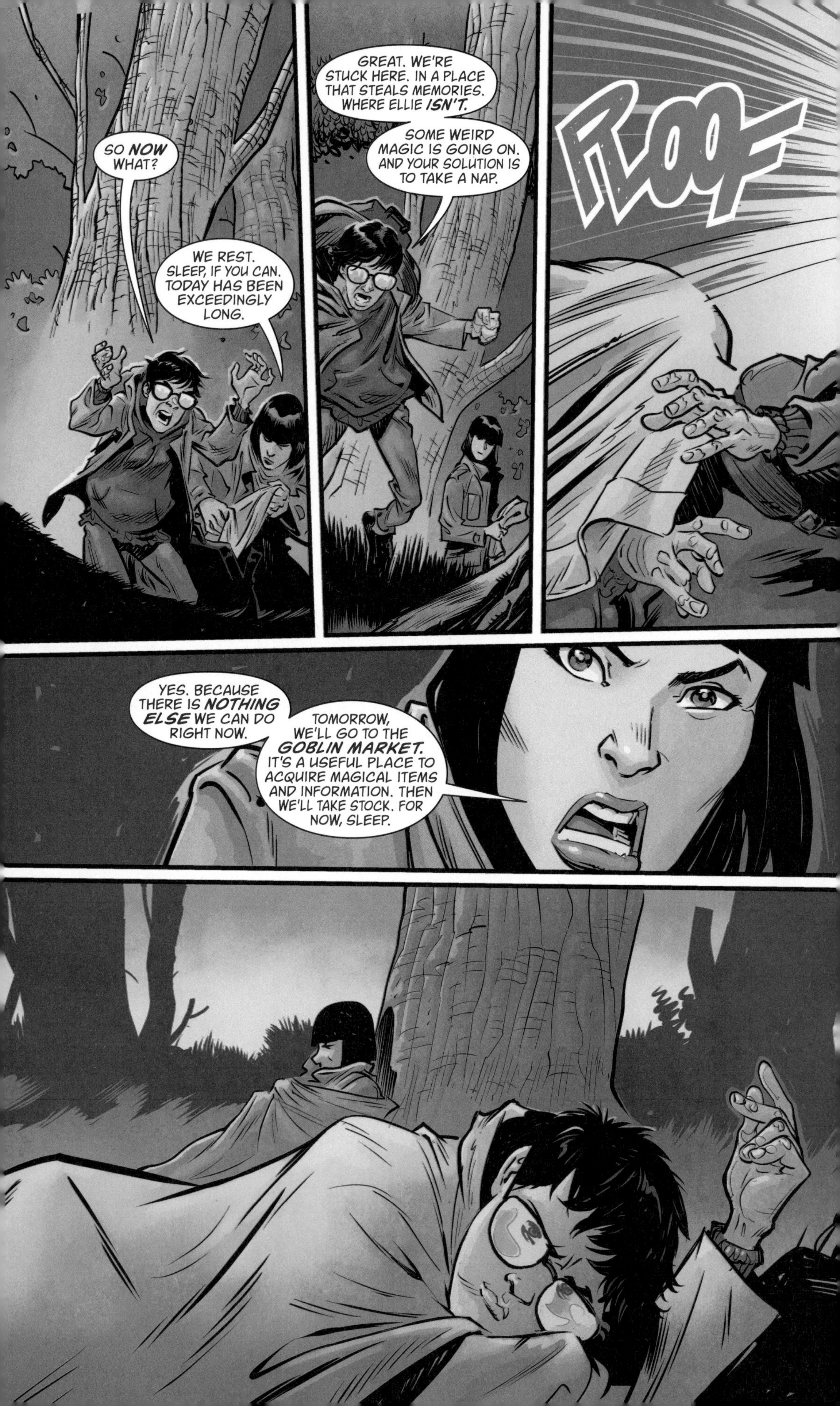
SO NOW WHAT?
WE REST. SLEEP, IF YOU CAN. TODAY HAS BEEN EXCEEDINGLY LONG.
GREAT. WE'RE STUCK HERE. IN A PLACE THAT STEALS MEMORIES. WHERE ELLIE ISN'T.
SOME WEIRD MAGIC IS GOING ON. AND YOUR SOLUTION IS TO TAKE A NAP.
FLOOF
YES. BECAUSE THERE IS NOTHING ELSE WE CAN DO RIGHT NOW.
TOMORROW, WE'LL GO TO THE GOBLIN MARKET. IT'S A USEFUL PLACE TO ACQUIRE MAGICAL ITEMS AND INFORMATION. THEN WE'LL TAKE STOCK. FOR NOW, SLEEP.

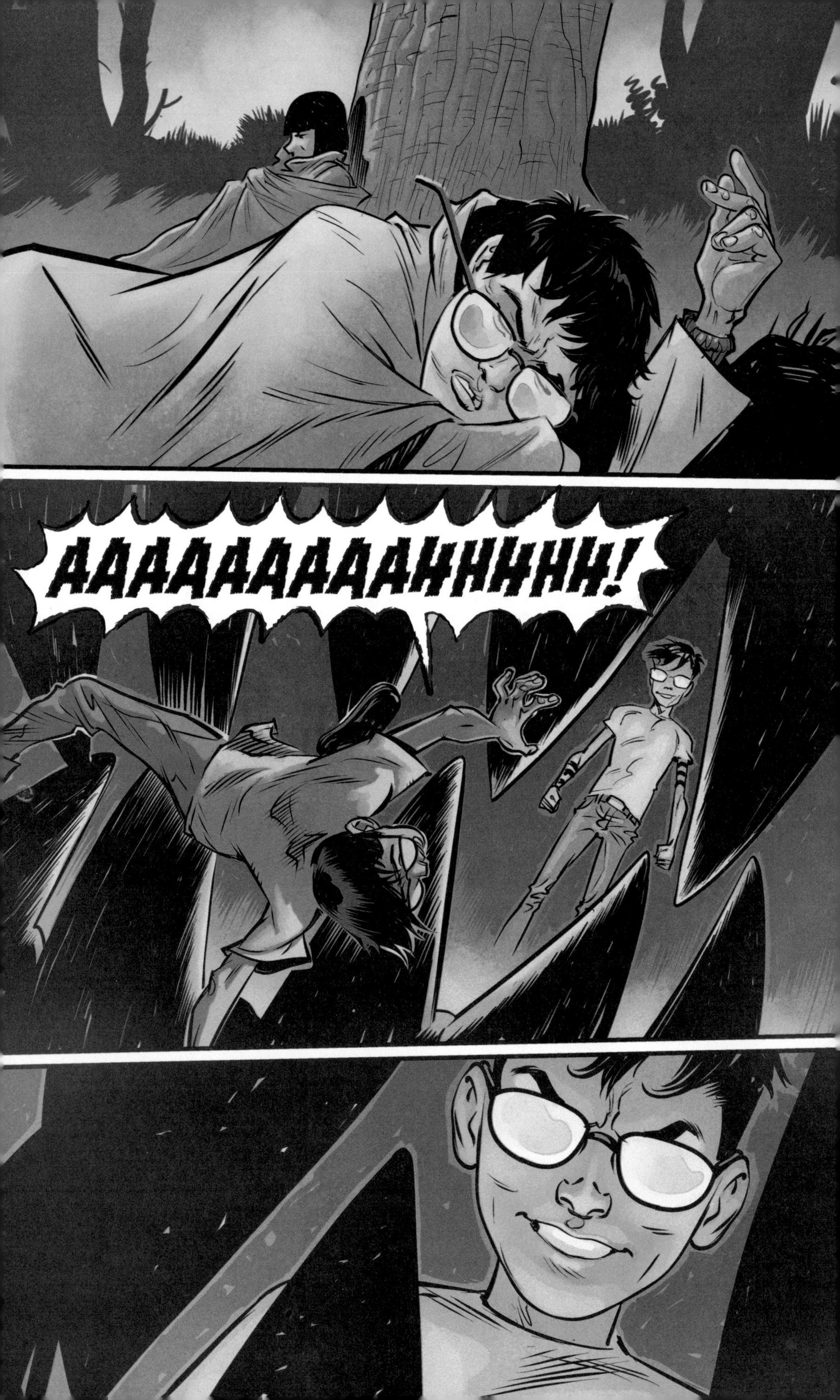
AAAAAAAAAAHHHHH!

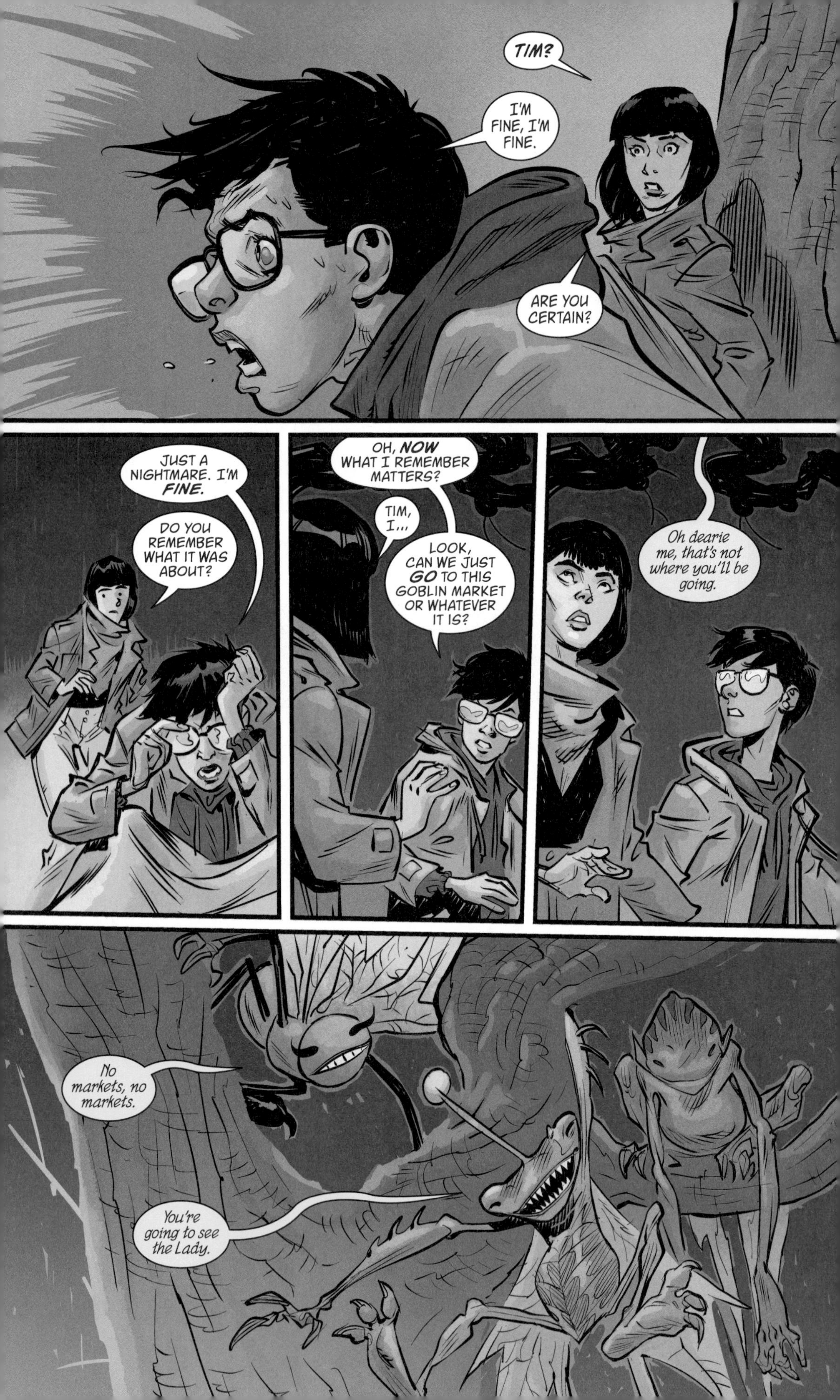
TIM?
I'M FINE, I'M FINE.
ARE YOU CERTAIN?
JUST A NIGHTMARE. I'M FINE.
DO YOU REMEMBER WHAT IT WAS ABOUT?
OH, NOW WHAT I REMEMBER MATTERS?
TIM, I...
LOOK, CAN WE JUST GO TO THIS GOBLIN MARKET OR WHATEVER IT IS?
Oh dearie me, that's not where you'll be going.
No markets, no markets.
You're going to see the Lady.

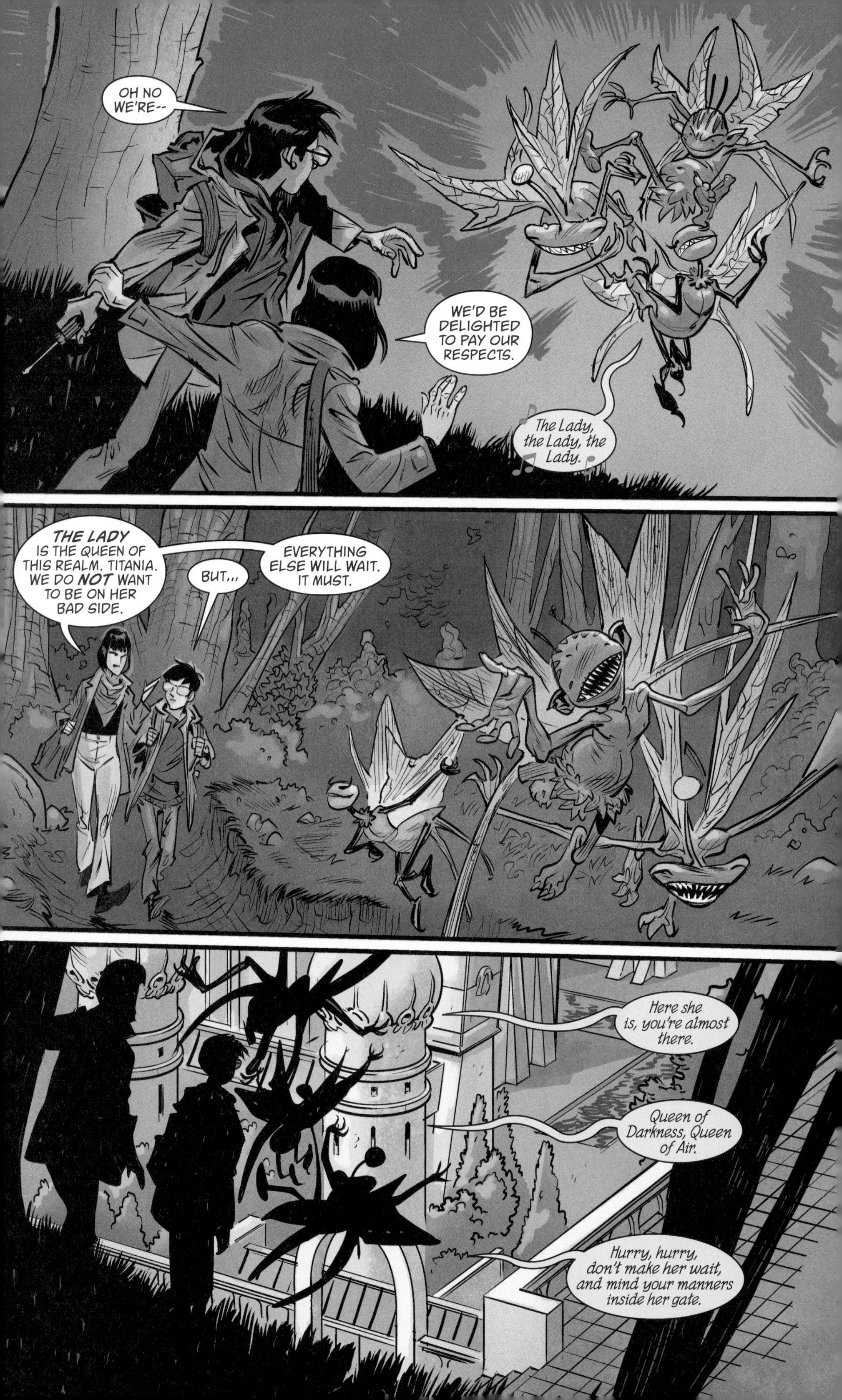
OH NO WE'RE--
WE'D BE DELIGHTED TO PAY OUR RESPECTS.
The Lady, the Lady, the Lady.
THE LADY IS THE QUEEN OF THIS REALM. TITANIA. WE DO NOT WANT TO BE ON HER BAD SIDE.
BUT...
EVERYTHING ELSE WILL WAIT. IT MUST.
Here she is, you're almost there.
Queen of Darkness, Queen of Air.
Hurry, hurry, don't make her wait, and mind your manners inside her gate.

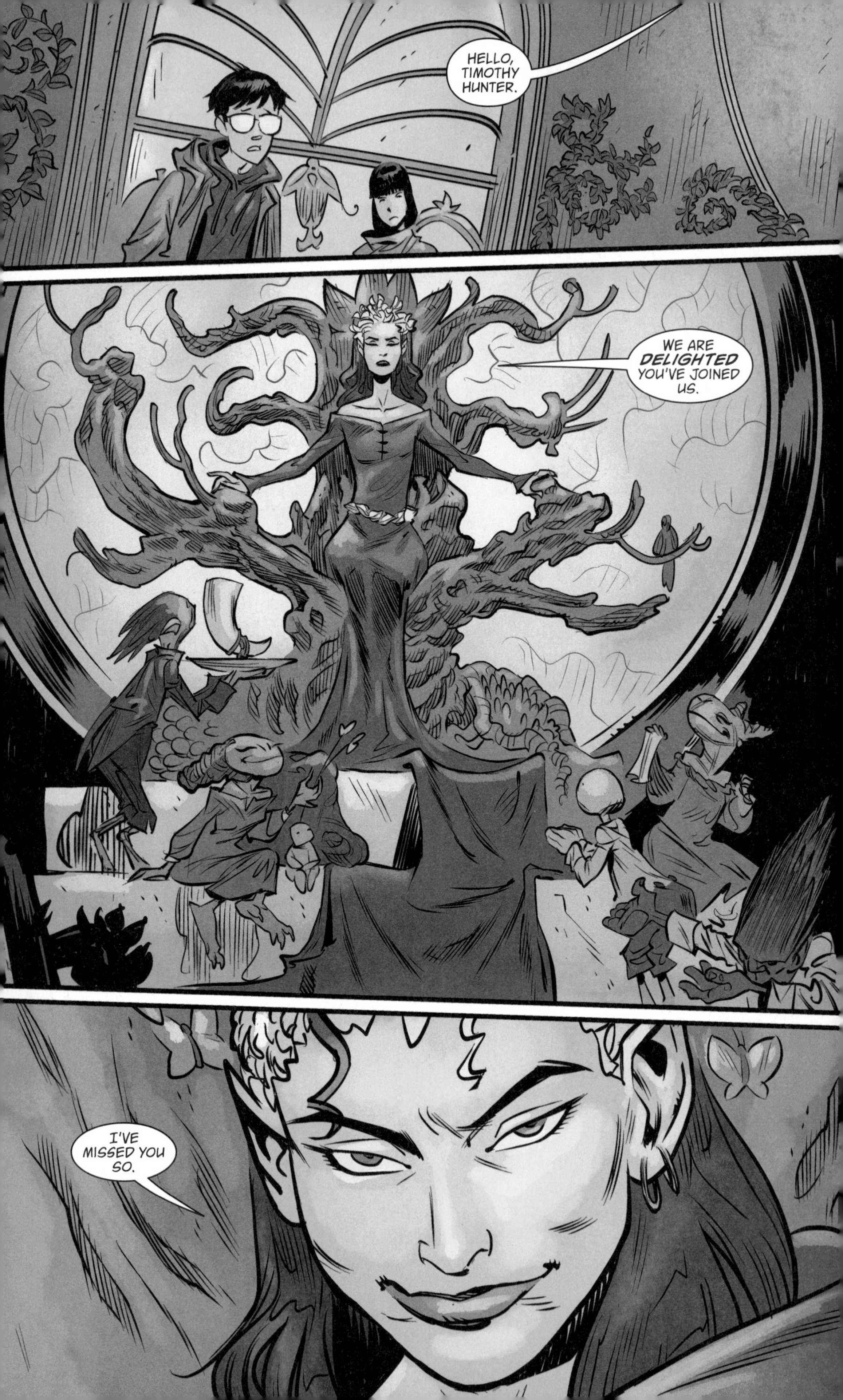
HELLO, TIMOTHY HUNTER.
WE ARE DELIGHTED YOU'VE JOINED US.
I'VE MISSED YOU SO.

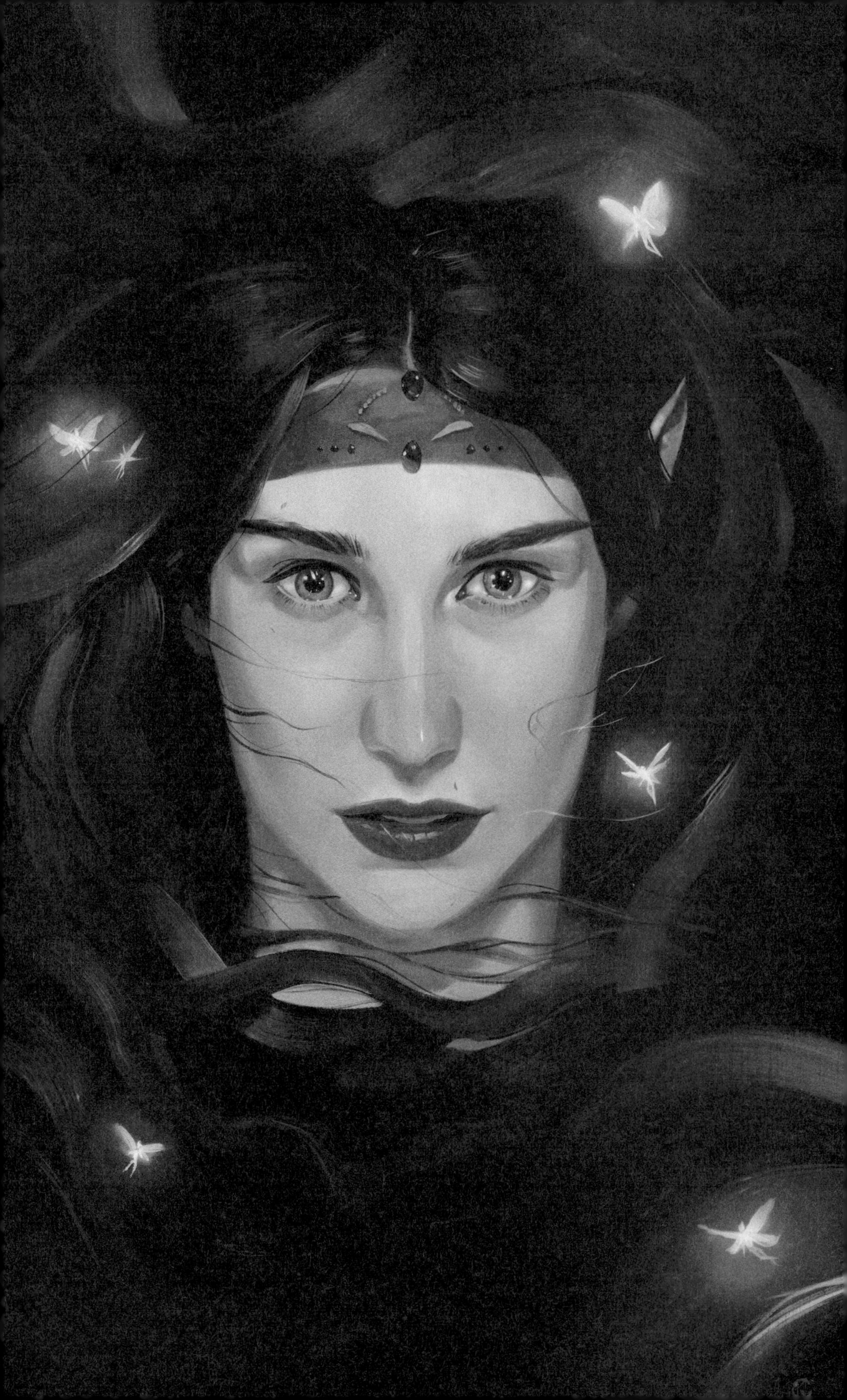

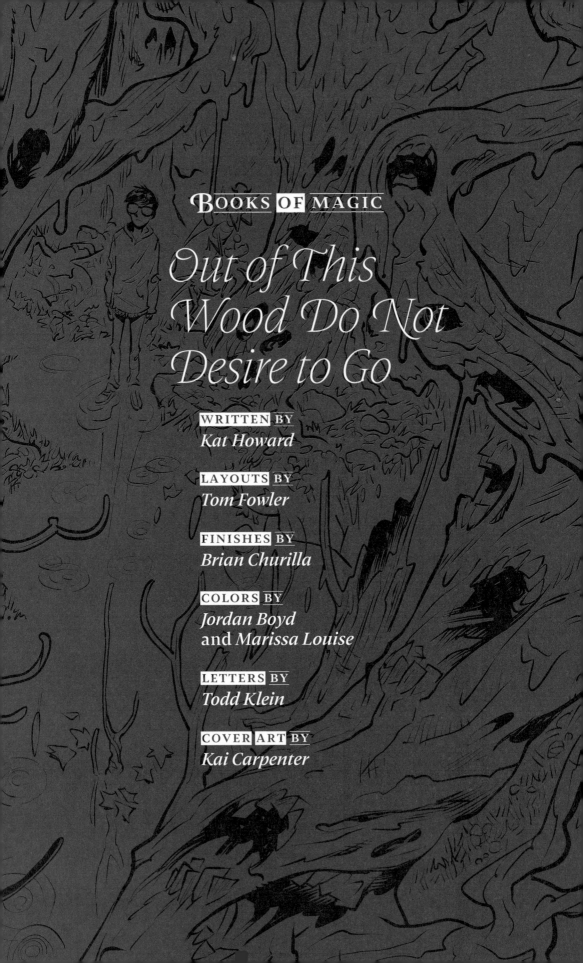

BOOKS OF MAGIC

Out of This Wood Do Not Desire to Go

WRITTEN BY
Kat Howard

LAYOUTS BY
Tom Fowler

FINISHES BY
Brian Churilla

COLORS BY
Jordan Boyd and *Marissa Louise*

LETTERS BY
Todd Klein

COVER ART BY
Kai Carpenter

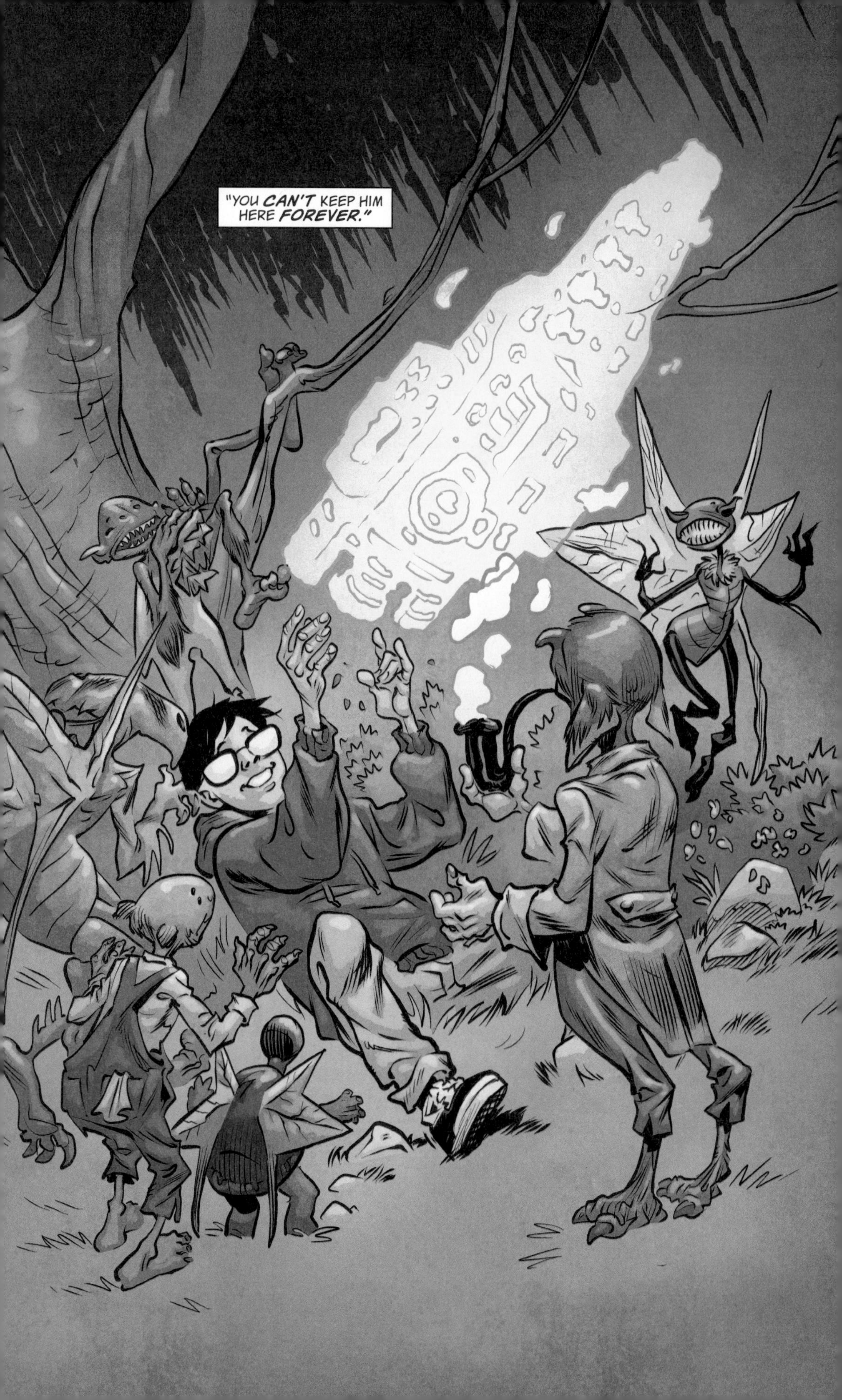
"YOU CAN'T KEEP HIM HERE FOREVER."

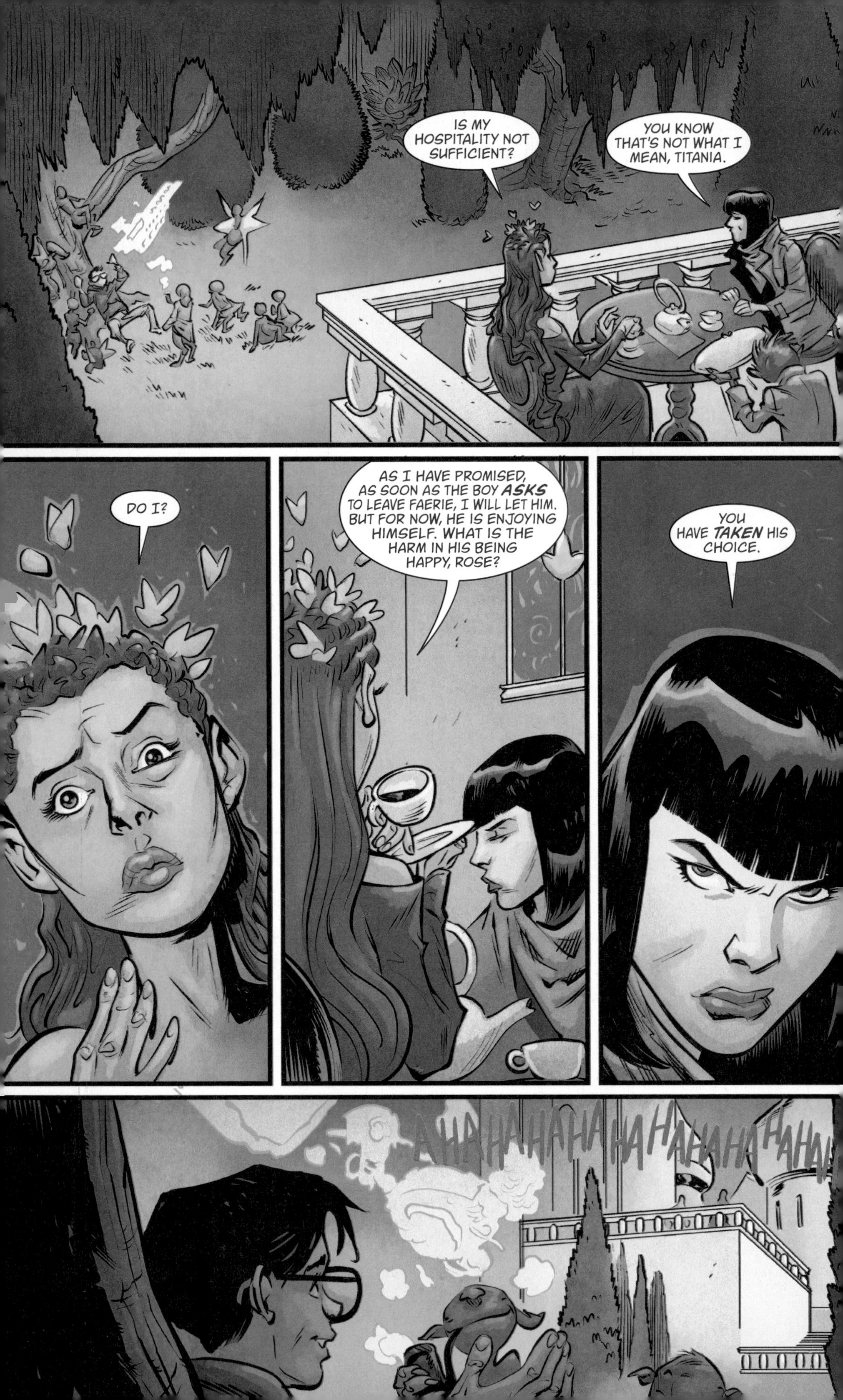
IS MY HOSPITALITY NOT SUFFICIENT?
YOU KNOW THAT'S NOT WHAT I MEAN, TITANIA.
DO I?
AS I HAVE PROMISED, AS SOON AS THE BOY ASKS TO LEAVE FAERIE, I WILL LET HIM. BUT FOR NOW, HE IS ENJOYING HIMSELF. WHAT IS THE HARM IN HIS BEING HAPPY, ROSE?
YOU HAVE TAKEN HIS CHOICE.
AHAHAHAHAHAHAHAHAHAHAHAHA

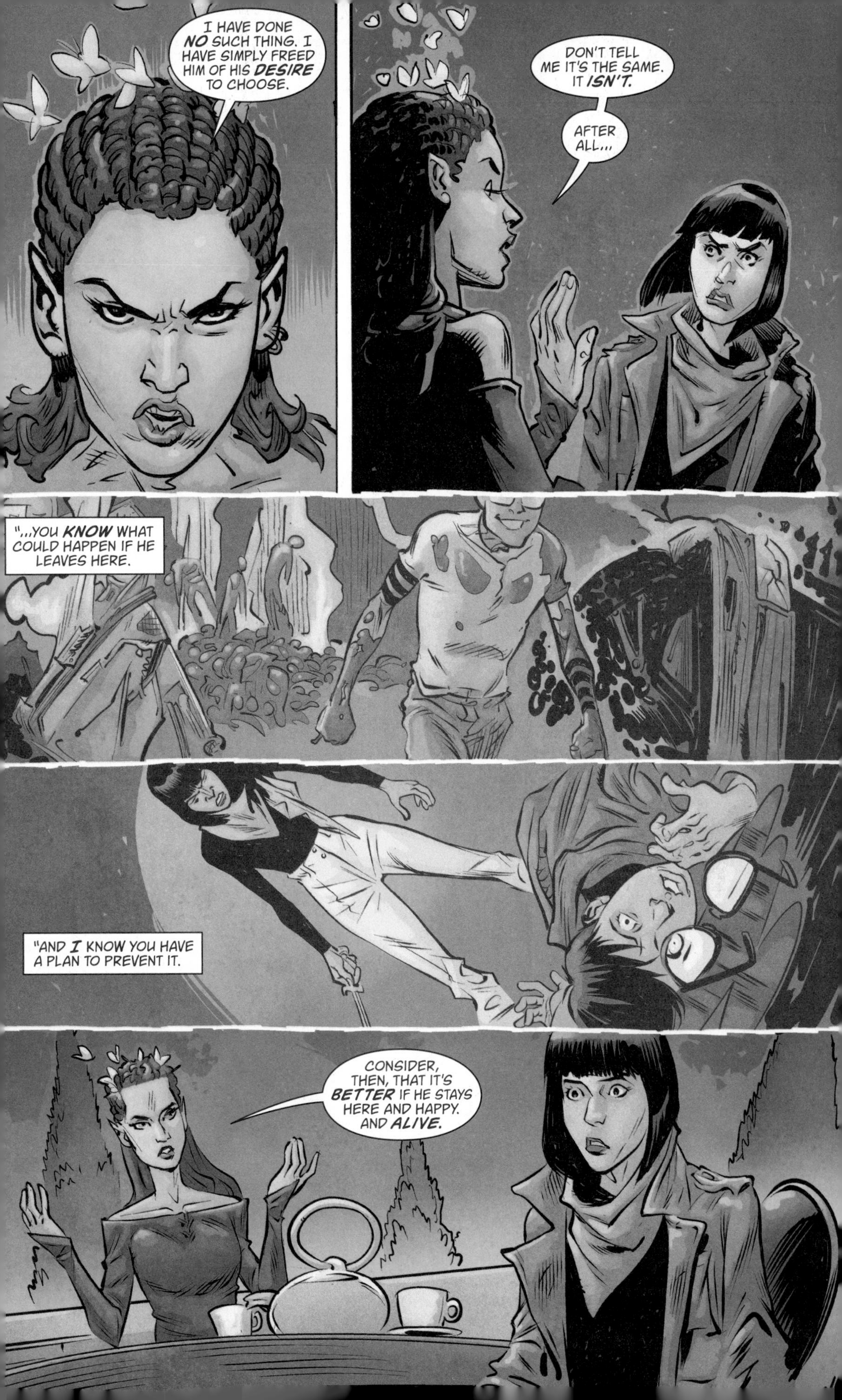
I HAVE DONE NO SUCH THING. I HAVE SIMPLY FREED HIM OF HIS DESIRE TO CHOOSE.
DON'T TELL ME IT'S THE SAME. IT ISN'T.
AFTER ALL...
"...YOU KNOW WHAT COULD HAPPEN IF HE LEAVES HERE.
"AND I KNOW YOU HAVE A PLAN TO PREVENT IT.
CONSIDER, THEN, THAT IT'S BETTER IF HE STAYS HERE AND HAPPY. AND ALIVE.

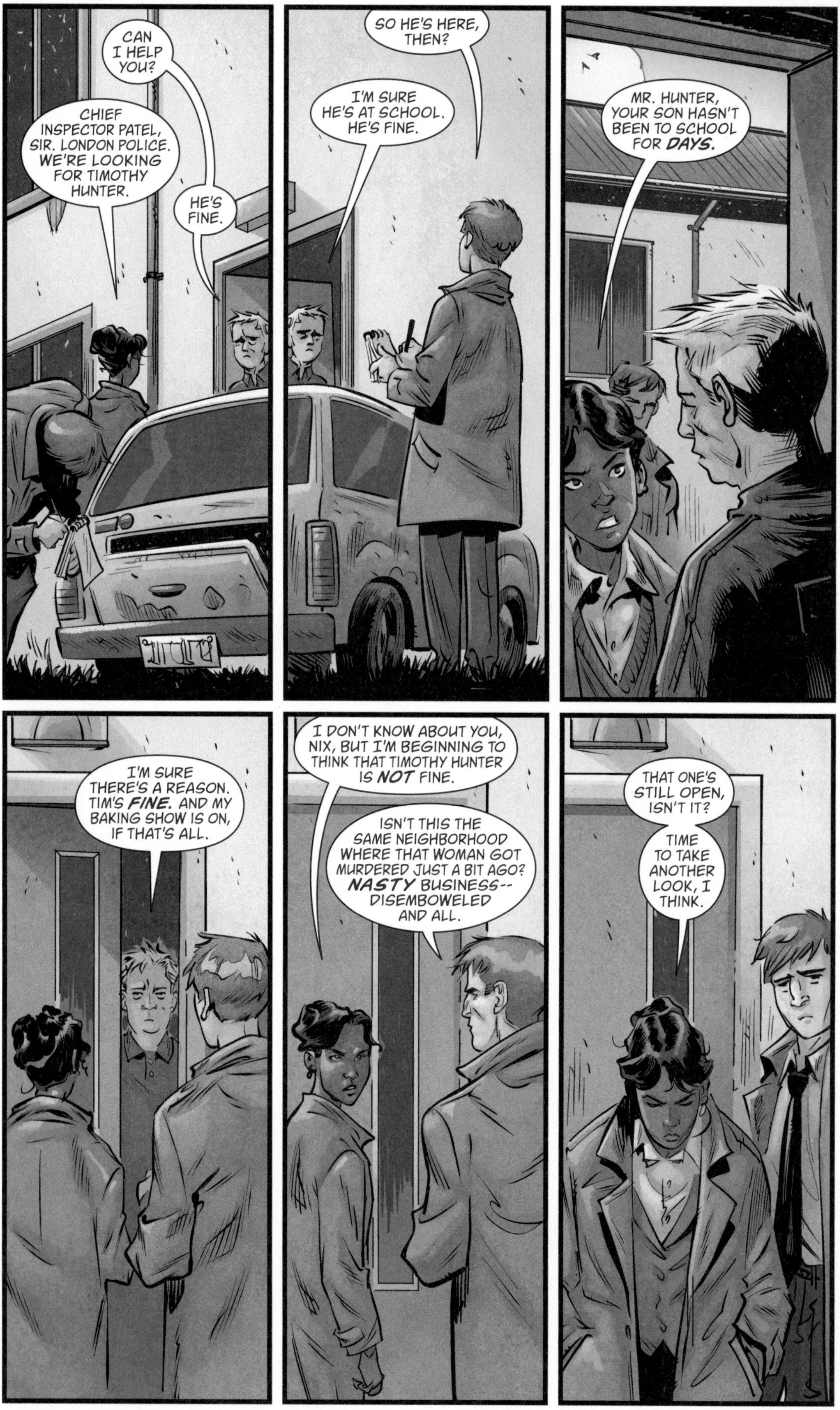
CAN I HELP YOU?
CHIEF INSPECTOR PATEL, SIR. LONDON POLICE. WE'RE LOOKING FOR TIMOTHY HUNTER.
HE'S FINE.
SO HE'S HERE, THEN?
I'M SURE HE'S AT SCHOOL. HE'S FINE.
MR. HUNTER, YOUR SON HASN'T BEEN TO SCHOOL FOR DAYS.
I'M SURE THERE'S A REASON. TIM'S FINE. AND MY BAKING SHOW IS ON, IF THAT'S ALL.
I DON'T KNOW ABOUT YOU, NIX, BUT I'M BEGINNING TO THINK THAT TIMOTHY HUNTER IS NOT FINE.
ISN'T THIS THE SAME NEIGHBORHOOD WHERE THAT WOMAN GOT MURDERED JUST A BIT AGO? NASTY BUSINESS-- DISEMBOWELED AND ALL.
THAT ONE'S STILL OPEN, ISN'T IT?
TIME TO TAKE ANOTHER LOOK, I THINK.

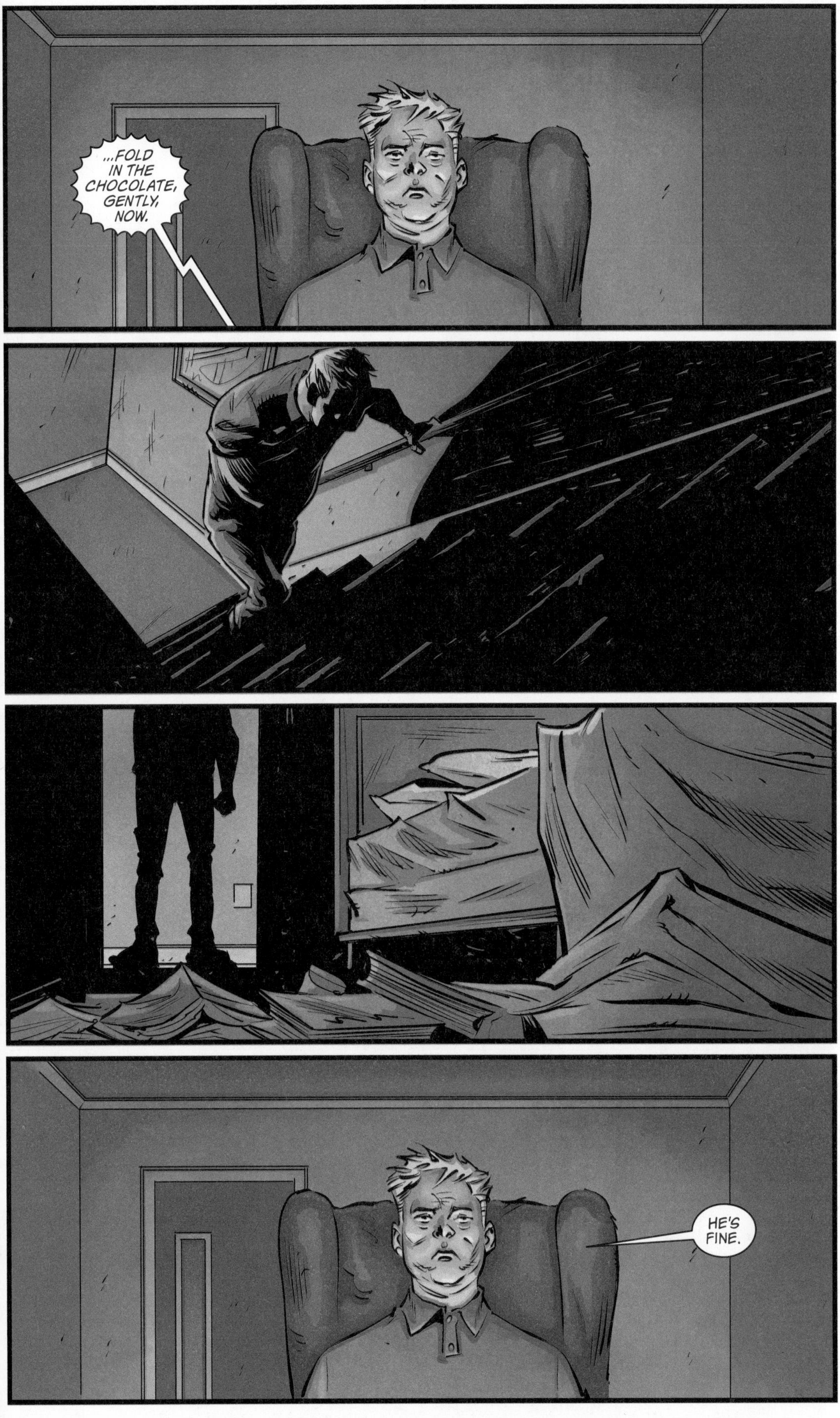
...FOLD IN THE CHOCOLATE, GENTLY, NOW.
HE'S FINE.

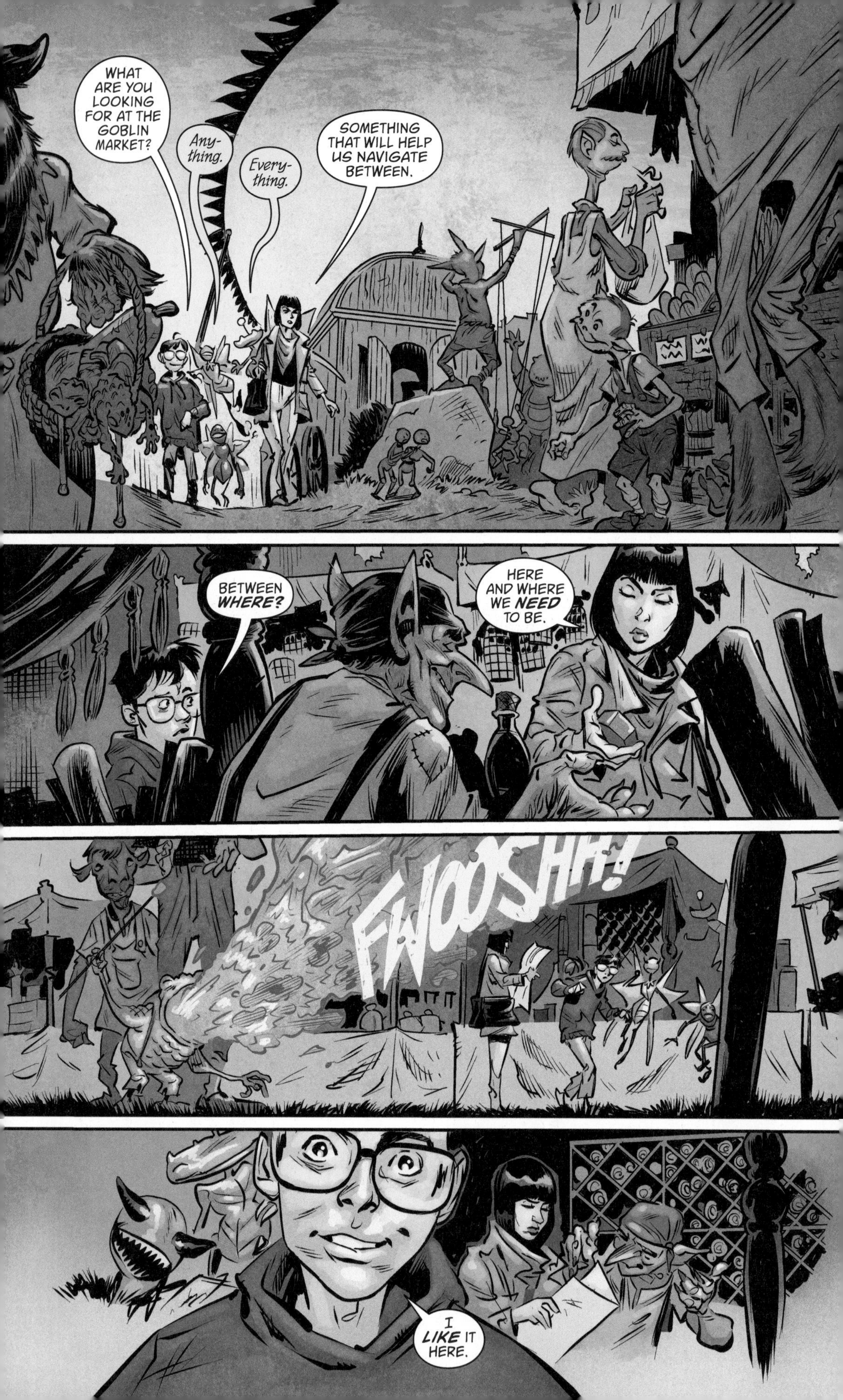
WHAT ARE YOU LOOKING FOR AT THE GOBLIN MARKET?
Any- thing.
Every- thing.
SOMETHING THAT WILL HELP US NAVIGATE BETWEEN.
BETWEEN **WHERE?**
HERE AND WHERE WE **NEED** TO BE.
FWOOSHH!
I **LIKE** IT HERE.

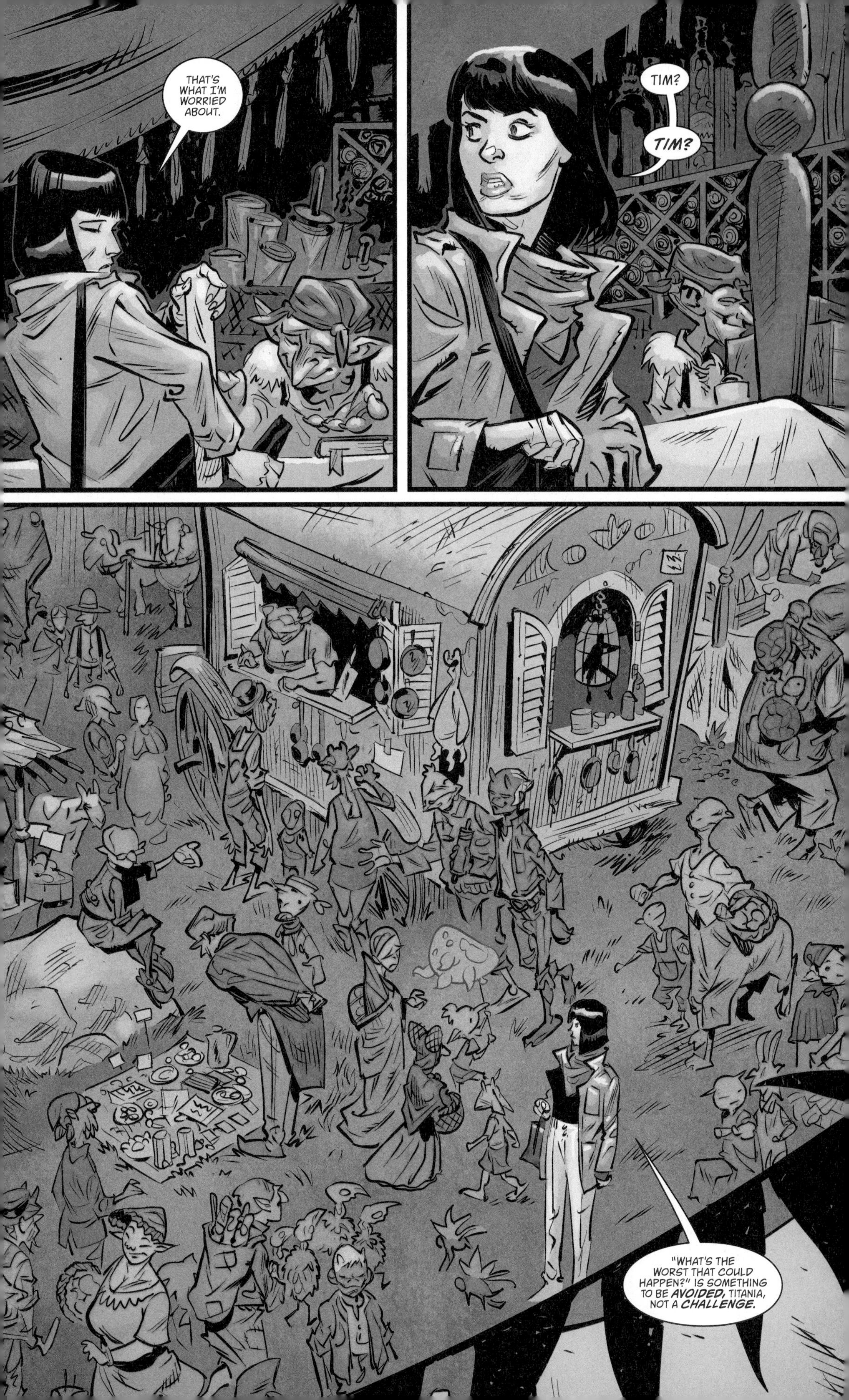
THAT'S WHAT I'M WORRIED ABOUT.
TIM?
TIM?
"WHAT'S THE WORST THAT COULD HAPPEN?" IS SOMETHING TO BE AVOIDED, TITANIA, NOT A CHALLENGE.

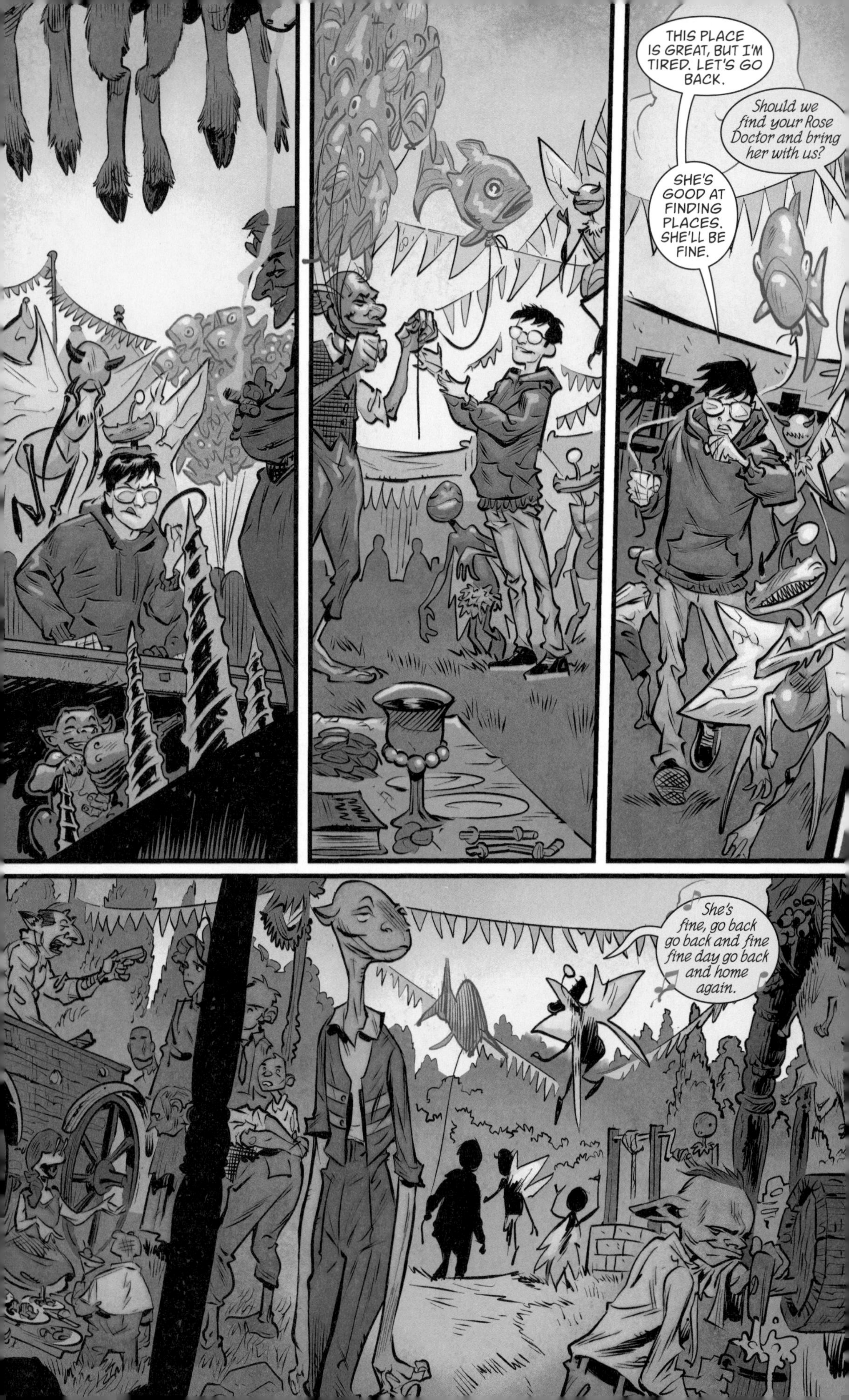
THIS PLACE IS GREAT, BUT I'M TIRED. LET'S GO BACK.
Should we find your Rose Doctor and bring her with us?
SHE'S GOOD AT FINDING PLACES. SHE'LL BE FINE.
She's fine, go back go back and fine fine day go back and home again.

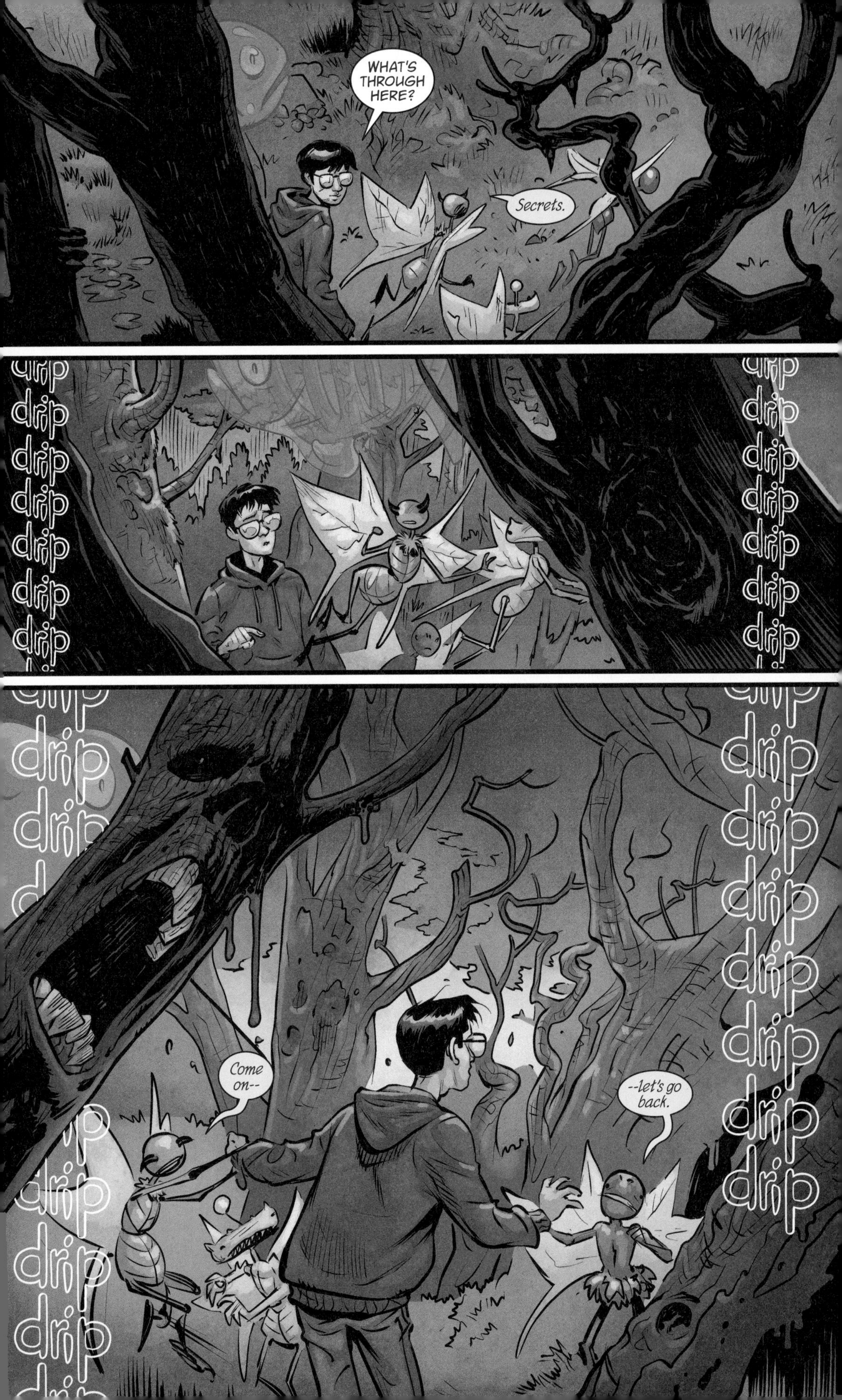
WHAT'S THROUGH HERE?
Secrets.
drip drip drip drip drip drip drip
drip drip drip drip drip drip drip
drip drip
drip drip drip drip drip drip drip drip
Come on--
--let's go back.
drip drip drip drip

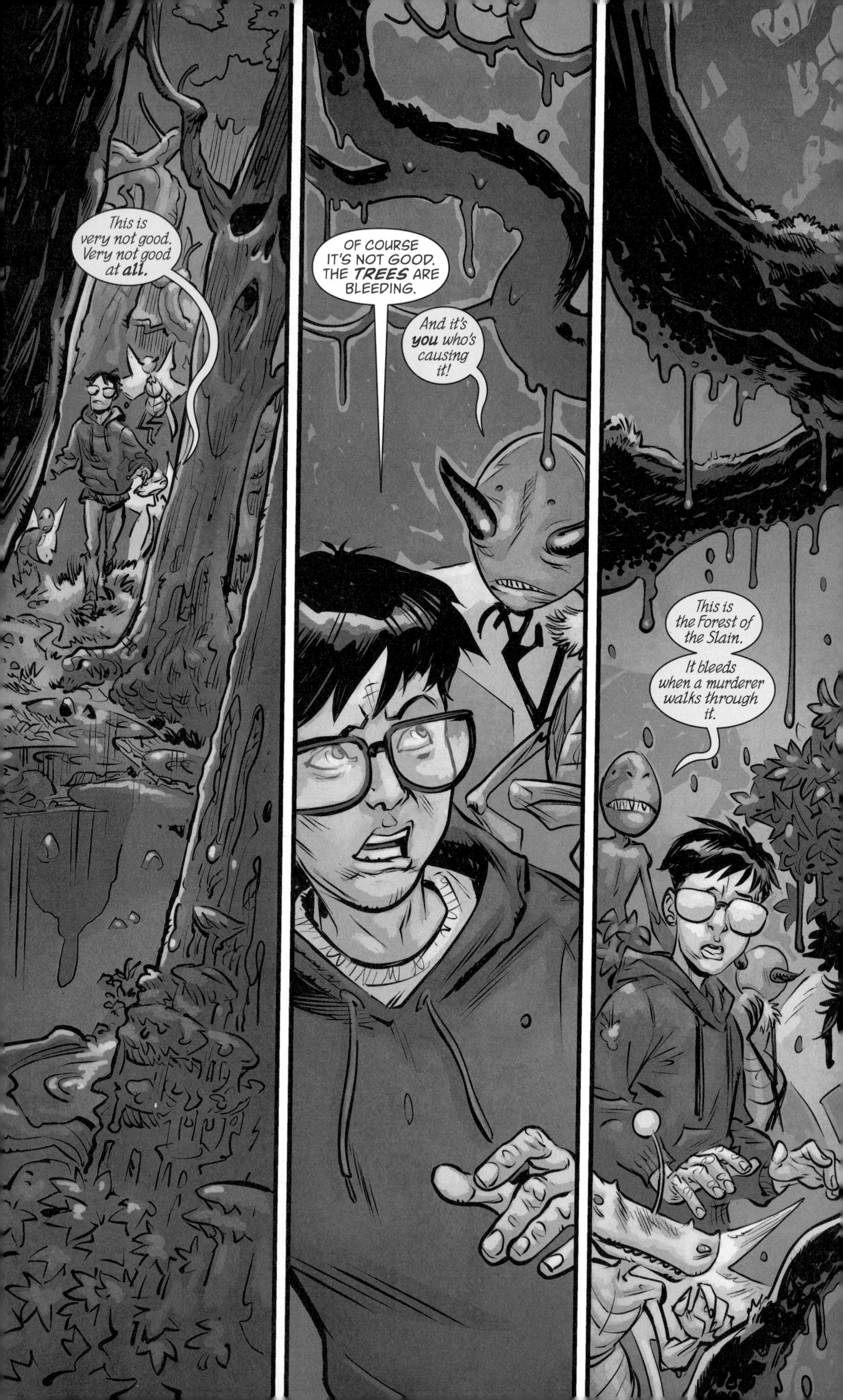
This is very not good. Very not good at **all.**
OF COURSE IT'S NOT GOOD. THE **TREES** ARE BLEEDING.
And it's **you** who's causing it!
This is the Forest of the Slain.
It bleeds when a murderer walks through it.

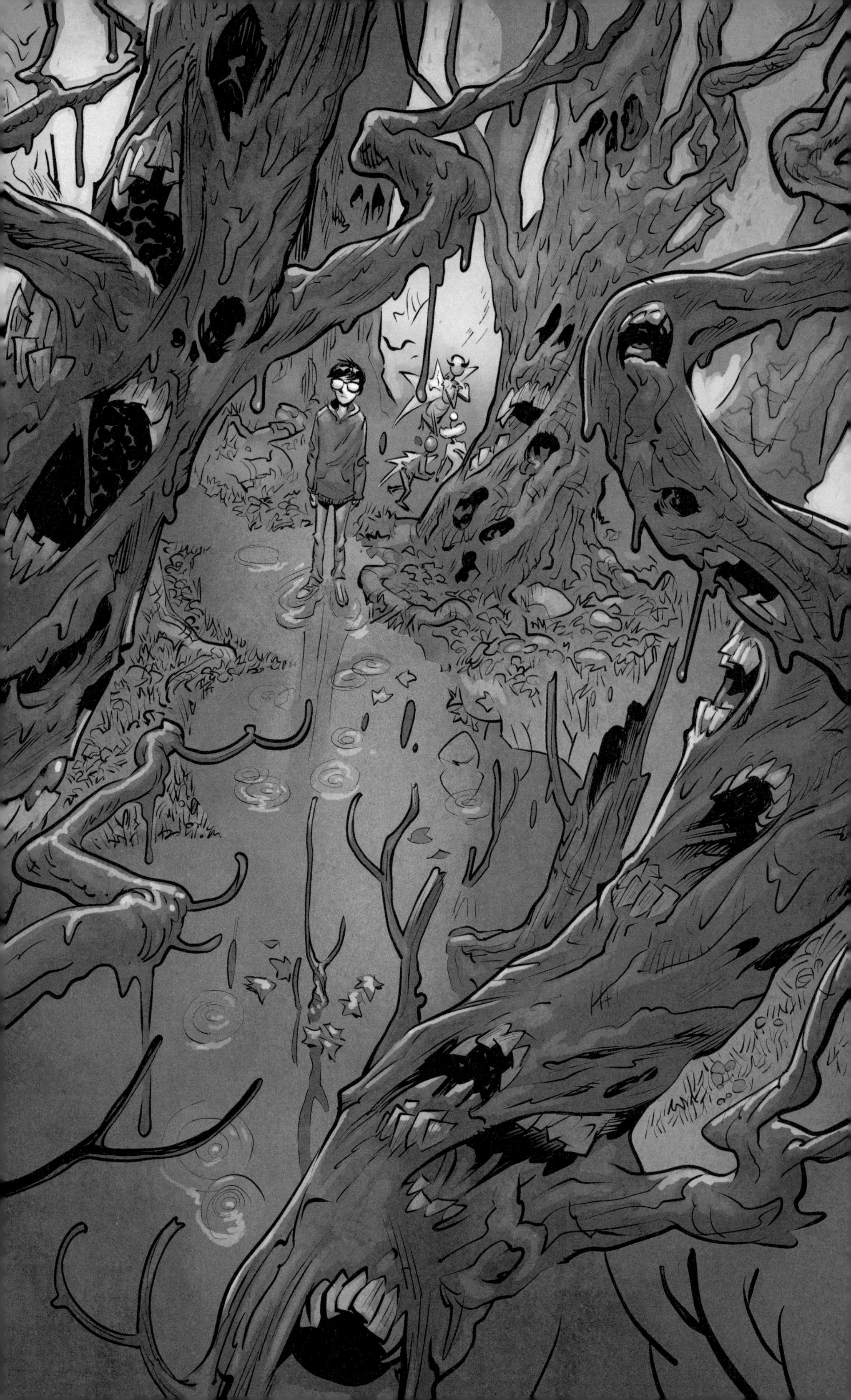

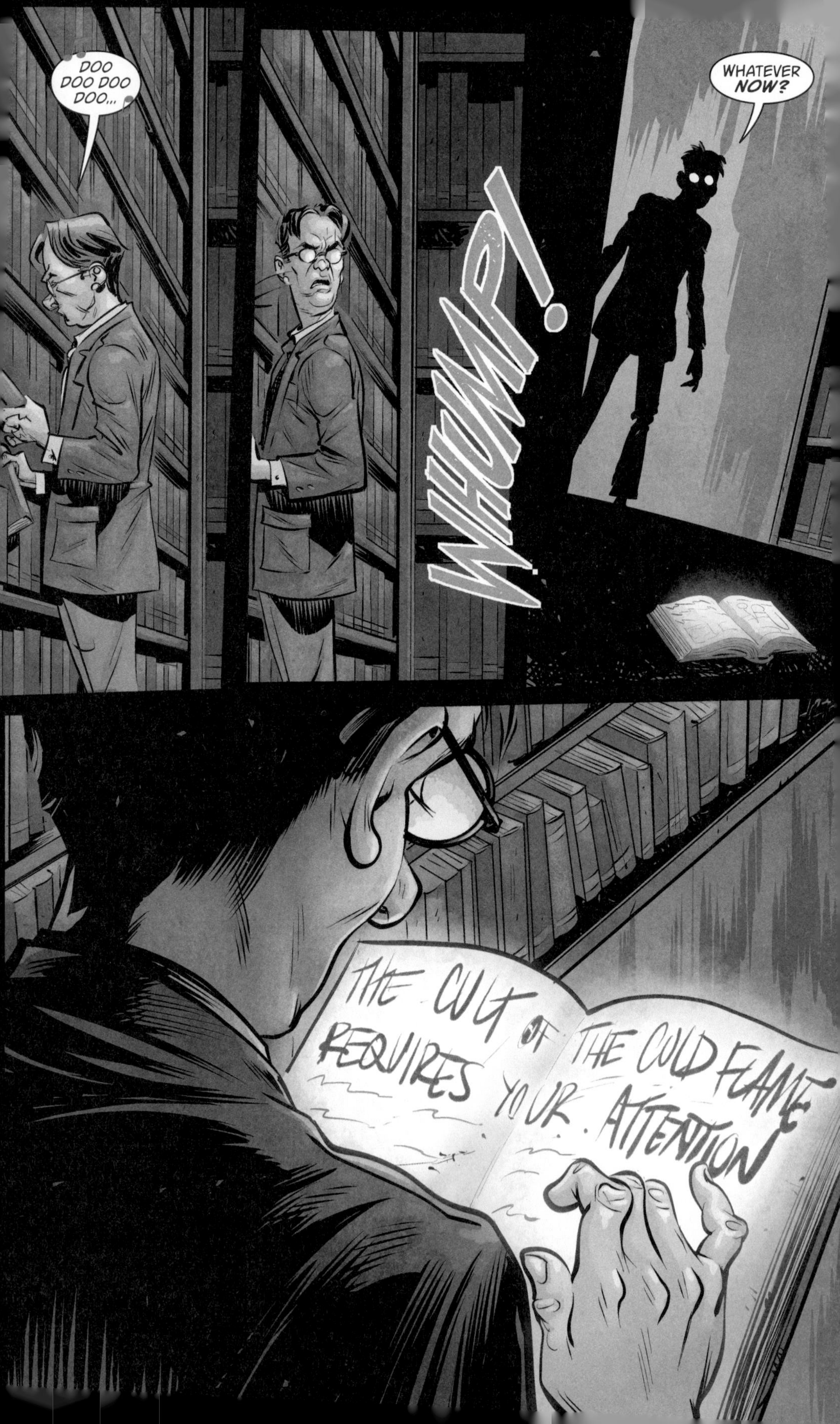
DOO DOO DOO DOO DOO...
WHUMP!
WHATEVER NOW?
THE CULT OF THE COLD FLAME REQUIRES YOUR ATTENTION

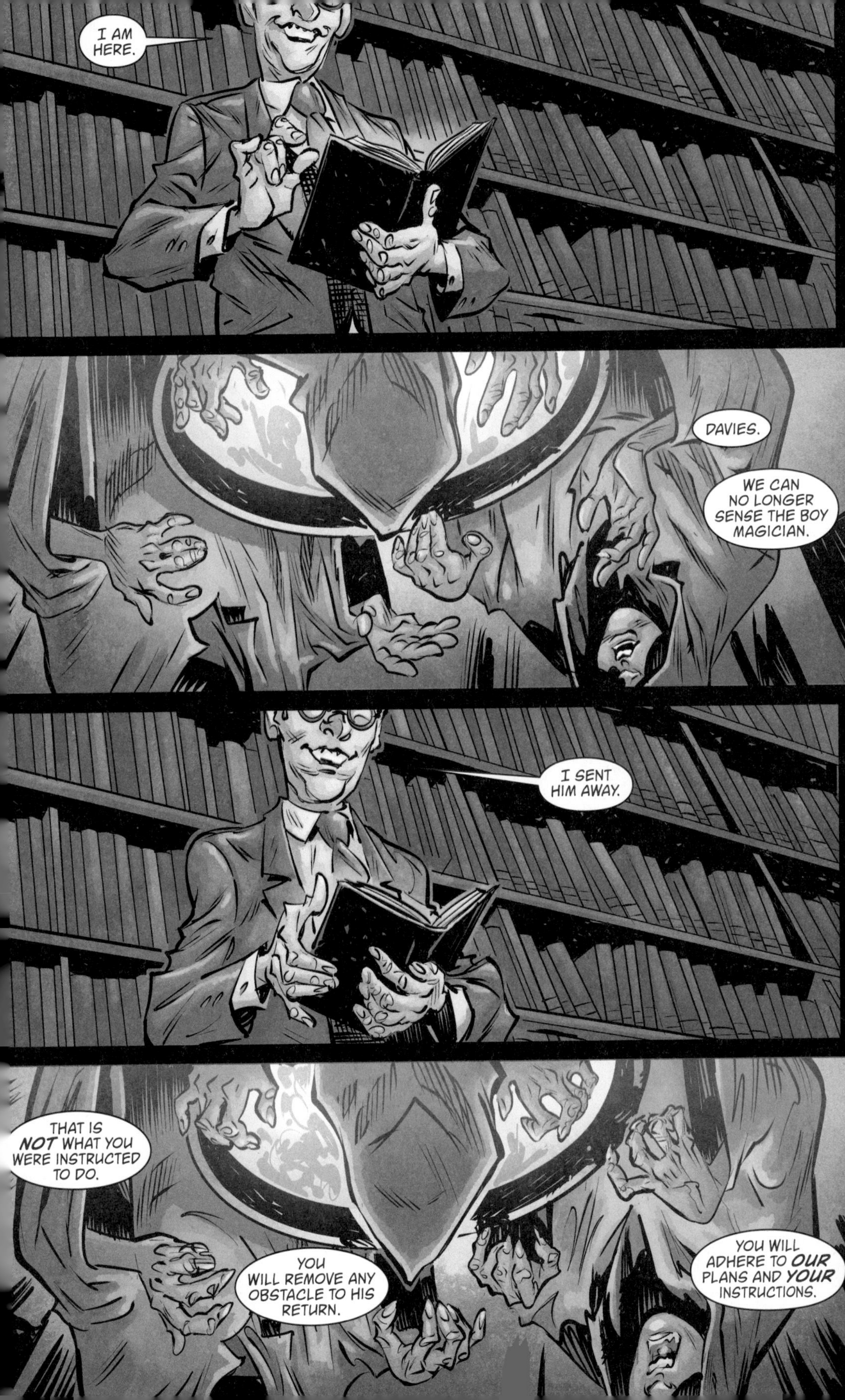
I AM HERE.
DAVIES.
WE CAN NO LONGER SENSE THE BOY MAGICIAN.
I SENT HIM AWAY.
THAT IS ***NOT*** WHAT YOU WERE INSTRUCTED TO DO.
YOU WILL REMOVE ANY OBSTACLE TO HIS RETURN.
YOU WILL ADHERE TO ***OUR*** PLANS AND ***YOUR*** INSTRUCTIONS.

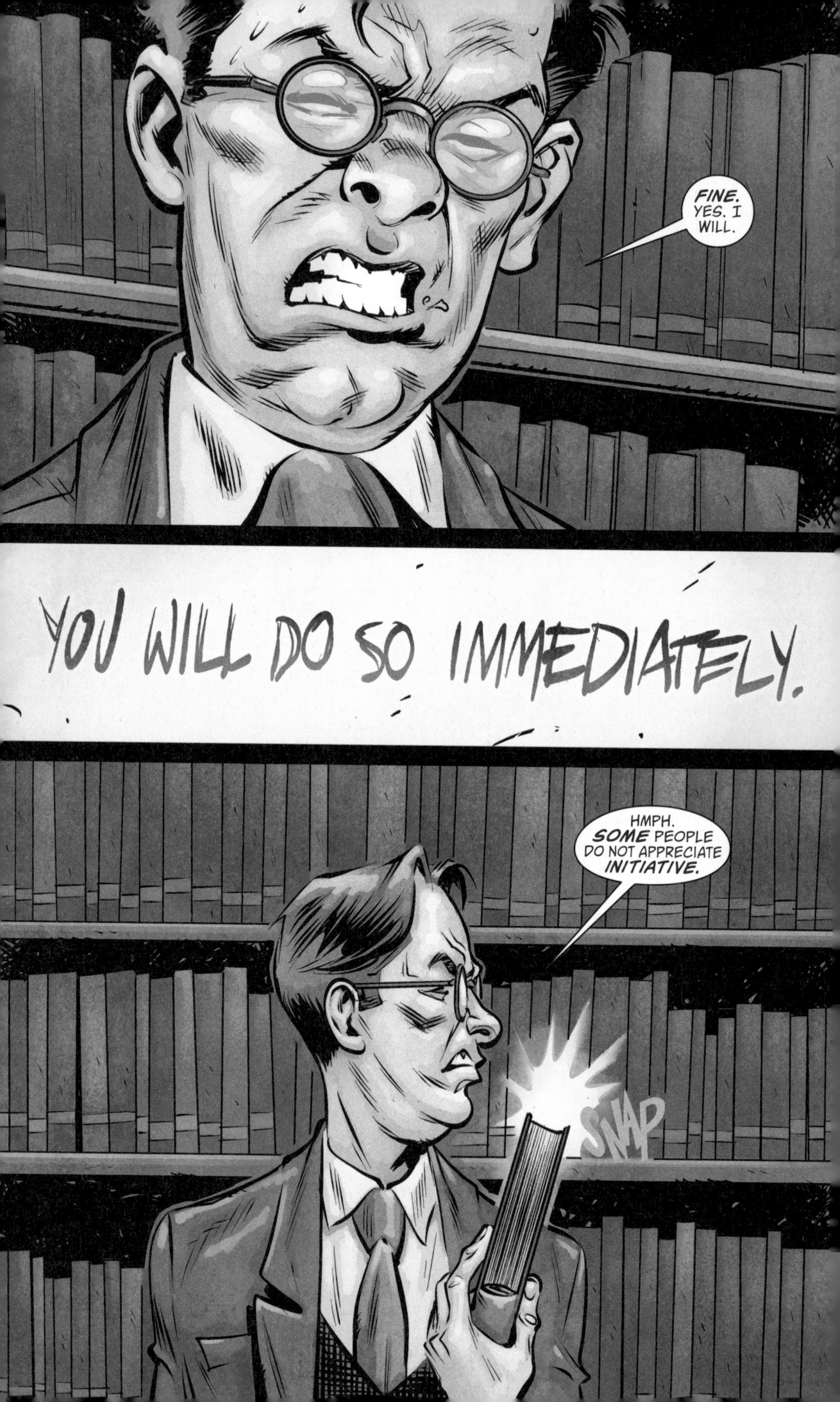
FINE. YES. I WILL.
YOU WILL DO SO IMMEDIATELY.
HMPH. SOME PEOPLE DO NOT APPRECIATE INITIATIVE.
SNAP

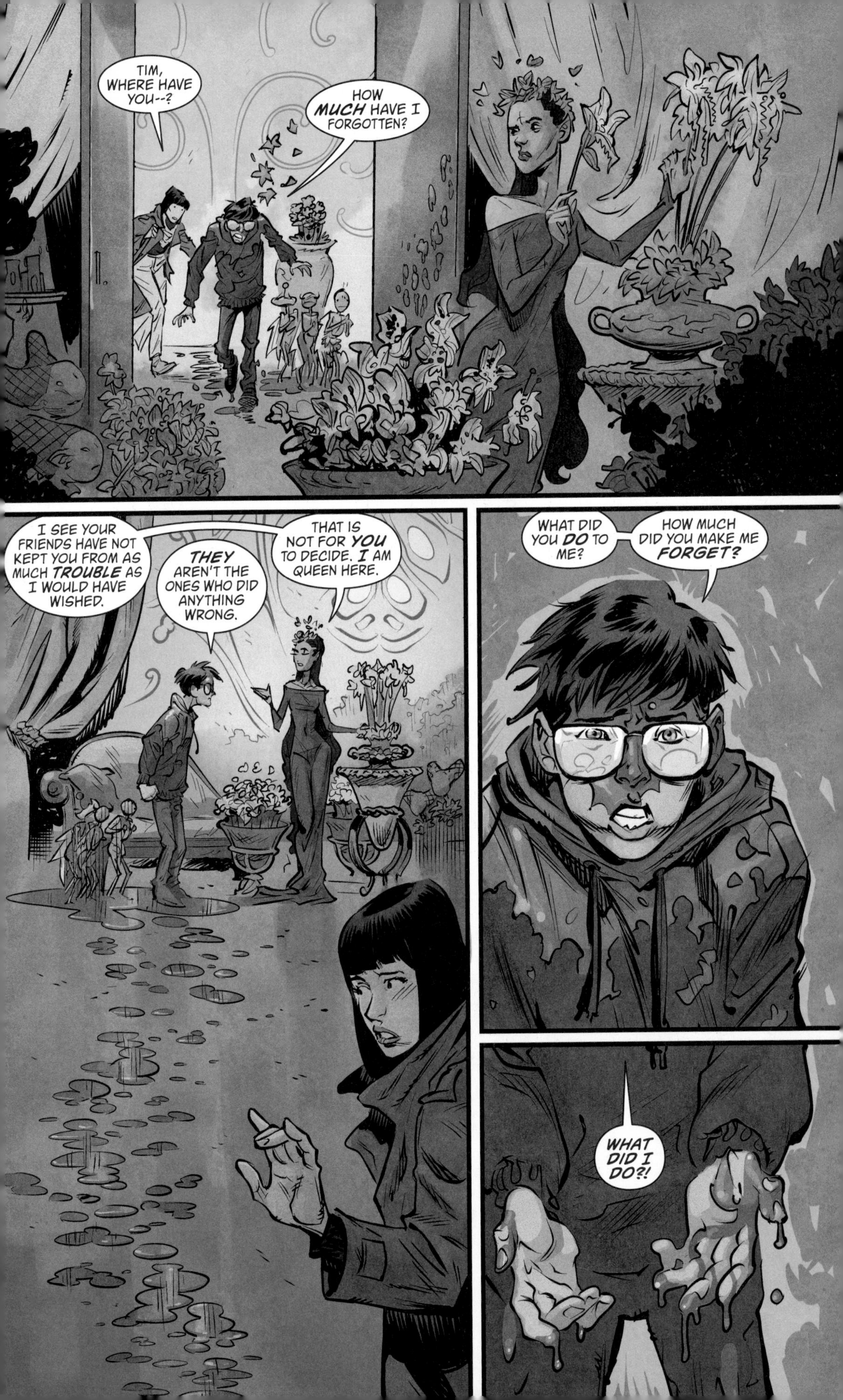
TIM, WHERE HAVE YOU--?
HOW MUCH HAVE I FORGOTTEN?
I SEE YOUR FRIENDS HAVE NOT KEPT YOU FROM AS MUCH TROUBLE AS I WOULD HAVE WISHED.
THEY AREN'T THE ONES WHO DID ANYTHING WRONG.
THAT IS NOT FOR YOU TO DECIDE. I AM QUEEN HERE.
WHAT DID YOU DO TO ME?
HOW MUCH DID YOU MAKE ME FORGET?
WHAT DID I DO?!

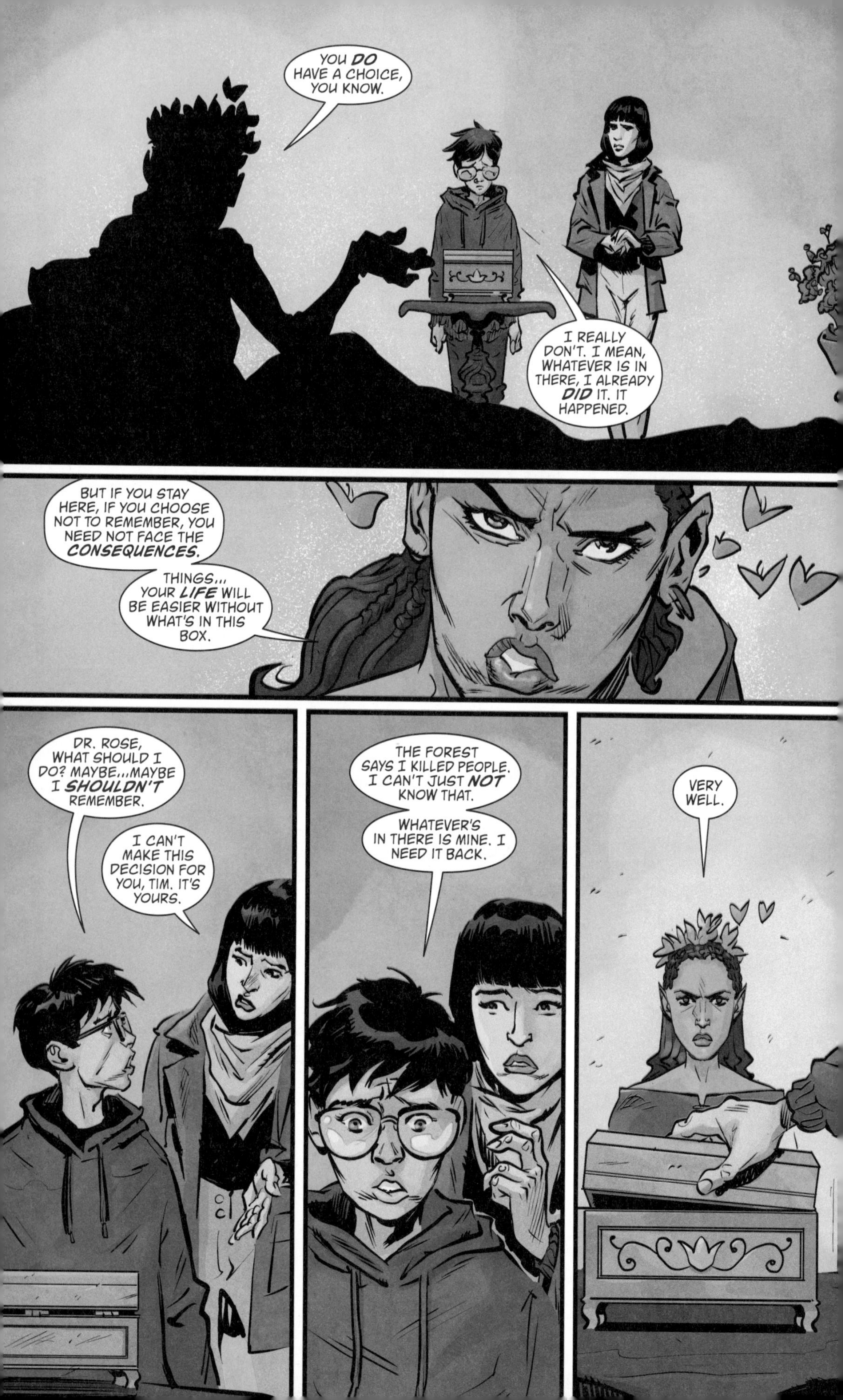
YOU DO HAVE A CHOICE, YOU KNOW.
I REALLY DON'T. I MEAN, WHATEVER IS IN THERE, I ALREADY DID IT. IT HAPPENED.
BUT IF YOU STAY HERE, IF YOU CHOOSE NOT TO REMEMBER, YOU NEED NOT FACE THE CONSEQUENCES.
THINGS... YOUR LIFE WILL BE EASIER WITHOUT WHAT'S IN THIS BOX.
DR. ROSE, WHAT SHOULD I DO? MAYBE...MAYBE I SHOULDN'T REMEMBER.
I CAN'T MAKE THIS DECISION FOR YOU, TIM. IT'S YOURS.
THE FOREST SAYS I KILLED PEOPLE. I CAN'T JUST NOT KNOW THAT.
WHATEVER'S IN THERE IS MINE. I NEED IT BACK.
VERY WELL.

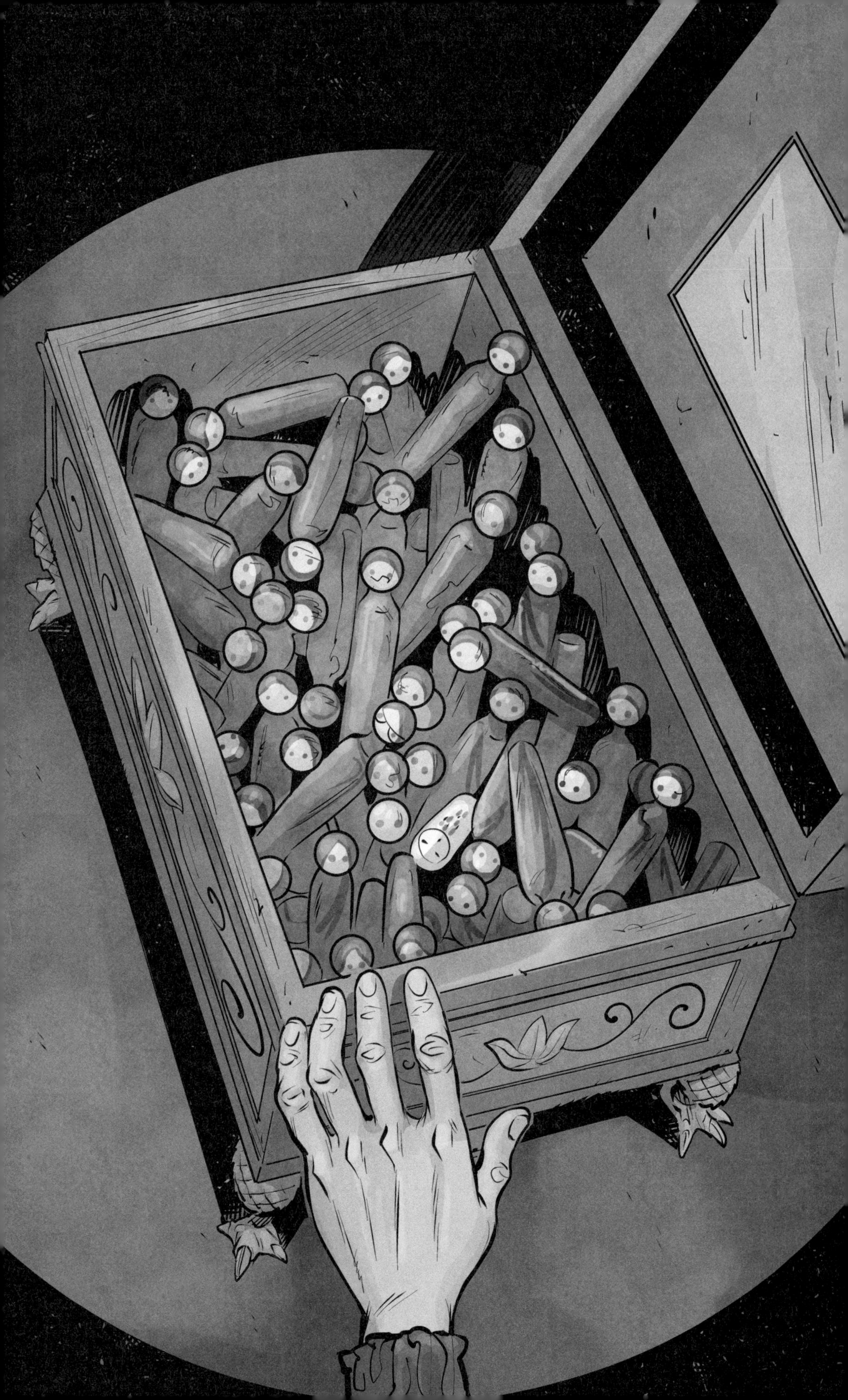

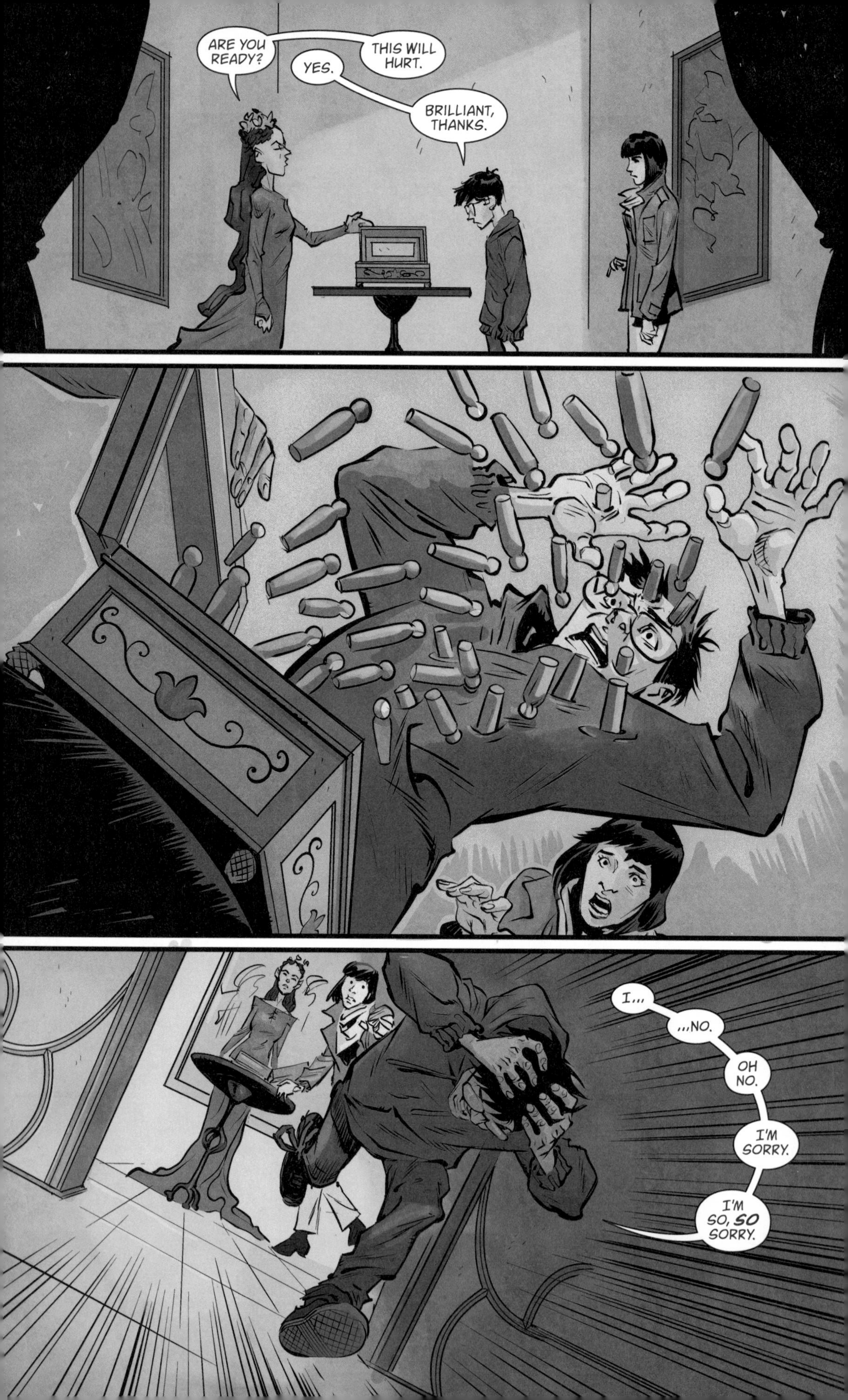
ARE YOU READY?
THIS WILL HURT.
YES.
BRILLIANT, THANKS.
I...
...NO.
OH NO.
I'M SORRY.
I'M SO, **SO** SORRY.

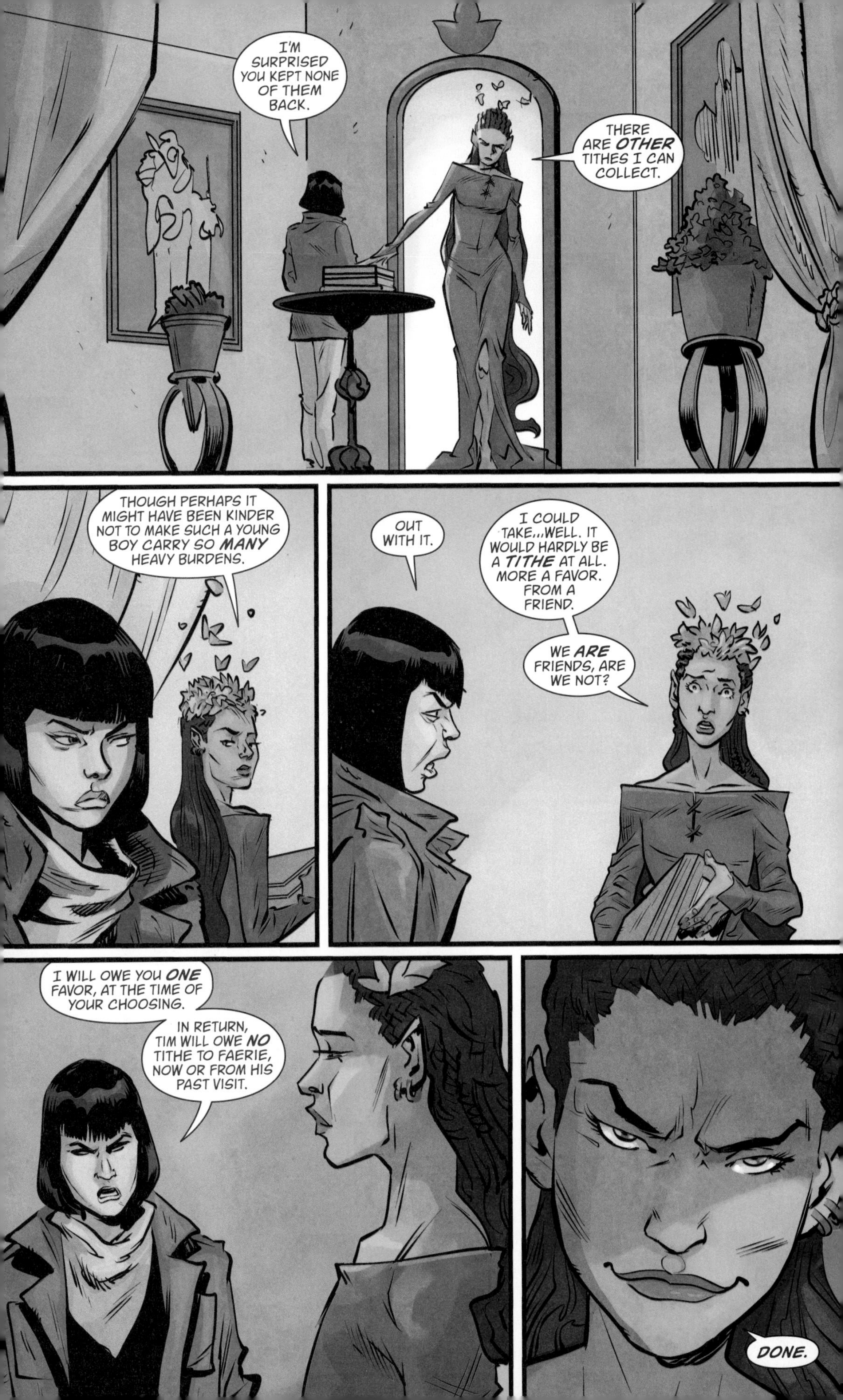
I'M SURPRISED YOU KEPT NONE OF THEM BACK.
THERE ARE OTHER TITHES I CAN COLLECT.
THOUGH PERHAPS IT MIGHT HAVE BEEN KINDER NOT TO MAKE SUCH A YOUNG BOY CARRY SO MANY HEAVY BURDENS.
OUT WITH IT.
I COULD TAKE...WELL. IT WOULD HARDLY BE A TITHE AT ALL. MORE A FAVOR. FROM A FRIEND.
WE ARE FRIENDS, ARE WE NOT?
I WILL OWE YOU ONE FAVOR, AT THE TIME OF YOUR CHOOSING.
IN RETURN, TIM WILL OWE NO TITHE TO FAERIE, NOW OR FROM HIS PAST VISIT.
DONE.

HAVE WE HAD THIS CONVERSATION BEFORE? THE ONE WHERE YOU TELL ME IT'S FINE WHAT I DID. WHAT I'VE *DONE.*

NOT *FINE,* PRECISELY, TIM. BUT THERE WERE REASONS.

DID MY REASONS MAKE ANYONE LESS DEAD?

THAT'S NOT...

...NO. THEY DID NOT.

DIDN'T THINK SO.

THEN, WHATEVER. WE'RE NOT WASTING TIME HAVING IT NOW.

WE NEED TO *GO.* WE NEED TO HELP ELLIE.

I AGREE. BUT THIS IS TITANIA'S WORLD, AND SO YOU NEED HER PERMISSION TO LEAVE.

YOU'LL NEED TO ASK, AND ASK CAREFULLY.

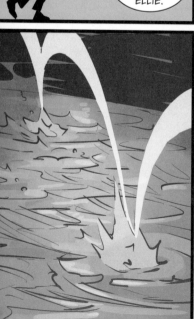

FINE. YOU CAN TELL ME ON THE WAY.

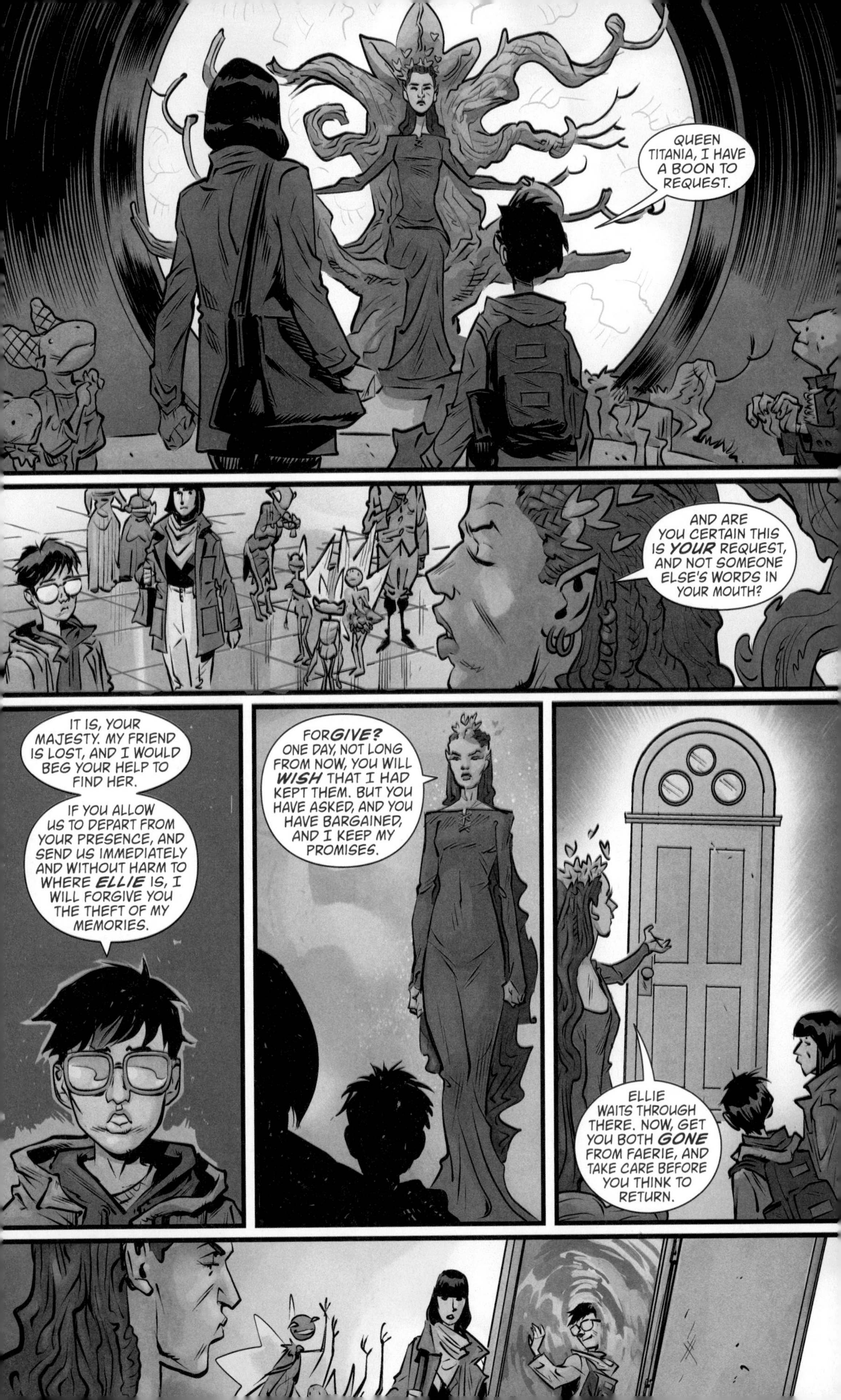
QUEEN TITANIA, I HAVE A BOON TO REQUEST.
AND ARE YOU CERTAIN THIS IS YOUR REQUEST, AND NOT SOMEONE ELSE'S WORDS IN YOUR MOUTH?
IT IS, YOUR MAJESTY. MY FRIEND IS LOST, AND I WOULD BEG YOUR HELP TO FIND HER.
IF YOU ALLOW US TO DEPART FROM YOUR PRESENCE, AND SEND US IMMEDIATELY AND WITHOUT HARM TO WHERE ELLIE IS, I WILL FORGIVE YOU THE THEFT OF MY MEMORIES.
FORGIVE? ONE DAY, NOT LONG FROM NOW, YOU WILL WISH THAT I HAD KEPT THEM. BUT YOU HAVE ASKED, AND YOU HAVE BARGAINED, AND I KEEP MY PROMISES.
ELLIE WAITS THROUGH THERE. NOW, GET YOU BOTH GONE FROM FAERIE, AND TAKE CARE BEFORE YOU THINK TO RETURN.

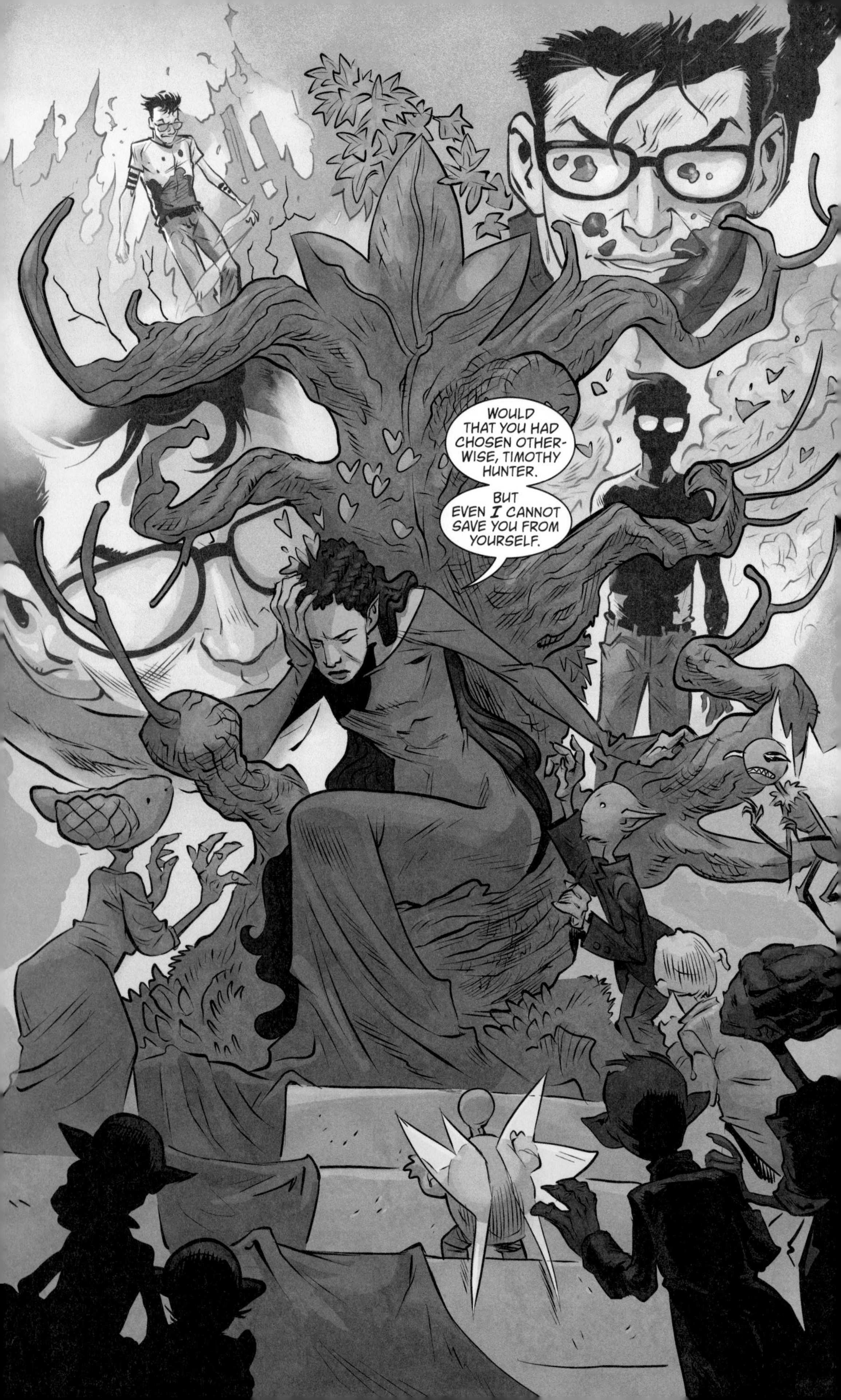
WOULD THAT YOU HAD CHOSEN OTHER-WISE, TIMOTHY HUNTER.
BUT EVEN I CANNOT SAVE YOU FROM YOURSELF.

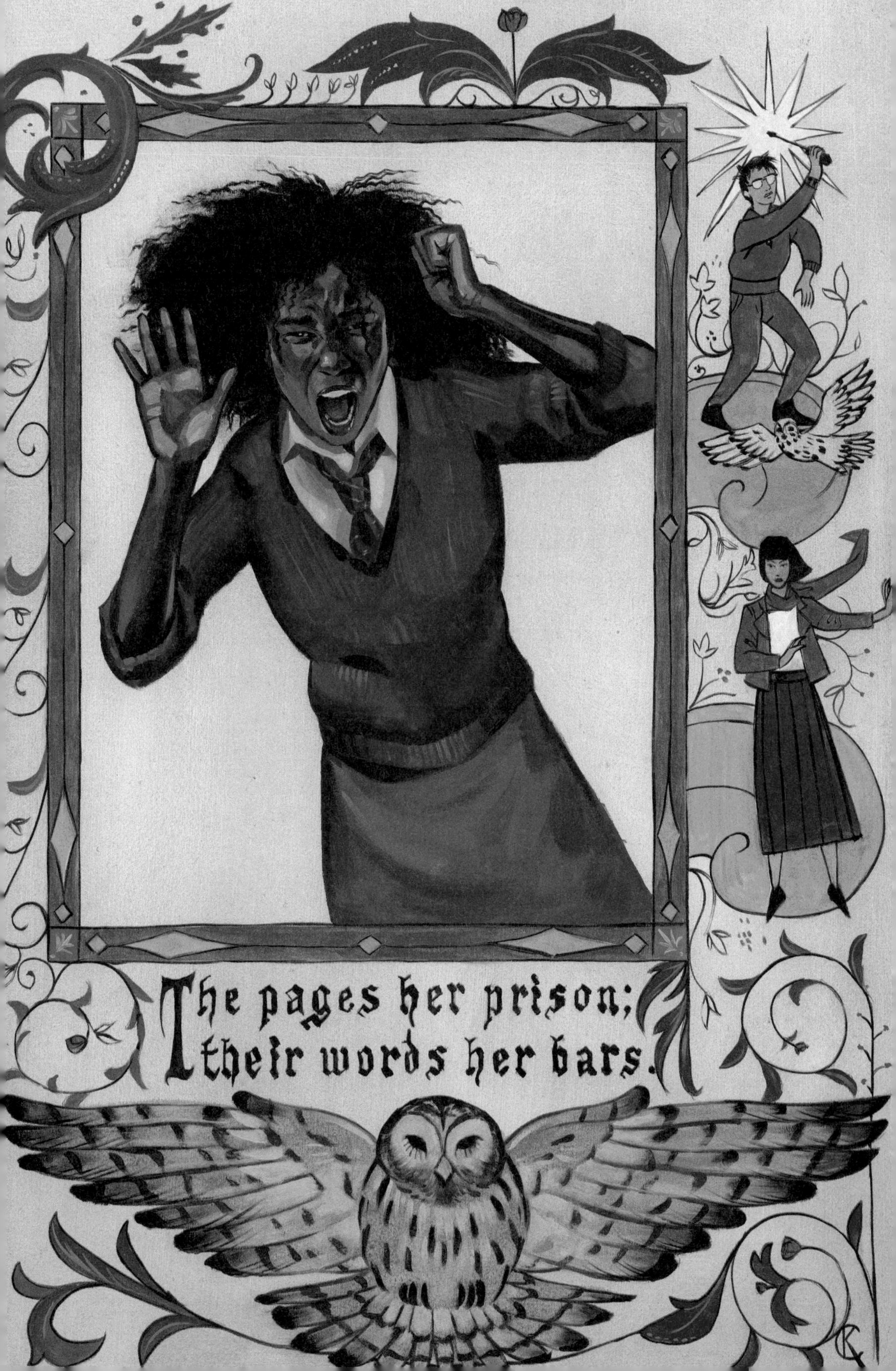
The pages her prison;
their words her bars.

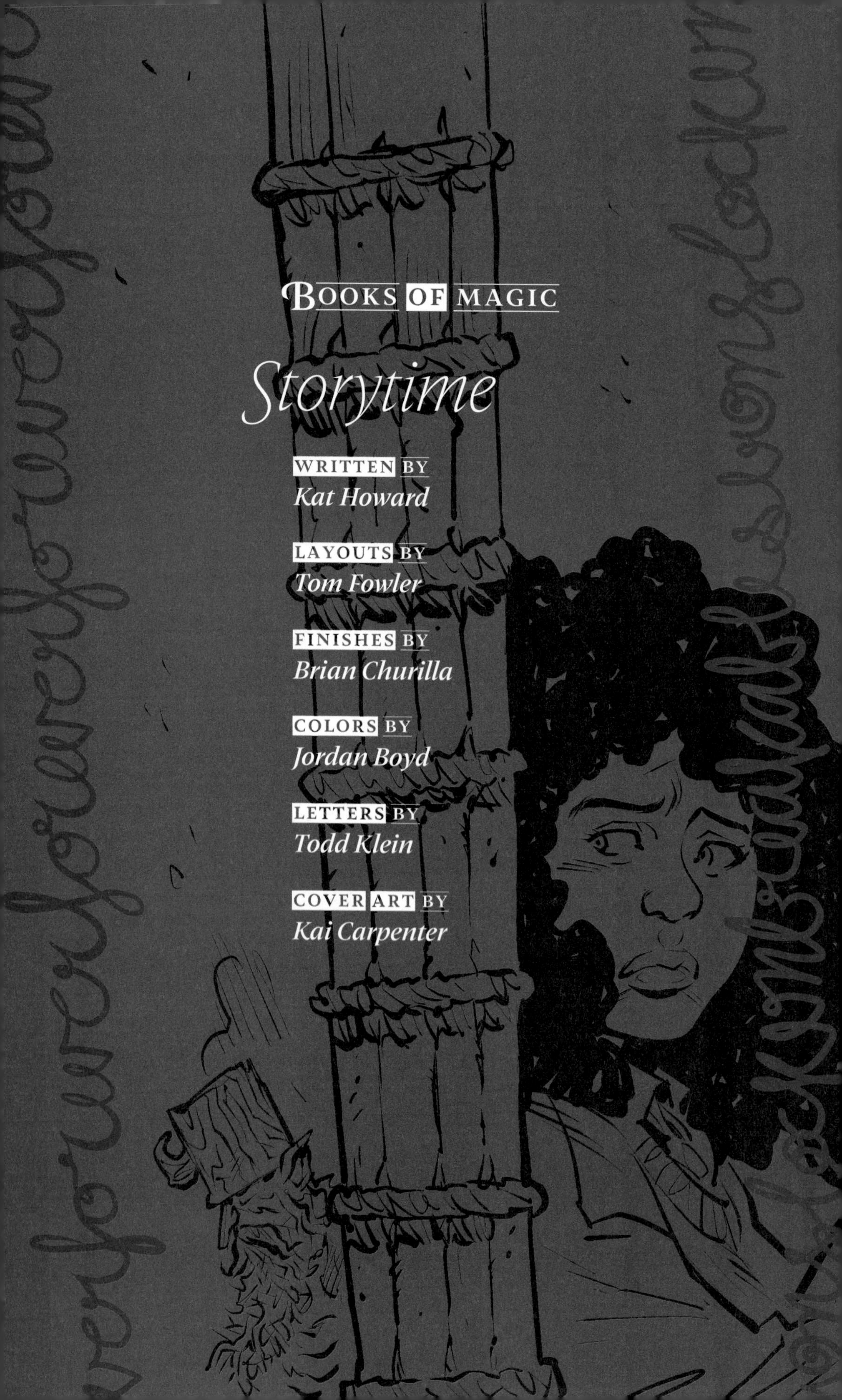

BOOKS OF MAGIC

Storytime

WRITTEN BY
Kat Howard

LAYOUTS BY
Tom Fowler

FINISHES BY
Brian Churilla

COLORS BY
Jordan Boyd

LETTERS BY
Todd Klein

COVER ART BY
Kai Carpenter

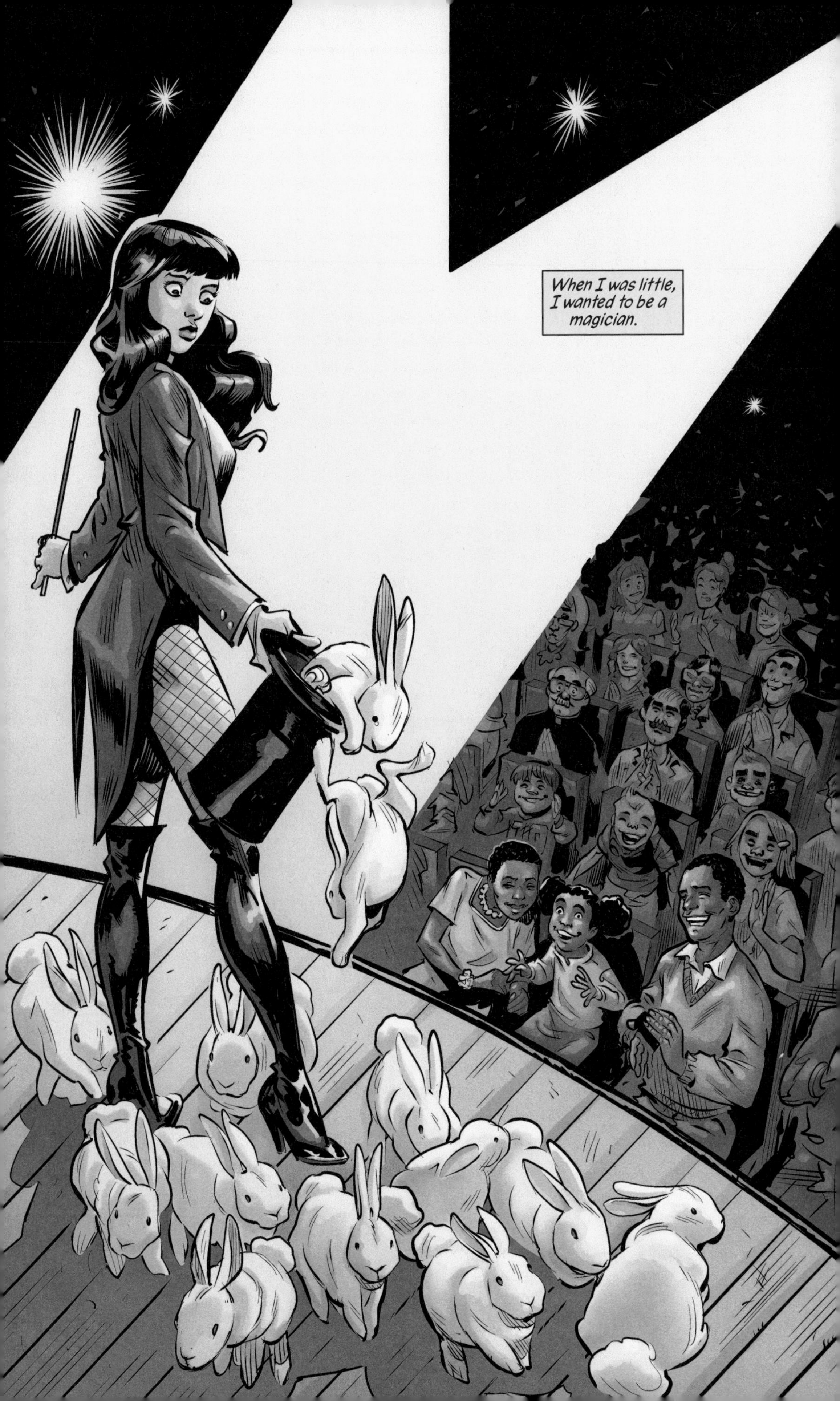
When I was little, I wanted to be a magician.

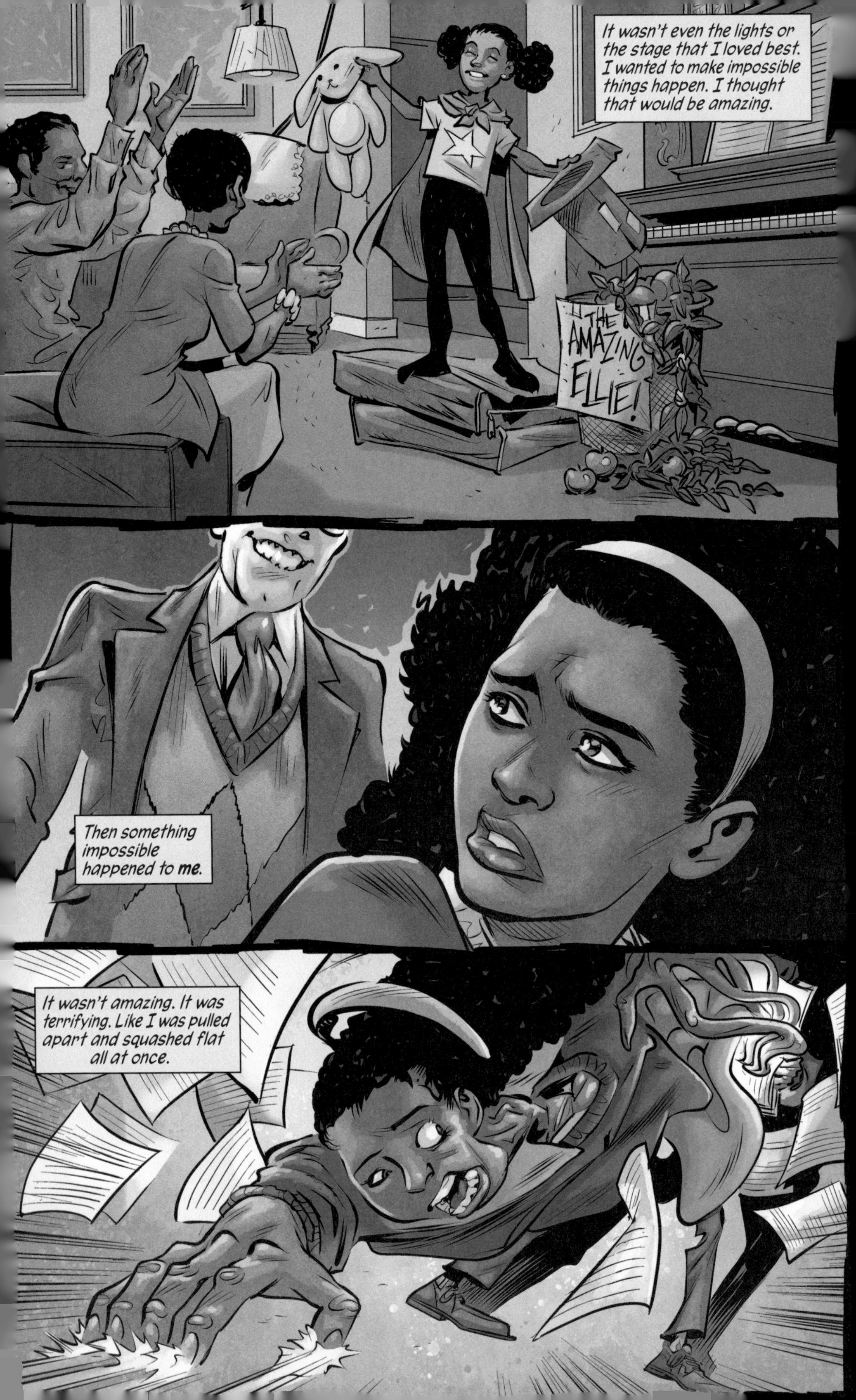
It wasn't even the lights or the stage that I loved best. I wanted to make impossible things happen. I thought that would be amazing.
THE AMAZING ELLIE!
Then something impossible happened to **me**.
It wasn't amazing. It was terrifying. Like I was pulled apart and squashed flat all at once.

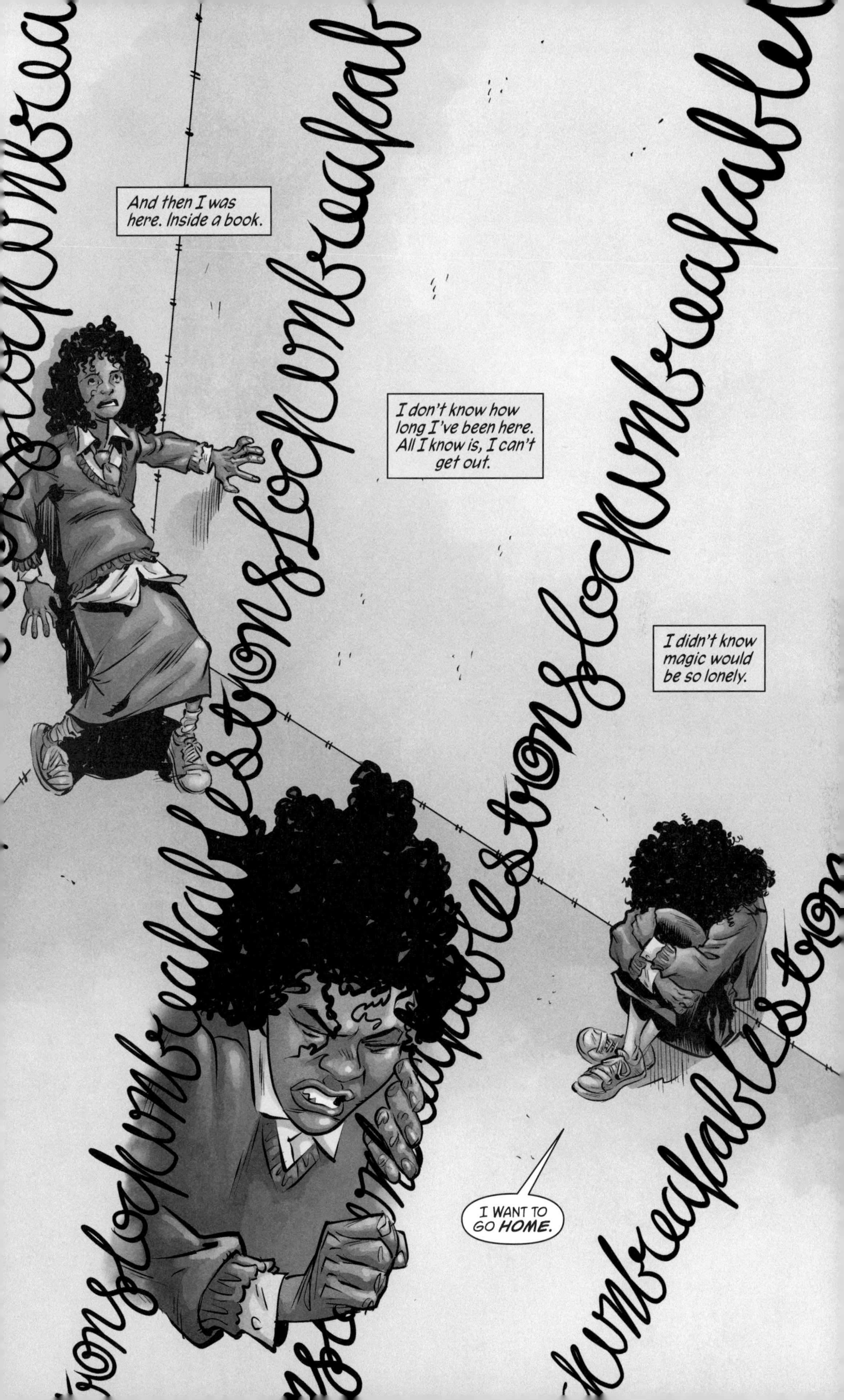
And then I was here. Inside a book.
I don't know how long I've been here. All I know is, I can't get out.
I didn't know magic would be so lonely.
I WANT TO GO HOME.

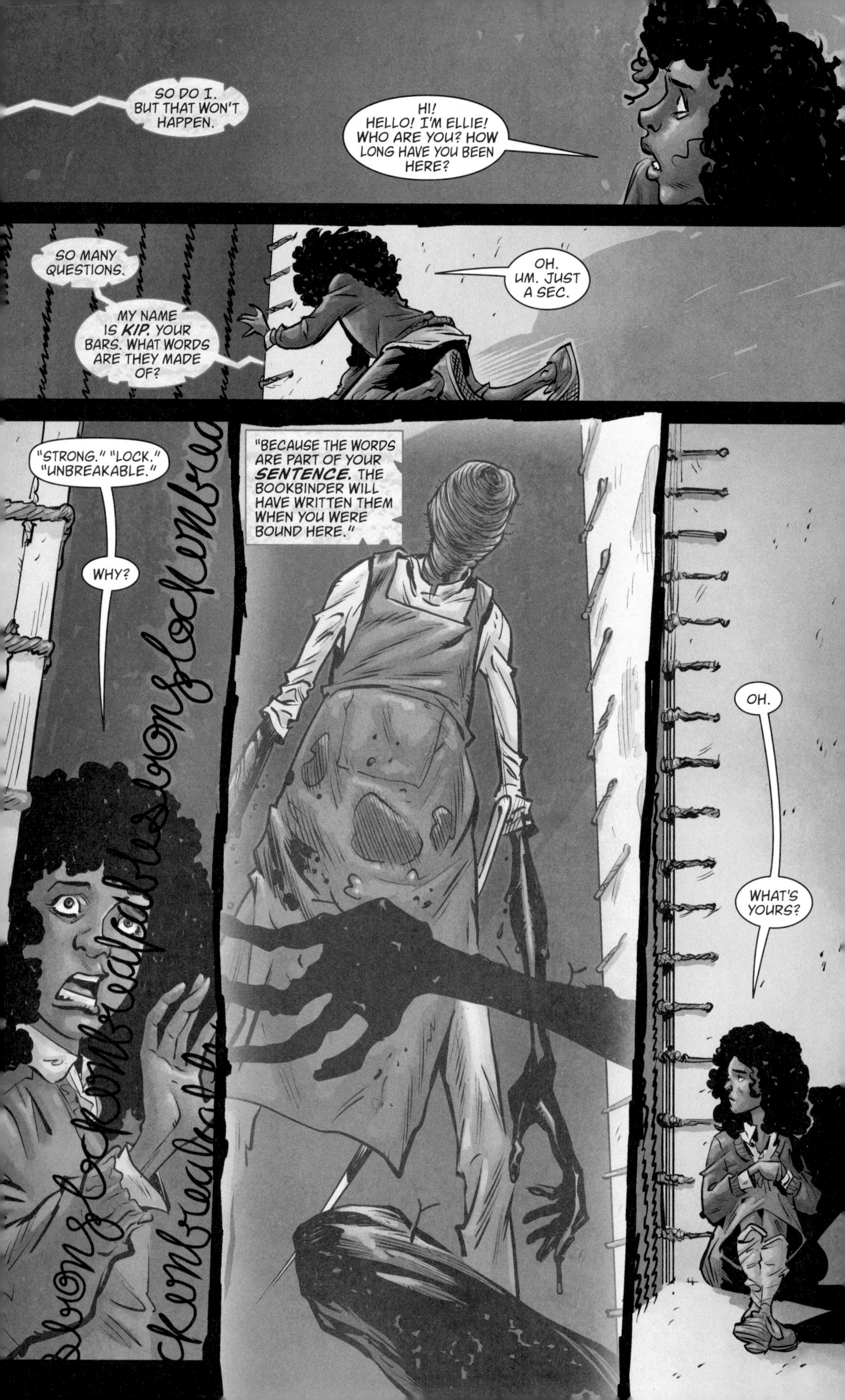
SO DO I. BUT THAT WON'T HAPPEN.
HI! HELLO! I'M ELLIE! WHO ARE YOU? HOW LONG HAVE YOU BEEN HERE?
SO MANY QUESTIONS.
MY NAME IS KIP. YOUR BARS. WHAT WORDS ARE THEY MADE OF?
OH. UM. JUST A SEC.
"STRONG." "LOCK." "UNBREAKABLE."
WHY?
"BECAUSE THE WORDS ARE PART OF YOUR SENTENCE. THE BOOKBINDER WILL HAVE WRITTEN THEM WHEN YOU WERE BOUND HERE."
OH.
WHAT'S YOURS?

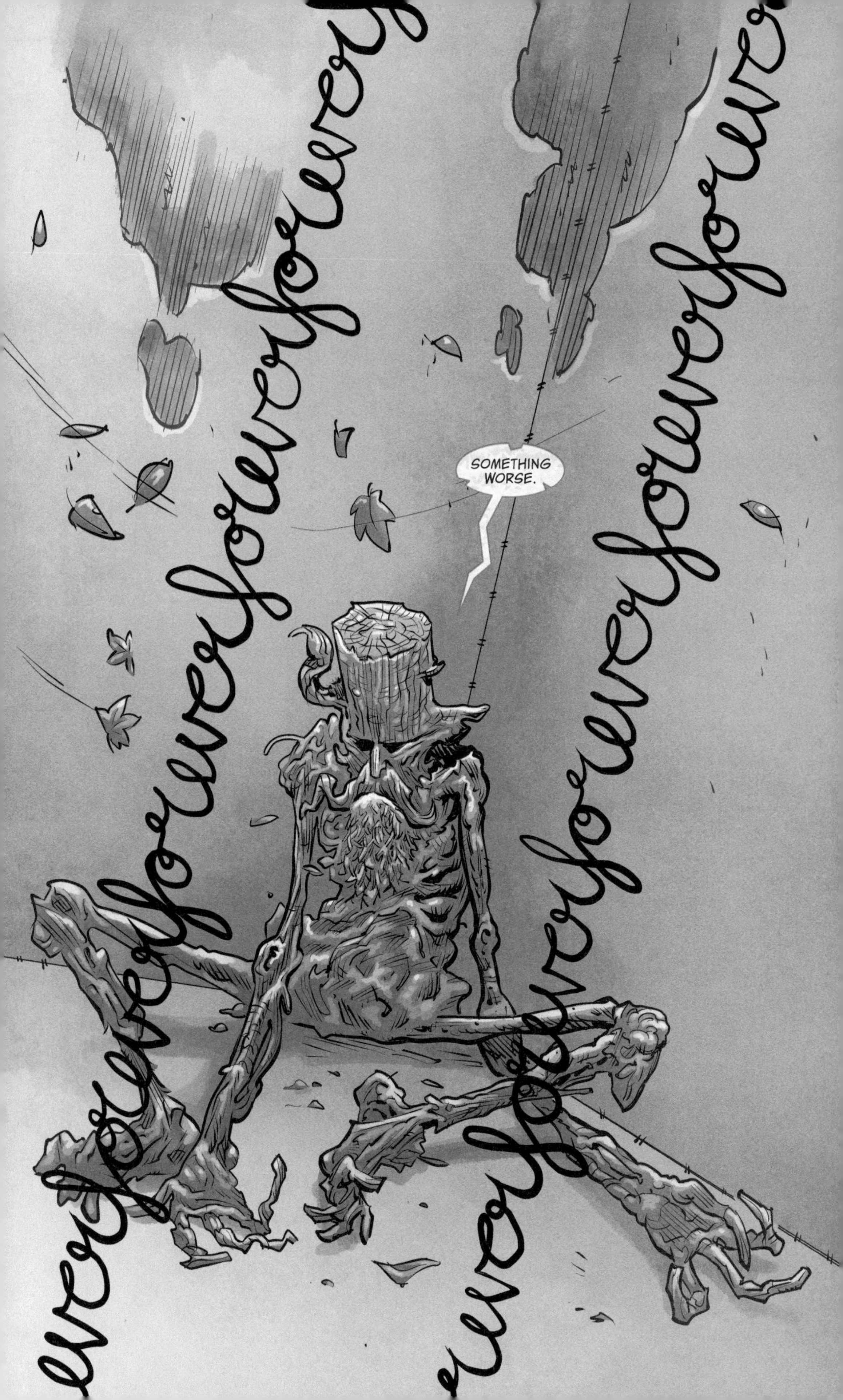
SOMETHING WORSE.

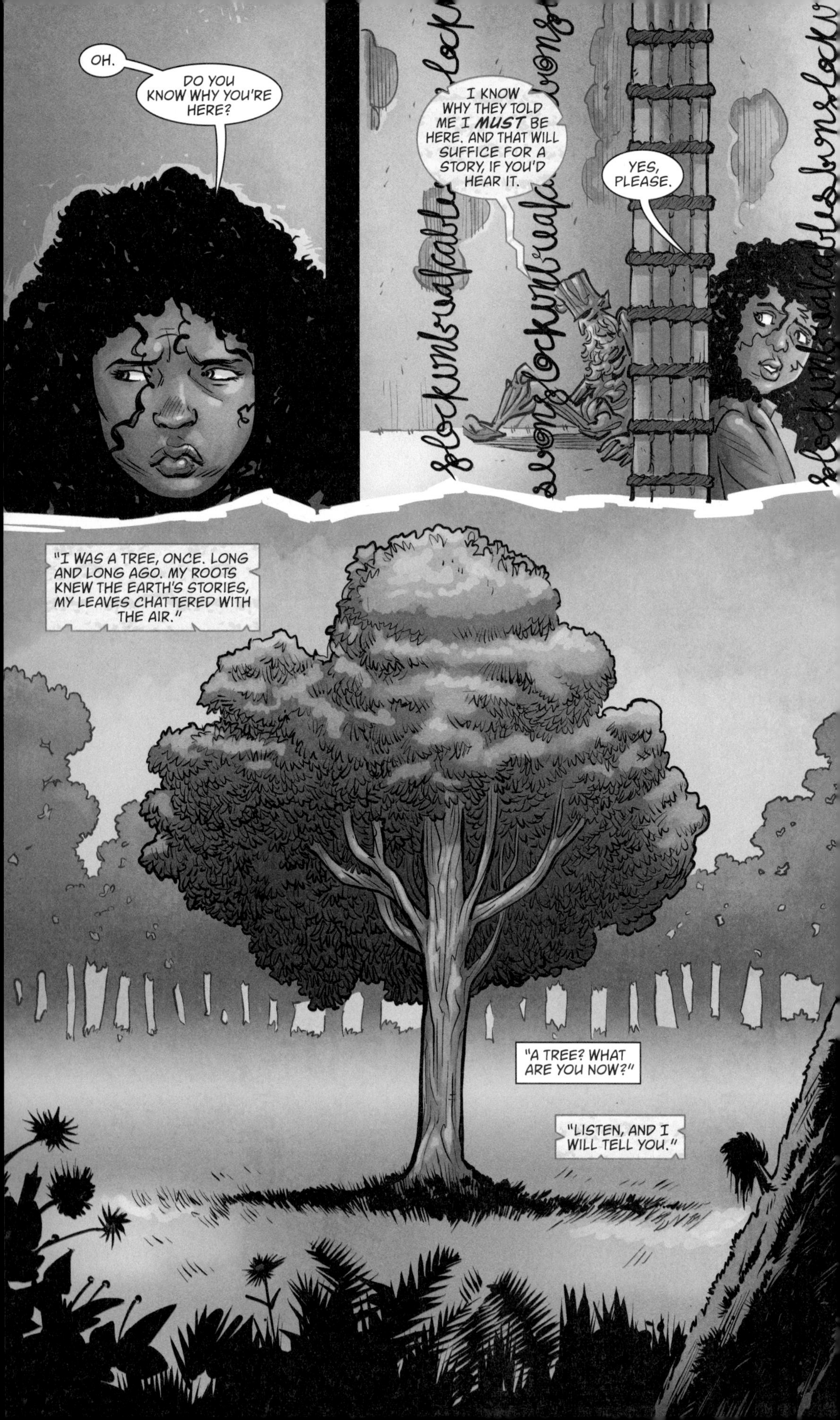
OH.
DO YOU KNOW WHY YOU'RE HERE?
I KNOW WHY THEY TOLD ME I *MUST* BE HERE. AND THAT WILL SUFFICE FOR A STORY, IF YOU'D HEAR IT.
YES, PLEASE.
"I WAS A TREE, ONCE. LONG AND LONG AGO. MY ROOTS KNEW THE EARTH'S STORIES, MY LEAVES CHATTERED WITH THE AIR."
"A TREE? WHAT ARE YOU NOW?"
"LISTEN, AND I WILL TELL YOU."

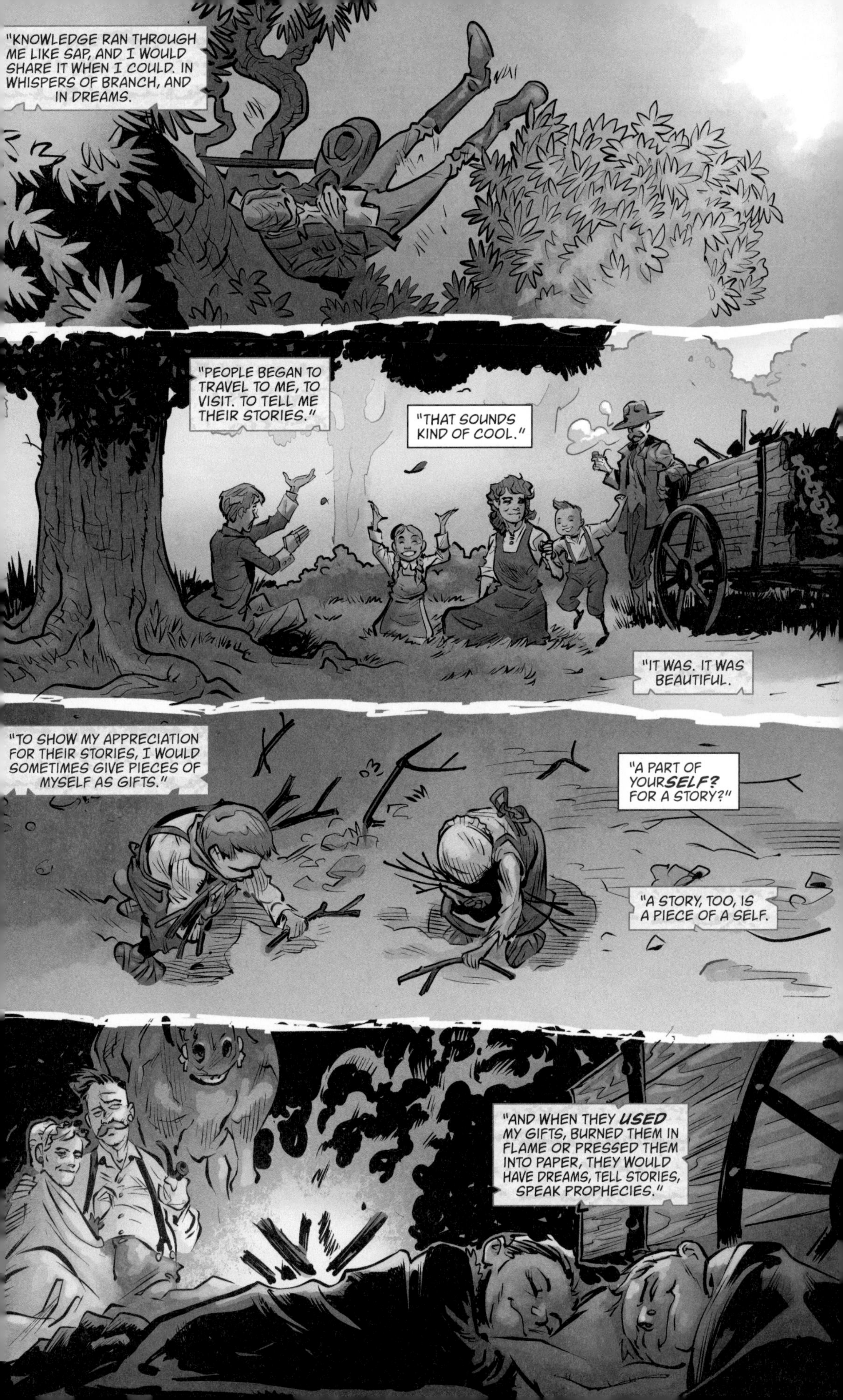
"KNOWLEDGE RAN THROUGH ME LIKE SAP, AND I WOULD SHARE IT WHEN I COULD. IN WHISPERS OF BRANCH, AND IN DREAMS.
"PEOPLE BEGAN TO TRAVEL TO ME, TO VISIT. TO TELL ME THEIR STORIES."
"THAT SOUNDS KIND OF COOL."
"IT WAS. IT WAS BEAUTIFUL.
"TO SHOW MY APPRECIATION FOR THEIR STORIES, I WOULD SOMETIMES GIVE PIECES OF MYSELF AS GIFTS."
"A PART OF YOUR *SELF?* FOR A STORY?"
"A STORY, TOO, IS A PIECE OF A SELF.
"AND WHEN THEY *USED* MY GIFTS, BURNED THEM IN FLAME OR PRESSED THEM INTO PAPER, THEY WOULD HAVE DREAMS, TELL STORIES, SPEAK PROPHECIES."

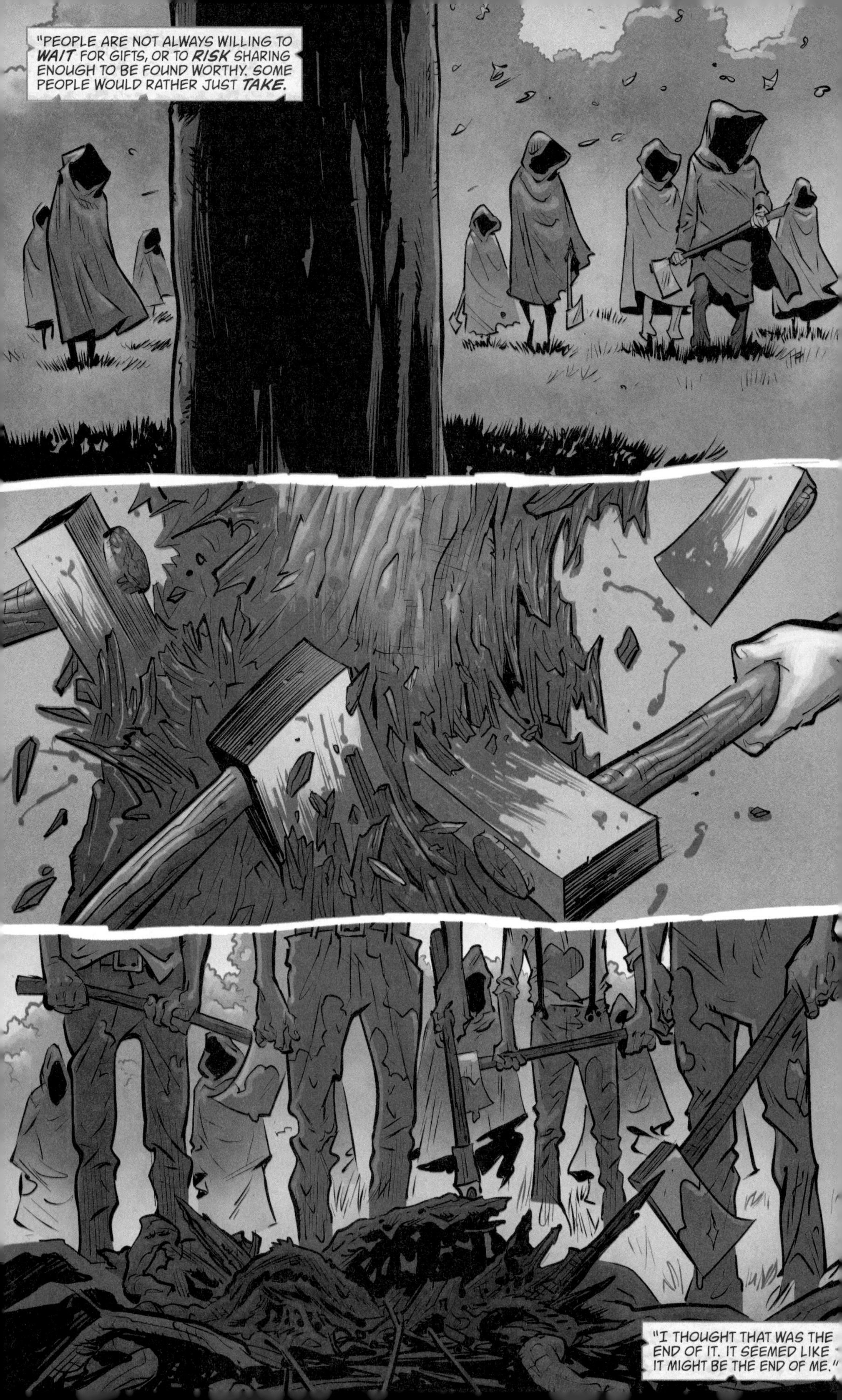
"PEOPLE ARE NOT ALWAYS WILLING TO WAIT FOR GIFTS, OR TO RISK SHARING ENOUGH TO BE FOUND WORTHY. SOME PEOPLE WOULD RATHER JUST TAKE.
"I THOUGHT THAT WAS THE END OF IT. IT SEEMED LIKE IT MIGHT BE THE END OF ME."

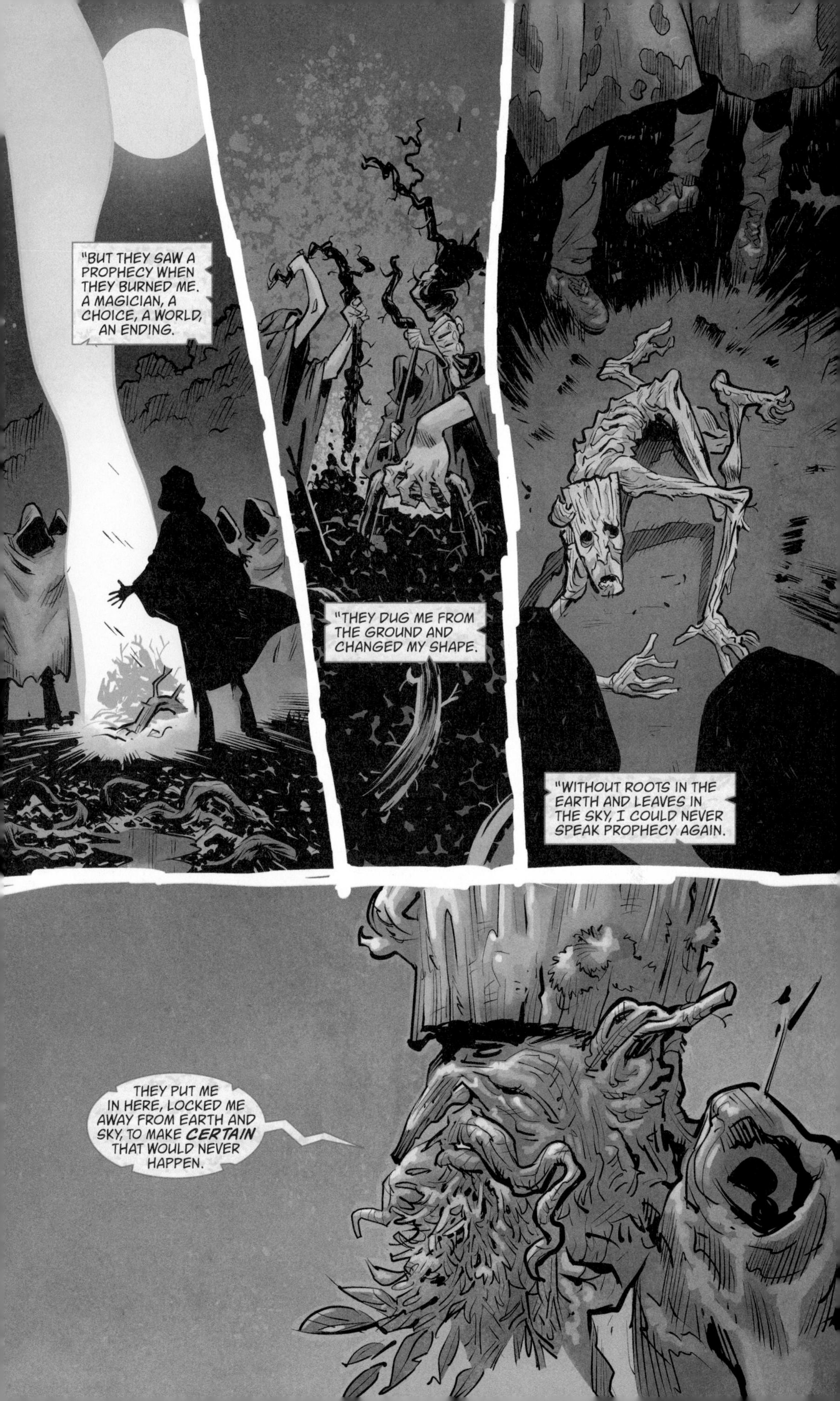
"BUT THEY SAW A PROPHECY WHEN THEY BURNED ME. A MAGICIAN, A CHOICE, A WORLD, AN ENDING.
"THEY DUG ME FROM THE GROUND AND CHANGED MY SHAPE.
"WITHOUT ROOTS IN THE EARTH AND LEAVES IN THE SKY, I COULD NEVER SPEAK PROPHECY AGAIN.
THEY PUT ME IN HERE, LOCKED ME AWAY FROM EARTH AND SKY, TO MAKE *CERTAIN* THAT WOULD NEVER HAPPEN.

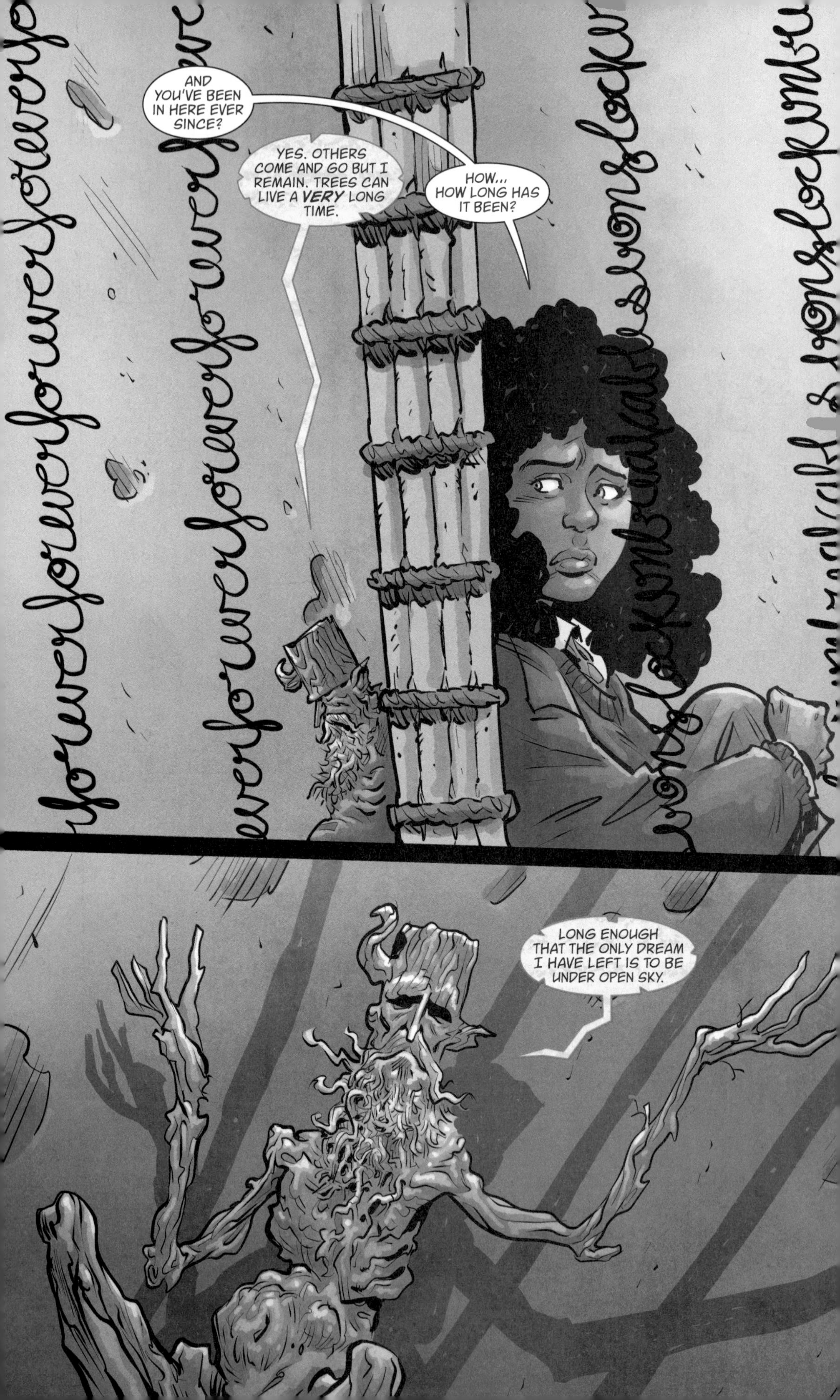
AND YOU'VE BEEN IN HERE EVER SINCE?
YES. OTHERS COME AND GO BUT I REMAIN. TREES CAN LIVE A *VERY* LONG TIME.
HOW... HOW LONG HAS IT BEEN?
LONG ENOUGH THAT THE ONLY DREAM I HAVE LEFT IS TO BE UNDER OPEN SKY.

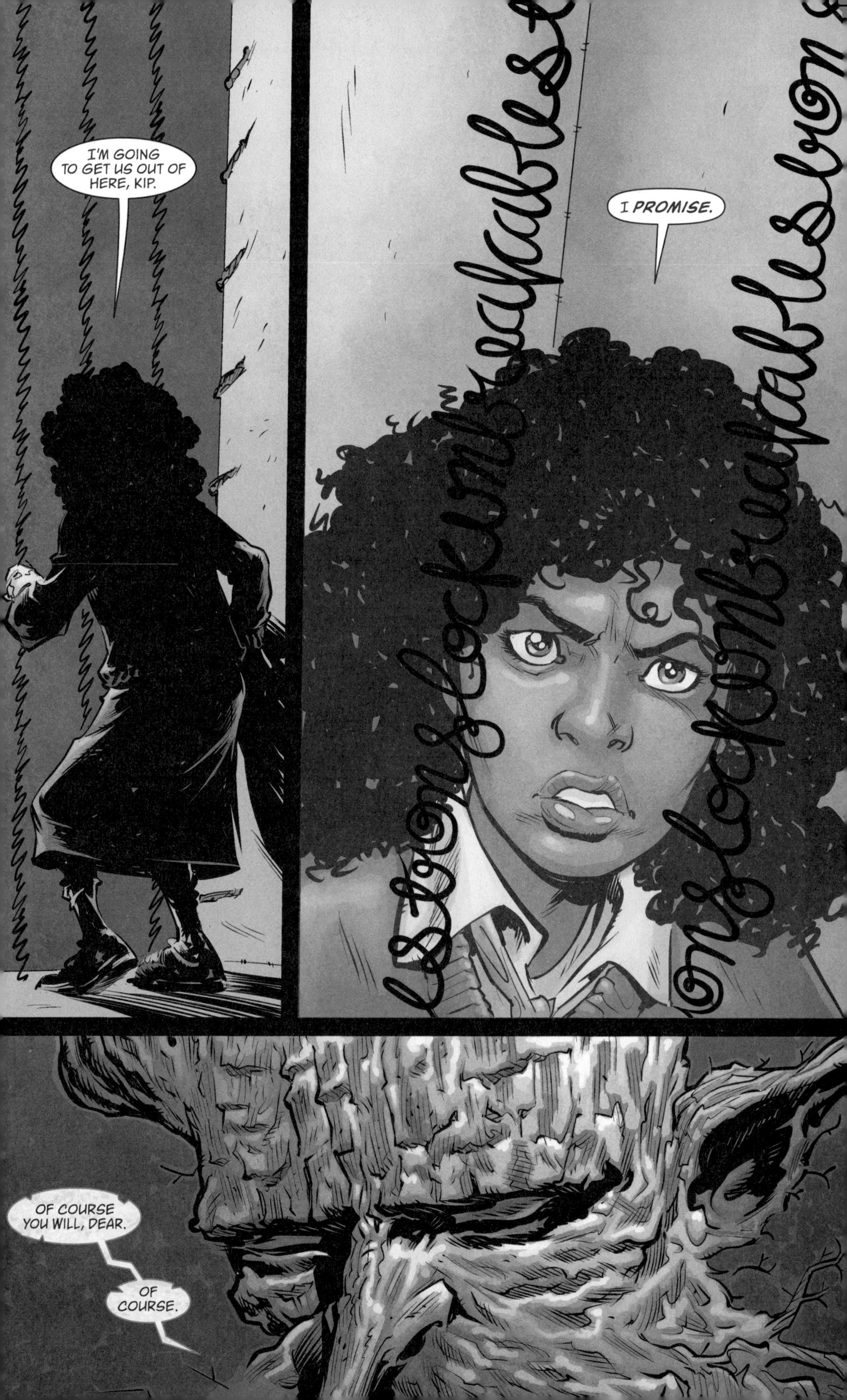

I'M GOING TO GET US OUT OF HERE, KIP.
I PROMISE.
OF COURSE YOU WILL, DEAR.
OF COURSE.

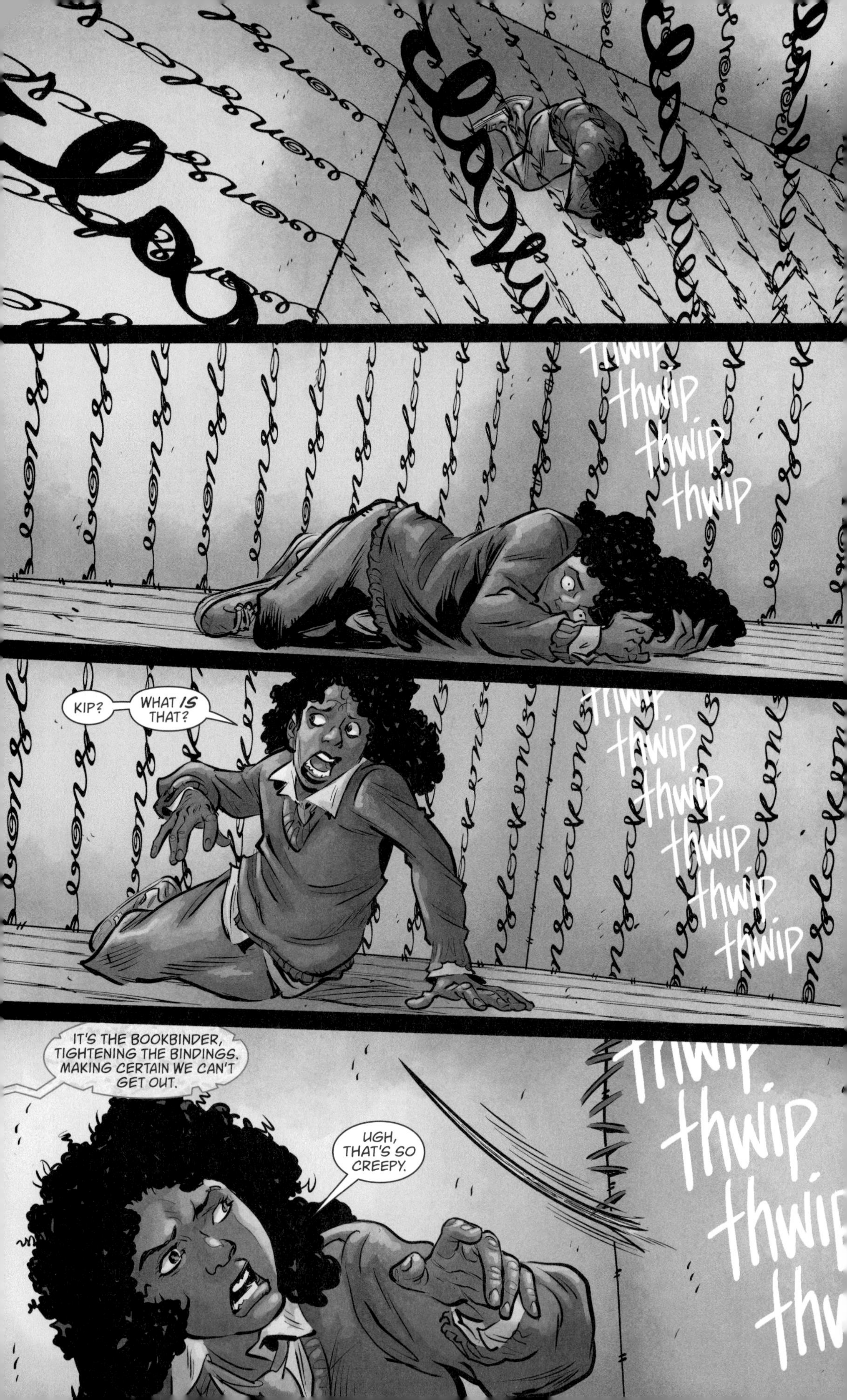
thwip
thwip
thwip
thwip
KIP?
WHAT IS THAT?
thwip
thwip
thwip
thwip
thwip
thwip
IT'S THE BOOKBINDER, TIGHTENING THE BINDINGS. MAKING CERTAIN WE CAN'T GET OUT.
UGH, THAT'S SO CREEPY.
thwip
thwip

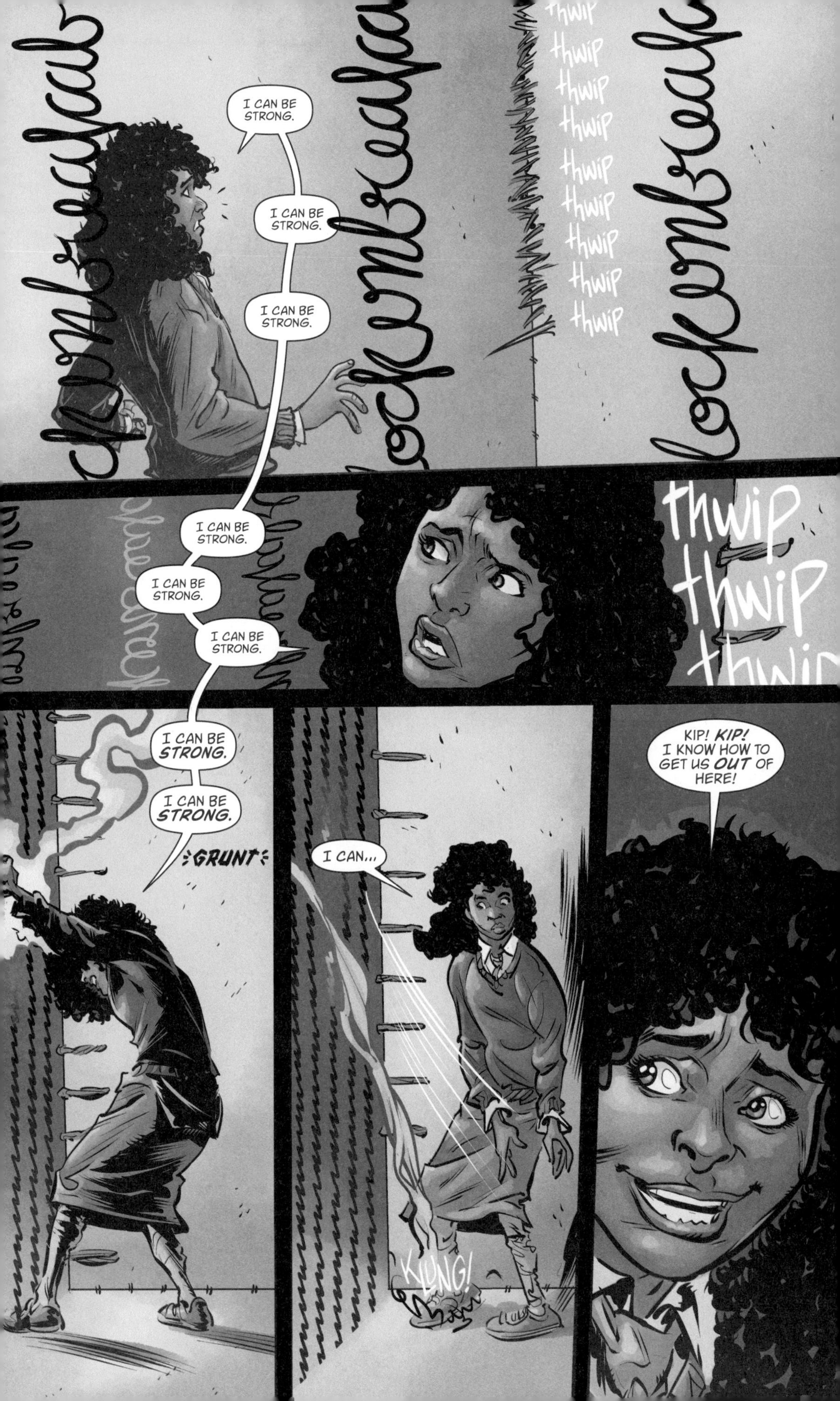

I CAN BE STRONG.
I CAN BE STRONG.
I CAN BE STRONG.
thwip
thwip
thwip
thwip
thwip
thwip
thwip
thwip
I CAN BE STRONG.
I CAN BE STRONG.
I CAN BE STRONG.
thwip
thwip
I CAN BE STRONG.
I CAN BE STRONG.
GRUNT
I CAN...
KLUNG!
KIP! KIP! I KNOW HOW TO GET US OUT OF HERE!

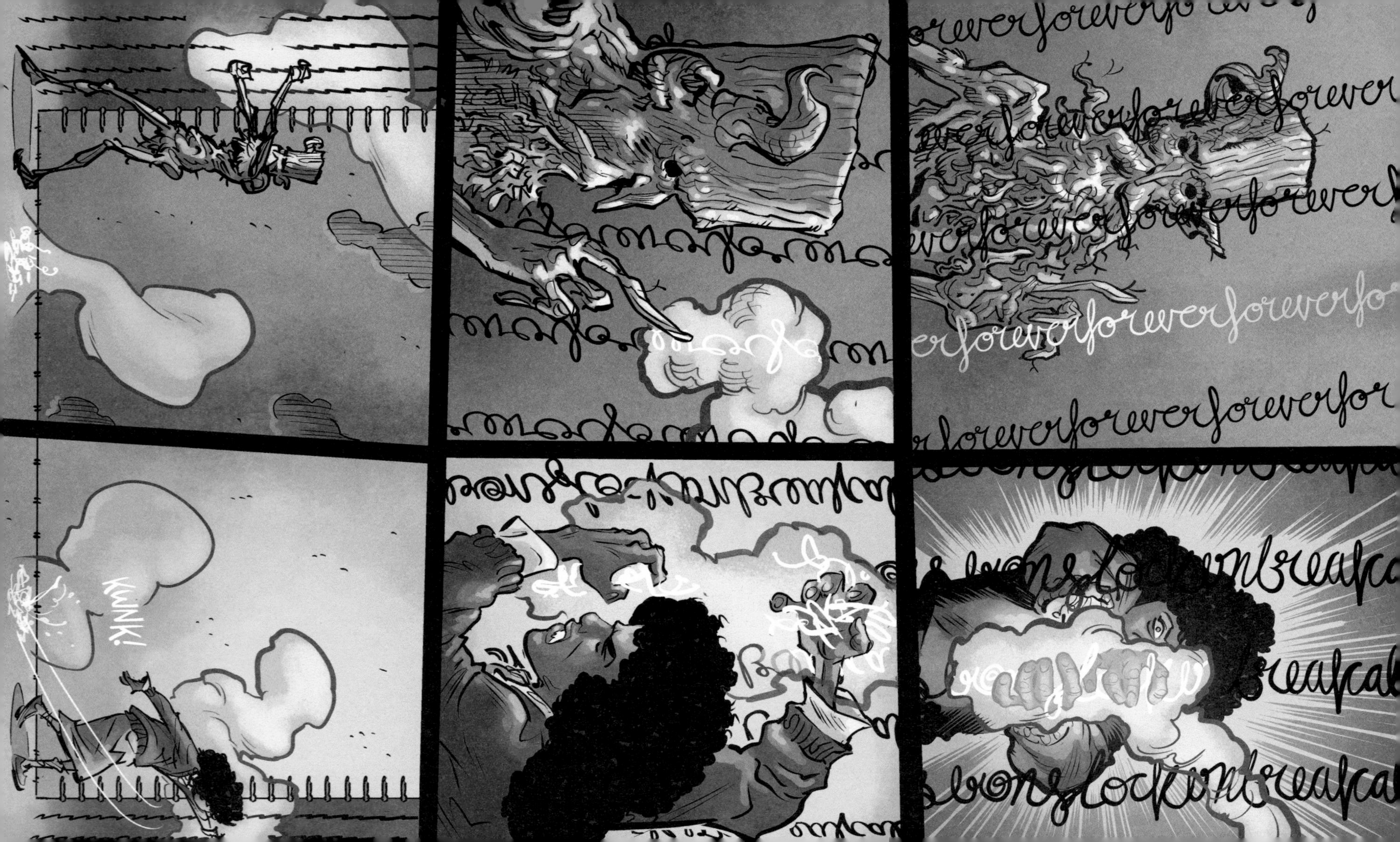
foreverforeverforever
KWNK!

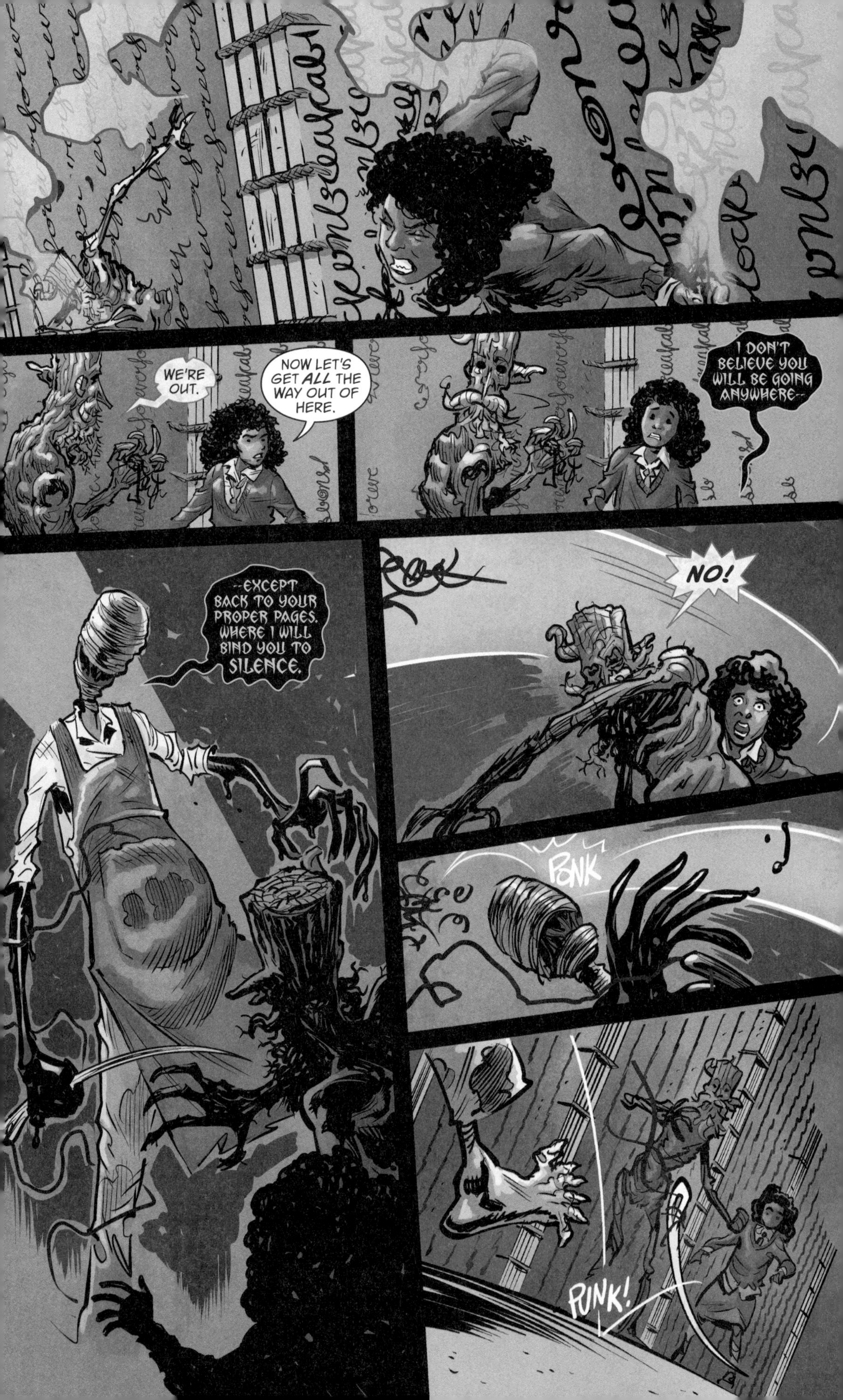
WE'RE OUT.
NOW LET'S GET ALL THE WAY OUT OF HERE.
I DON'T BELIEVE YOU WILL BE GOING ANYWHERE--
--EXCEPT BACK TO YOUR PROPER PAGES. WHERE I WILL BIND YOU TO SILENCE.
NO!
PONK
PUNK!

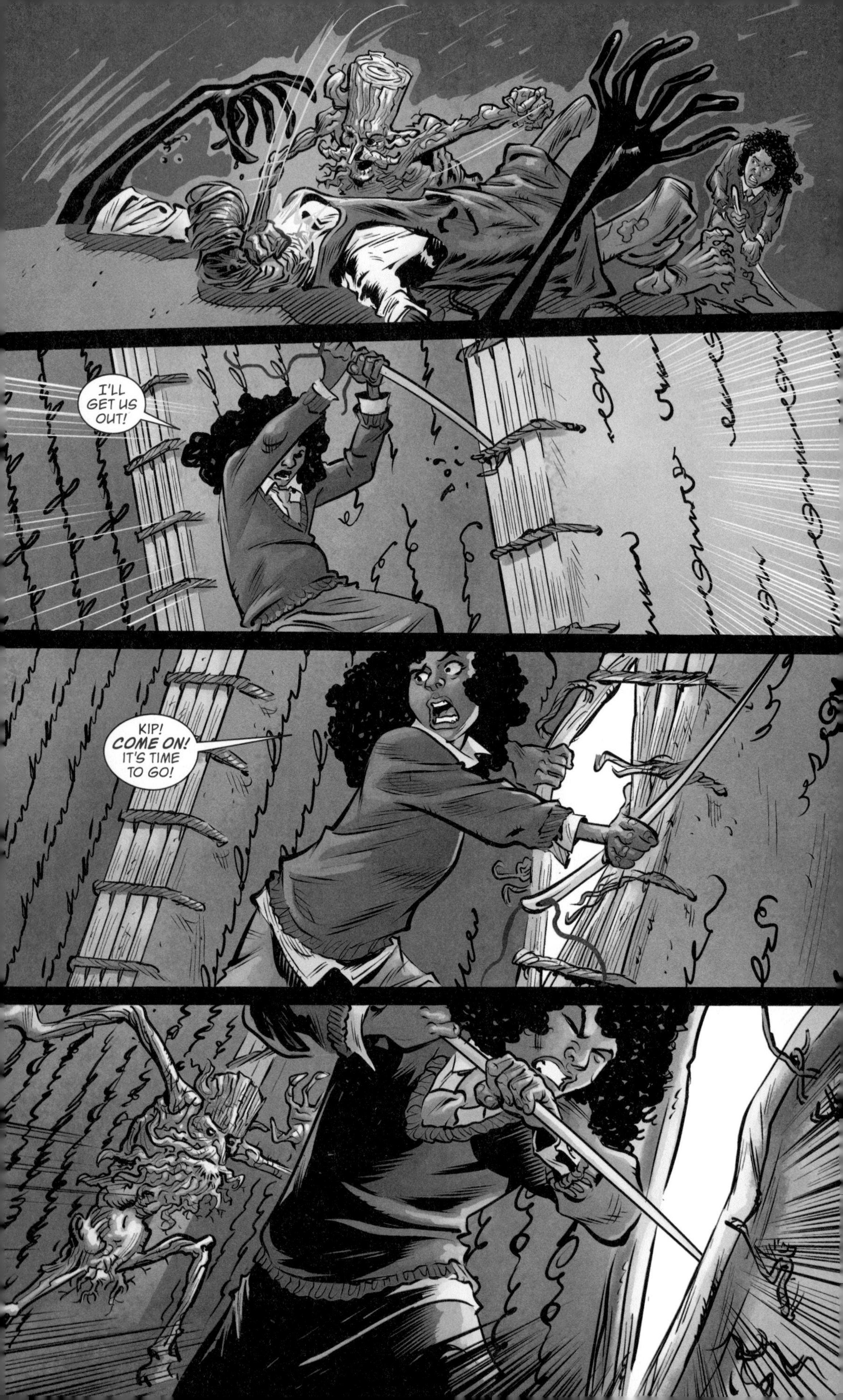
I'LL GET US OUT!
KIP! **COME ON!** IT'S TIME TO GO!

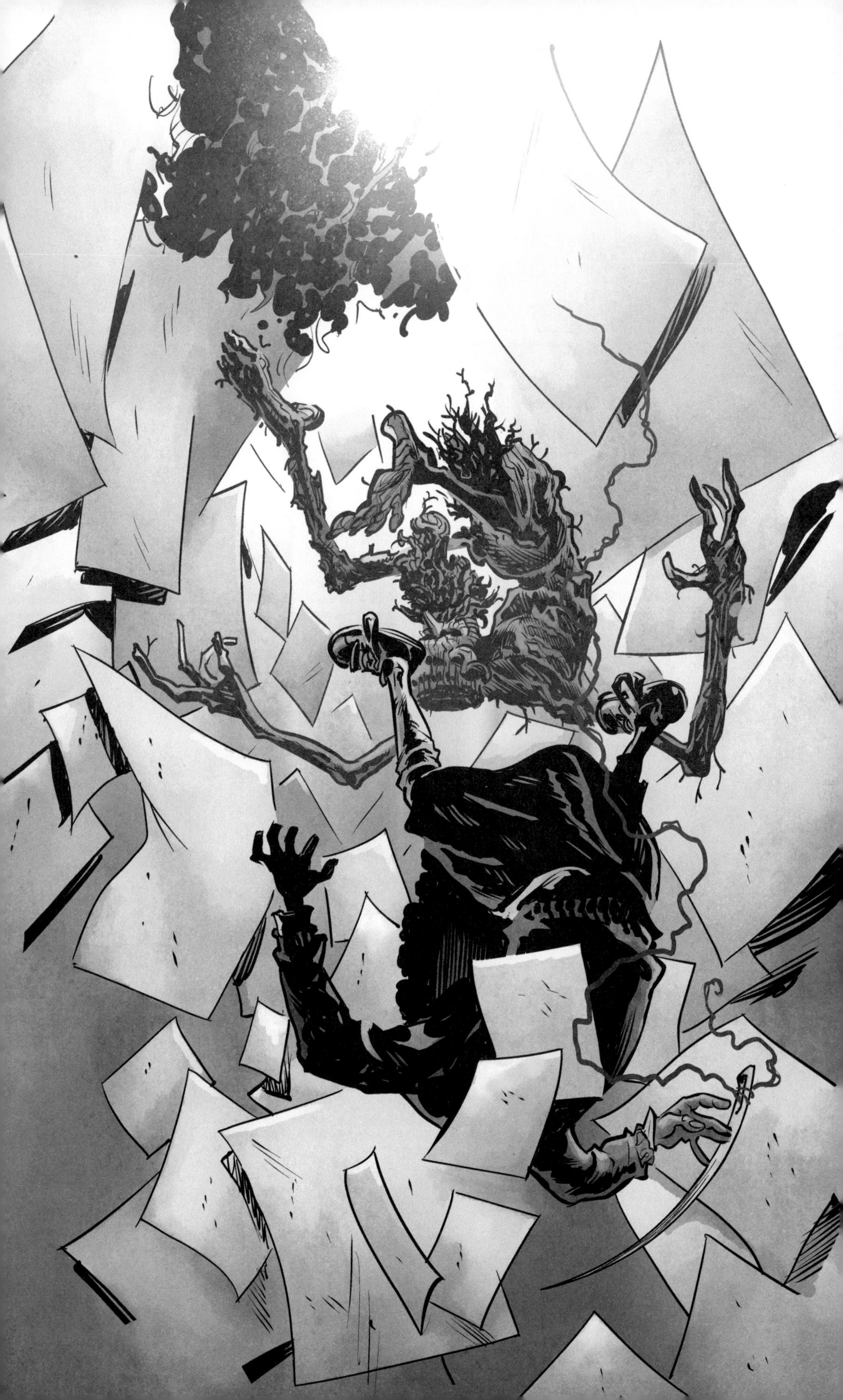

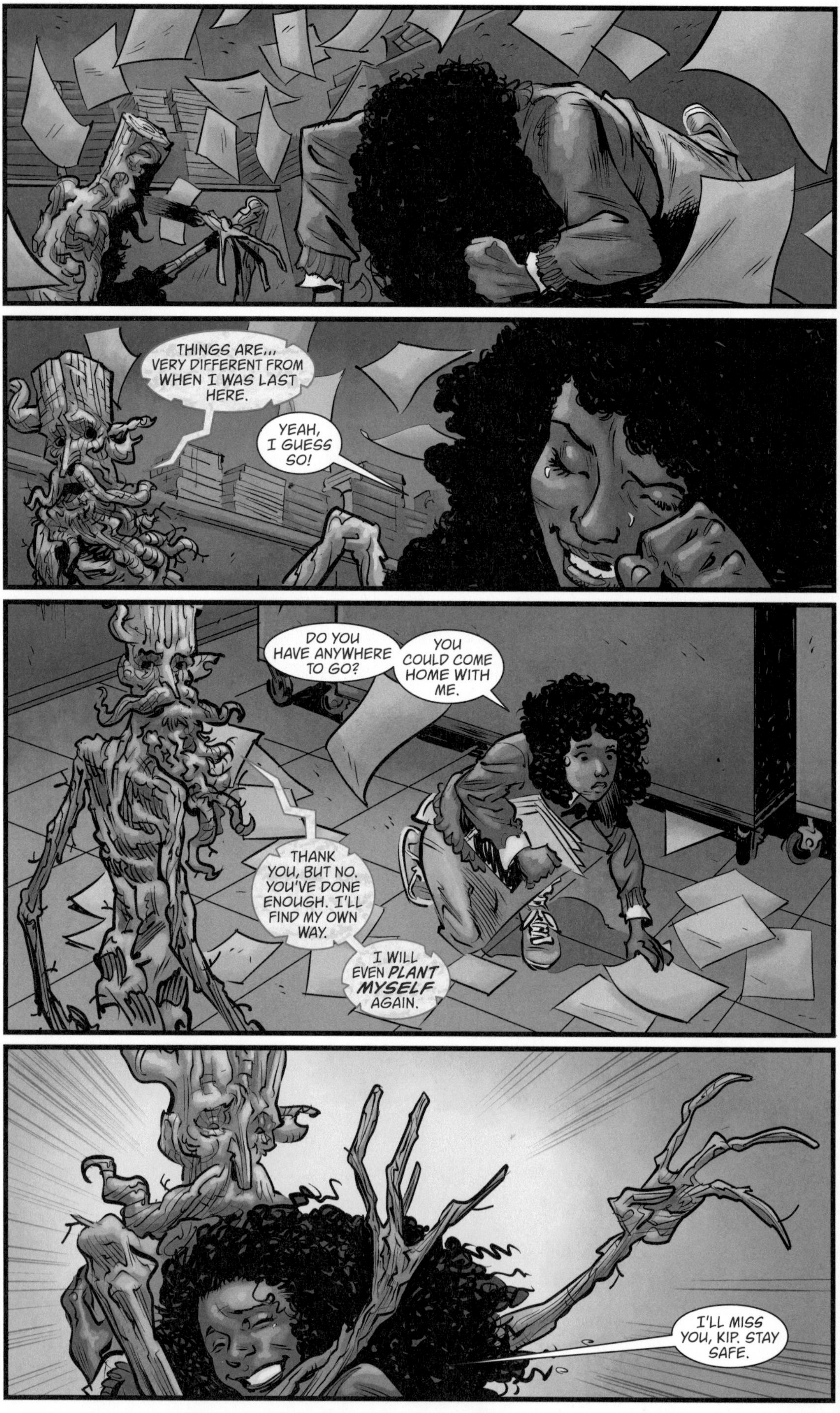
THINGS ARE... VERY DIFFERENT FROM WHEN I WAS LAST HERE.
YEAH, I GUESS SO!
DO YOU HAVE ANYWHERE TO GO?
YOU COULD COME HOME WITH ME.
THANK YOU, BUT NO. YOU'VE DONE ENOUGH. I'LL FIND MY OWN WAY.
I WILL EVEN PLANT MYSELF AGAIN.
I'LL MISS YOU, KIP. STAY SAFE.

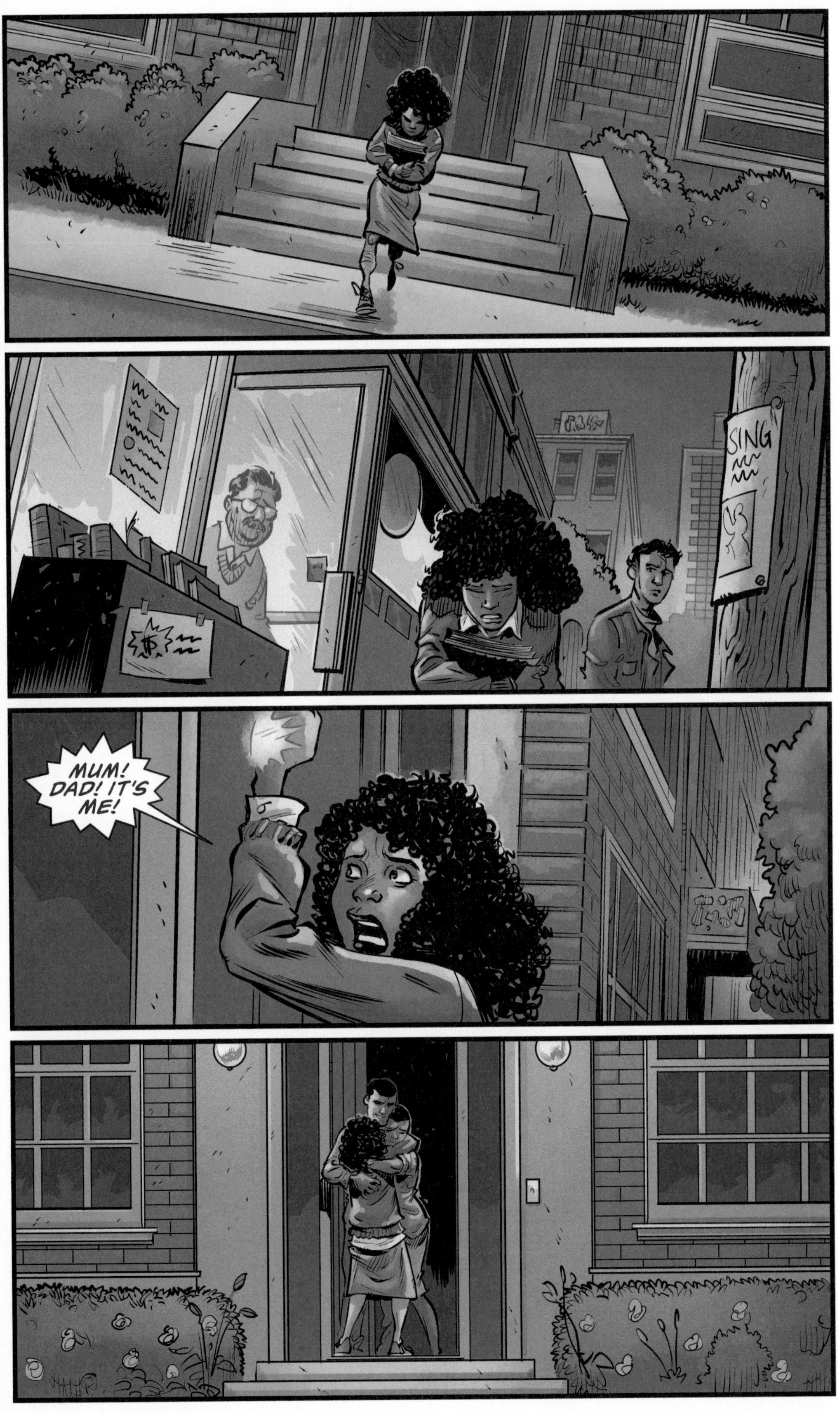
SING
MUM! DAD! IT'S ME!

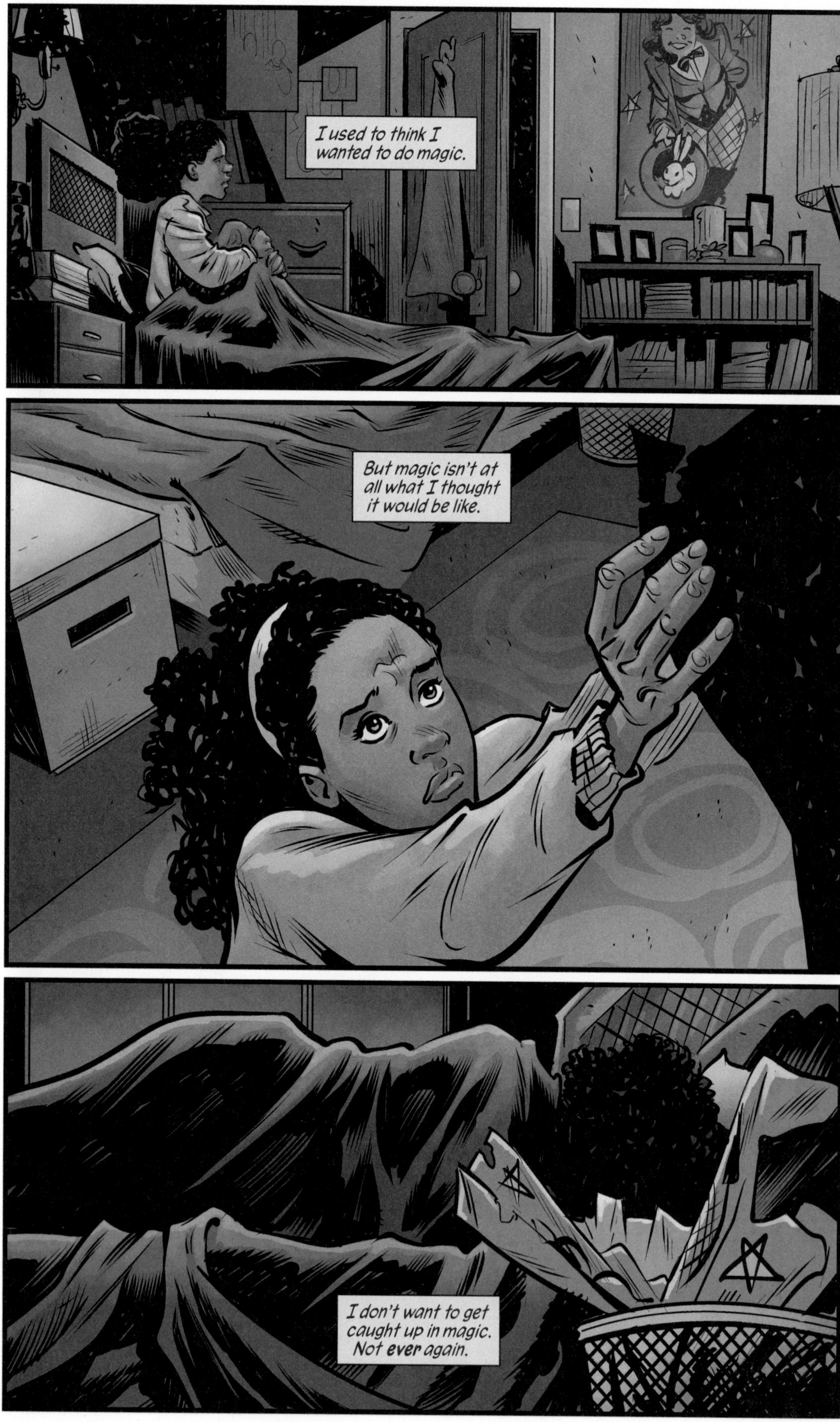
I used to think I wanted to do magic.
But magic isn't at all what I thought it would be like.
I don't want to get caught up in magic. Not **ever** again.

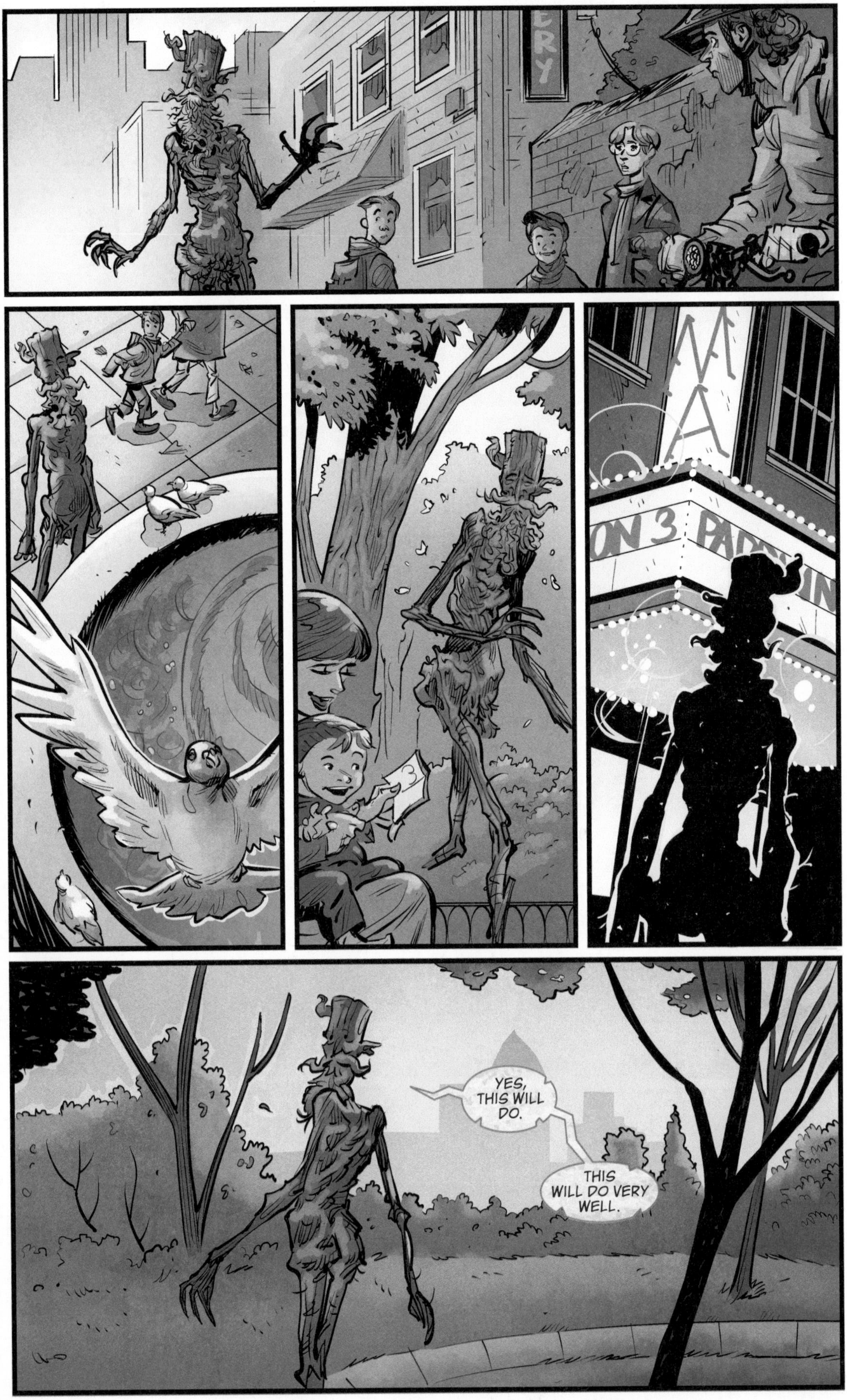
YES, THIS WILL DO.
THIS WILL DO VERY WELL.

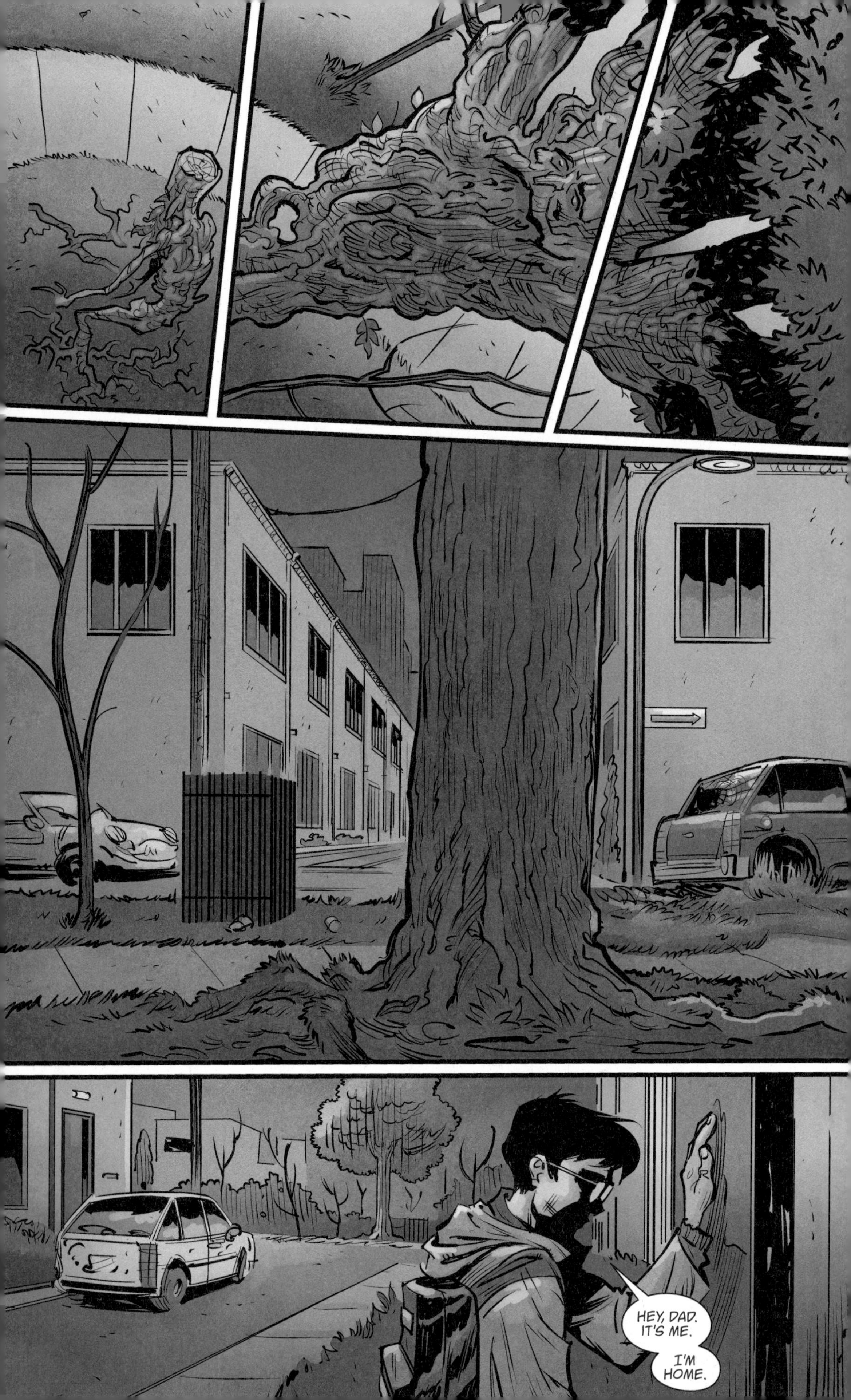
HEY, DAD. IT'S ME.
I'M HOME.

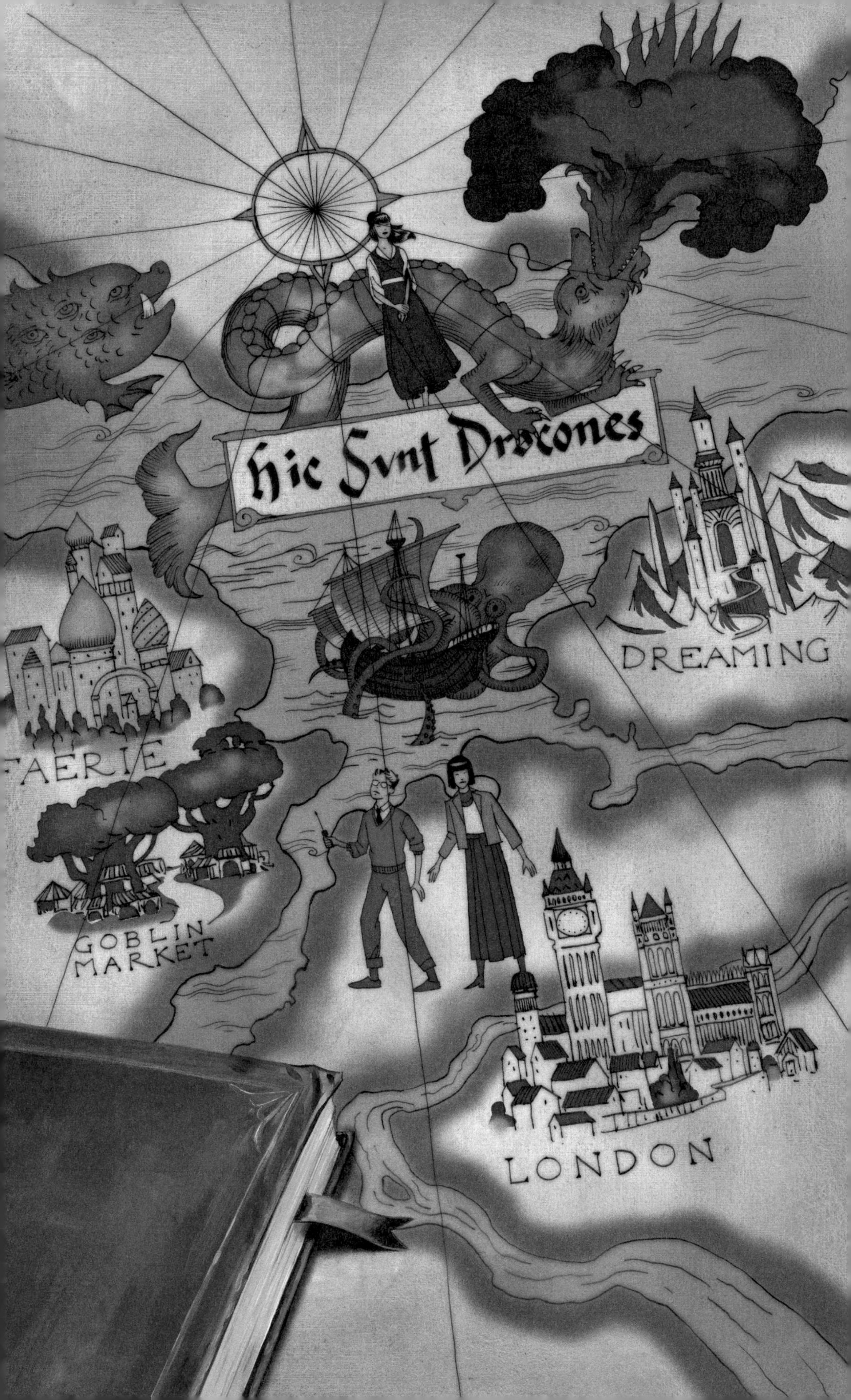

Hic Sunt Dracones
DREAMING
FAERIE
GOBLIN MARKET
LONDON

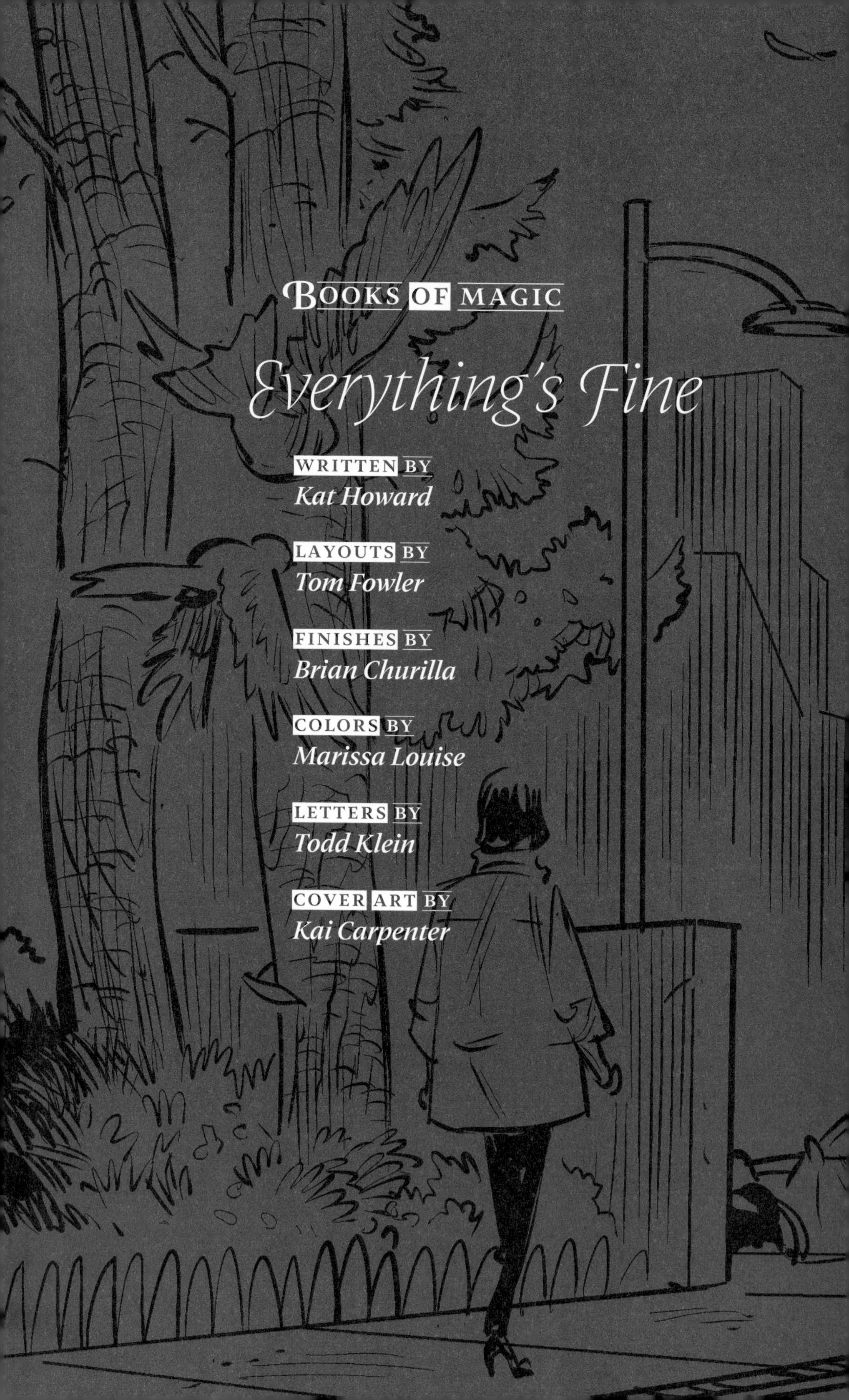

BOOKS OF MAGIC

Everything's Fine

WRITTEN BY
Kat Howard

LAYOUTS BY
Tom Fowler

FINISHES BY
Brian Churilla

COLORS BY
Marissa Louise

LETTERS BY
Todd Klein

COVER ART BY
Kai Carpenter

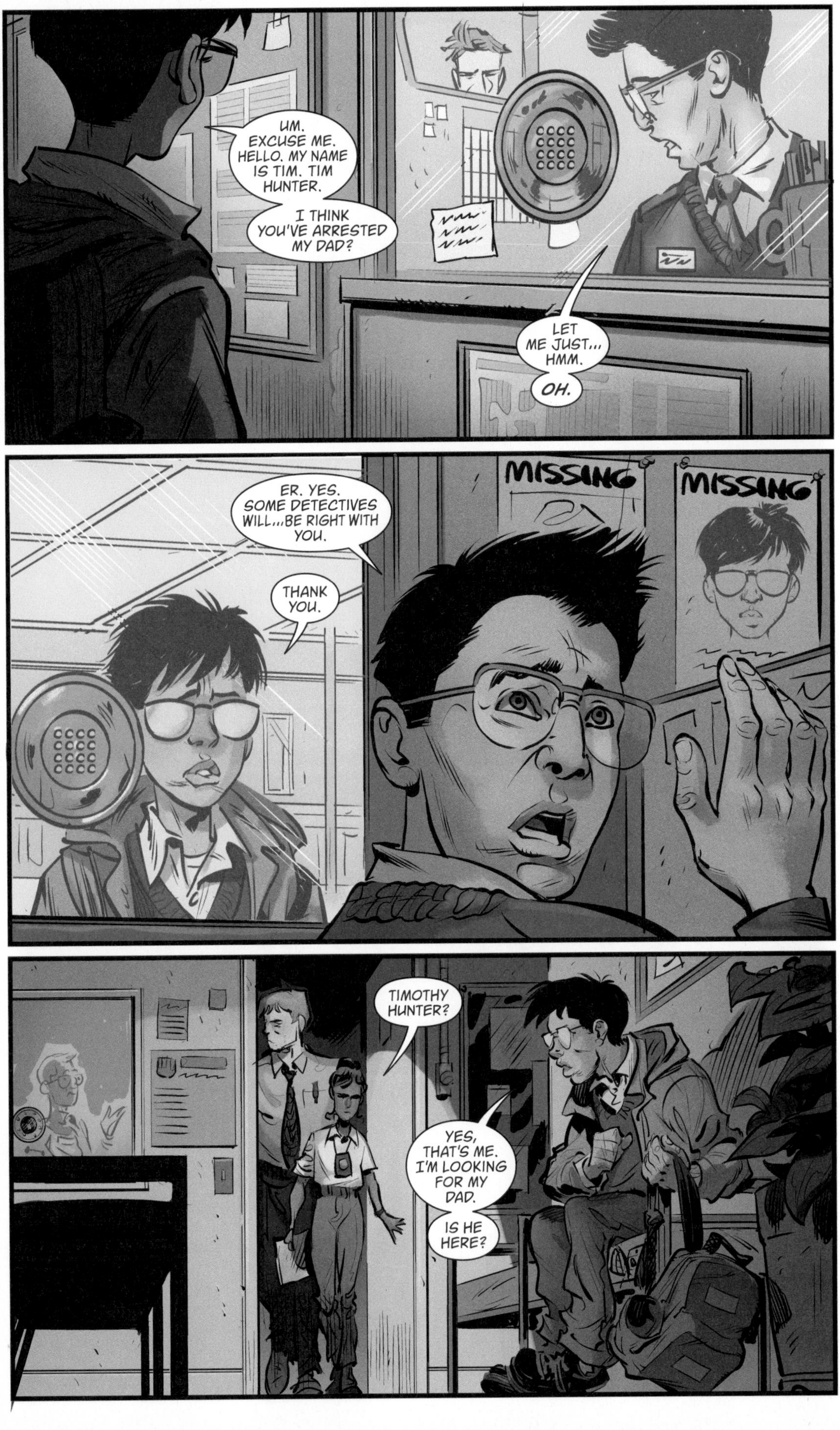
UM. EXCUSE ME. HELLO. MY NAME IS TIM. TIM HUNTER.
I THINK YOU'VE ARRESTED MY DAD?
LET ME JUST... HMM.
OH.
ER. YES. SOME DETECTIVES WILL...BE RIGHT WITH YOU.
THANK YOU.
MISSING
MISSING
TIMOTHY HUNTER?
YES, THAT'S ME. I'M LOOKING FOR MY DAD.
IS HE HERE?

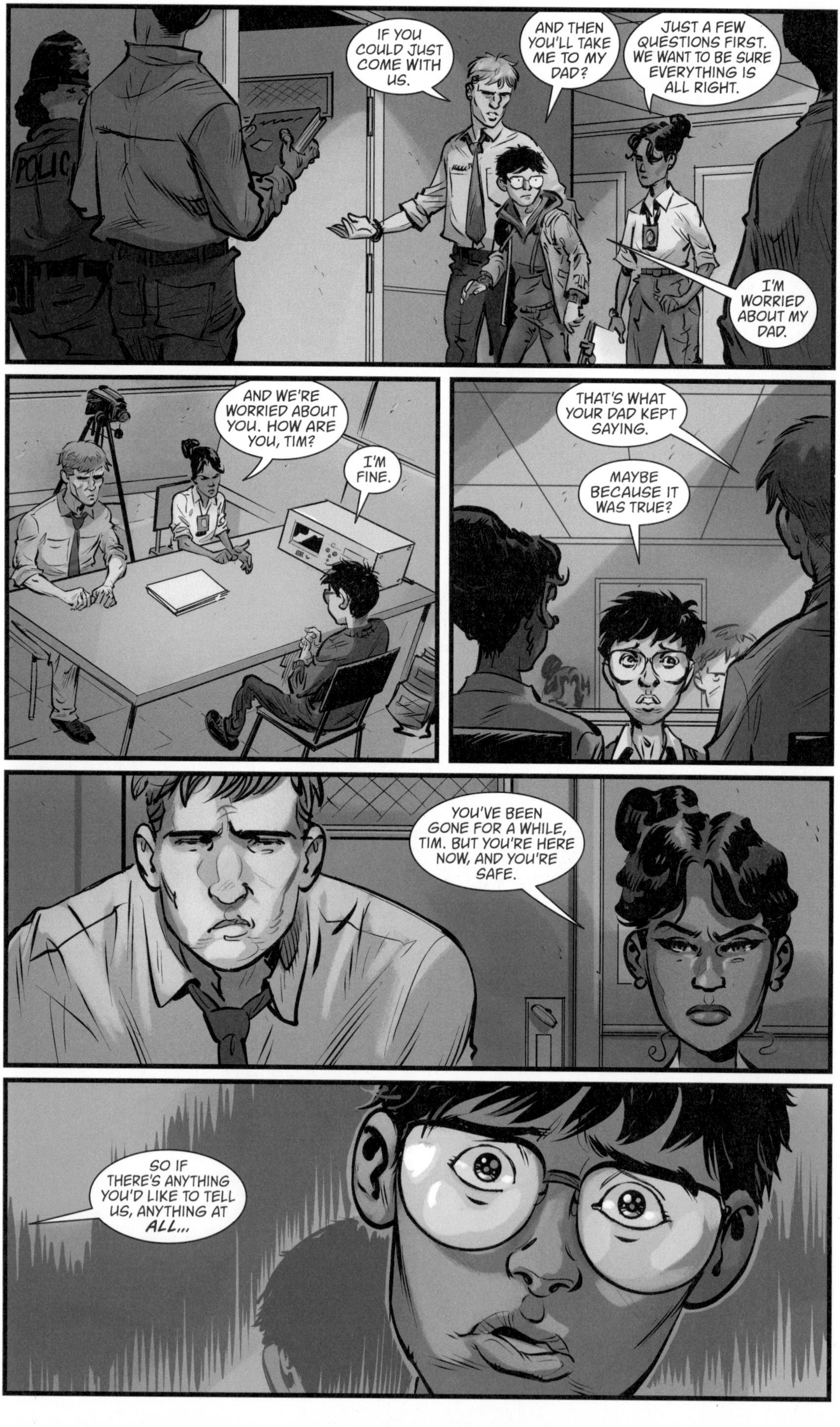
IF YOU COULD JUST COME WITH US.
AND THEN YOU'LL TAKE ME TO MY DAD?
JUST A FEW QUESTIONS FIRST. WE WANT TO BE SURE EVERYTHING IS ALL RIGHT.
I'M WORRIED ABOUT MY DAD.
AND WE'RE WORRIED ABOUT YOU. HOW ARE YOU, TIM?
I'M FINE.
THAT'S WHAT YOUR DAD KEPT SAYING.
MAYBE BECAUSE IT WAS TRUE?
YOU'VE BEEN GONE FOR A WHILE, TIM. BUT YOU'RE HERE NOW, AND YOU'RE SAFE.
SO IF THERE'S ANYTHING YOU'D LIKE TO TELL US, ANYTHING AT *ALL*...

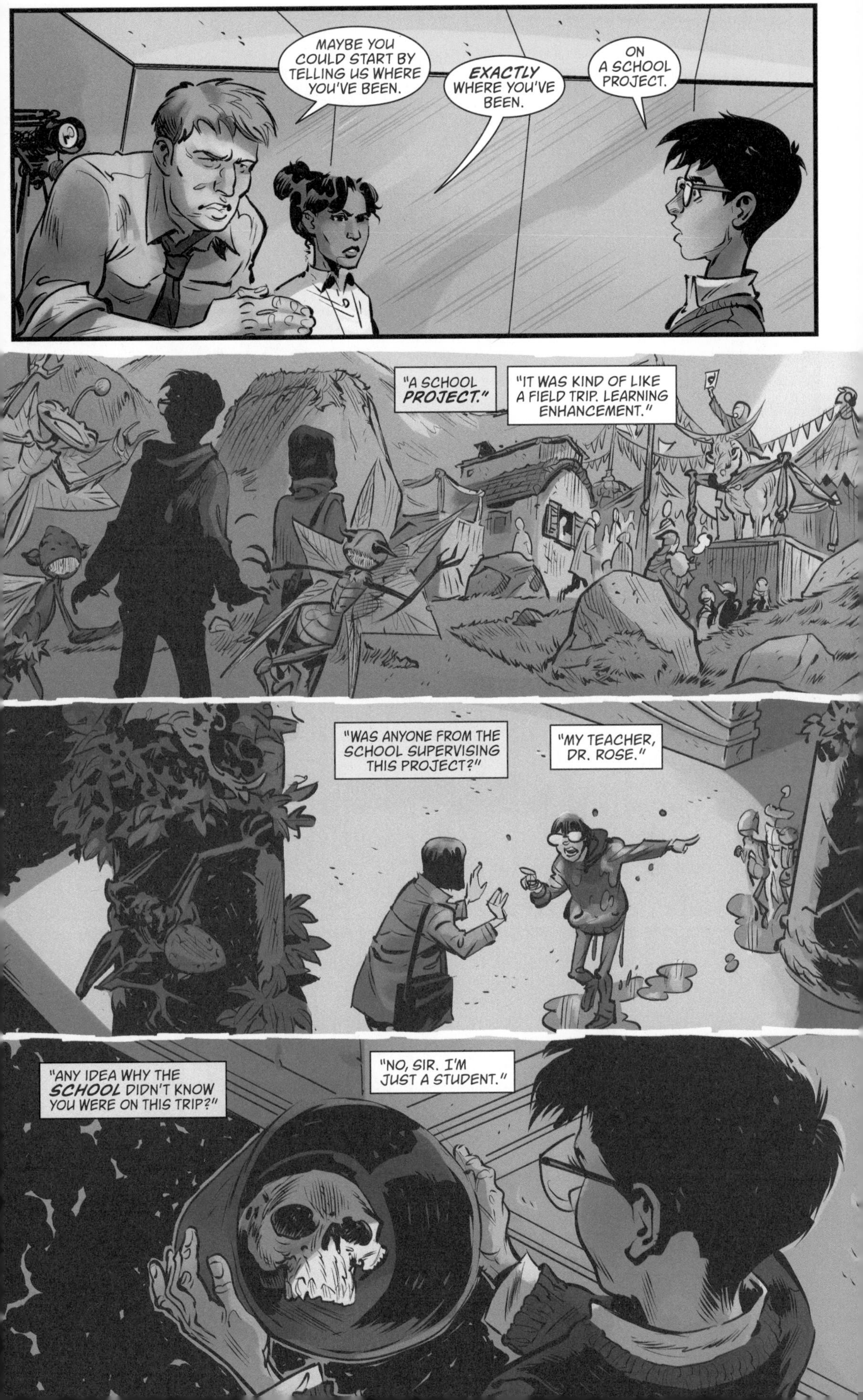
MAYBE YOU COULD START BY TELLING US WHERE YOU'VE BEEN.
EXACTLY WHERE YOU'VE BEEN.
ON A SCHOOL PROJECT.
"A SCHOOL PROJECT."
"IT WAS KIND OF LIKE A FIELD TRIP. LEARNING ENHANCEMENT."
"WAS ANYONE FROM THE SCHOOL SUPERVISING THIS PROJECT?"
"MY TEACHER, DR. ROSE."
"ANY IDEA WHY THE SCHOOL DIDN'T KNOW YOU WERE ON THIS TRIP?"
"NO, SIR. I'M JUST A STUDENT."

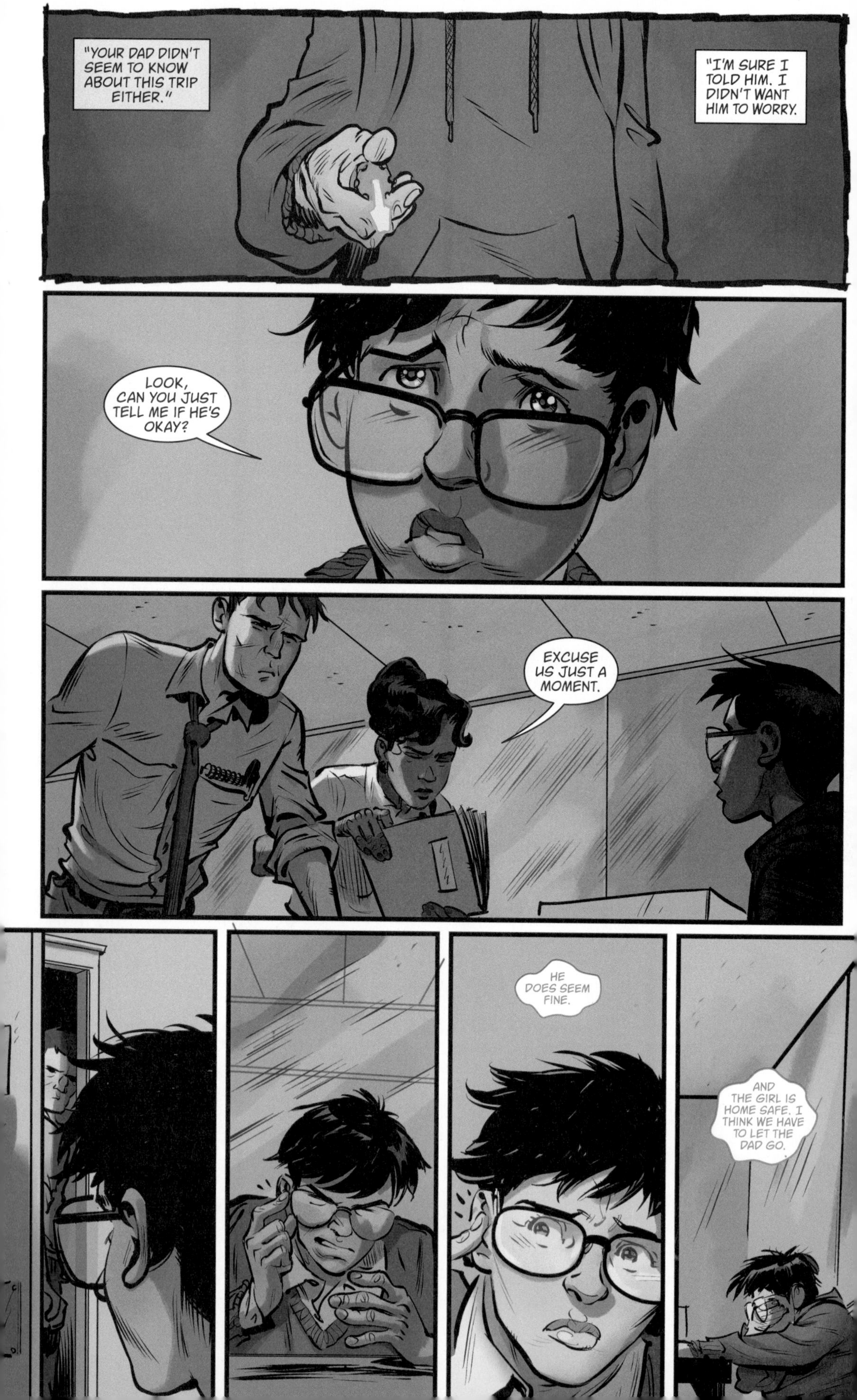
"YOUR DAD DIDN'T SEEM TO KNOW ABOUT THIS TRIP EITHER."
"I'M SURE I TOLD HIM. I DIDN'T WANT HIM TO WORRY.
LOOK, CAN YOU JUST TELL ME IF HE'S OKAY?
EXCUSE US JUST A MOMENT.
HE DOES SEEM FINE.
AND THE GIRL IS HOME SAFE. I THINK WE HAVE TO LET THE DAD GO.

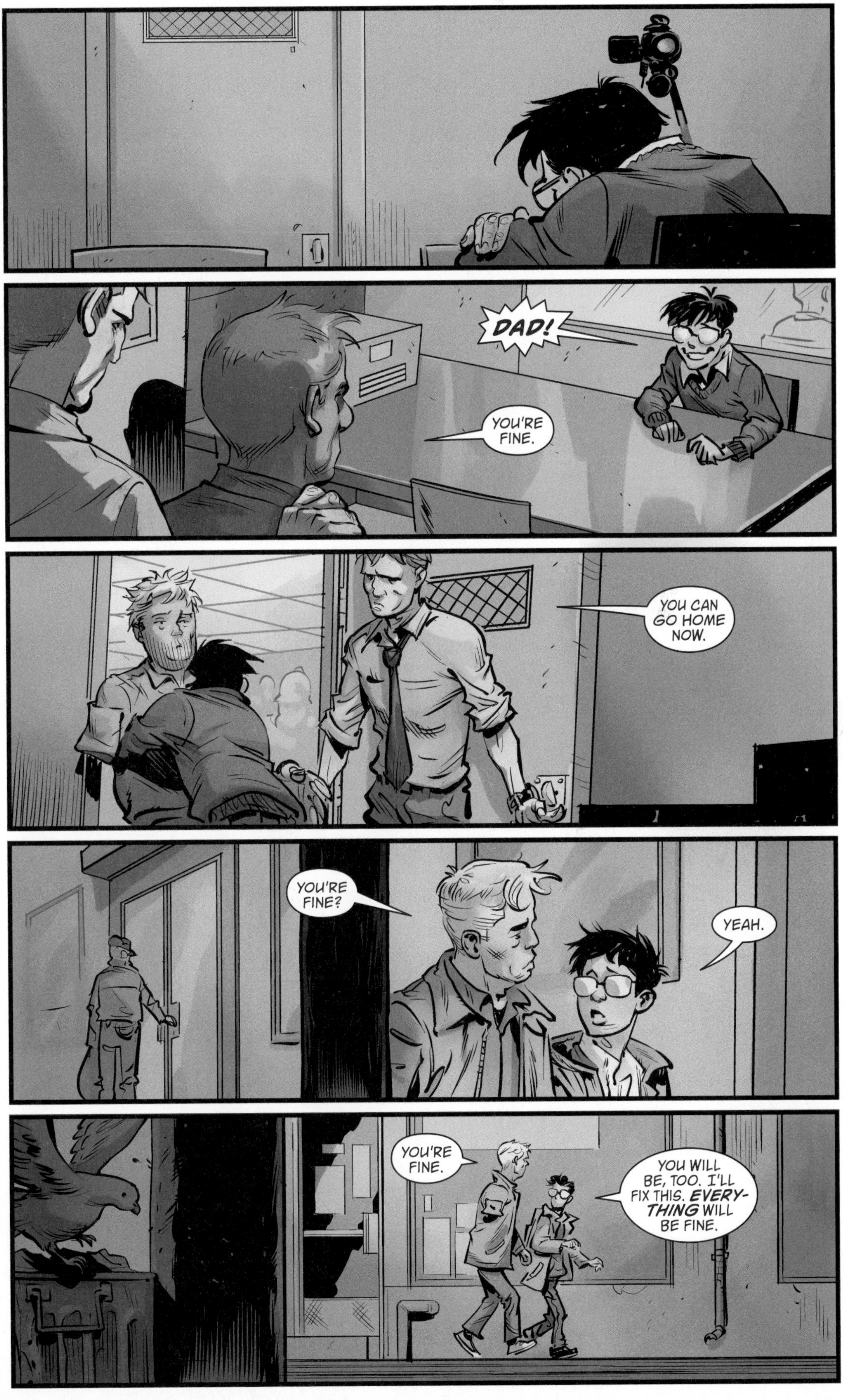
DAD!
YOU'RE FINE.
YOU CAN GO HOME NOW.
YOU'RE FINE?
YEAH.
YOU'RE FINE.
YOU WILL BE, TOO. I'LL FIX THIS. EVERYTHING WILL BE FINE.

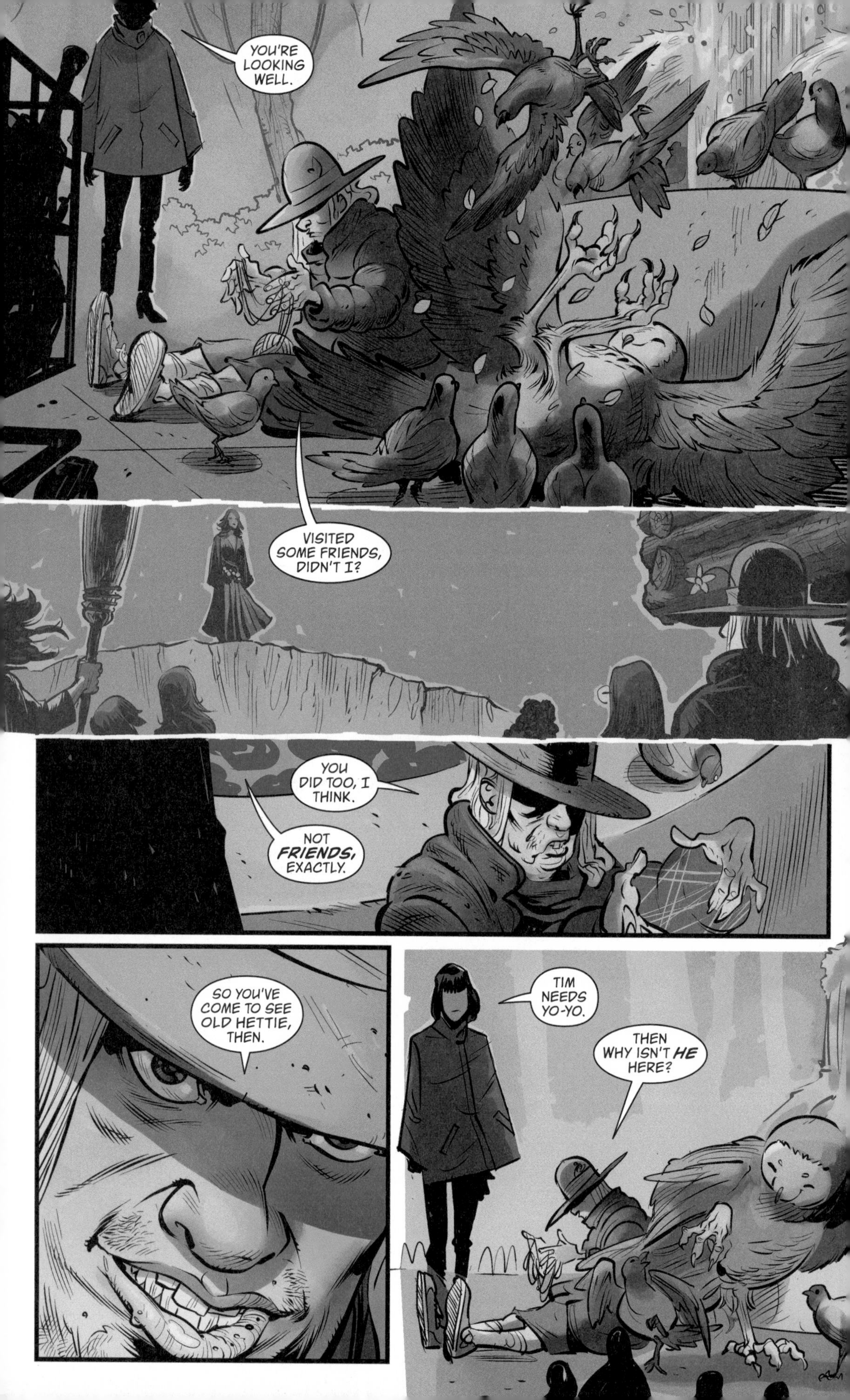
YOU'RE LOOKING WELL.
VISITED SOME FRIENDS, DIDN'T I?
YOU DID TOO, I THINK.
NOT *FRIENDS,* EXACTLY.
SO YOU'VE COME TO SEE OLD HETTIE, THEN.
TIM NEEDS YO-YO.
THEN WHY ISN'T *HE* HERE?

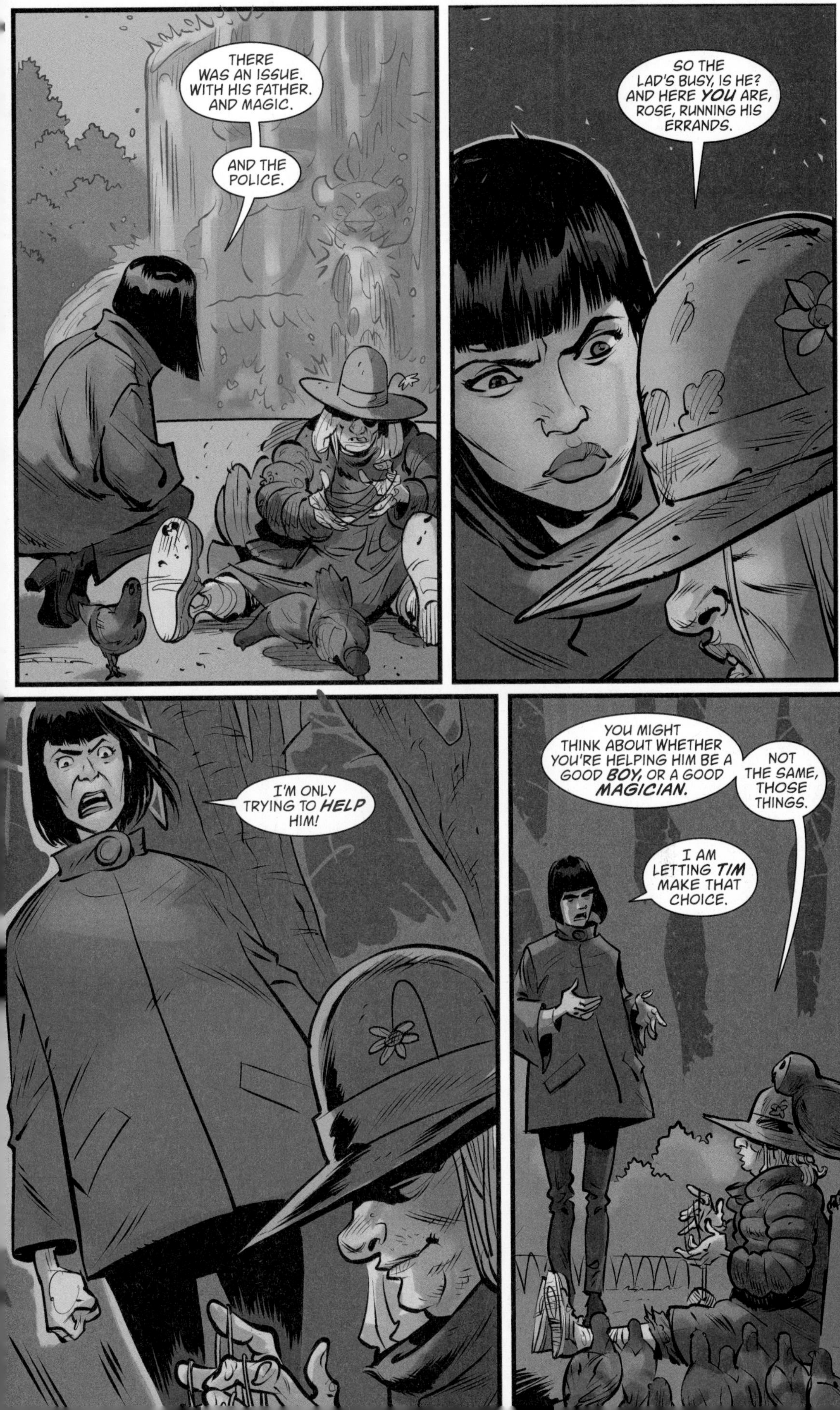

THERE WAS AN ISSUE. WITH HIS FATHER. AND MAGIC.
AND THE POLICE.
SO THE LAD'S BUSY, IS HE? AND HERE YOU ARE, ROSE, RUNNING HIS ERRANDS.
I'M ONLY TRYING TO HELP HIM!
YOU MIGHT THINK ABOUT WHETHER YOU'RE HELPING HIM BE A GOOD BOY, OR A GOOD MAGICIAN.
NOT THE SAME, THOSE THINGS.
I AM LETTING TIM MAKE THAT CHOICE.

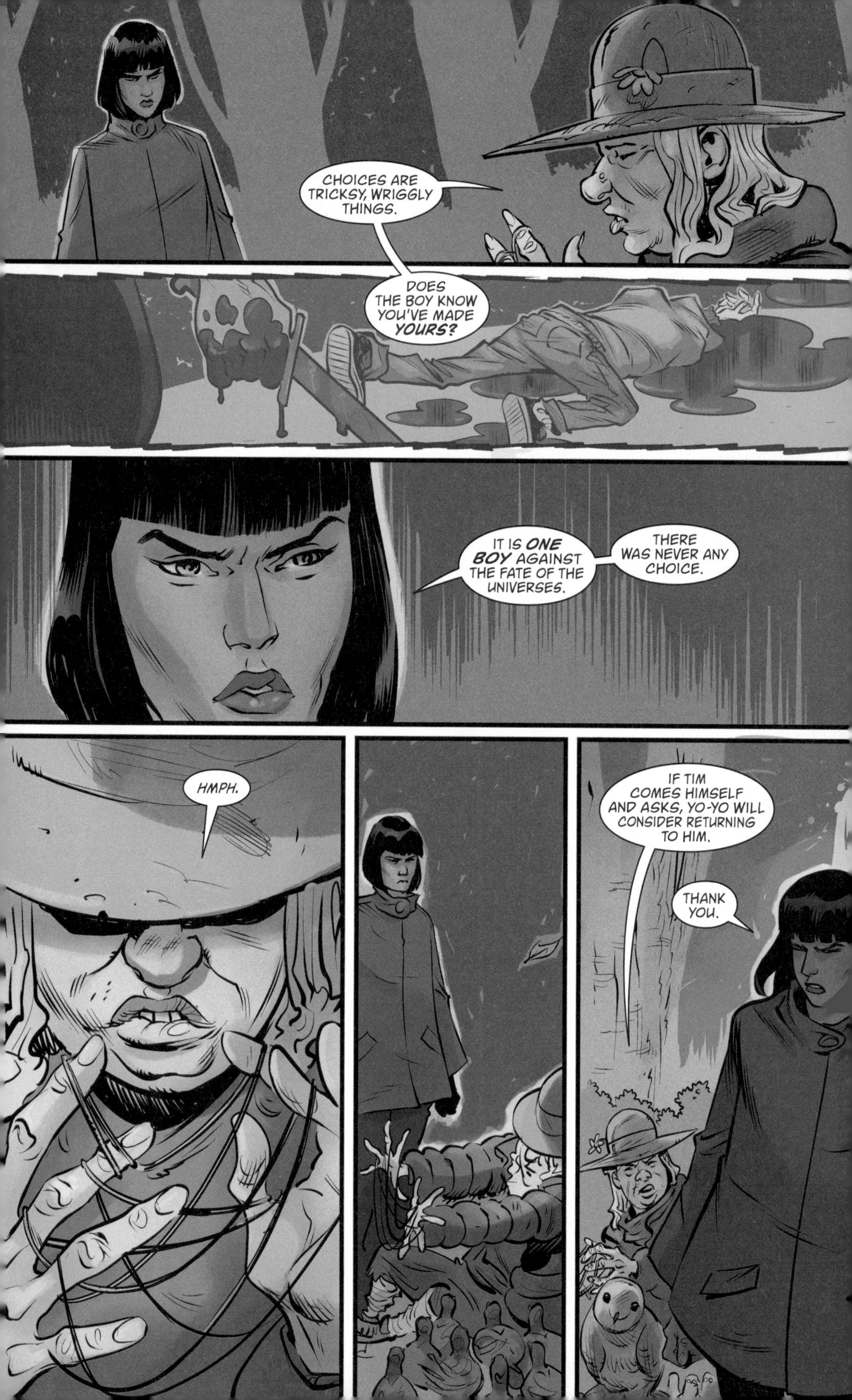
CHOICES ARE TRICKSY, WRIGGLY THINGS.
DOES THE BOY KNOW YOU'VE MADE YOURS?
IT IS ONE BOY AGAINST THE FATE OF THE UNIVERSES.
THERE WAS NEVER ANY CHOICE.
HMPH.
IF TIM COMES HIMSELF AND ASKS, YO-YO WILL CONSIDER RETURNING TO HIM.
THANK YOU.

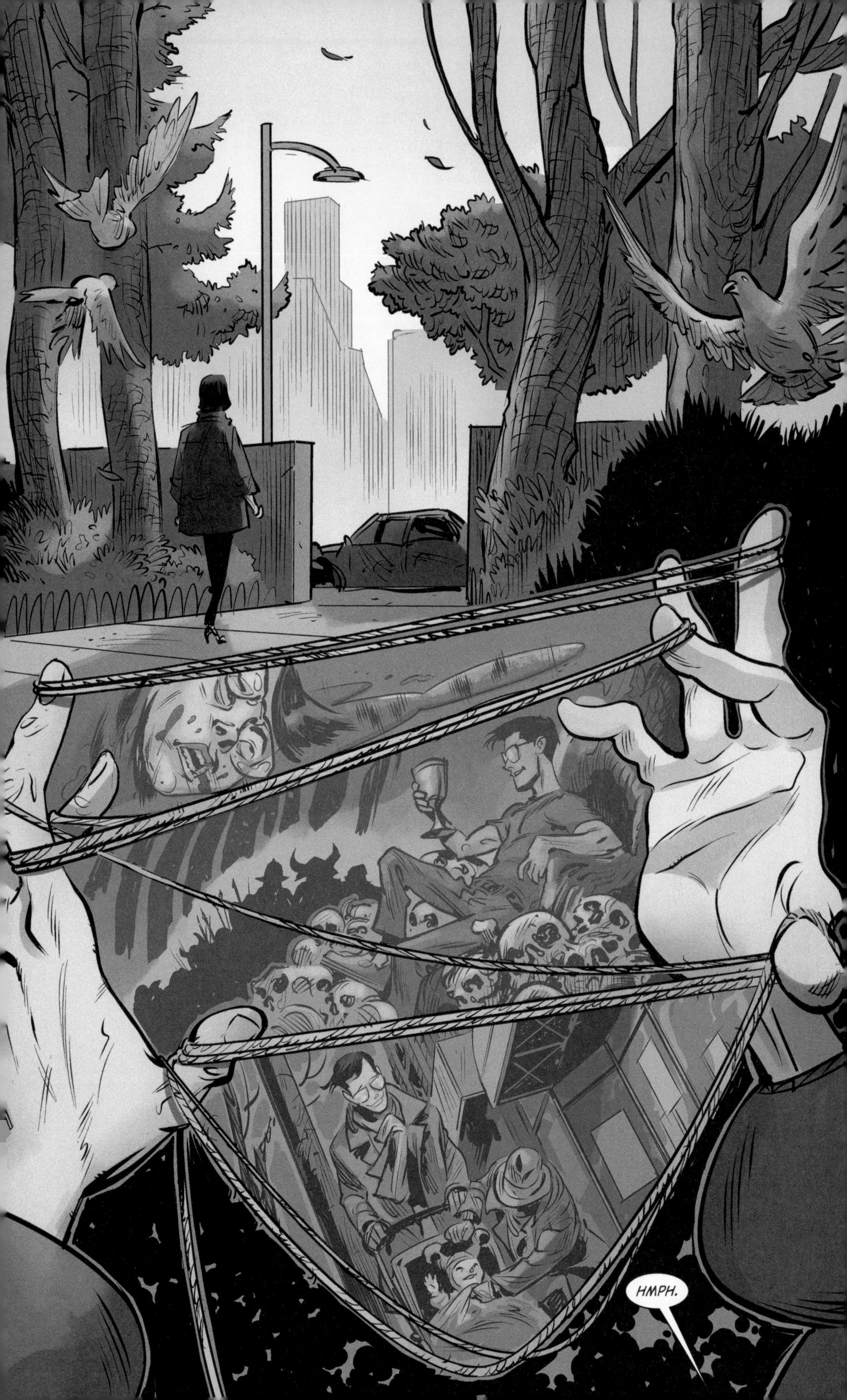
HMPH.

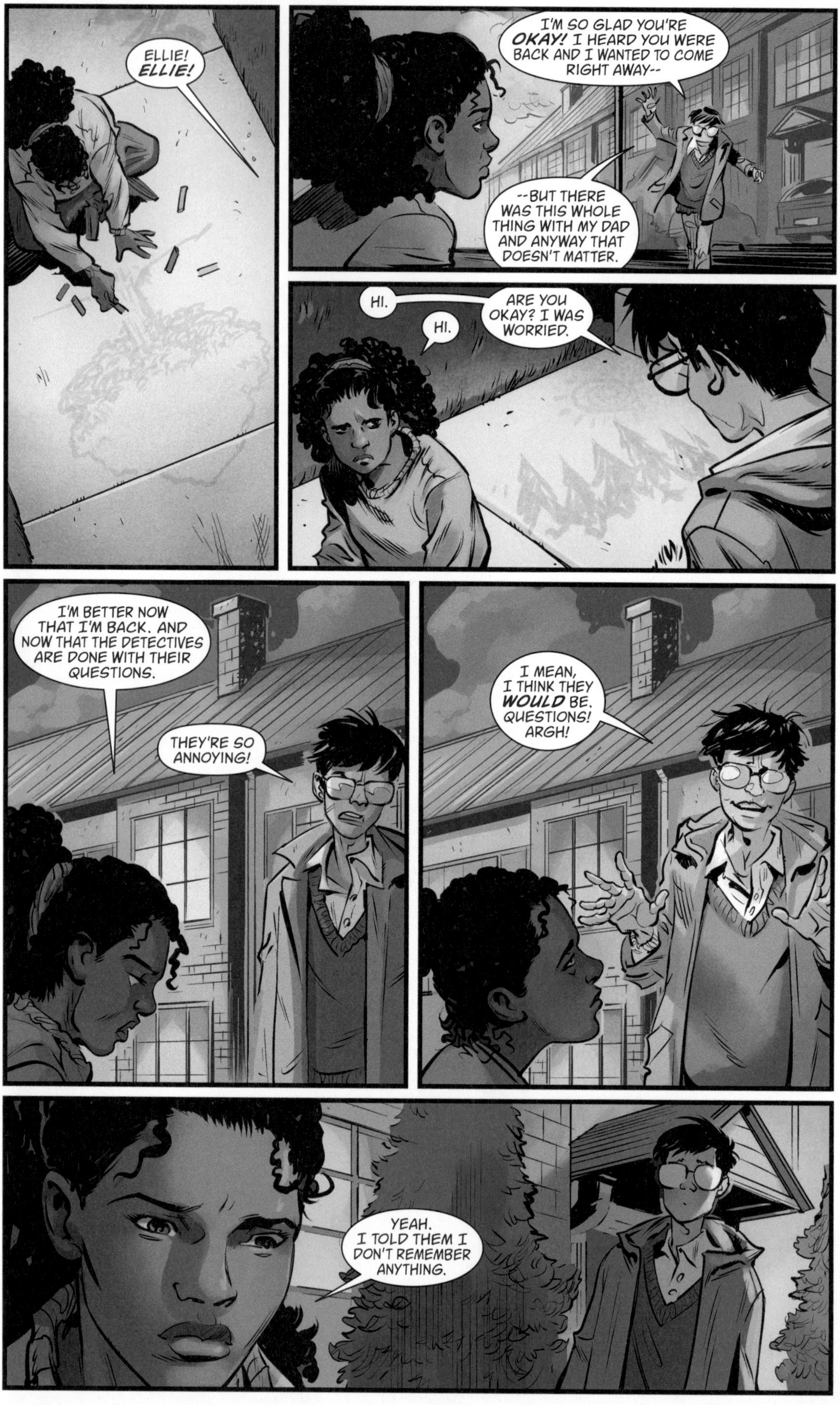
ELLIE! ELLIE!
I'M SO GLAD YOU'RE OKAY! I HEARD YOU WERE BACK AND I WANTED TO COME RIGHT AWAY--
--BUT THERE WAS THIS WHOLE THING WITH MY DAD AND ANYWAY THAT DOESN'T MATTER.
HI.
HI.
ARE YOU OKAY? I WAS WORRIED.
I'M BETTER NOW THAT I'M BACK. AND NOW THAT THE DETECTIVES ARE DONE WITH THEIR QUESTIONS.
THEY'RE SO ANNOYING!
I MEAN, I THINK THEY WOULD BE. QUESTIONS! ARGH!
YEAH. I TOLD THEM I DON'T REMEMBER ANYTHING.

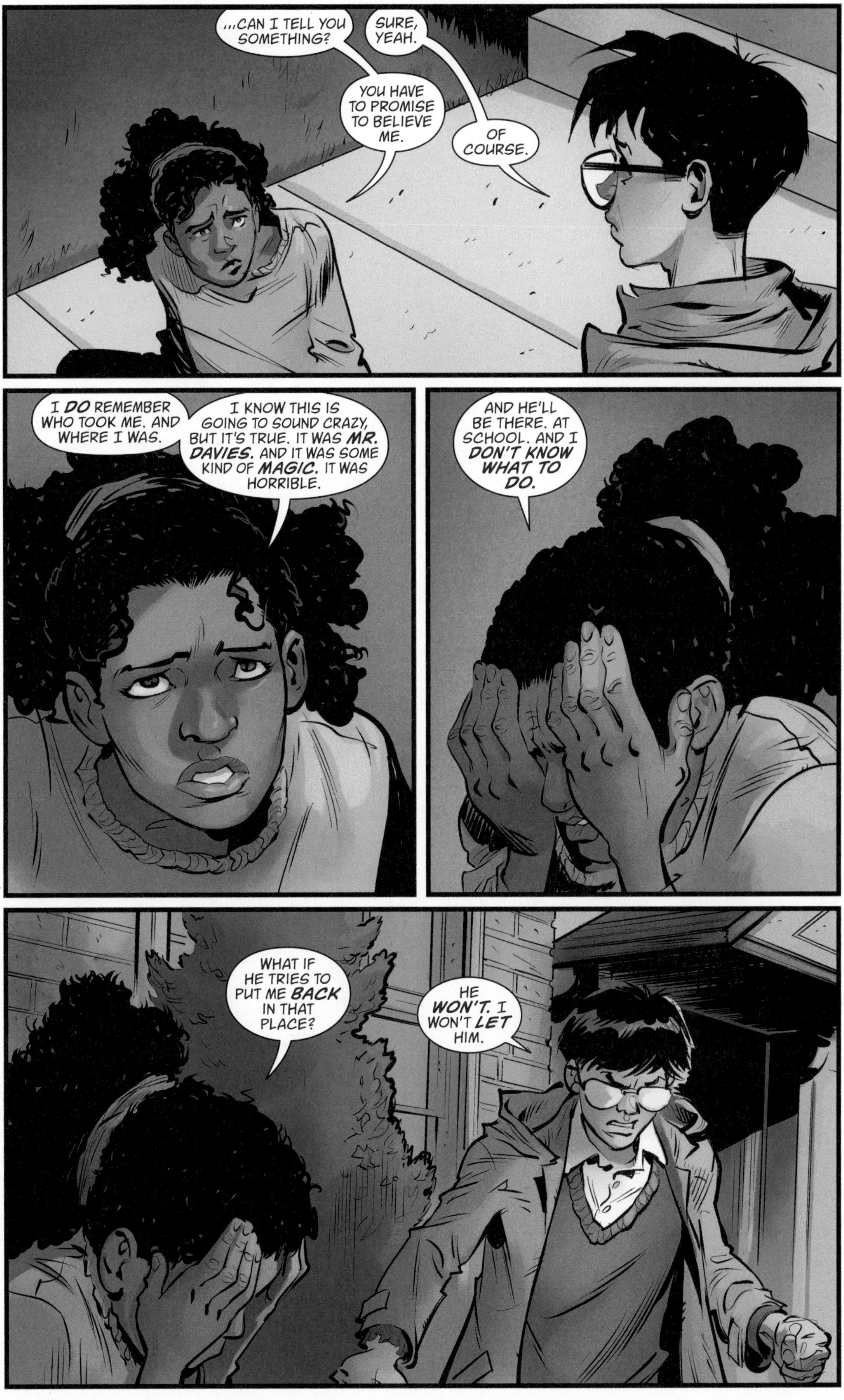
...CAN I TELL YOU SOMETHING?
SURE, YEAH.
YOU HAVE TO PROMISE TO BELIEVE ME.
OF COURSE.
I DO REMEMBER WHO TOOK ME. AND WHERE I WAS.
I KNOW THIS IS GOING TO SOUND CRAZY, BUT IT'S TRUE. IT WAS MR. DAVIES. AND IT WAS SOME KIND OF MAGIC. IT WAS HORRIBLE.
AND HE'LL BE THERE. AT SCHOOL. AND I DON'T KNOW WHAT TO DO.
WHAT IF HE TRIES TO PUT ME BACK IN THAT PLACE?
HE WON'T. I WON'T LET HIM.

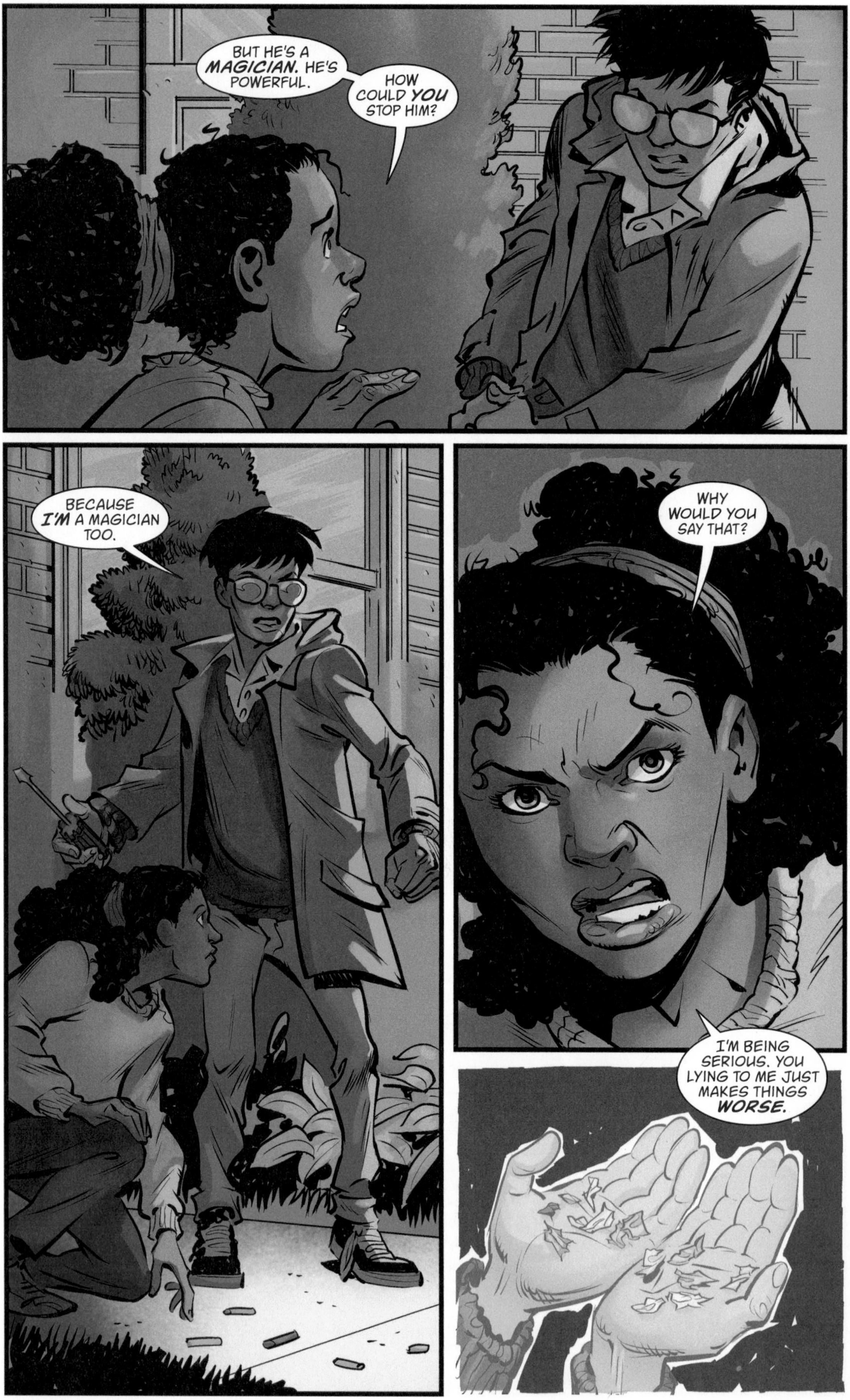
BUT HE'S A MAGICIAN. HE'S POWERFUL.
HOW COULD YOU STOP HIM?
BECAUSE I'M A MAGICIAN TOO.
WHY WOULD YOU SAY THAT?
I'M BEING SERIOUS. YOU LYING TO ME JUST MAKES THINGS WORSE.

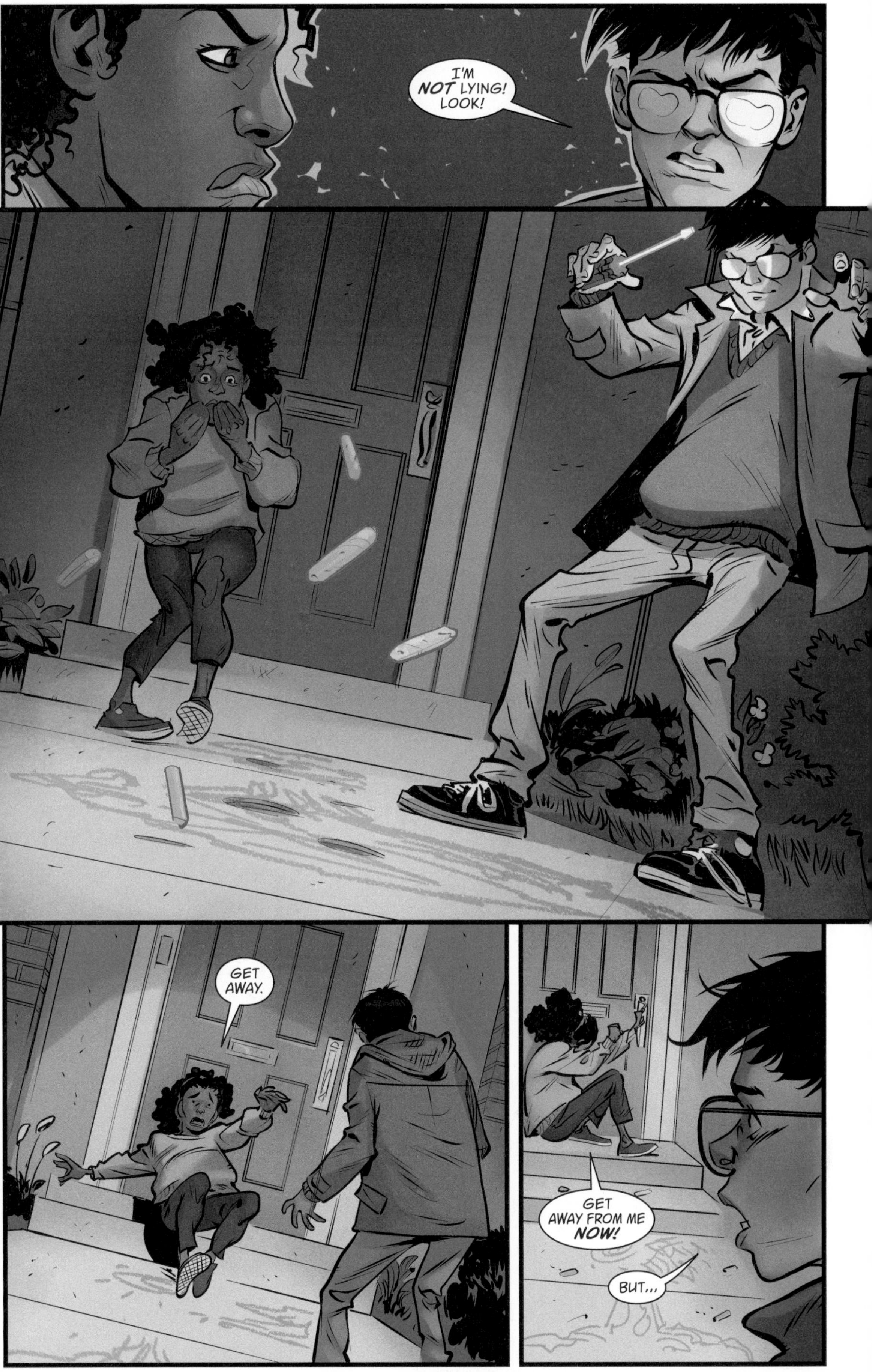

I'M NOT LYING! LOOK!
GET AWAY.
GET AWAY FROM ME NOW!
BUT...

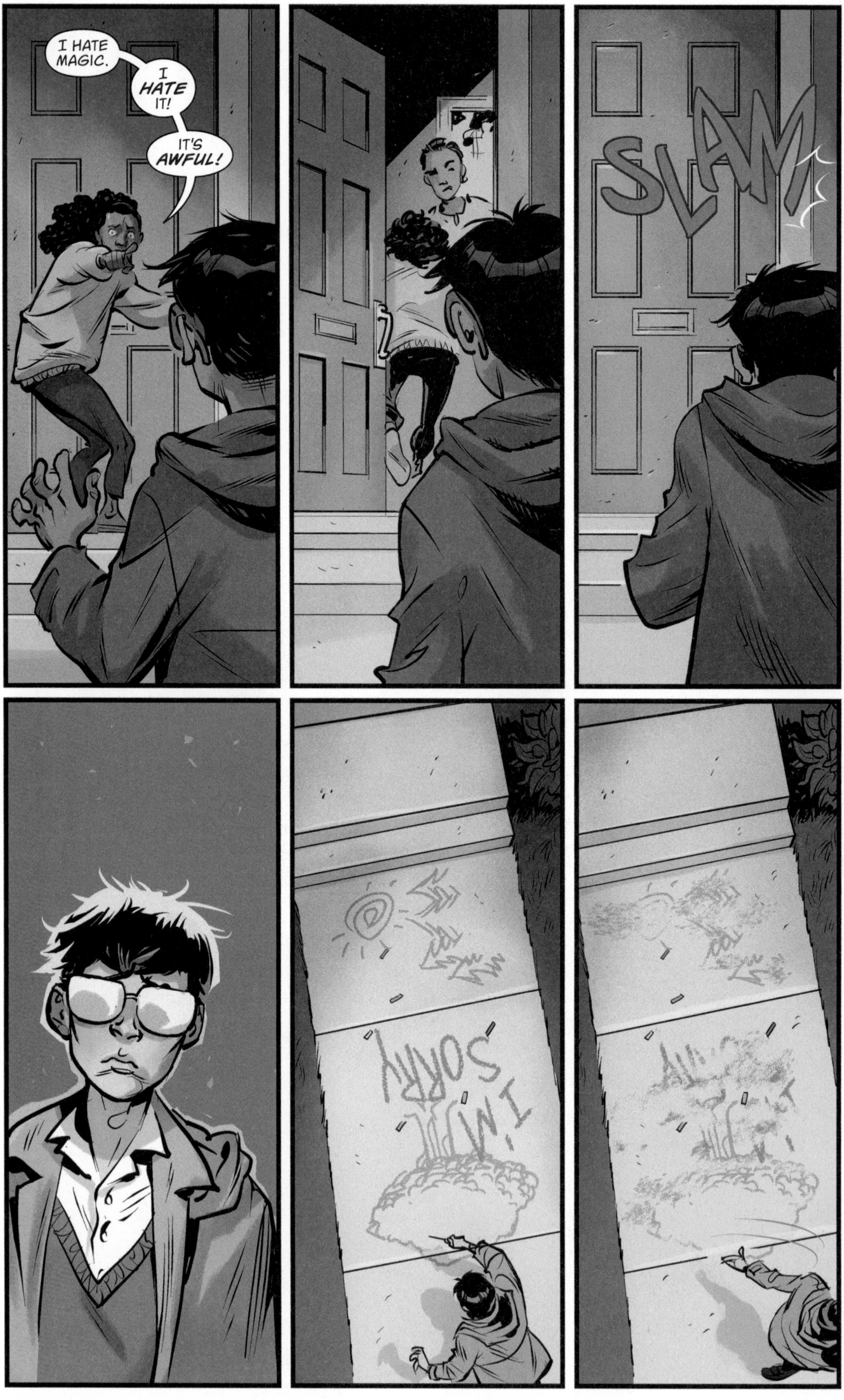
I HATE MAGIC.
I HATE IT!
IT'S AWFUL!
SLAM
SORRY

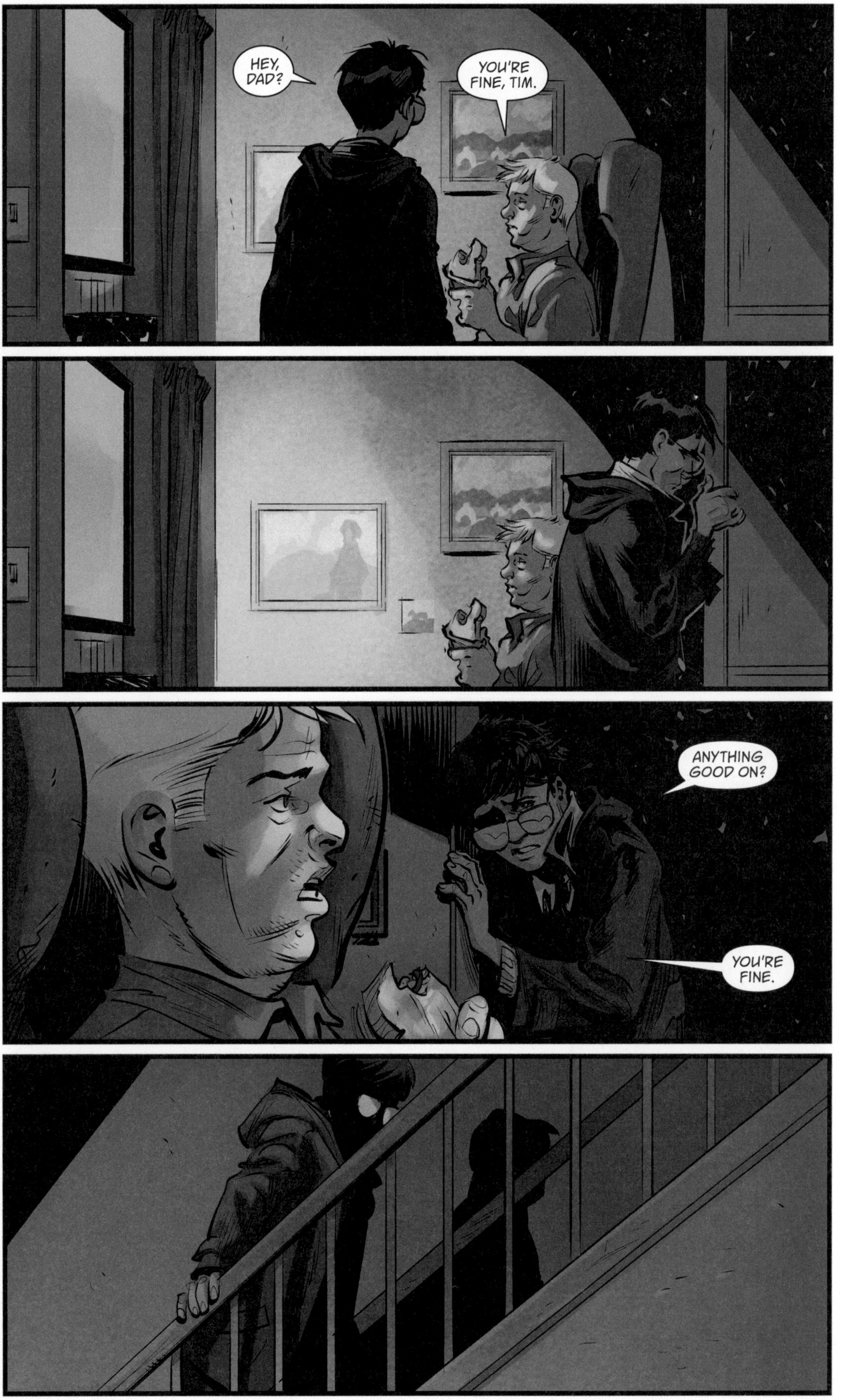
HEY, DAD?
YOU'RE FINE, TIM.
ANYTHING GOOD ON?
YOU'RE FINE.

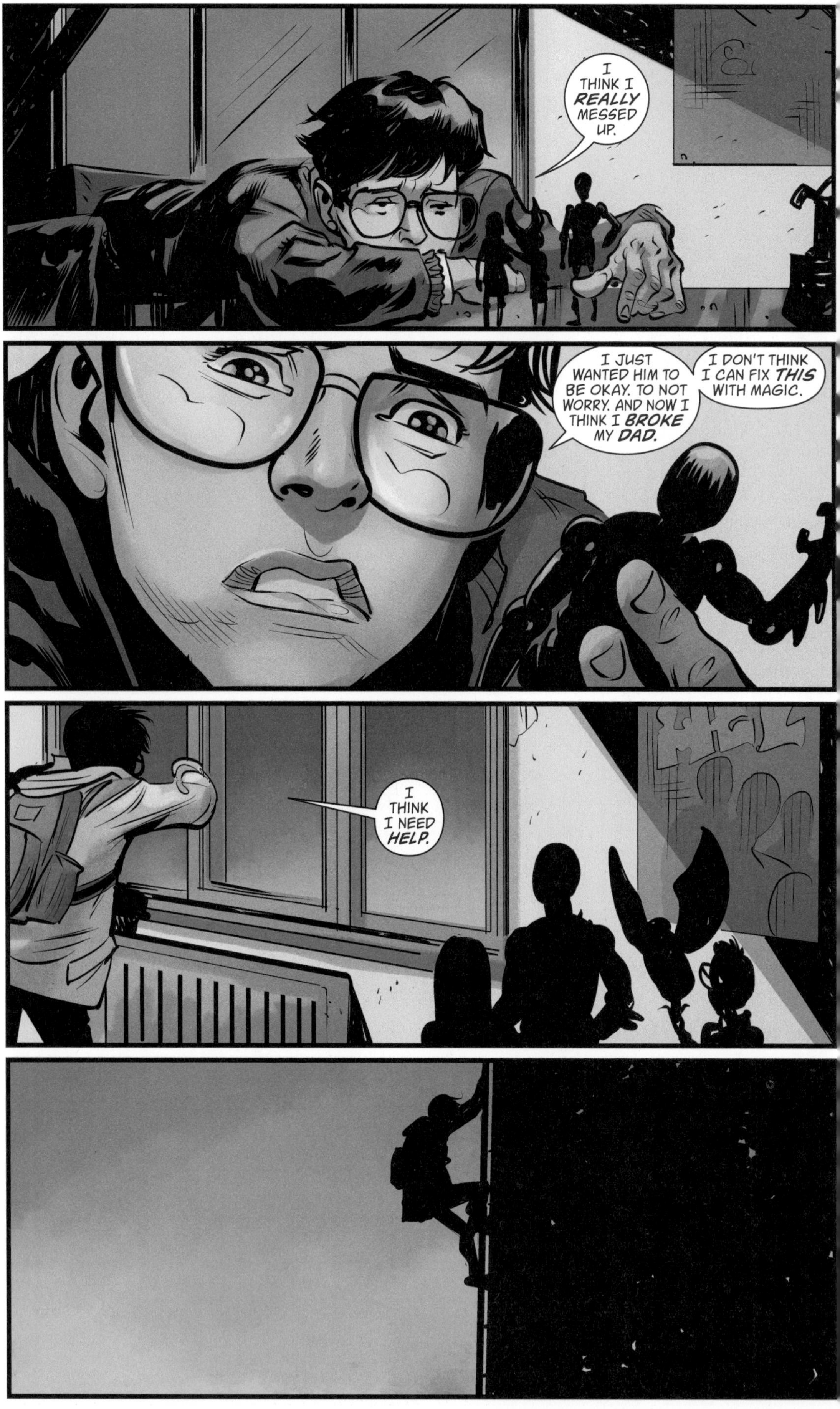
I THINK I REALLY MESSED UP.
I JUST WANTED HIM TO BE OKAY. TO NOT WORRY. AND NOW I THINK I BROKE MY DAD.
I DON'T THINK I CAN FIX THIS WITH MAGIC.
I THINK I NEED HELP.

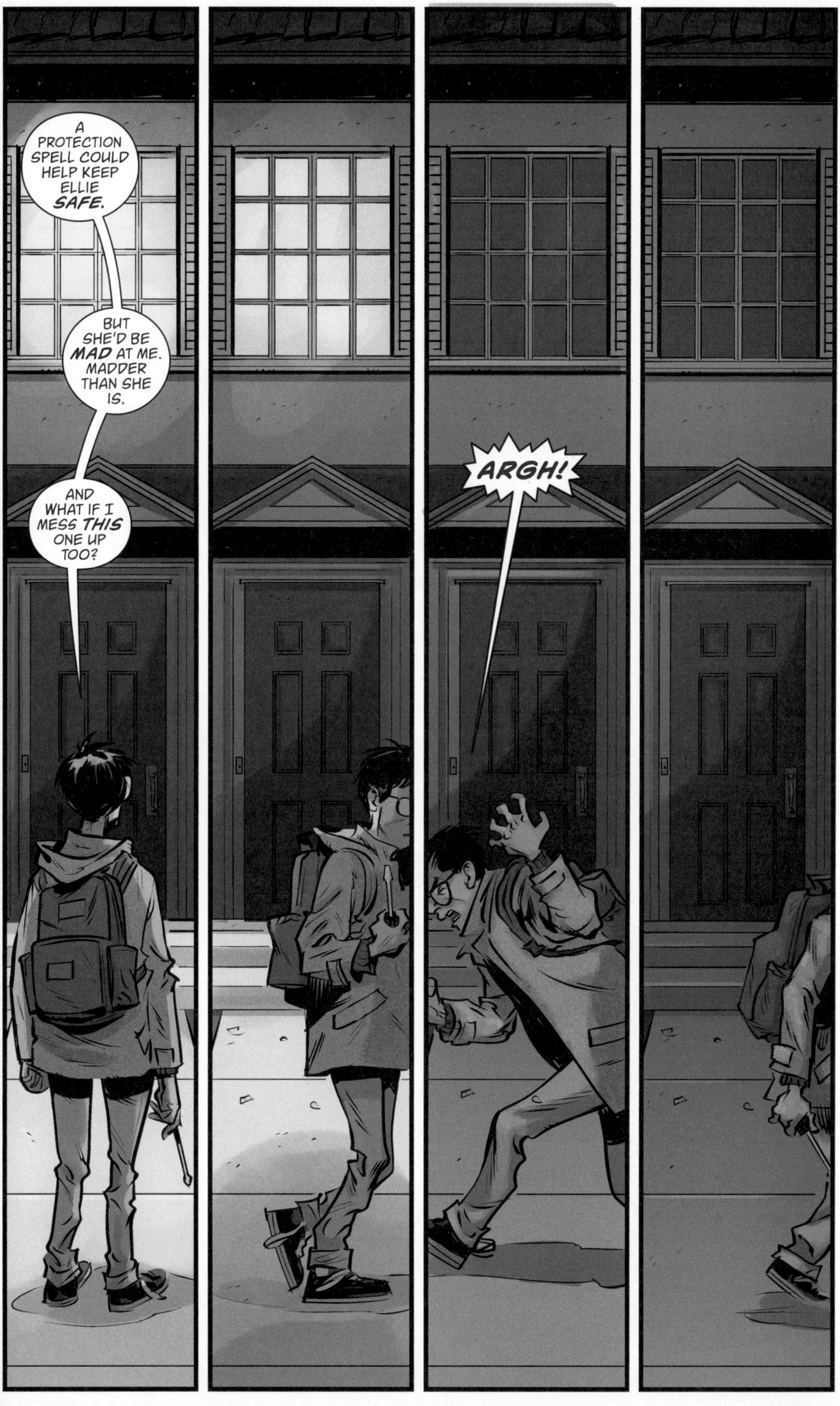
A PROTECTION SPELL COULD HELP KEEP ELLIE SAFE.
BUT SHE'D BE MAD AT ME. MADDER THAN SHE IS.
AND WHAT IF I MESS THIS ONE UP TOO?
ARGH!

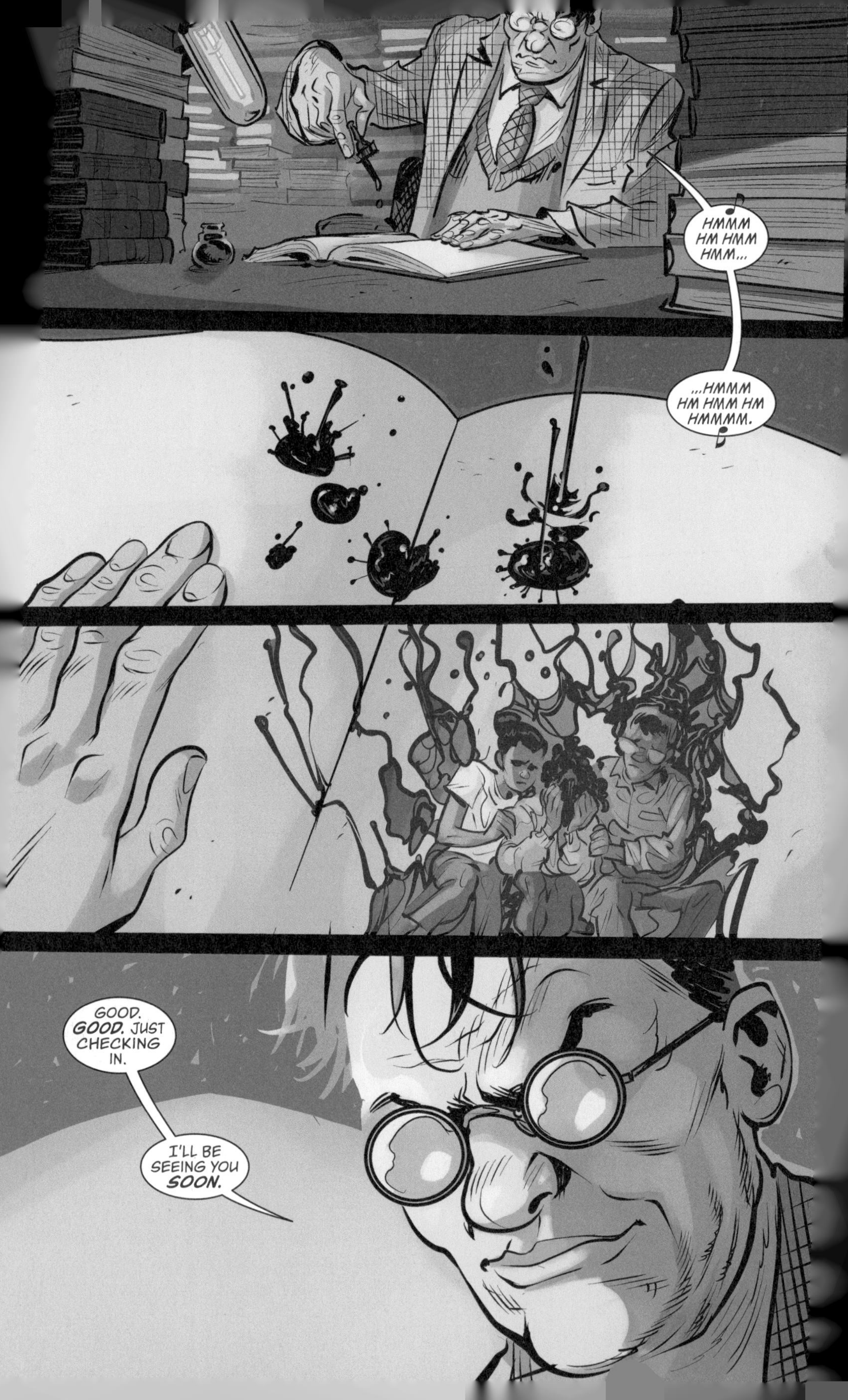
HMMM HM HMM HMM...
...HMMM HM HMM HM HMMMM.
GOOD. GOOD. JUST CHECKING IN.
I'LL BE SEEING YOU SOON.

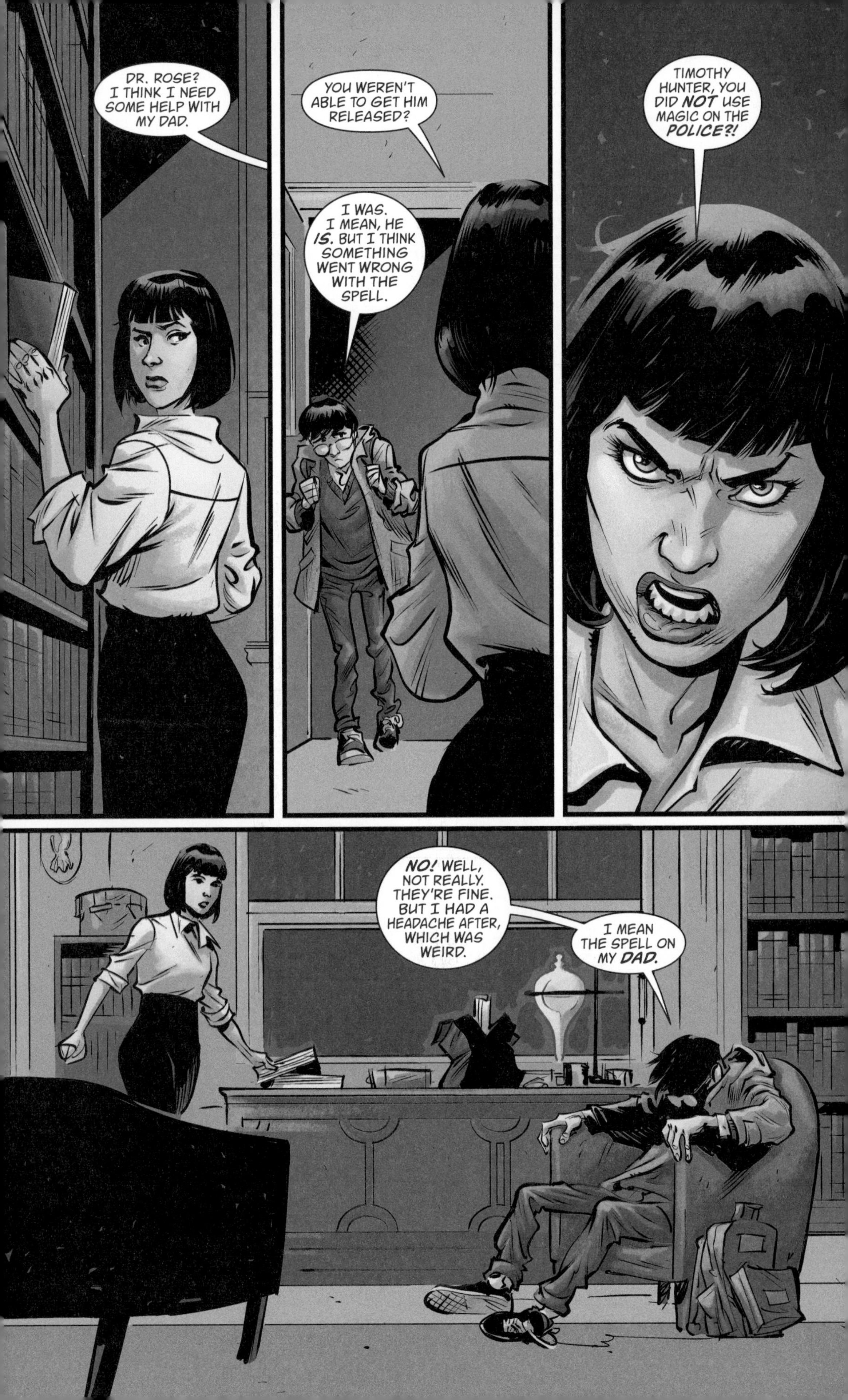
DR. ROSE? I THINK I NEED SOME HELP WITH MY DAD.
YOU WEREN'T ABLE TO GET HIM RELEASED?
I WAS. I MEAN, HE *IS.* BUT I THINK SOMETHING WENT WRONG WITH THE SPELL.
TIMOTHY HUNTER, YOU DID **NOT** USE MAGIC ON THE ***POLICE?!***
NO! WELL, NOT REALLY. THEY'RE FINE. BUT I HAD A HEADACHE AFTER, WHICH WAS WEIRD.
I MEAN THE SPELL ON MY ***DAD.***

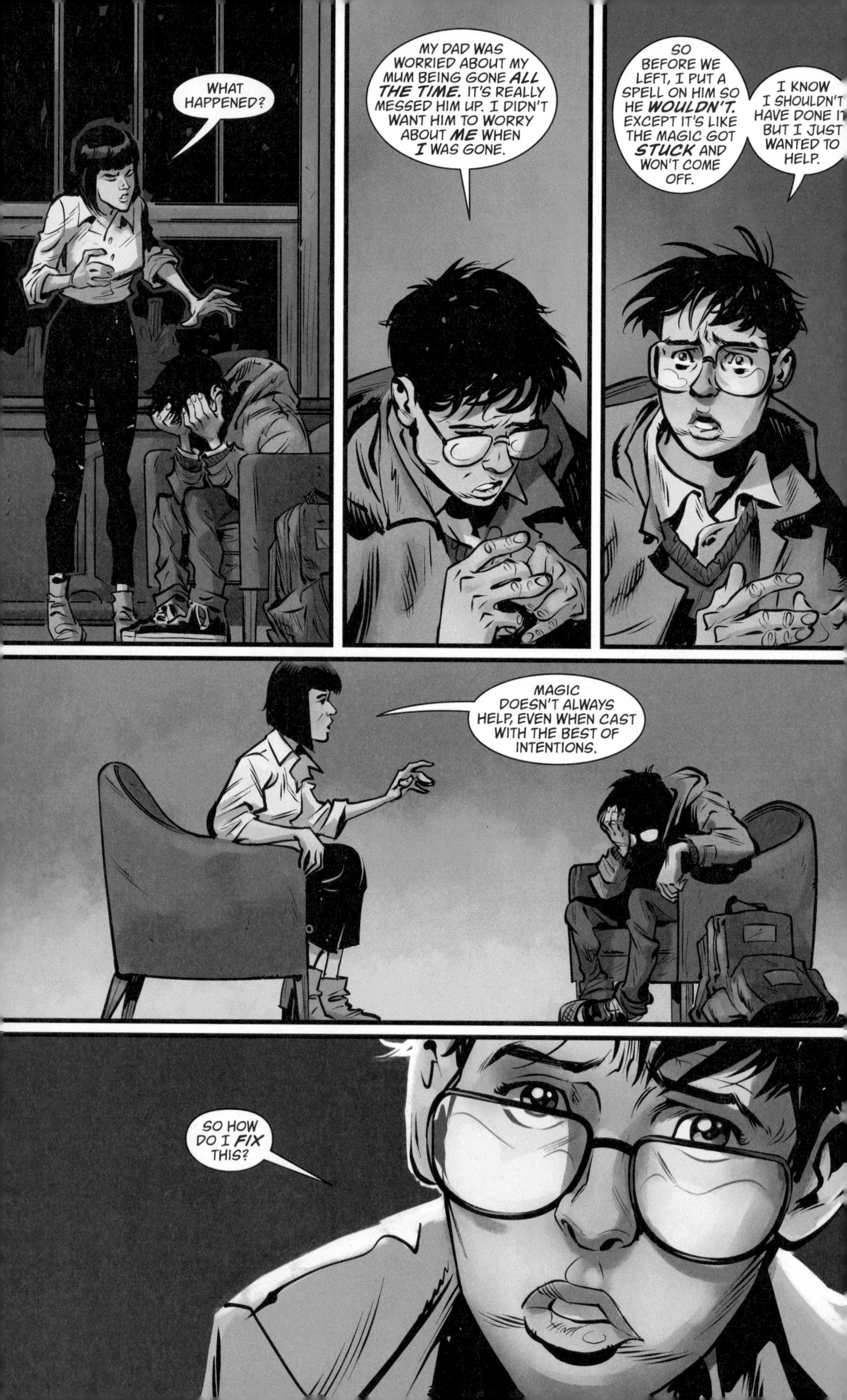
WHAT HAPPENED?
MY DAD WAS WORRIED ABOUT MY MUM BEING GONE ALL THE TIME. IT'S REALLY MESSED HIM UP. I DIDN'T WANT HIM TO WORRY ABOUT ME WHEN I WAS GONE.
SO BEFORE WE LEFT, I PUT A SPELL ON HIM SO HE WOULDN'T. EXCEPT IT'S LIKE THE MAGIC GOT STUCK AND WON'T COME OFF.
I KNOW I SHOULDN'T HAVE DONE IT BUT I JUST WANTED TO HELP.
MAGIC DOESN'T ALWAYS HELP, EVEN WHEN CAST WITH THE BEST OF INTENTIONS.
SO HOW DO I FIX THIS?

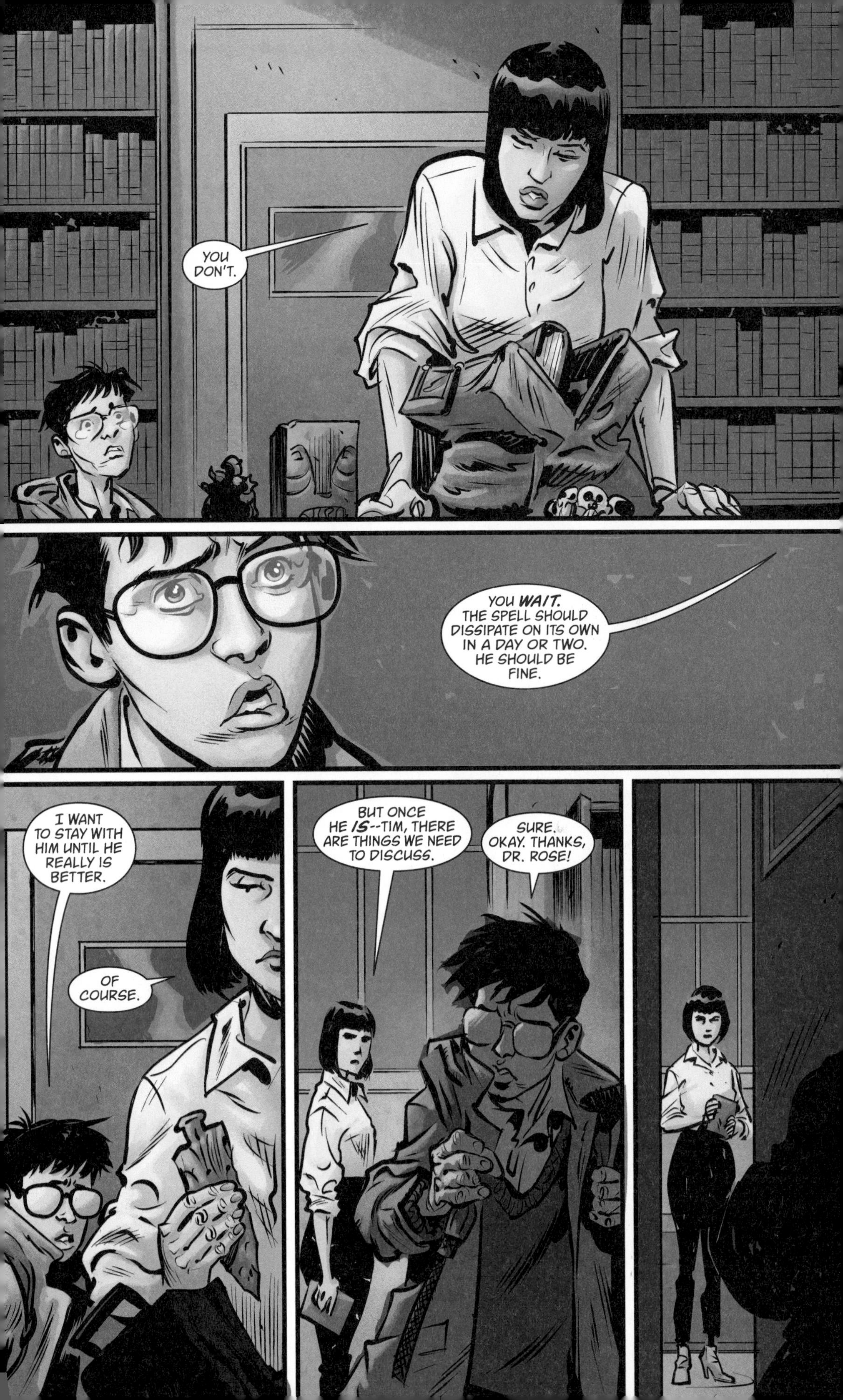
YOU DON'T.
YOU **WAIT.** THE SPELL SHOULD DISSIPATE ON ITS OWN IN A DAY OR TWO. HE SHOULD BE FINE.
I WANT TO STAY WITH HIM UNTIL HE REALLY IS BETTER.
OF COURSE.
BUT ONCE HE *IS*--TIM, THERE ARE THINGS WE NEED TO DISCUSS.
SURE. OKAY. THANKS, DR. ROSE!

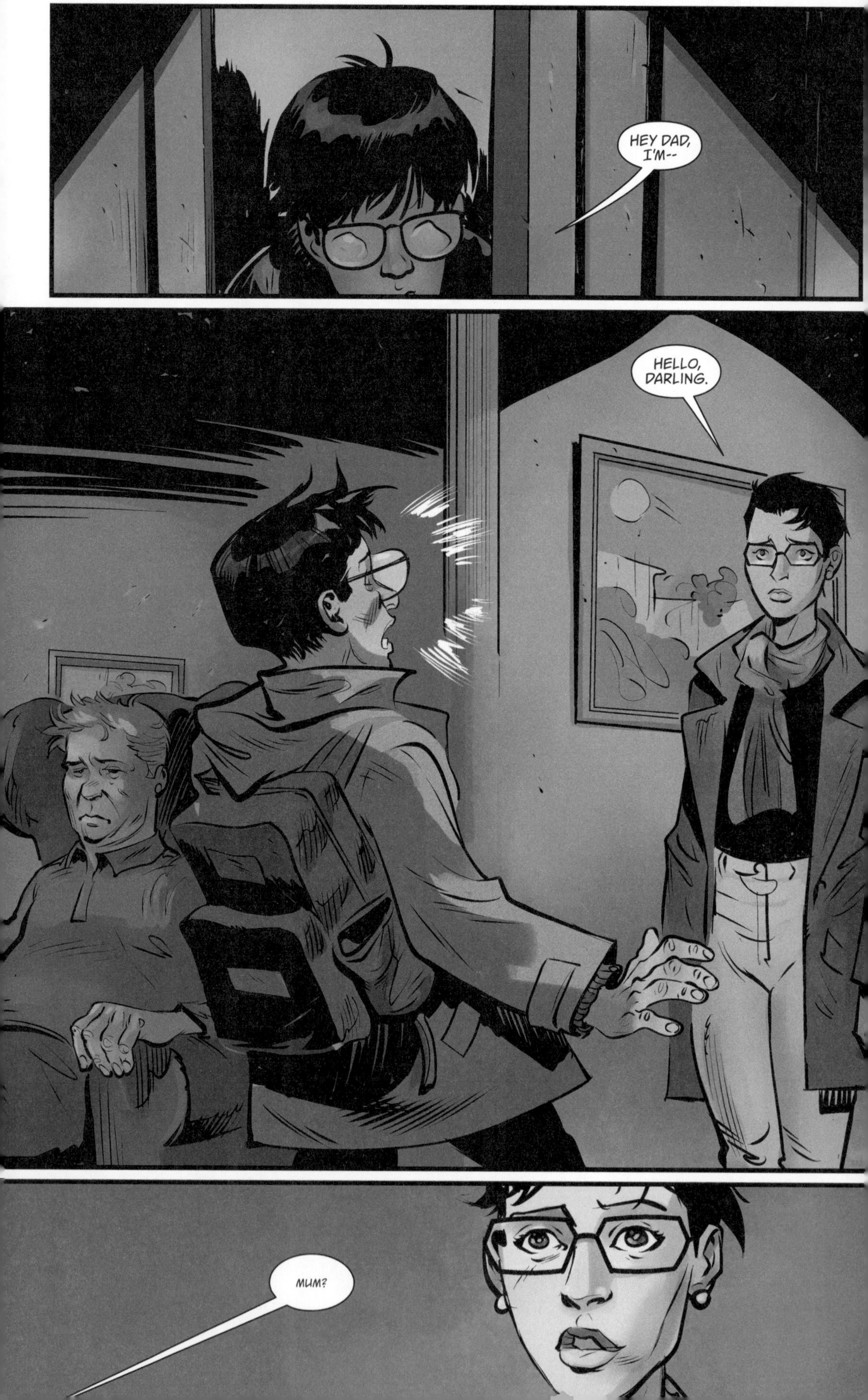
HEY DAD, I'M--
HELLO, DARLING.
MUM?

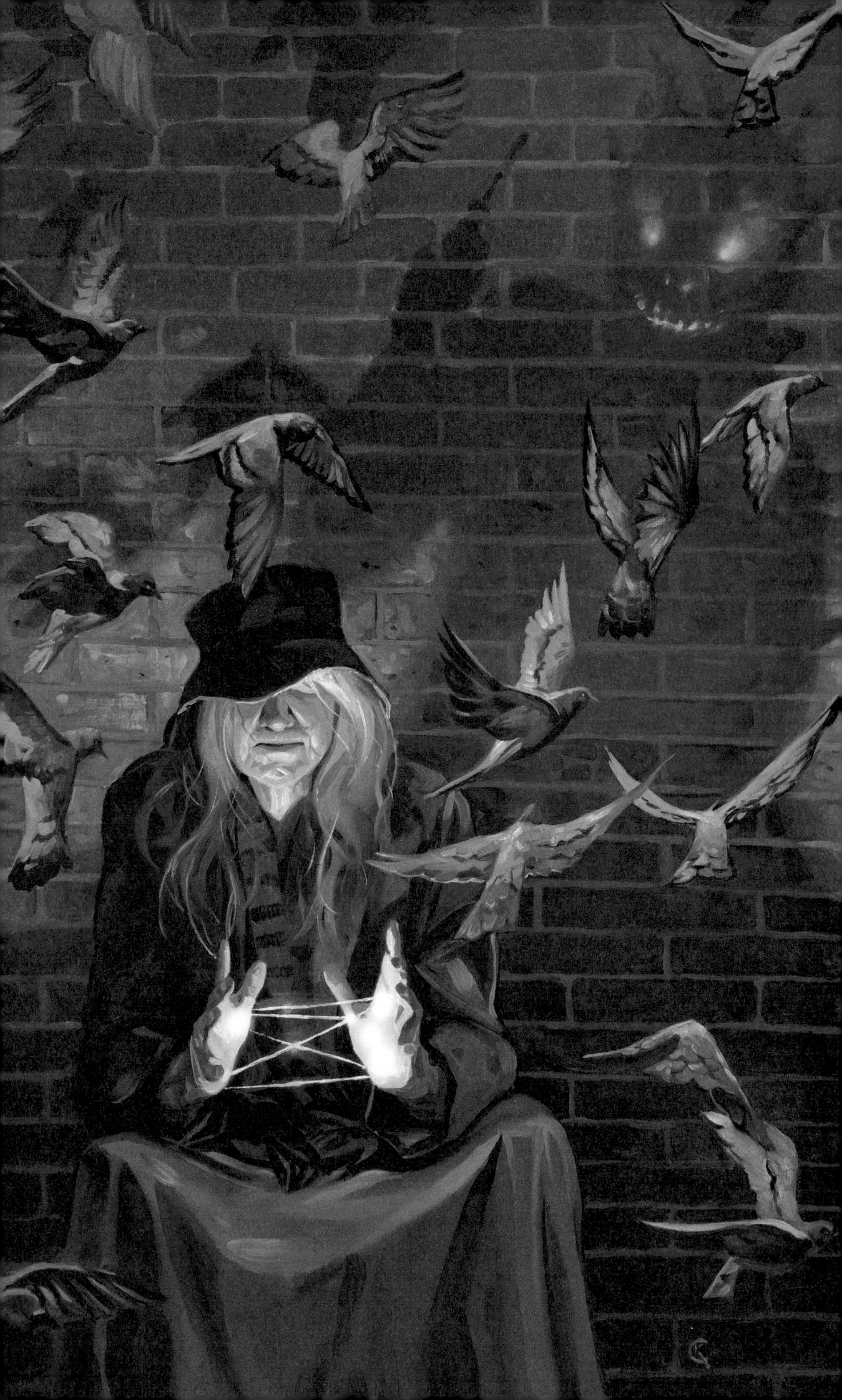

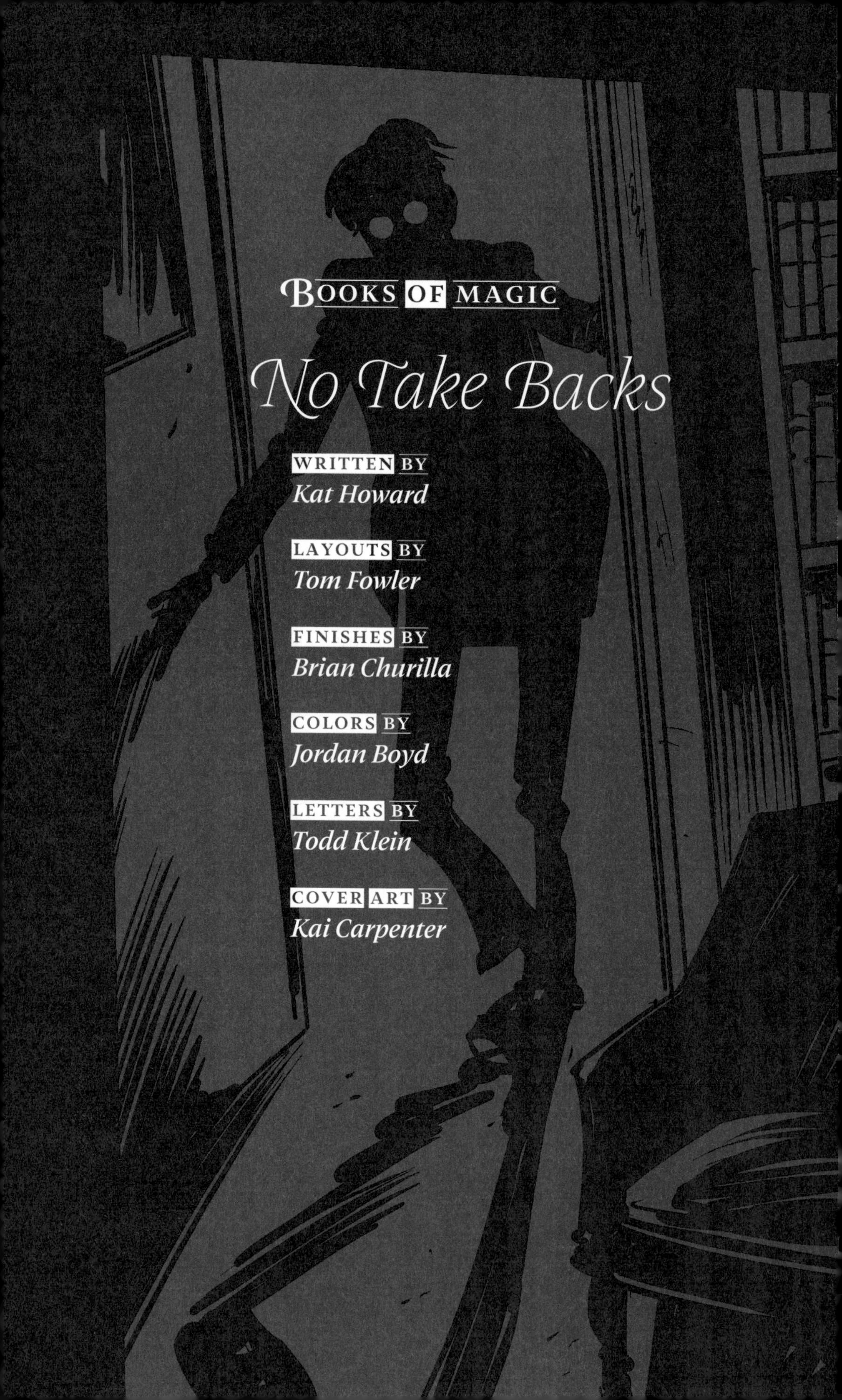

BOOKS OF MAGIC

No Take Backs

WRITTEN BY
Kat Howard

LAYOUTS BY
Tom Fowler

FINISHES BY
Brian Churilla

COLORS BY
Jordan Boyd

LETTERS BY
Todd Klein

COVER ART BY
Kai Carpenter

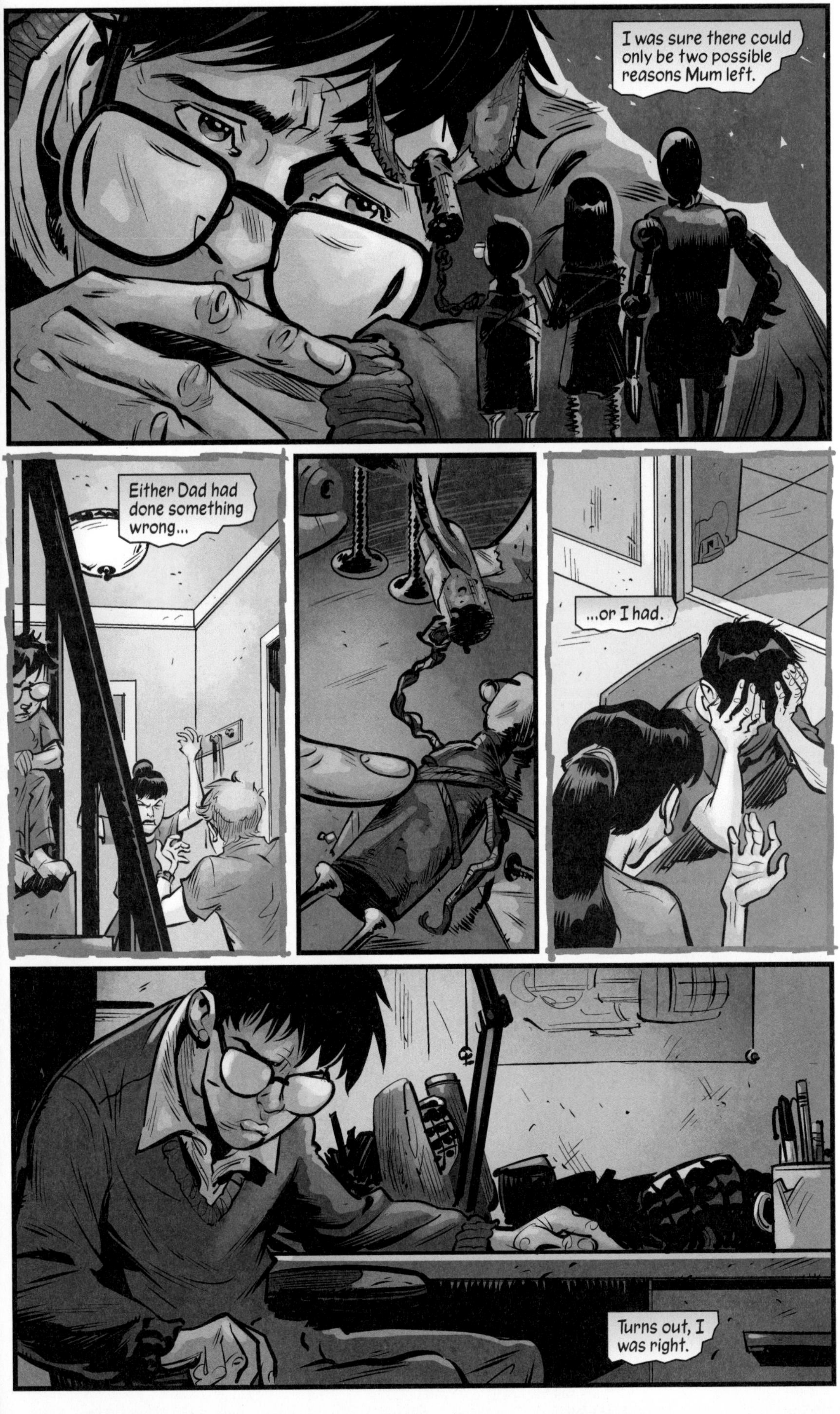
I was sure there could only be two possible reasons Mum left.
Either Dad had done something wrong...
...or I had.
Turns out, I was right.

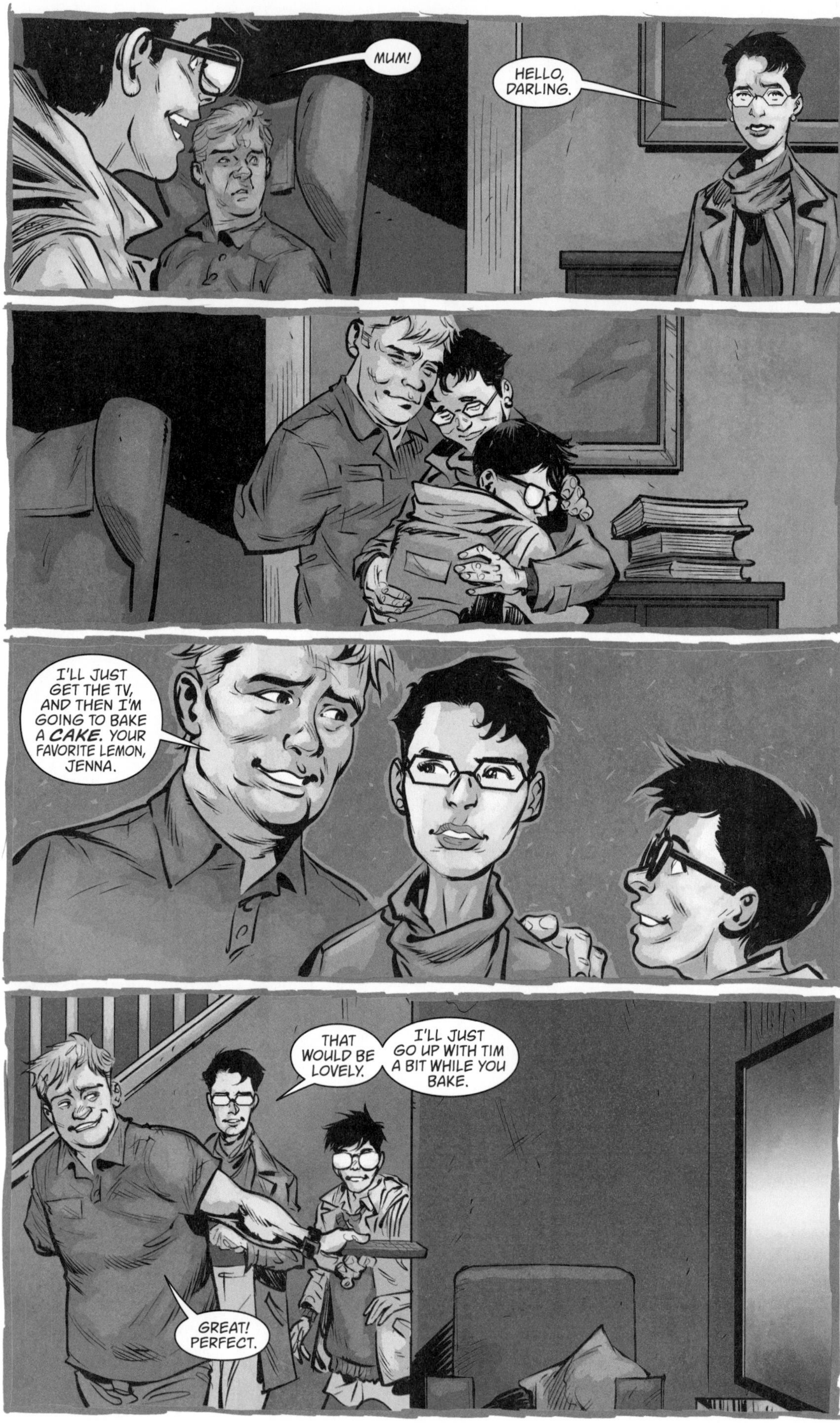
MUM!
HELLO, DARLING.
I'LL JUST GET THE TV, AND THEN I'M GOING TO BAKE A **CAKE**. YOUR FAVORITE LEMON, JENNA.
THAT WOULD BE LOVELY.
I'LL JUST GO UP WITH TIM A BIT WHILE YOU BAKE.
GREAT! PERFECT.

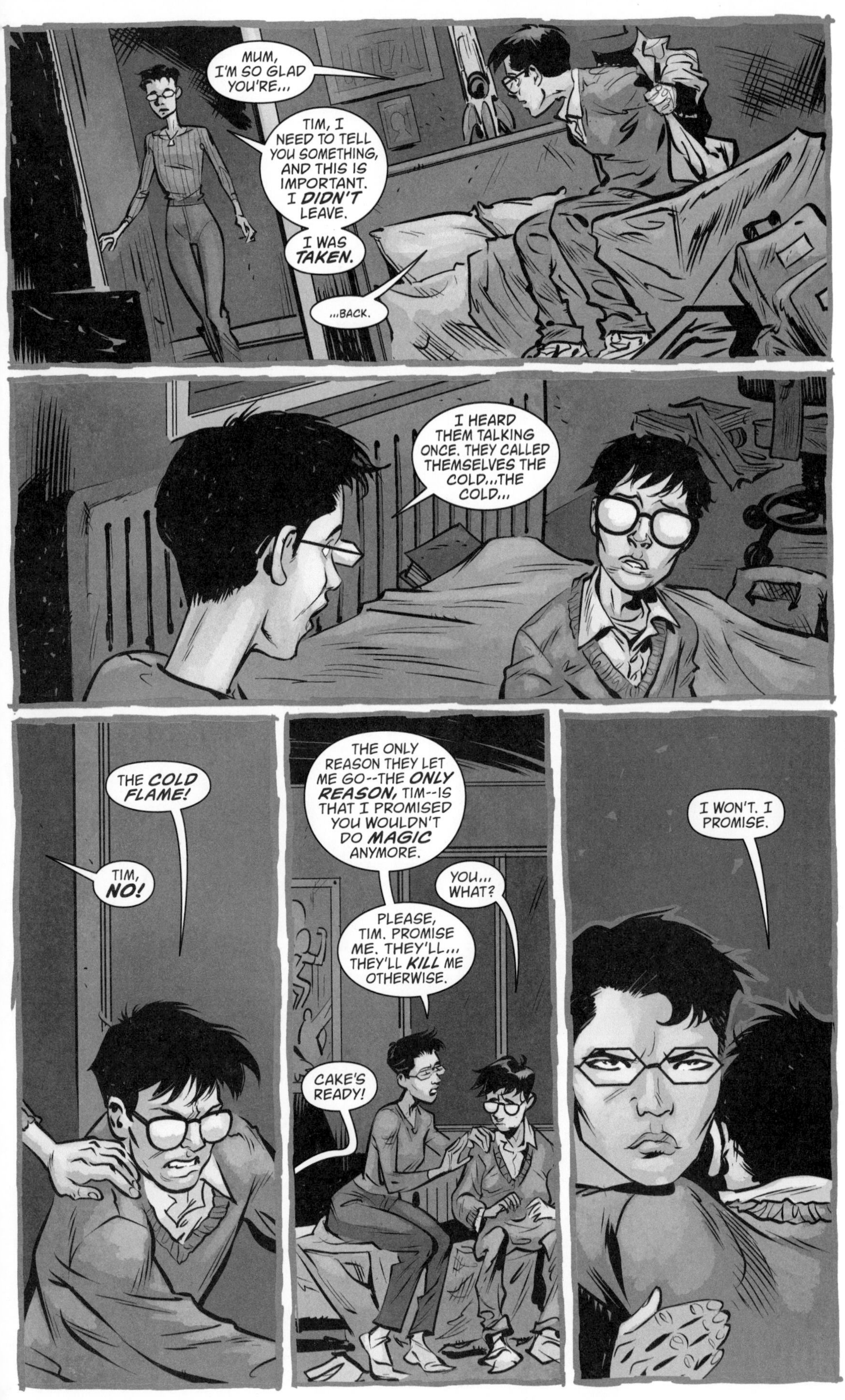
MUM, I'M SO GLAD YOU'RE...
TIM, I NEED TO TELL YOU SOMETHING, AND THIS IS IMPORTANT. I *DIDN'T* LEAVE.
I WAS *TAKEN.*
...BACK.
I HEARD THEM TALKING ONCE. THEY CALLED THEMSELVES THE COLD...THE COLD...
THE *COLD FLAME!*
TIM, *NO!*
THE ONLY REASON THEY LET ME GO--THE *ONLY REASON,* TIM--IS THAT I PROMISED YOU WOULDN'T DO *MAGIC* ANYMORE.
YOU... WHAT?
PLEASE, TIM. PROMISE ME. THEY'LL... THEY'LL *KILL* ME OTHERWISE.
CAKE'S READY!
I WON'T. I PROMISE.

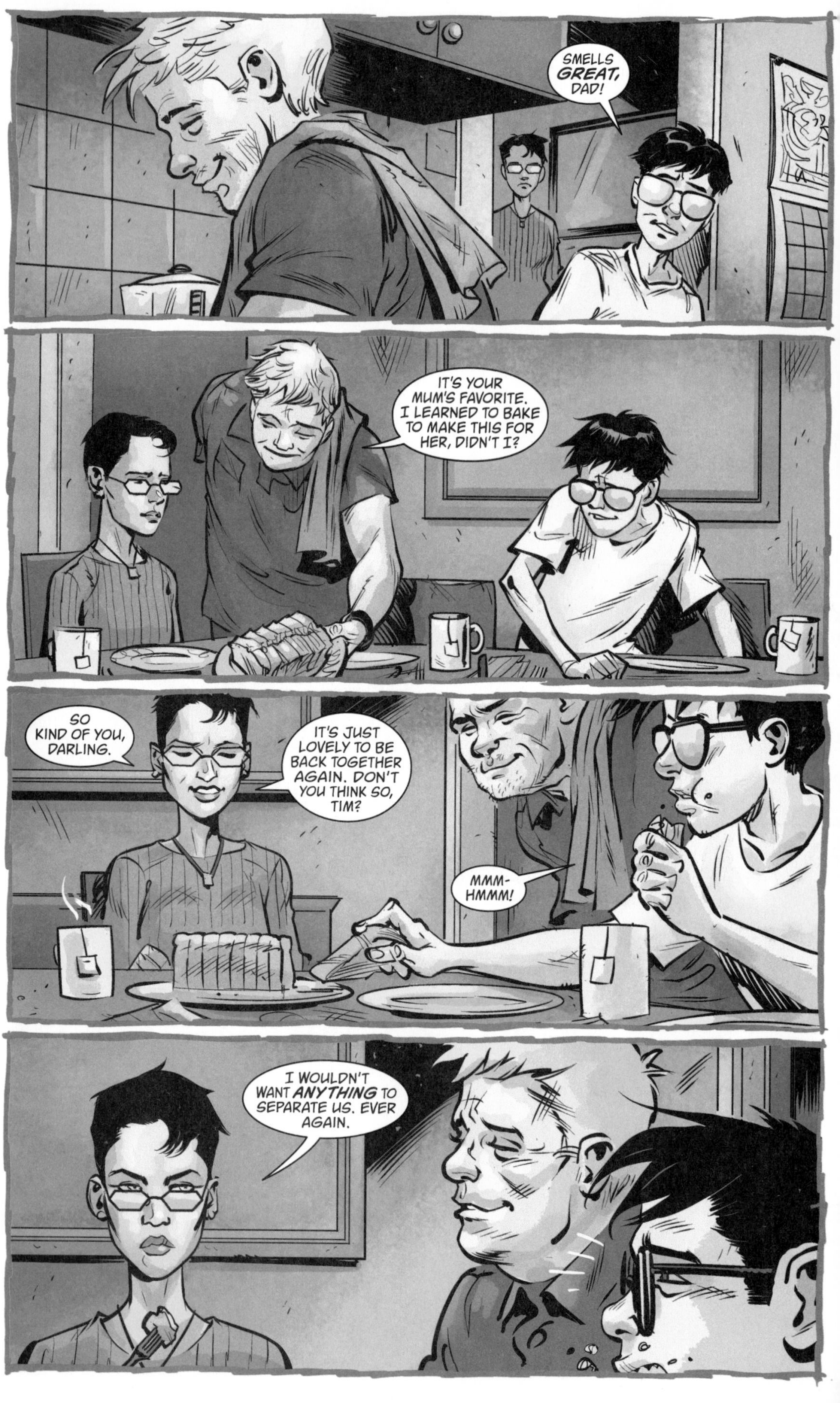
SMELLS GREAT, DAD!
IT'S YOUR MUM'S FAVORITE. I LEARNED TO BAKE TO MAKE THIS FOR HER, DIDN'T I?
SO KIND OF YOU, DARLING.
IT'S JUST LOVELY TO BE BACK TOGETHER AGAIN. DON'T YOU THINK SO, TIM?
MMM-HMMM!
I WOULDN'T WANT ANYTHING TO SEPARATE US. EVER AGAIN.

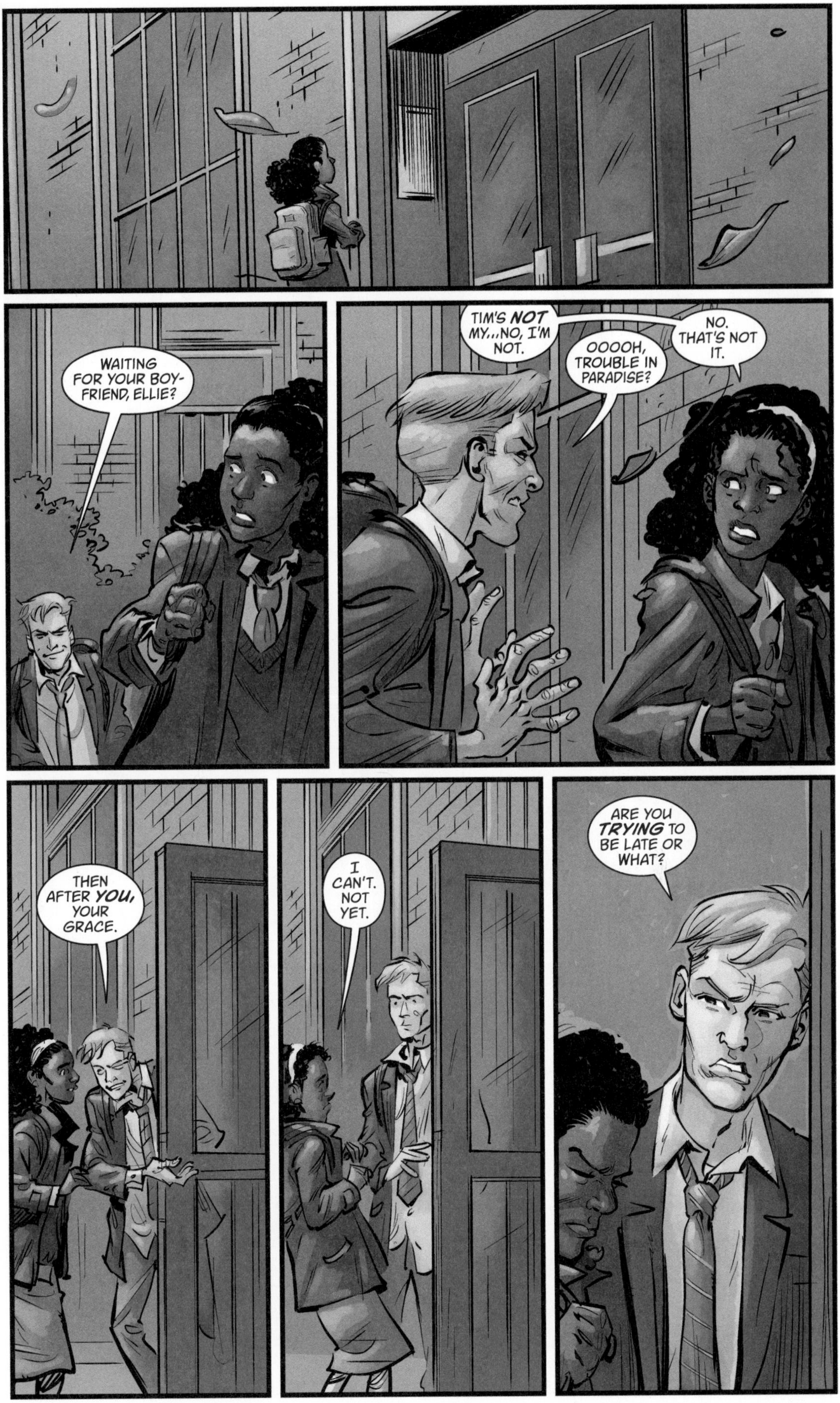
WAITING FOR YOUR BOY-FRIEND, ELLIE?
TIM'S NOT MY...NO, I'M NOT.
OOOOH, TROUBLE IN PARADISE?
NO. THAT'S NOT IT.
THEN AFTER YOU, YOUR GRACE.
I CAN'T. NOT YET.
ARE YOU TRYING TO BE LATE OR WHAT?

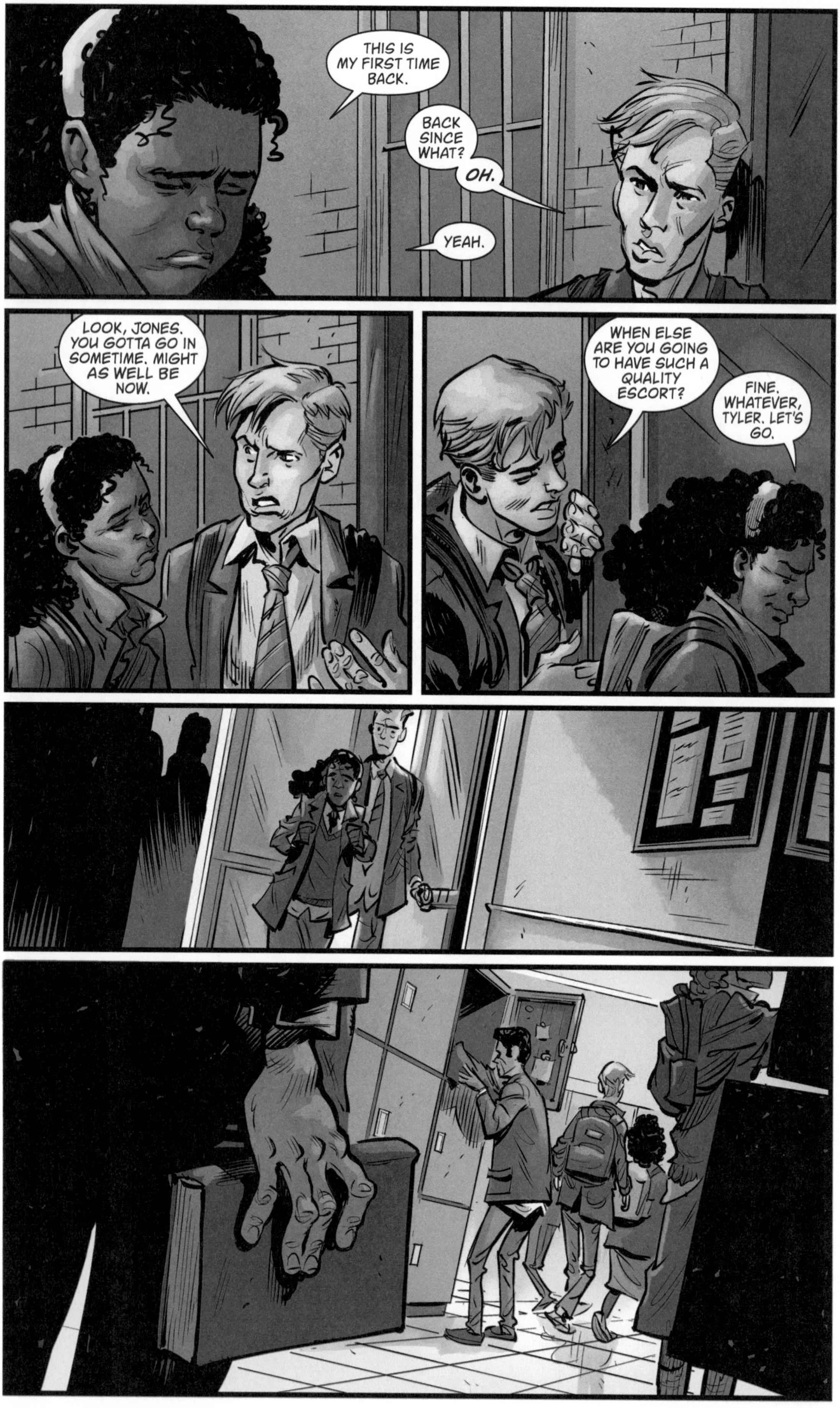
THIS IS MY FIRST TIME BACK.
BACK SINCE WHAT?
OH.
YEAH.
LOOK, JONES. YOU GOTTA GO IN SOMETIME. MIGHT AS WELL BE NOW.
WHEN ELSE ARE YOU GOING TO HAVE SUCH A QUALITY ESCORT?
FINE. WHATEVER, TYLER. LET'S GO.

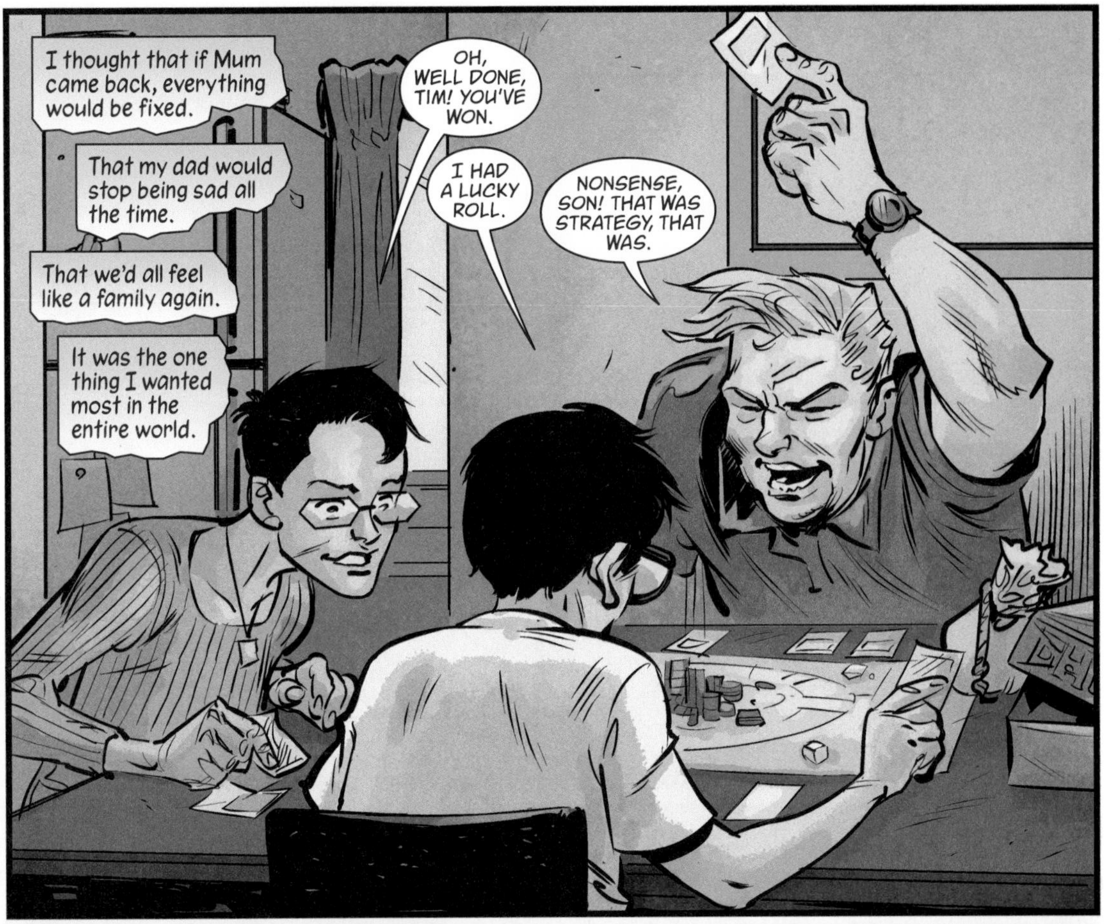
I thought that if Mum came back, everything would be fixed.
That my dad would stop being sad all the time.
That we'd all feel like a family again.
It was the one thing I wanted most in the entire world.
OH, WELL DONE, TIM! YOU'VE WON.
I HAD A LUCKY ROLL.
NONSENSE, SON! THAT WAS STRATEGY, THAT WAS.

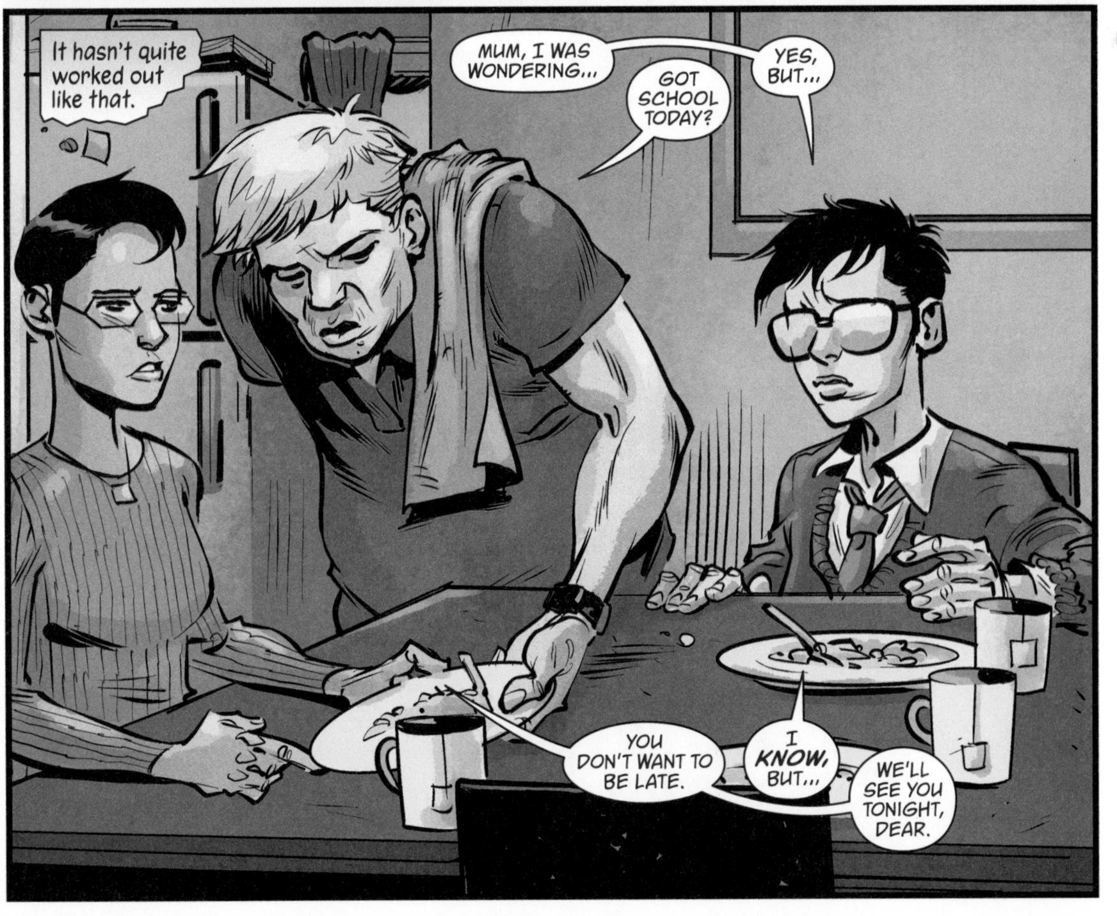
It hasn't quite worked out like that.
MUM, I WAS WONDERING...
YES, BUT...
GOT SCHOOL TODAY?
YOU DON'T WANT TO BE LATE.
I KNOW, BUT...
WE'LL SEE YOU TONIGHT, DEAR.

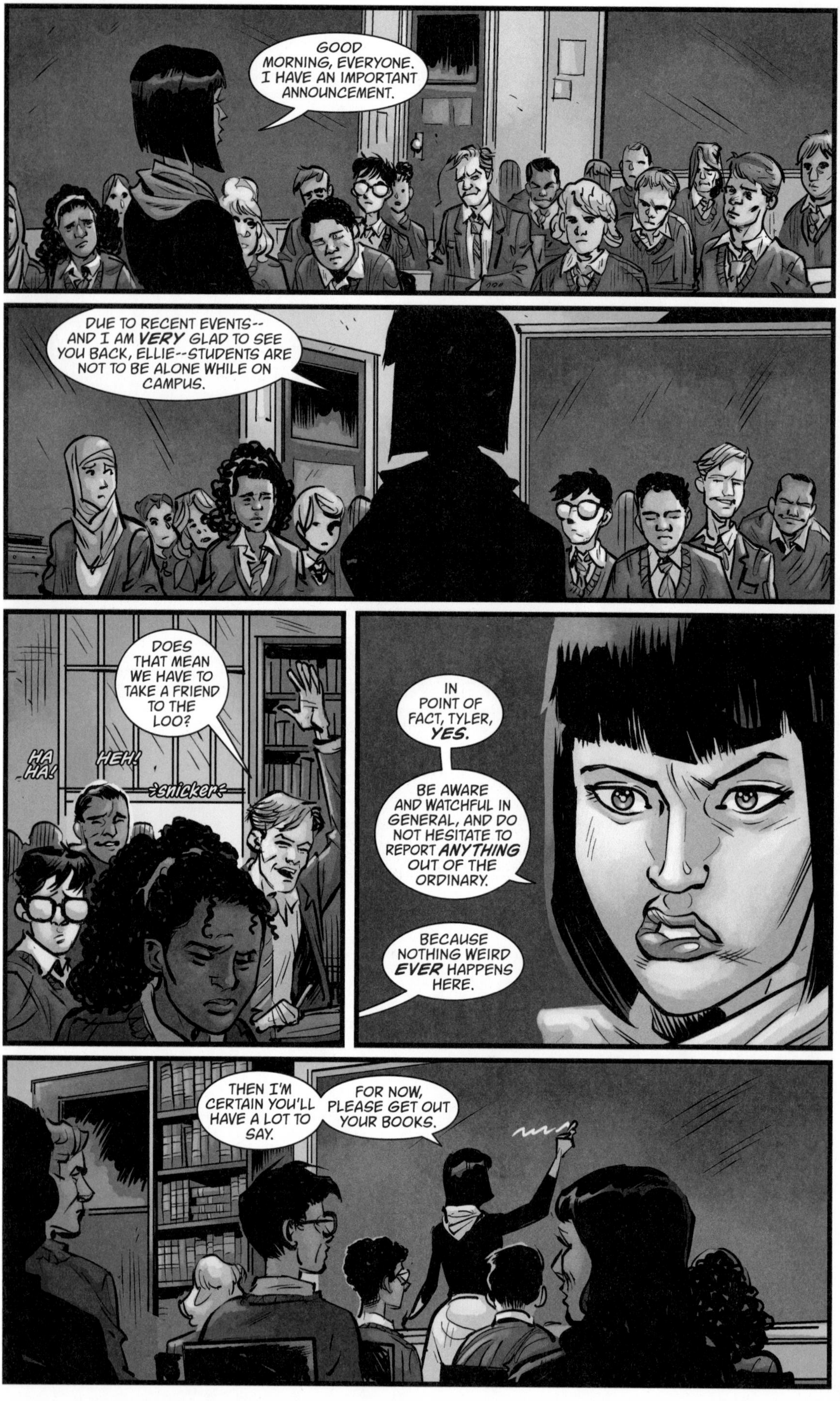
GOOD MORNING, EVERYONE. I HAVE AN IMPORTANT ANNOUNCEMENT.
DUE TO RECENT EVENTS-- AND I AM VERY GLAD TO SEE YOU BACK, ELLIE--STUDENTS ARE NOT TO BE ALONE WHILE ON CAMPUS.
DOES THAT MEAN WE HAVE TO TAKE A FRIEND TO THE LOO?
HA HA!
HEH!
snicker
IN POINT OF FACT, TYLER, YES.
BE AWARE AND WATCHFUL IN GENERAL, AND DO NOT HESITATE TO REPORT ANYTHING OUT OF THE ORDINARY.
BECAUSE NOTHING WEIRD EVER HAPPENS HERE.
THEN I'M CERTAIN YOU'LL HAVE A LOT TO SAY.
FOR NOW, PLEASE GET OUT YOUR BOOKS.

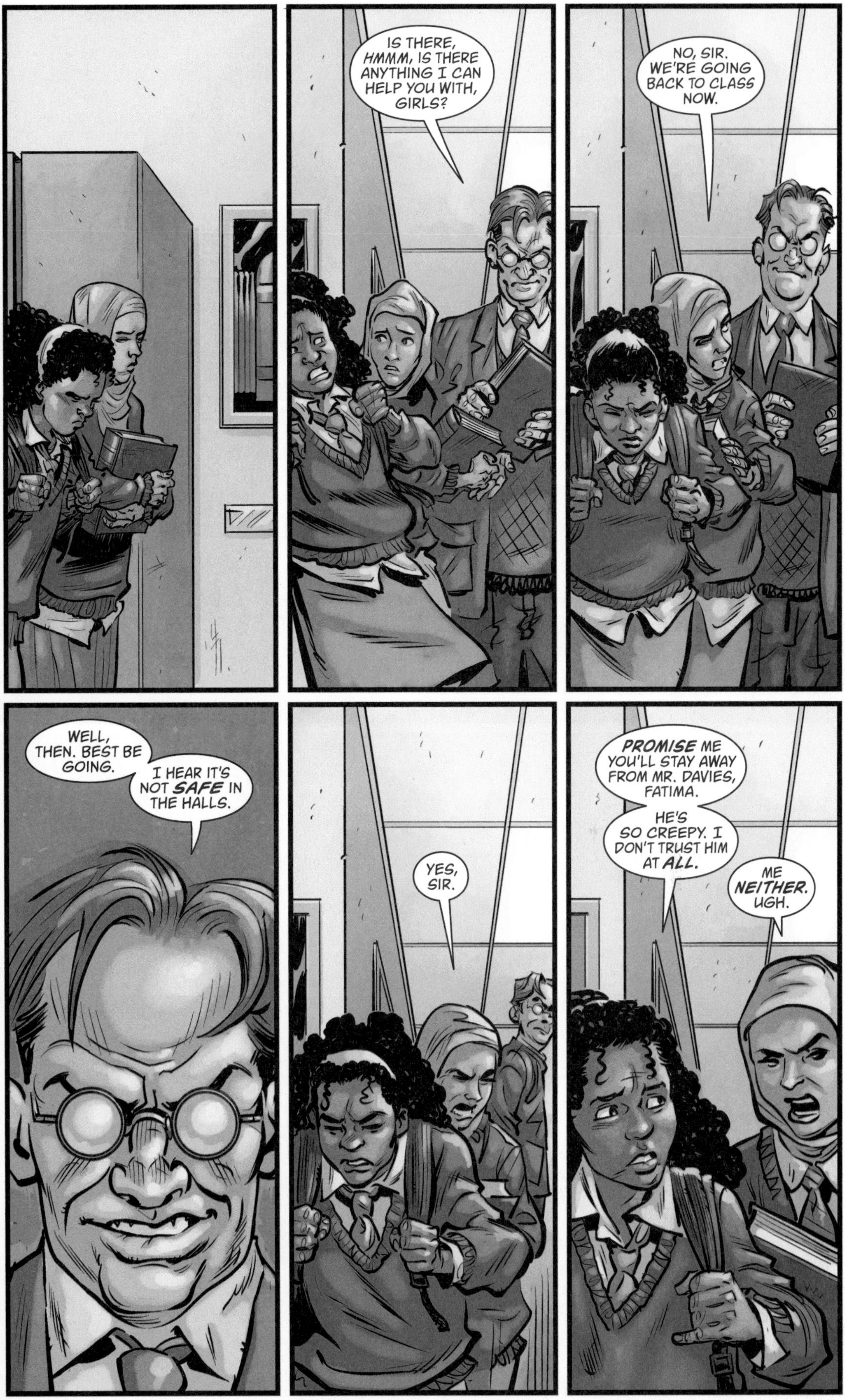
IS THERE, HMMM, IS THERE ANYTHING I CAN HELP YOU WITH, GIRLS?
NO, SIR. WE'RE GOING BACK TO CLASS NOW.
WELL, THEN. BEST BE GOING.
I HEAR IT'S NOT SAFE IN THE HALLS.
YES, SIR.
PROMISE ME YOU'LL STAY AWAY FROM MR. DAVIES, FATIMA.
HE'S SO CREEPY. I DON'T TRUST HIM AT ALL.
ME NEITHER. UGH.

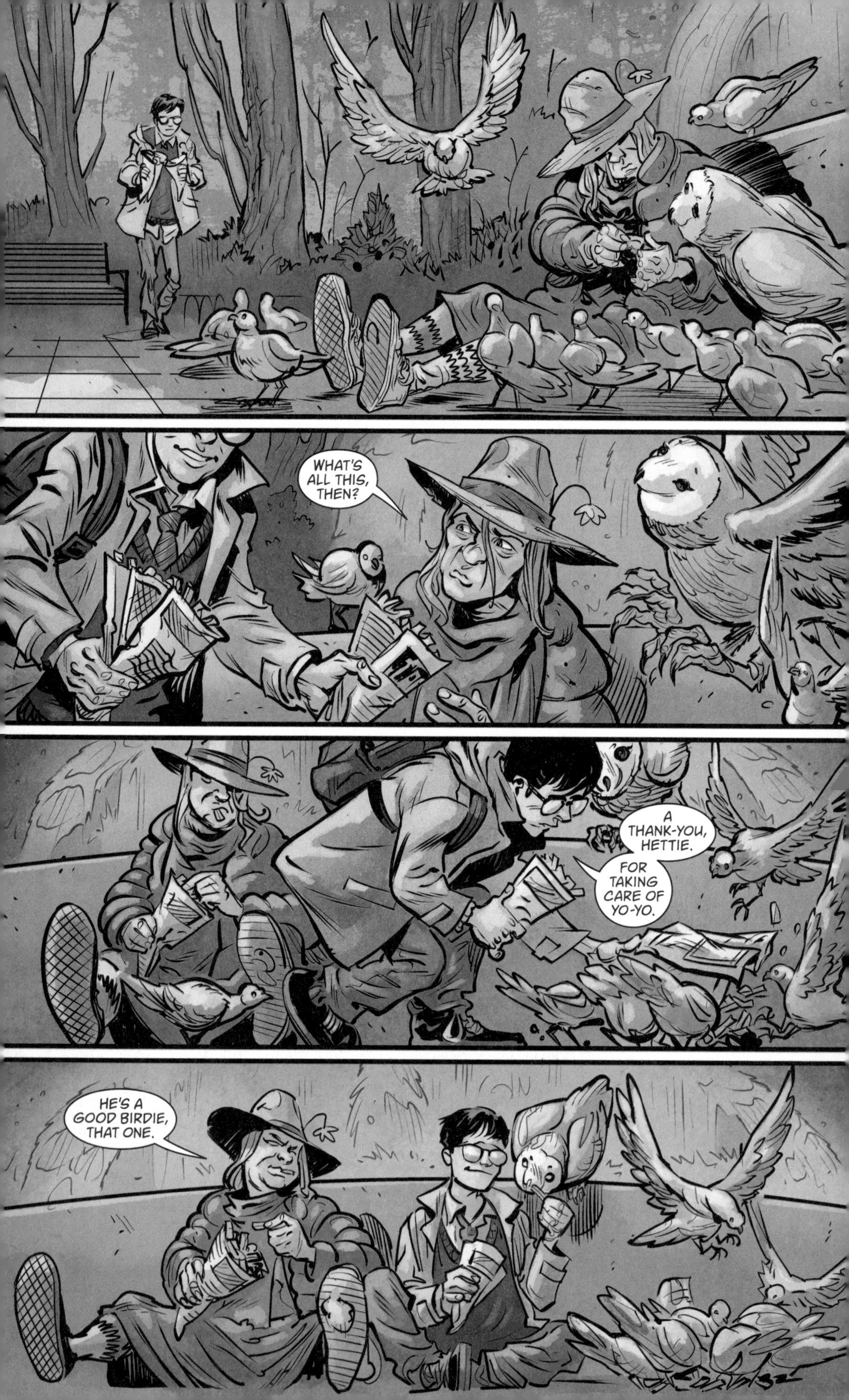
WHAT'S ALL THIS, THEN?
A THANK-YOU, HETTIE.
FOR TAKING CARE OF YO-YO.
HE'S A GOOD BIRDIE, THAT ONE.

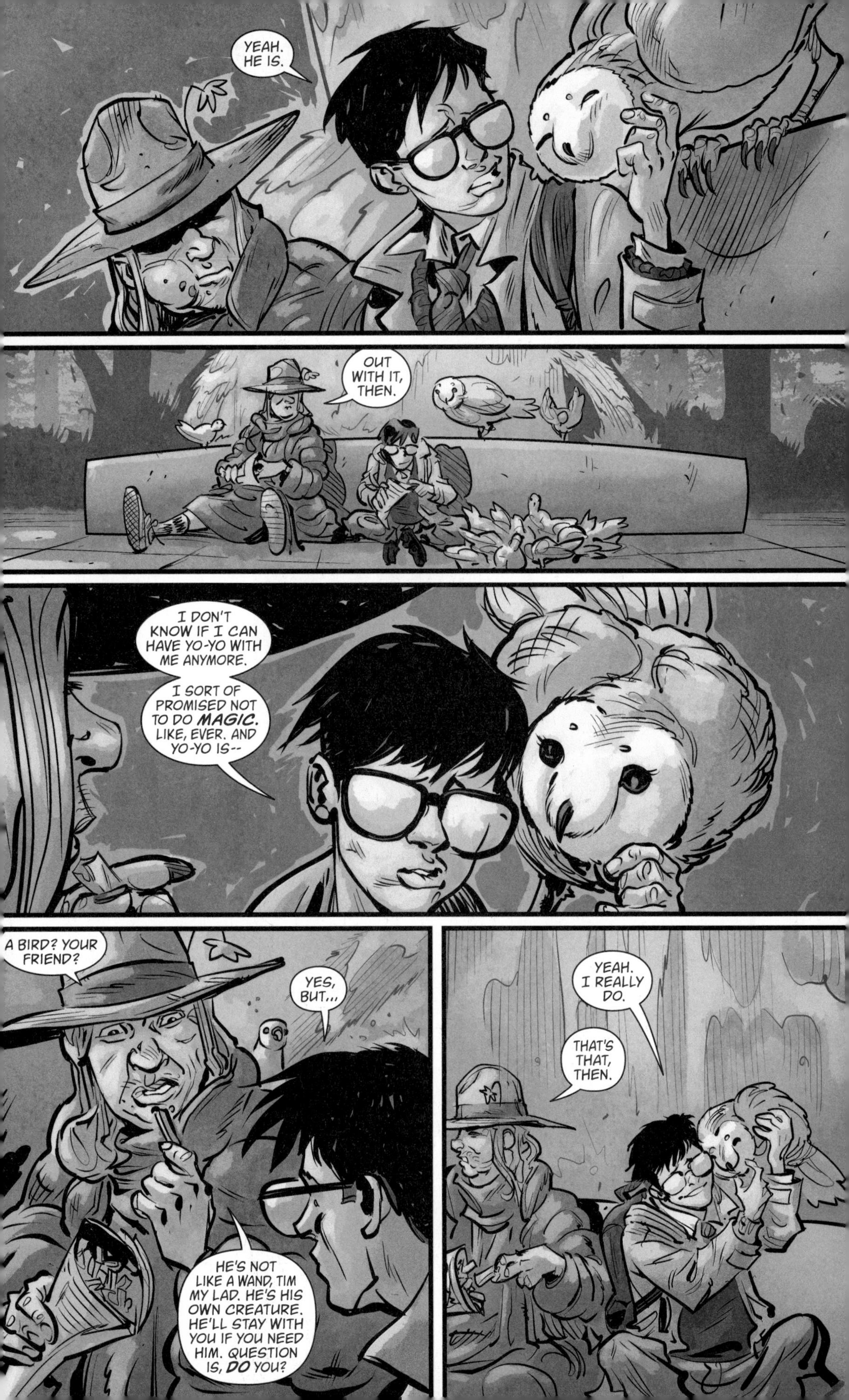
YEAH. HE IS.
OUT WITH IT, THEN.
I DON'T KNOW IF I CAN HAVE YO-YO WITH ME ANYMORE.
I SORT OF PROMISED NOT TO DO **MAGIC.** LIKE, EVER. AND YO-YO IS--
A BIRD? YOUR FRIEND?
YES, BUT...
HE'S NOT LIKE A WAND, TIM MY LAD. HE'S HIS OWN CREATURE. HE'LL STAY WITH YOU IF YOU NEED HIM. QUESTION IS, **DO** YOU?
YEAH. I REALLY DO.
THAT'S THAT, THEN.

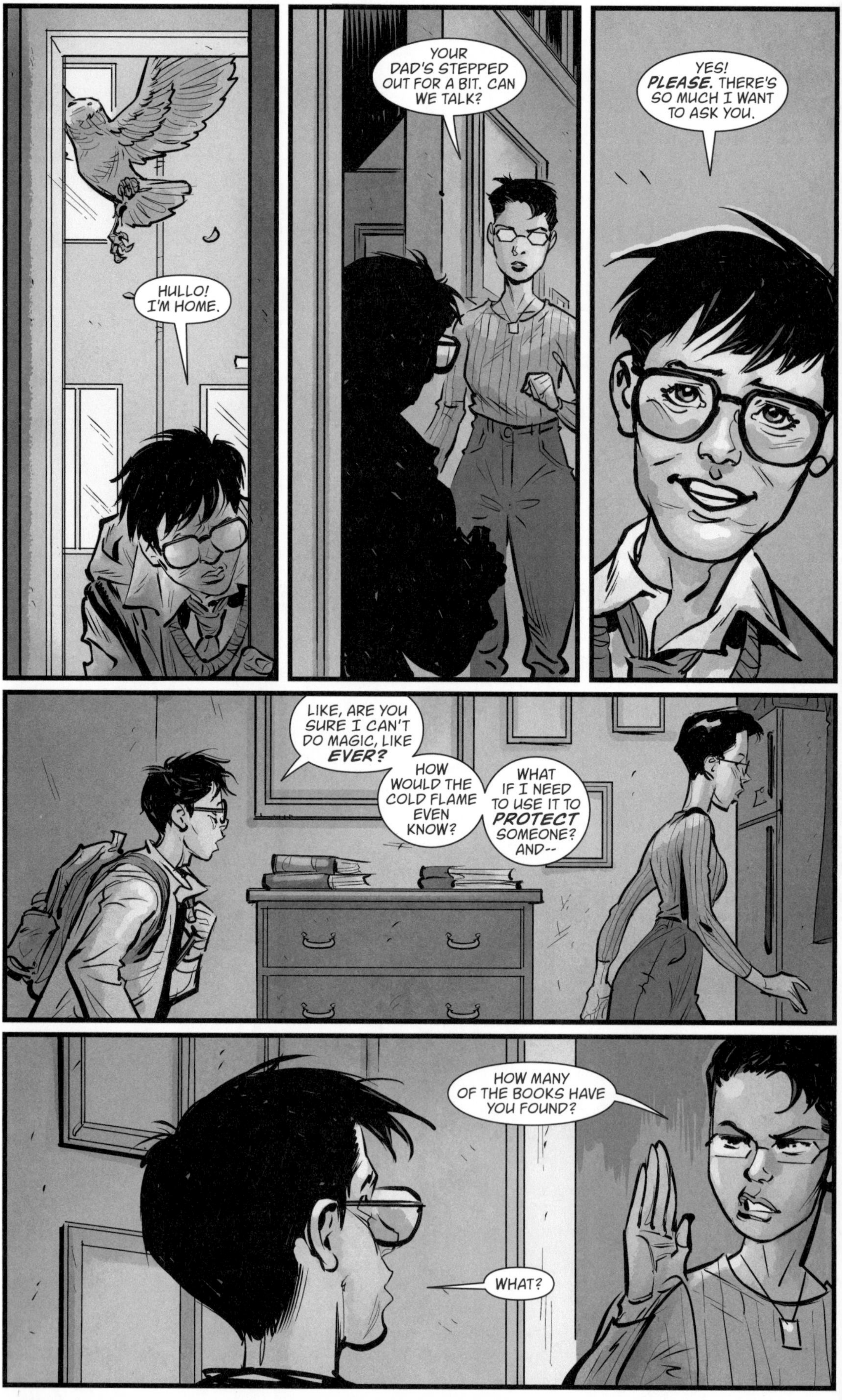
HULLO! I'M HOME.
YOUR DAD'S STEPPED OUT FOR A BIT. CAN WE TALK?
YES! PLEASE. THERE'S SO MUCH I WANT TO ASK YOU.
LIKE, ARE YOU SURE I CAN'T DO MAGIC, LIKE EVER?
HOW WOULD THE COLD FLAME EVEN KNOW?
WHAT IF I NEED TO USE IT TO PROTECT SOMEONE? AND--
HOW MANY OF THE BOOKS HAVE YOU FOUND?
WHAT?

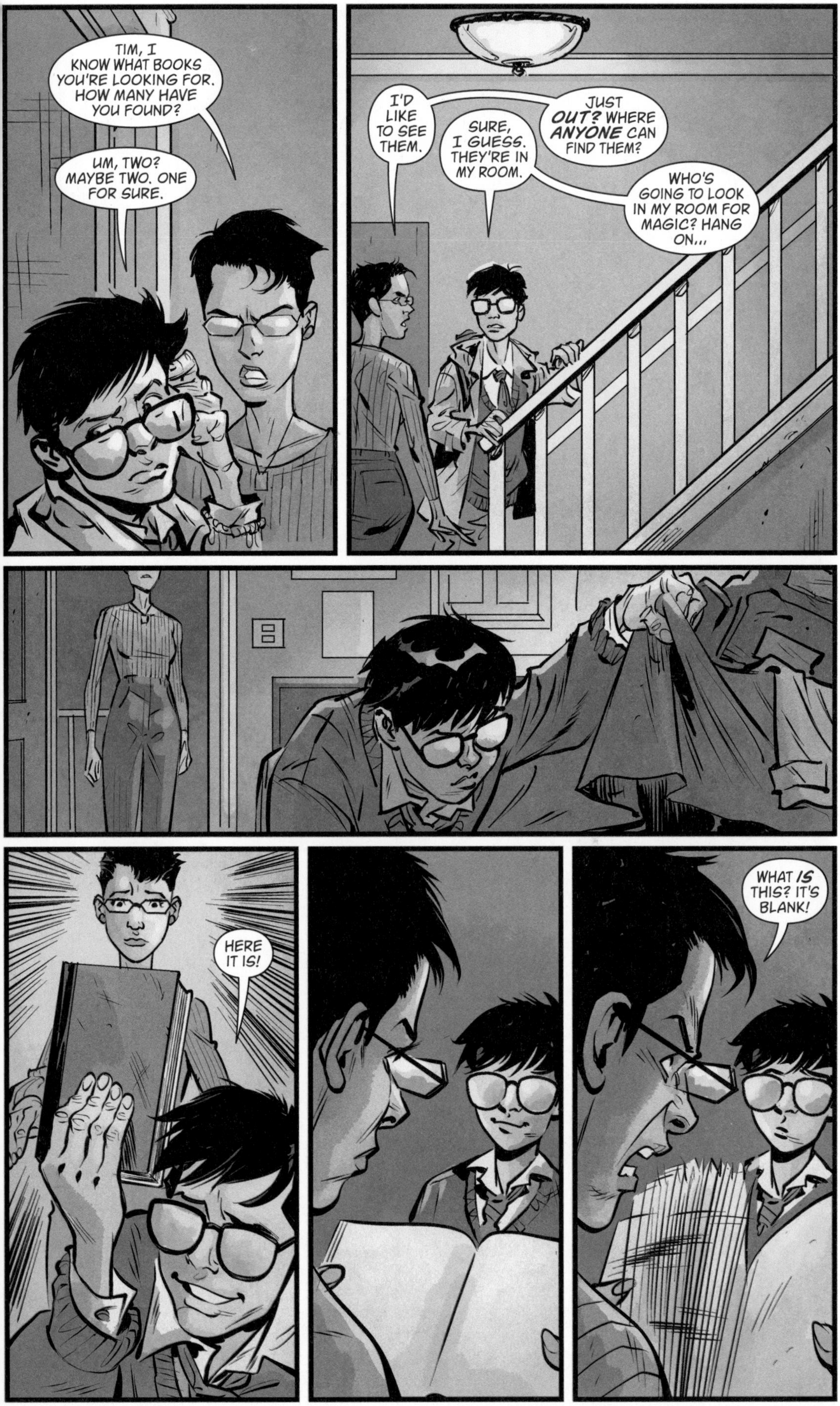
TIM, I KNOW WHAT BOOKS YOU'RE LOOKING FOR. HOW MANY HAVE YOU FOUND?
UM, TWO? MAYBE TWO. ONE FOR SURE.
I'D LIKE TO SEE THEM.
SURE, I GUESS. THEY'RE IN MY ROOM.
JUST OUT? WHERE ANYONE CAN FIND THEM?
WHO'S GOING TO LOOK IN MY ROOM FOR MAGIC? HANG ON...
HERE IT IS!
WHAT IS THIS? IT'S BLANK!

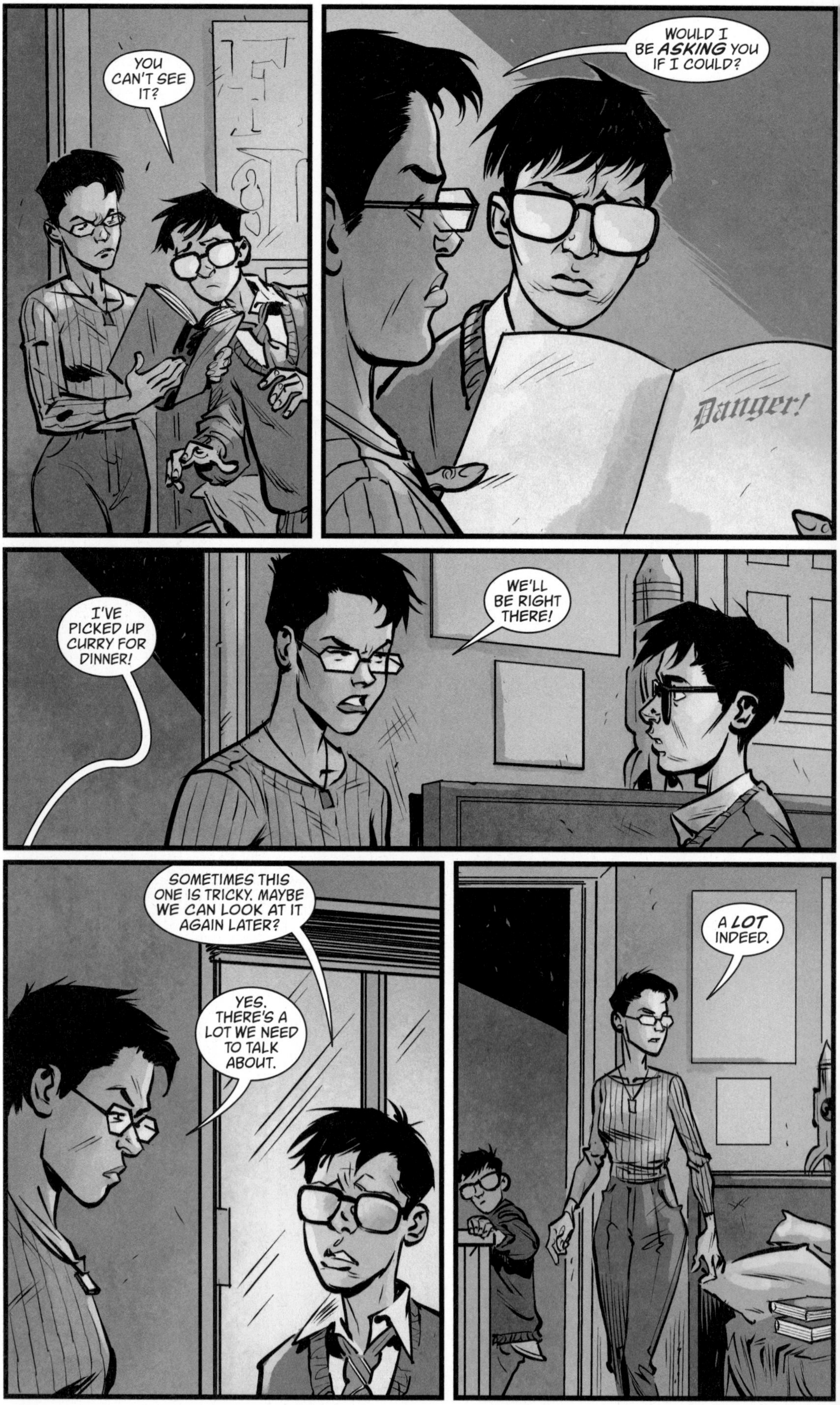
YOU CAN'T SEE IT?
WOULD I BE ASKING YOU IF I COULD?
Danger!
I'VE PICKED UP CURRY FOR DINNER!
WE'LL BE RIGHT THERE!
SOMETIMES THIS ONE IS TRICKY. MAYBE WE CAN LOOK AT IT AGAIN LATER?
YES. THERE'S A LOT WE NEED TO TALK ABOUT.
A LOT INDEED.

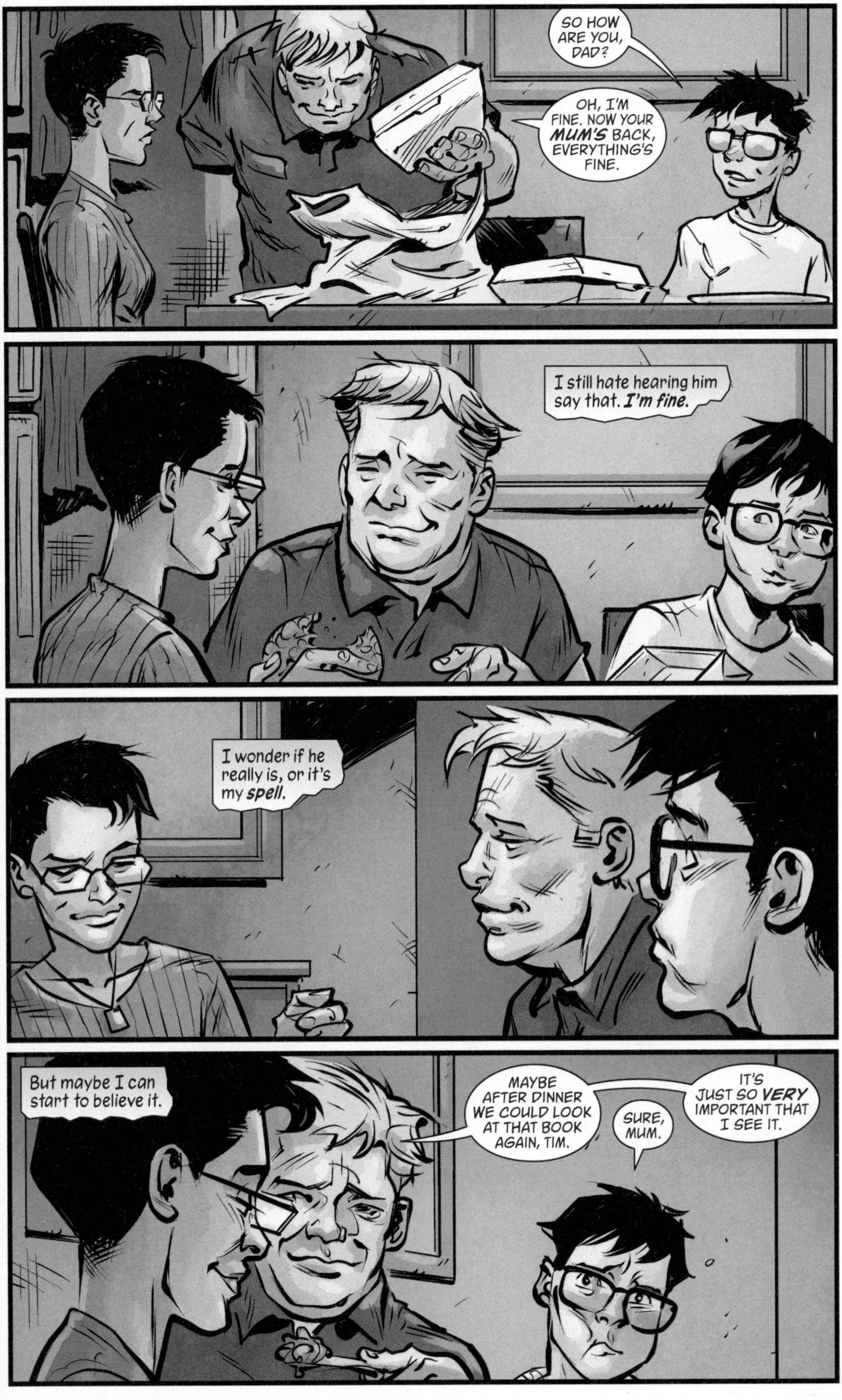
SO HOW ARE YOU, DAD?
OH, I'M FINE. NOW YOUR MUM'S BACK, EVERYTHING'S FINE.
I still hate hearing him say that. I'm fine.
I wonder if he really is, or it's my spell.
But maybe I can start to believe it.
MAYBE AFTER DINNER WE COULD LOOK AT THAT BOOK AGAIN, TIM.
IT'S JUST SO VERY IMPORTANT THAT I SEE IT.
SURE, MUM.

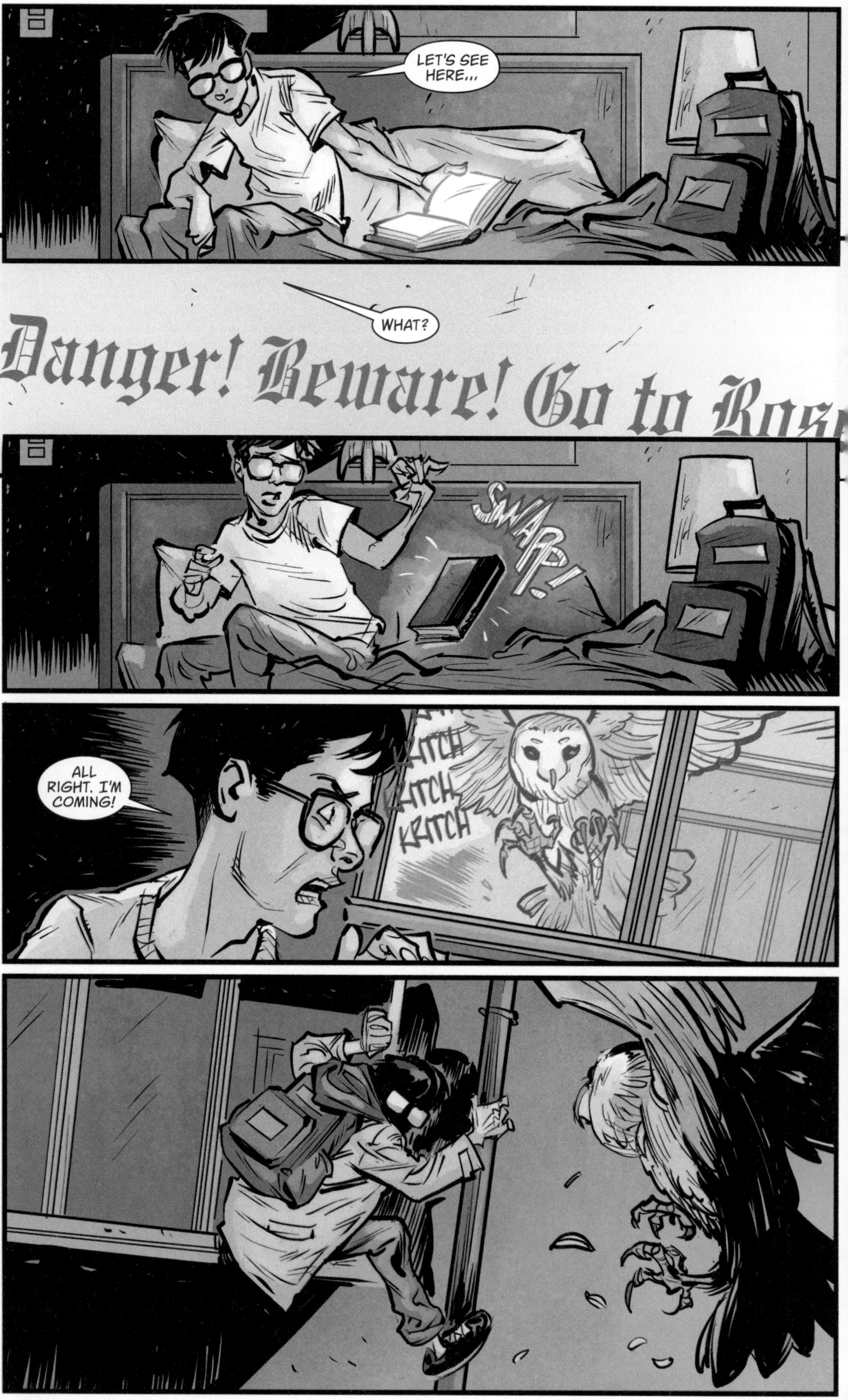
LET'S SEE HERE...
WHAT?
Danger! Beware! Go to
SWAP!
ALL RIGHT. I'M COMING!
KRITCH
KRITCH
KRITCH

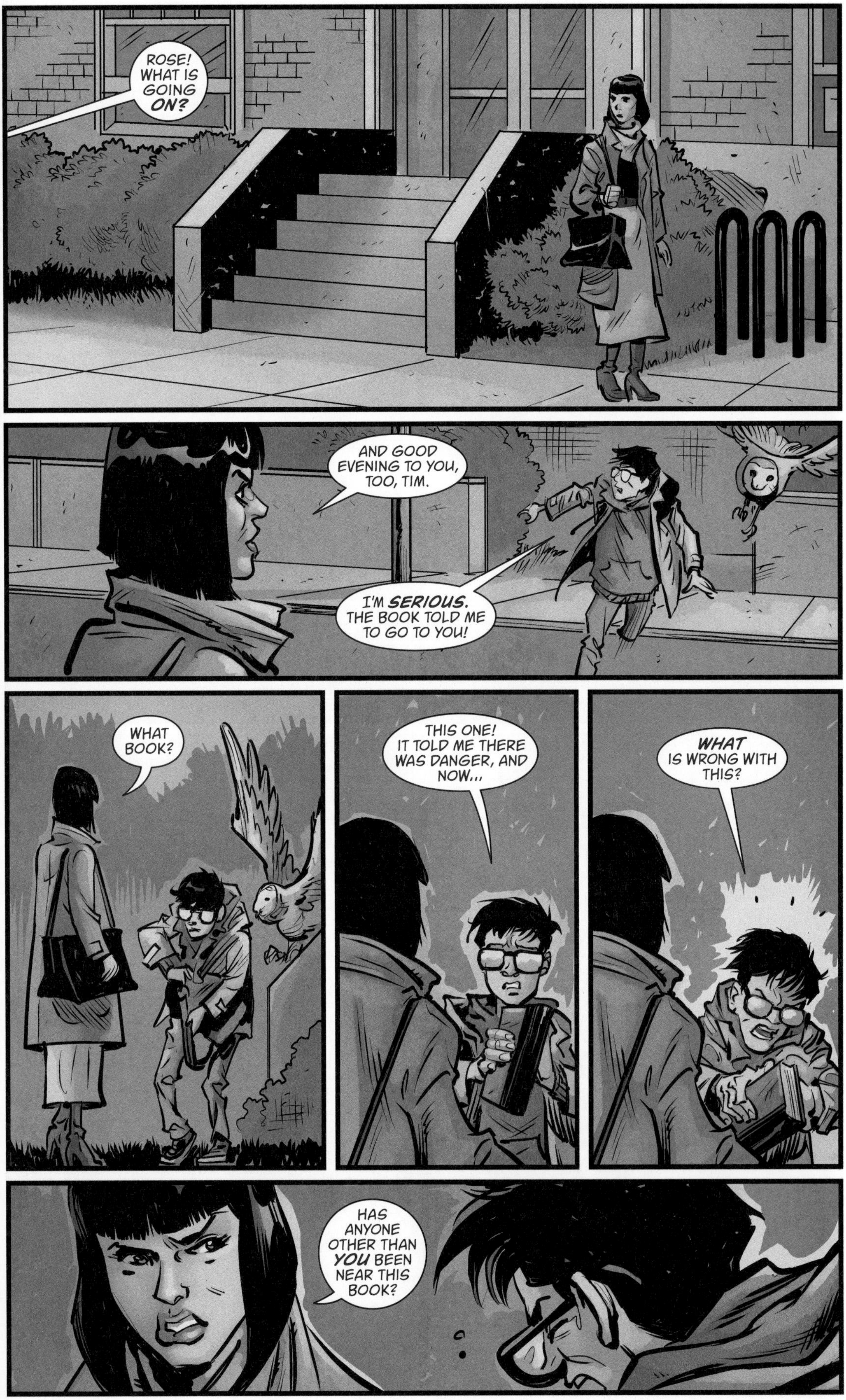
ROSE! WHAT IS GOING ON?
AND GOOD EVENING TO YOU, TOO, TIM.
I'M SERIOUS. THE BOOK TOLD ME TO GO TO YOU!
WHAT BOOK?
THIS ONE! IT TOLD ME THERE WAS DANGER, AND NOW...
WHAT IS WRONG WITH THIS?
HAS ANYONE OTHER THAN YOU BEEN NEAR THIS BOOK?

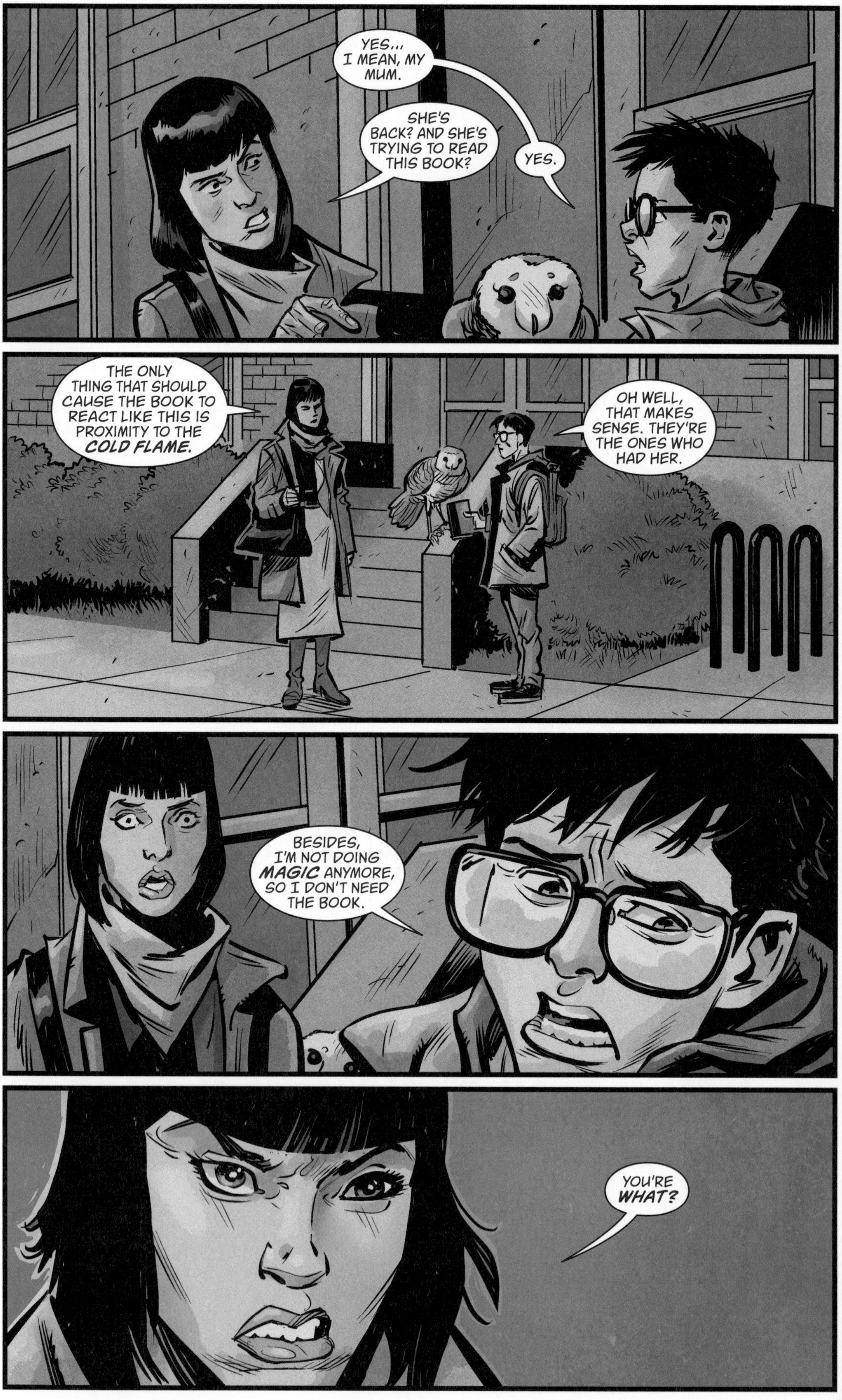
YES... I MEAN, MY MUM.
SHE'S BACK? AND SHE'S TRYING TO READ THIS BOOK?
YES.
THE ONLY THING THAT SHOULD CAUSE THE BOOK TO REACT LIKE THIS IS PROXIMITY TO THE COLD FLAME.
OH WELL, THAT MAKES SENSE. THEY'RE THE ONES WHO HAD HER.
BESIDES, I'M NOT DOING MAGIC ANYMORE, SO I DON'T NEED THE BOOK.
YOU'RE WHAT?

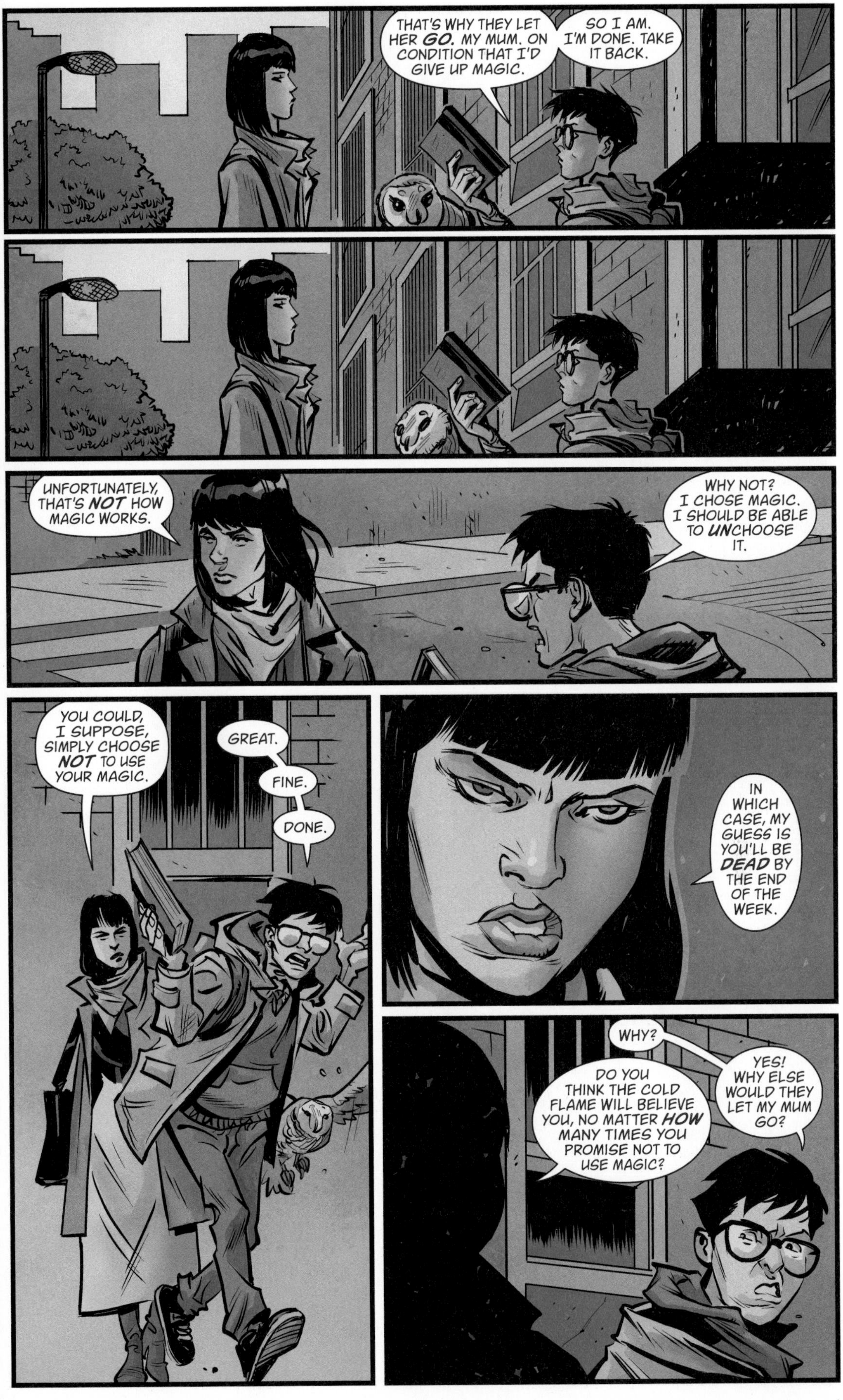

THAT'S WHY THEY LET HER GO. MY MUM. ON CONDITION THAT I'D GIVE UP MAGIC.
SO I AM. I'M DONE. TAKE IT BACK.
UNFORTUNATELY, THAT'S NOT HOW MAGIC WORKS.
WHY NOT? I CHOSE MAGIC. I SHOULD BE ABLE TO UNCHOOSE IT.
YOU COULD, I SUPPOSE, SIMPLY CHOOSE NOT TO USE YOUR MAGIC.
GREAT.
FINE.
DONE.
IN WHICH CASE, MY GUESS IS YOU'LL BE DEAD BY THE END OF THE WEEK.
WHY?
DO YOU THINK THE COLD FLAME WILL BELIEVE YOU, NO MATTER HOW MANY TIMES YOU PROMISE NOT TO USE MAGIC?
YES! WHY ELSE WOULD THEY LET MY MUM GO?

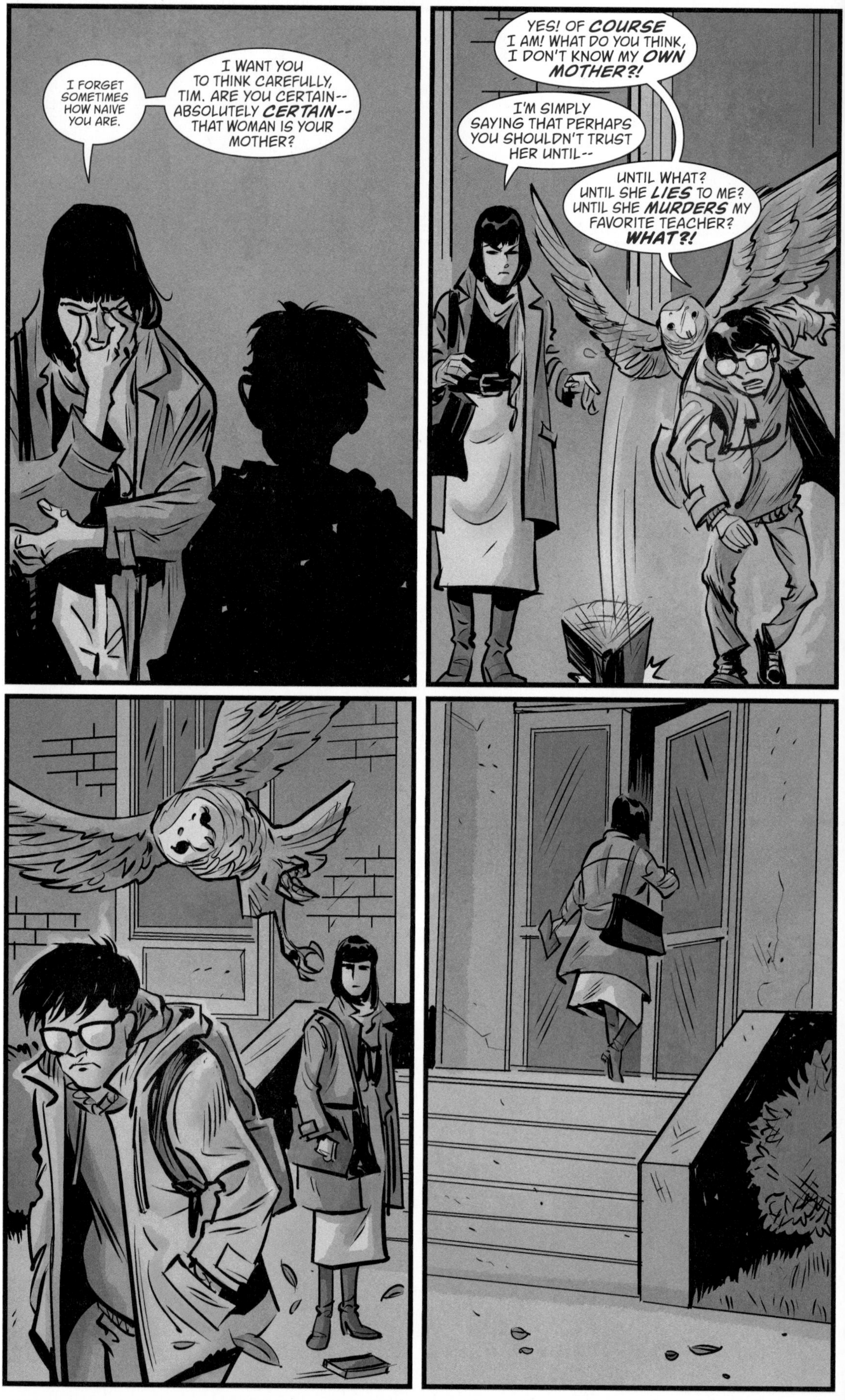
I FORGET SOMETIMES HOW NAIVE YOU ARE.
I WANT YOU TO THINK CAREFULLY, TIM. ARE YOU CERTAIN-- ABSOLUTELY CERTAIN-- THAT WOMAN IS YOUR MOTHER?
YES! OF COURSE I AM! WHAT DO YOU THINK, I DON'T KNOW MY OWN MOTHER?!
I'M SIMPLY SAYING THAT PERHAPS YOU SHOULDN'T TRUST HER UNTIL--
UNTIL WHAT? UNTIL SHE LIES TO ME? UNTIL SHE MURDERS MY FAVORITE TEACHER? WHAT?!

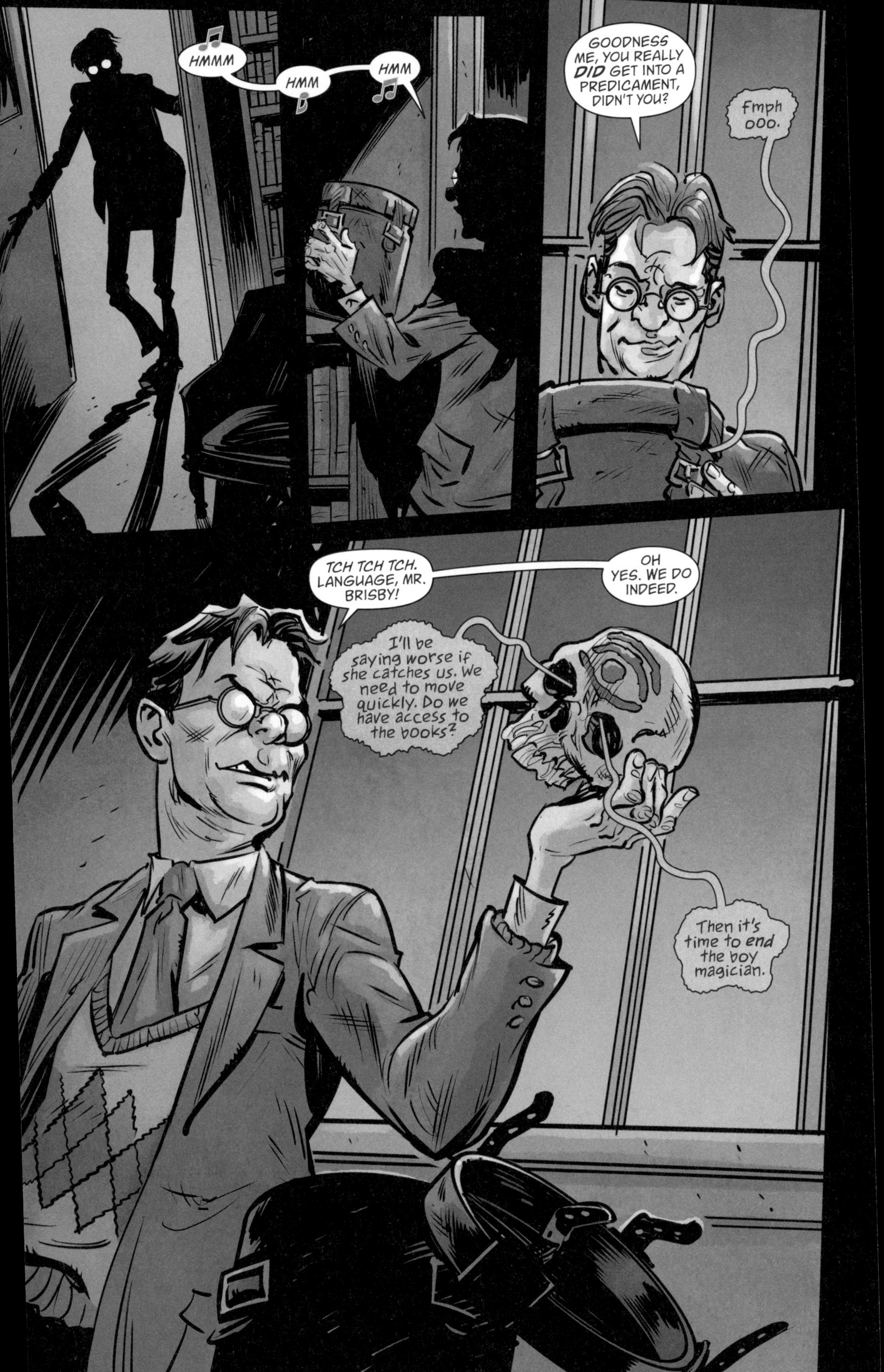
HMMM
HMM
HMM
GOODNESS ME, YOU REALLY DID GET INTO A PREDICAMENT, DIDN'T YOU?
Fmph ooo.
OH YES. WE DO INDEED.
I'll be saying worse if she catches us. We need to move quickly. Do we have access to the books?
TCH TCH TCH. LANGUAGE, MR. BRISBY!
Then it's time to end the boy magician.

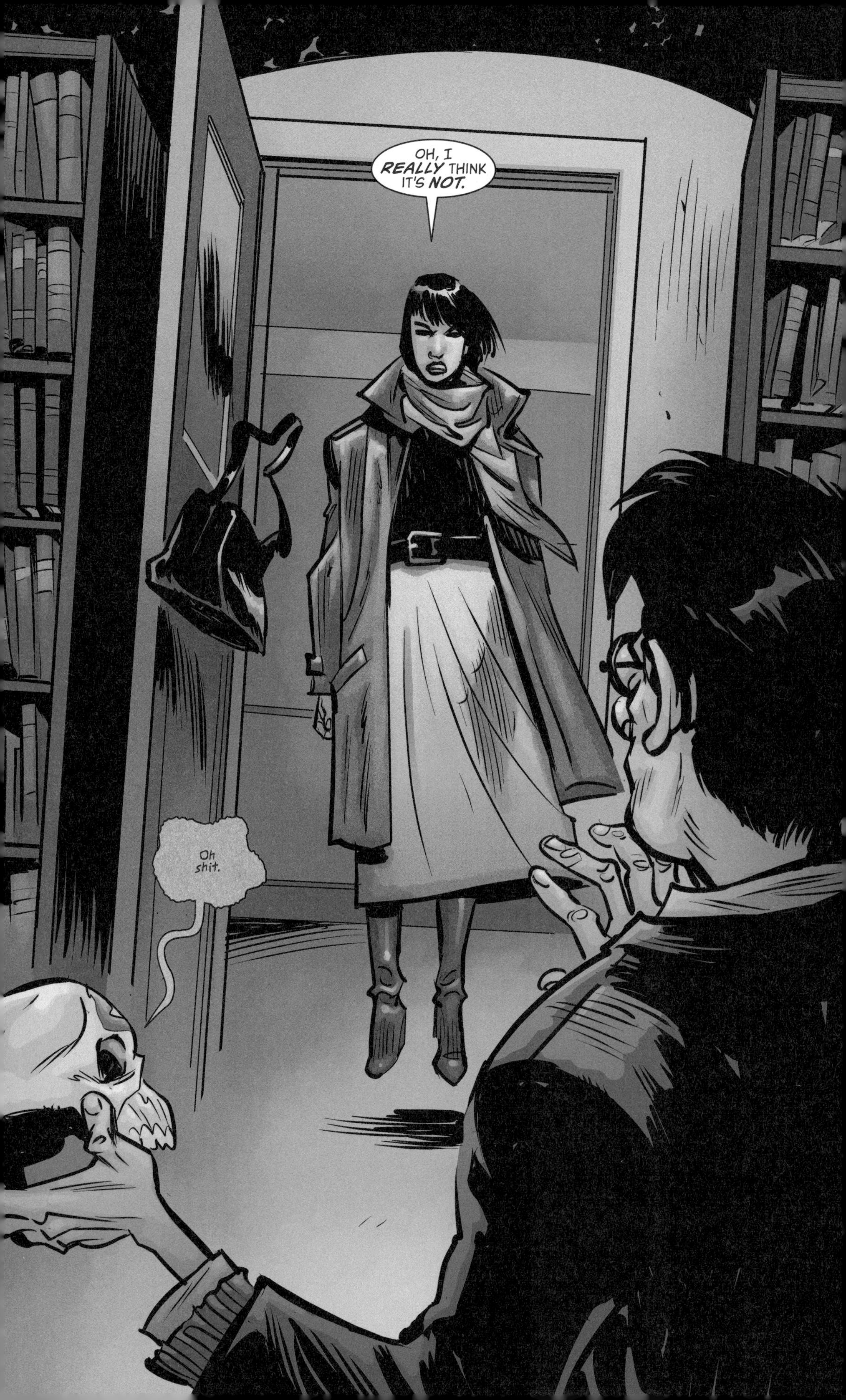
OH, I REALLY THINK IT'S NOT.
Oh shit.

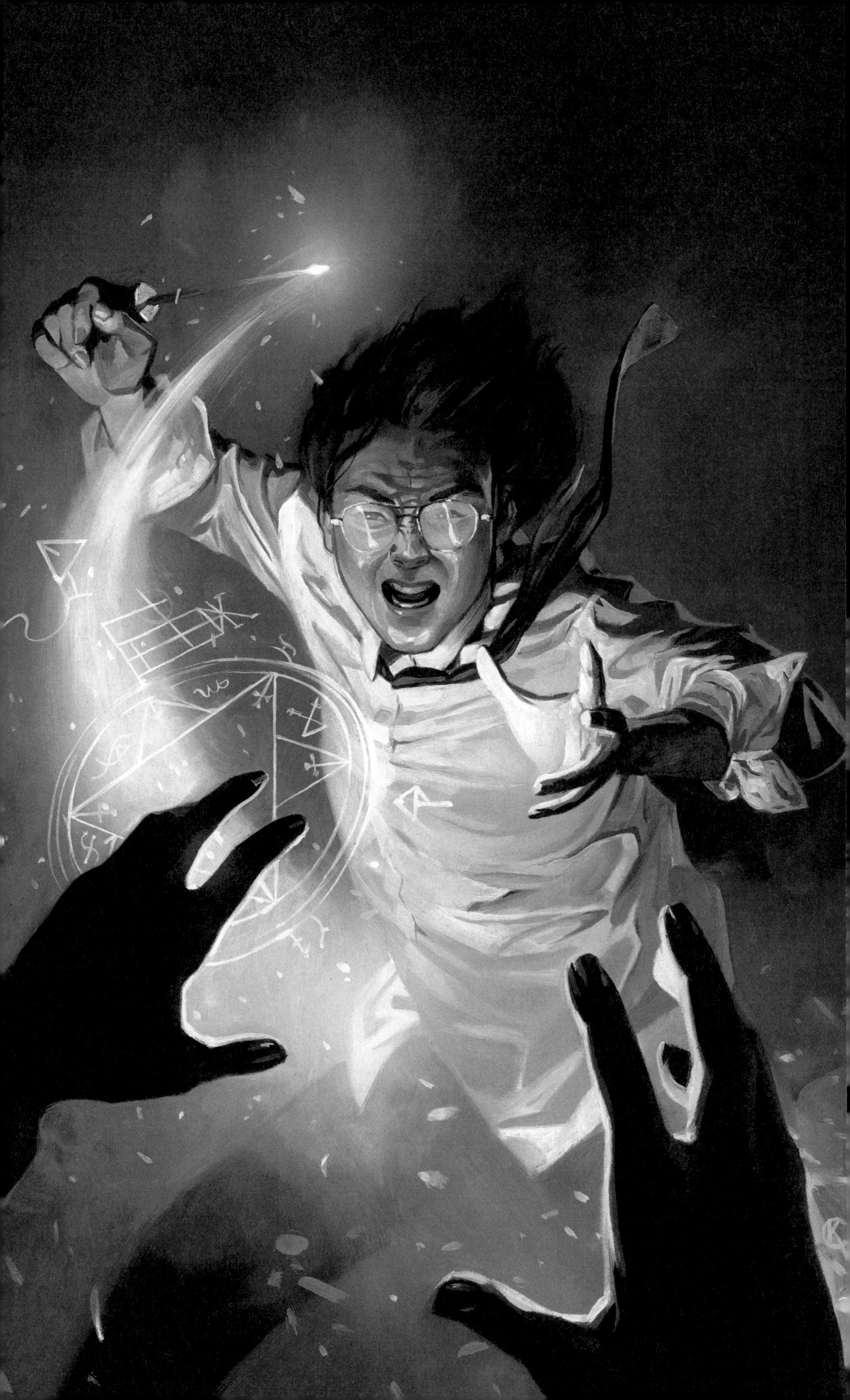

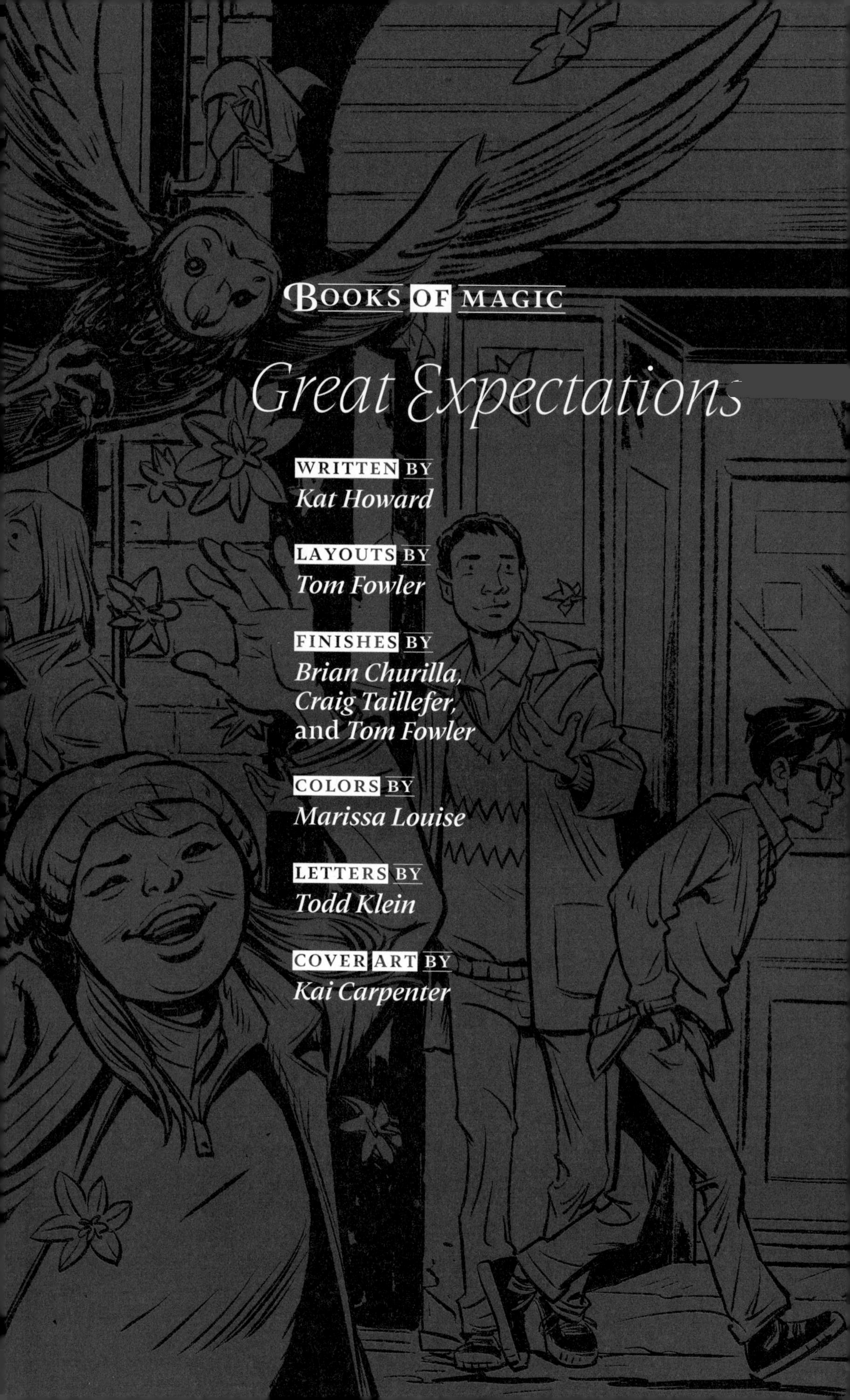

BOOKS OF MAGIC

Great Expectations

WRITTEN BY
Kat Howard

LAYOUTS BY
Tom Fowler

FINISHES BY
Brian Churilla,
Craig Taillefer,
and *Tom Fowler*

COLORS BY
Marissa Louise

LETTERS BY
Todd Klein

COVER ART BY
Kai Carpenter

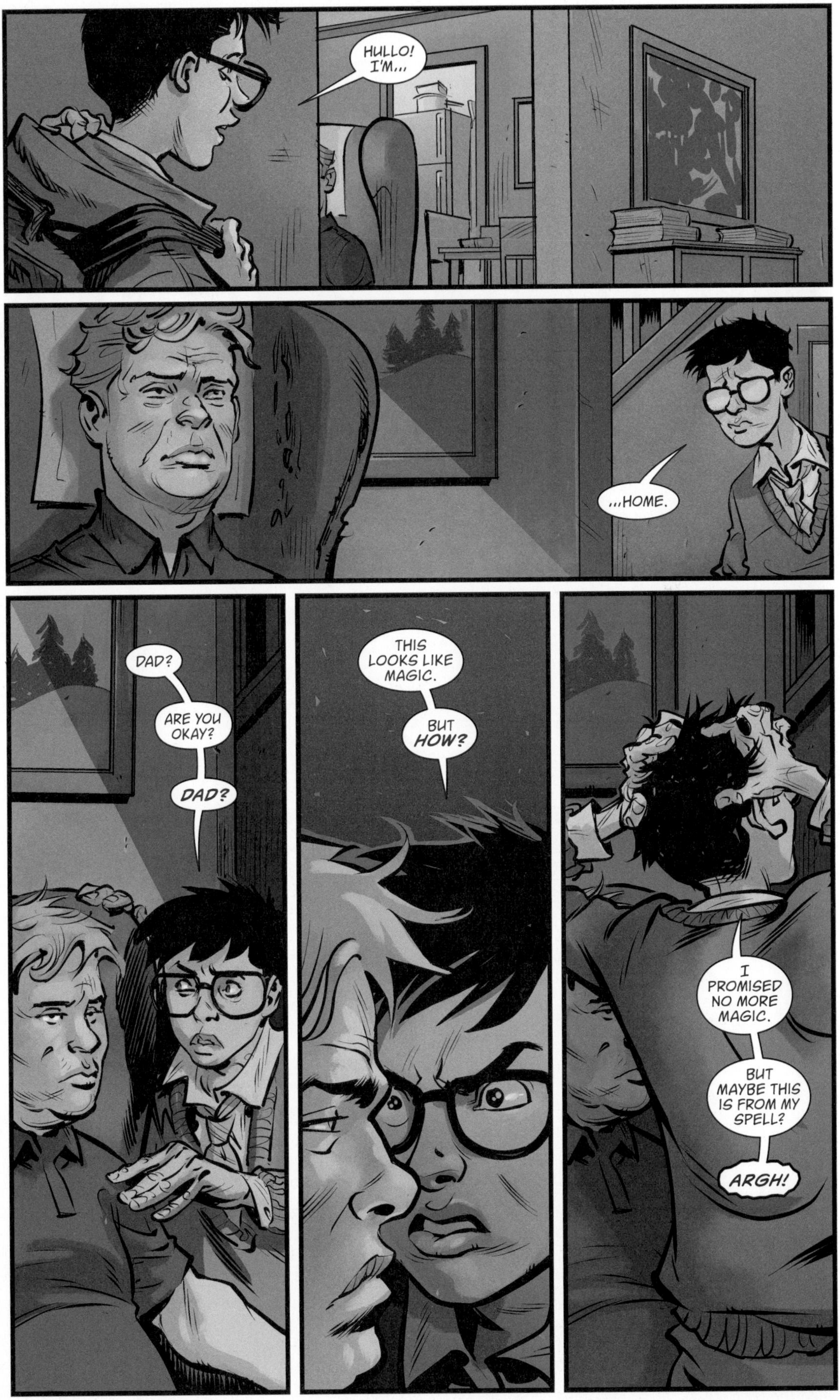
HULLO! I'M...
...HOME.
DAD?
ARE YOU OKAY?
DAD?
THIS LOOKS LIKE MAGIC.
BUT *HOW?*
I PROMISED NO MORE MAGIC.
BUT MAYBE THIS IS FROM MY SPELL?
ARGH!

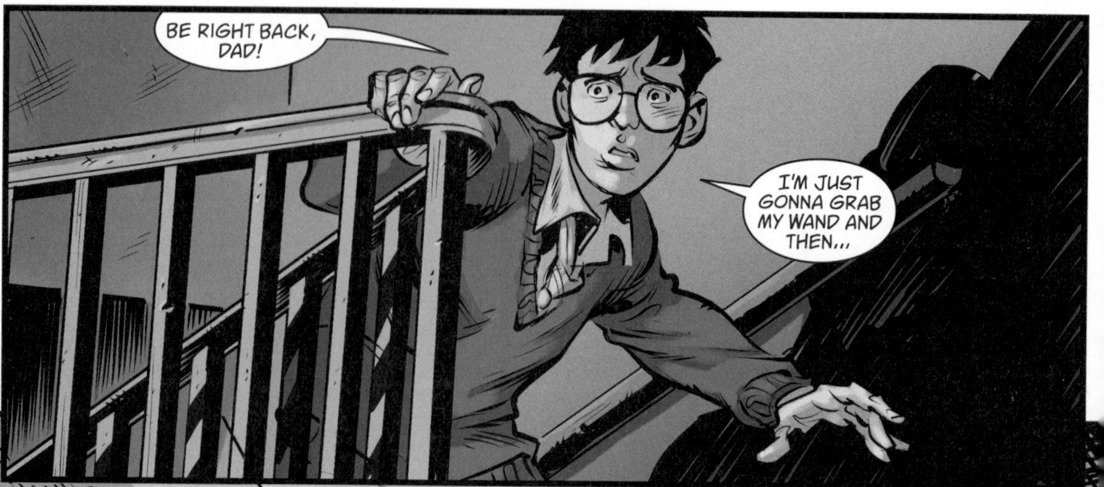
BE RIGHT BACK, DAD!
I'M JUST GONNA GRAB MY WAND AND THEN...

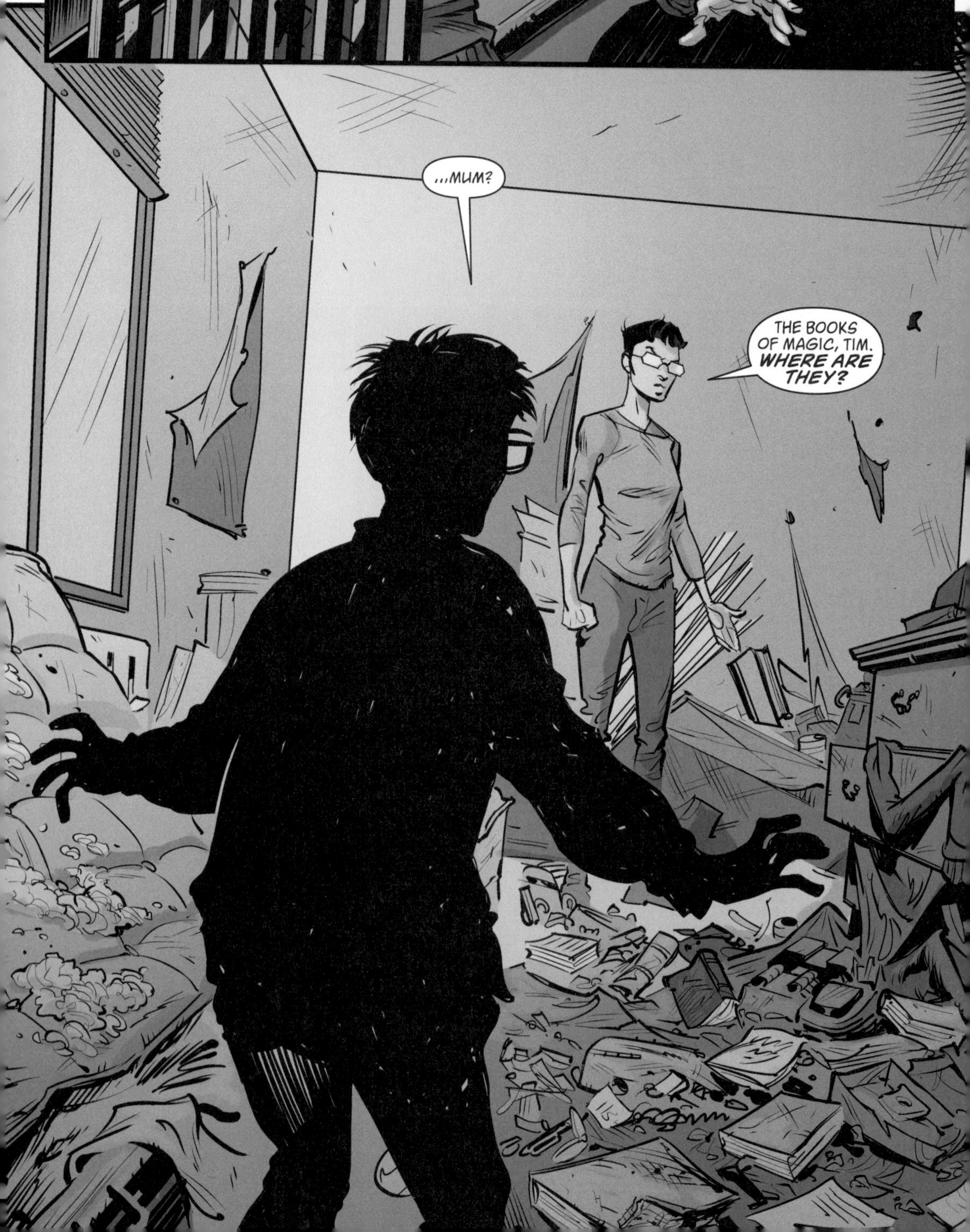
...MUM?
THE BOOKS OF MAGIC, TIM. *WHERE ARE THEY?*

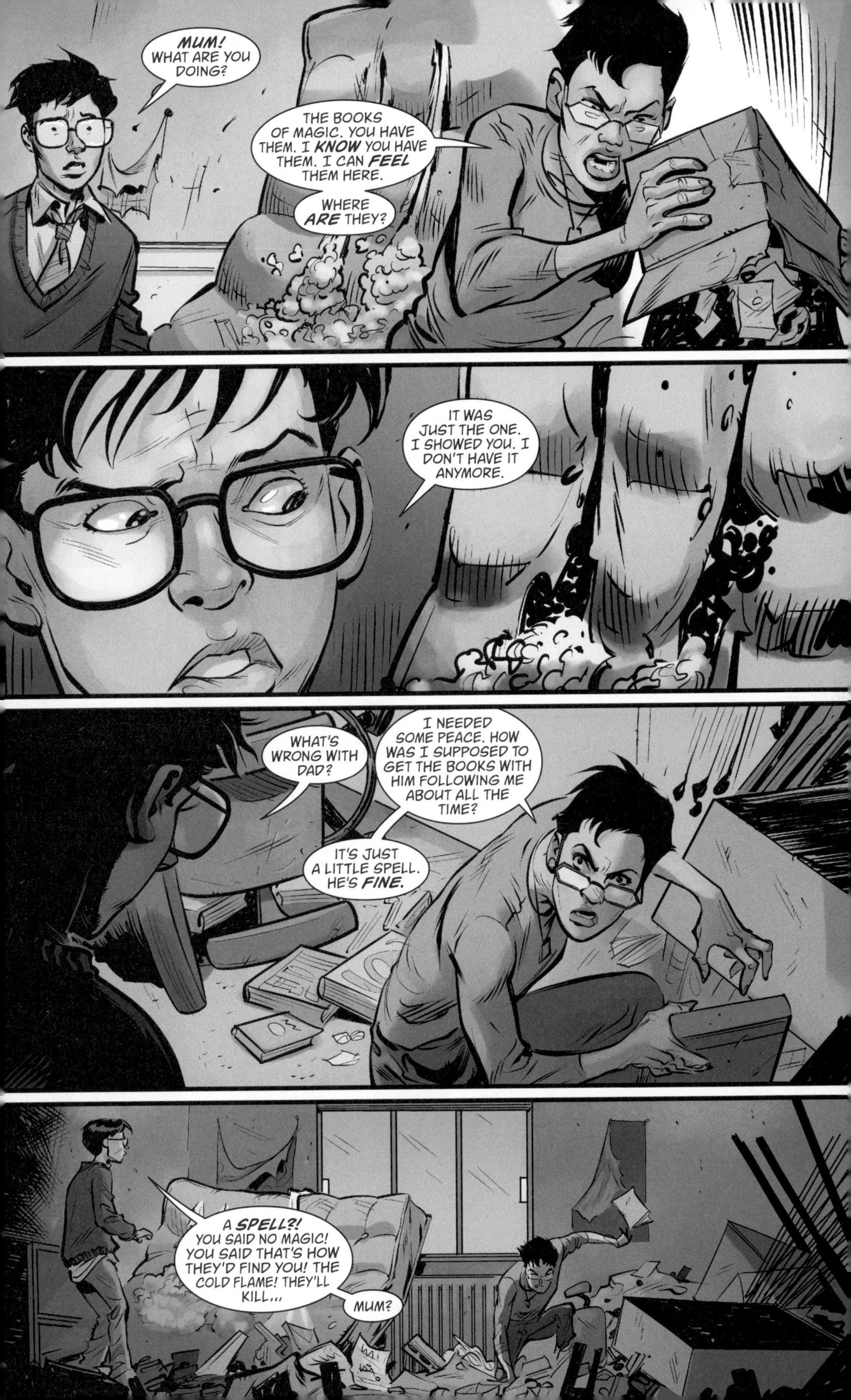
MUM! WHAT ARE YOU DOING?
THE BOOKS OF MAGIC. YOU HAVE THEM. I KNOW YOU HAVE THEM. I CAN FEEL THEM HERE.
WHERE ARE THEY?
IT WAS JUST THE ONE. I SHOWED YOU. I DON'T HAVE IT ANYMORE.
WHAT'S WRONG WITH DAD?
I NEEDED SOME PEACE. HOW WAS I SUPPOSED TO GET THE BOOKS WITH HIM FOLLOWING ME ABOUT ALL THE TIME?
IT'S JUST A LITTLE SPELL. HE'S FINE.
A SPELL?! YOU SAID NO MAGIC! YOU SAID THAT'S HOW THEY'D FIND YOU! THE COLD FLAME! THEY'LL KILL...
MUM?

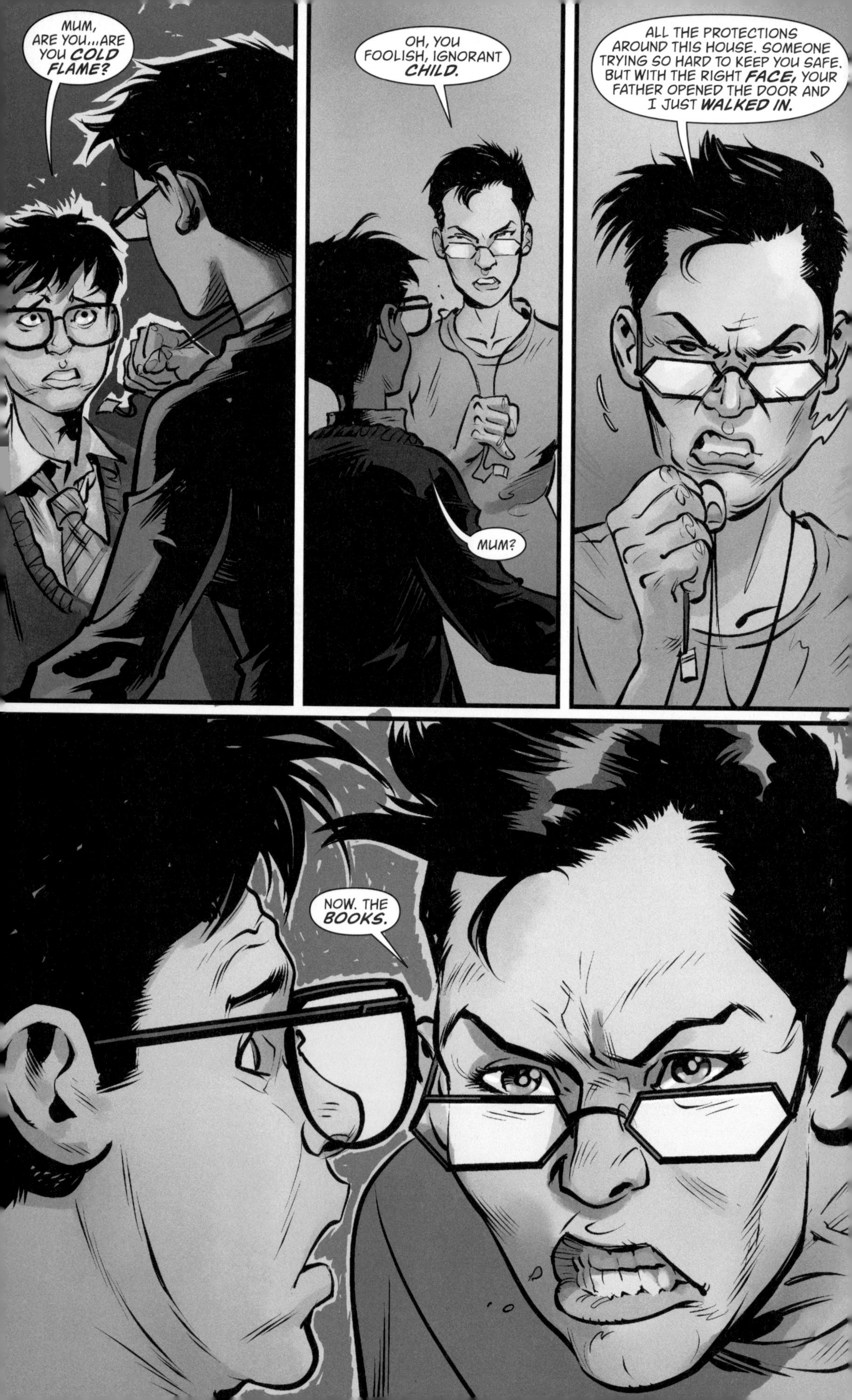
MUM, ARE YOU...ARE YOU ***COLD FLAME?***
OH, YOU FOOLISH, IGNORANT ***CHILD.***
MUM?
ALL THE PROTECTIONS AROUND THIS HOUSE. SOMEONE TRYING SO HARD TO KEEP YOU SAFE. BUT WITH THE RIGHT ***FACE,*** YOUR FATHER OPENED THE DOOR AND I JUST ***WALKED IN.***
NOW. THE ***BOOKS.***

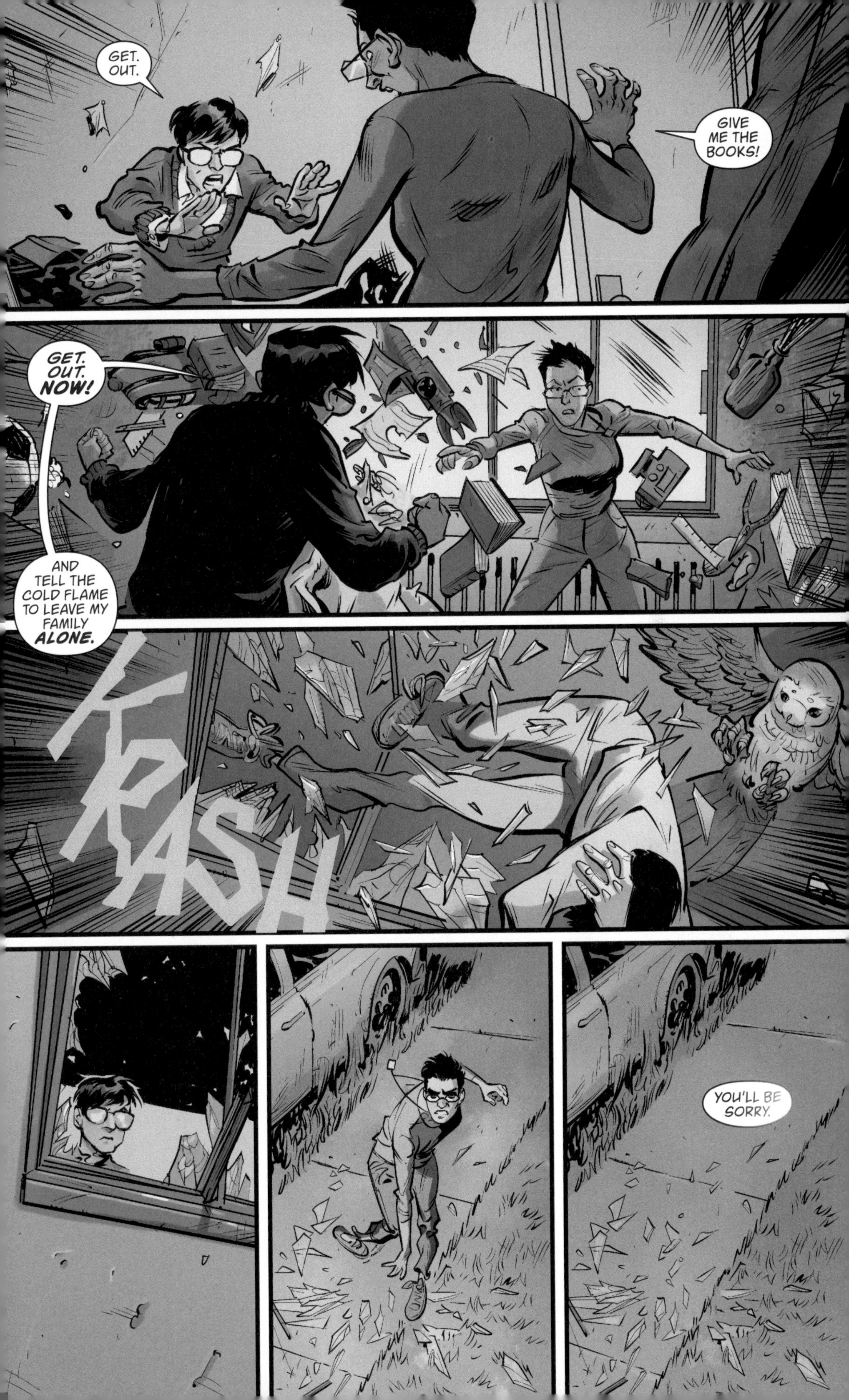
GET.
OUT.
GIVE
ME THE
BOOKS!
GET.
OUT.
NOW!
AND
TELL THE
COLD FLAME
TO LEAVE MY
FAMILY
ALONE.
KRASH
YOU'LL BE
SORRY.

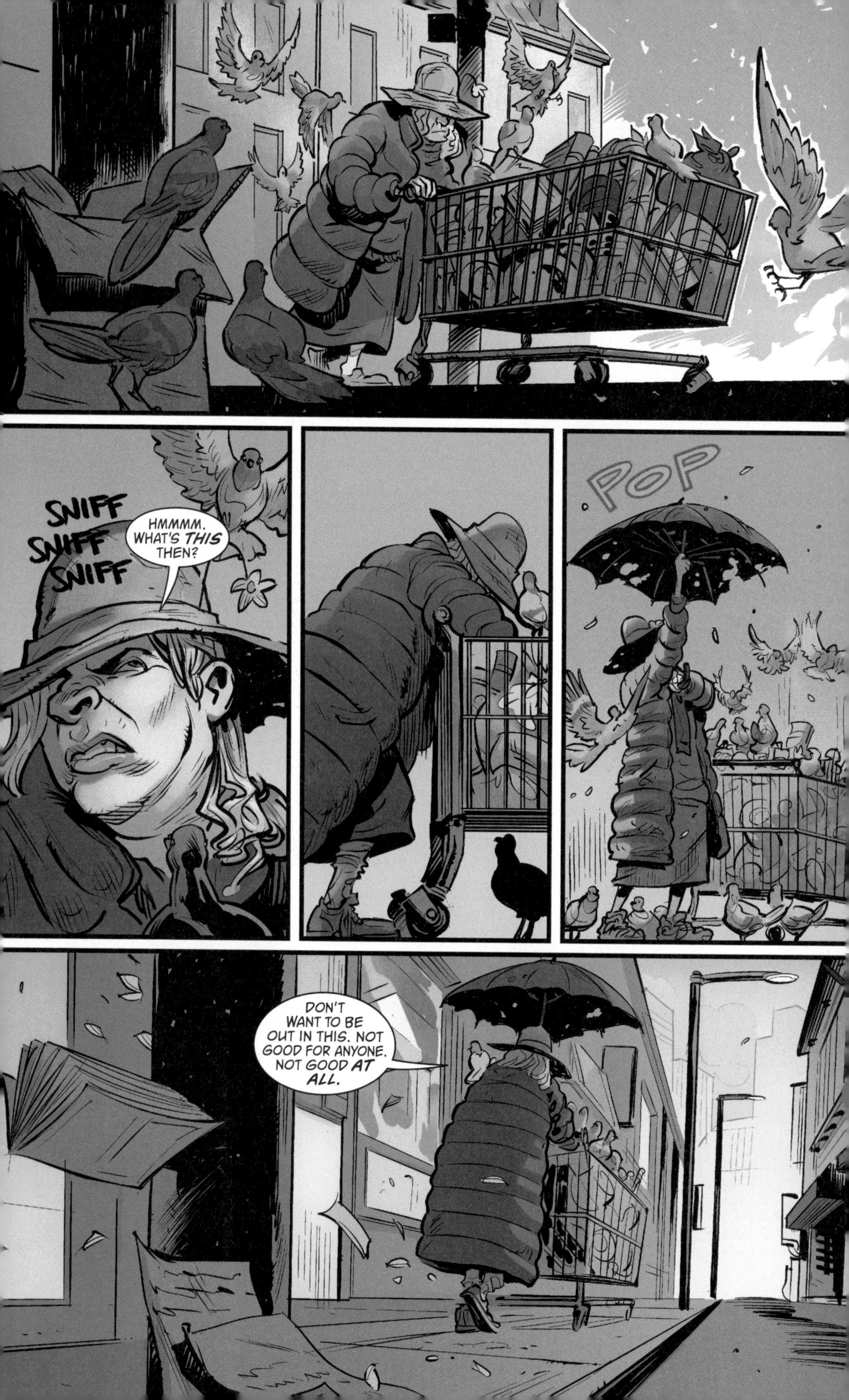
SNIFF
SNIFF
SNIFF
HMMMM. WHAT'S *THIS* THEN?
POP
DON'T WANT TO BE OUT IN THIS. NOT GOOD FOR ANYONE. NOT GOOD *AT ALL.*

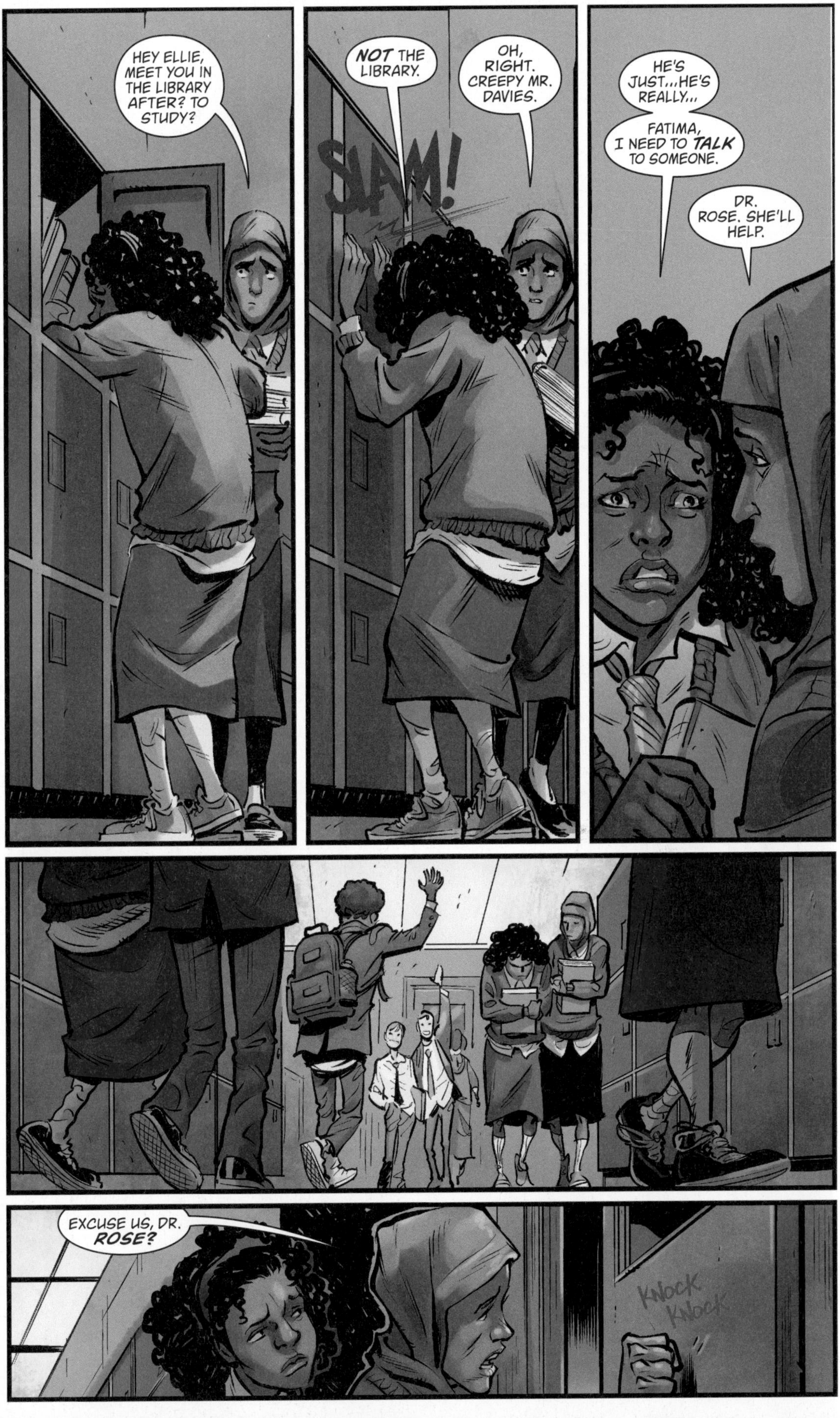
HEY ELLIE, MEET YOU IN THE LIBRARY AFTER? TO STUDY?
NOT THE LIBRARY.
OH, RIGHT. CREEPY MR. DAVIES.
SLAM!
HE'S JUST...HE'S REALLY...
FATIMA, I NEED TO TALK TO SOMEONE.
DR. ROSE. SHE'LL HELP.
EXCUSE US, DR. ROSE?
KNOCK KNOCK

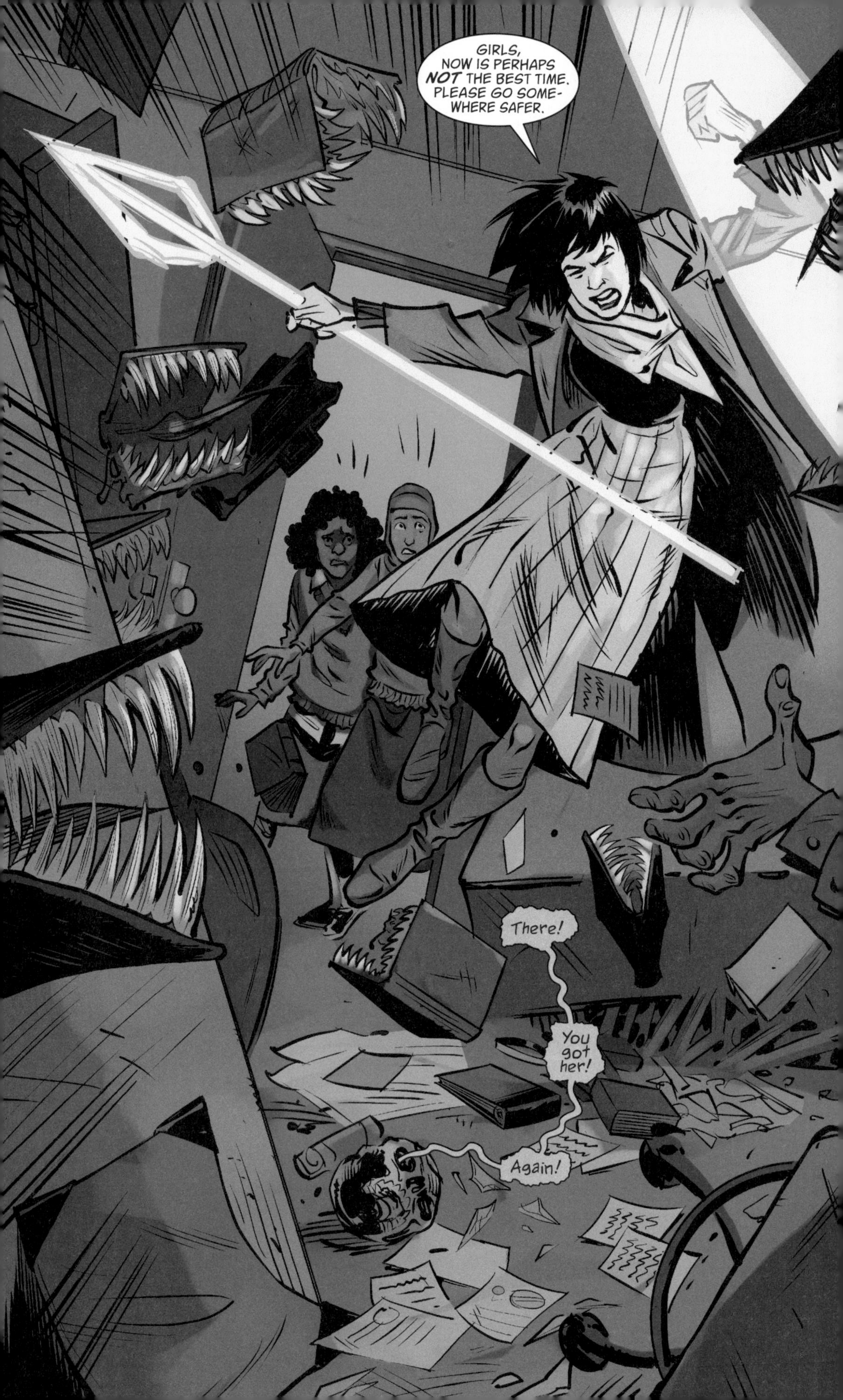
GIRLS, NOW IS PERHAPS NOT THE BEST TIME. PLEASE GO SOMEWHERE SAFER.
There!
You got her!
Again!

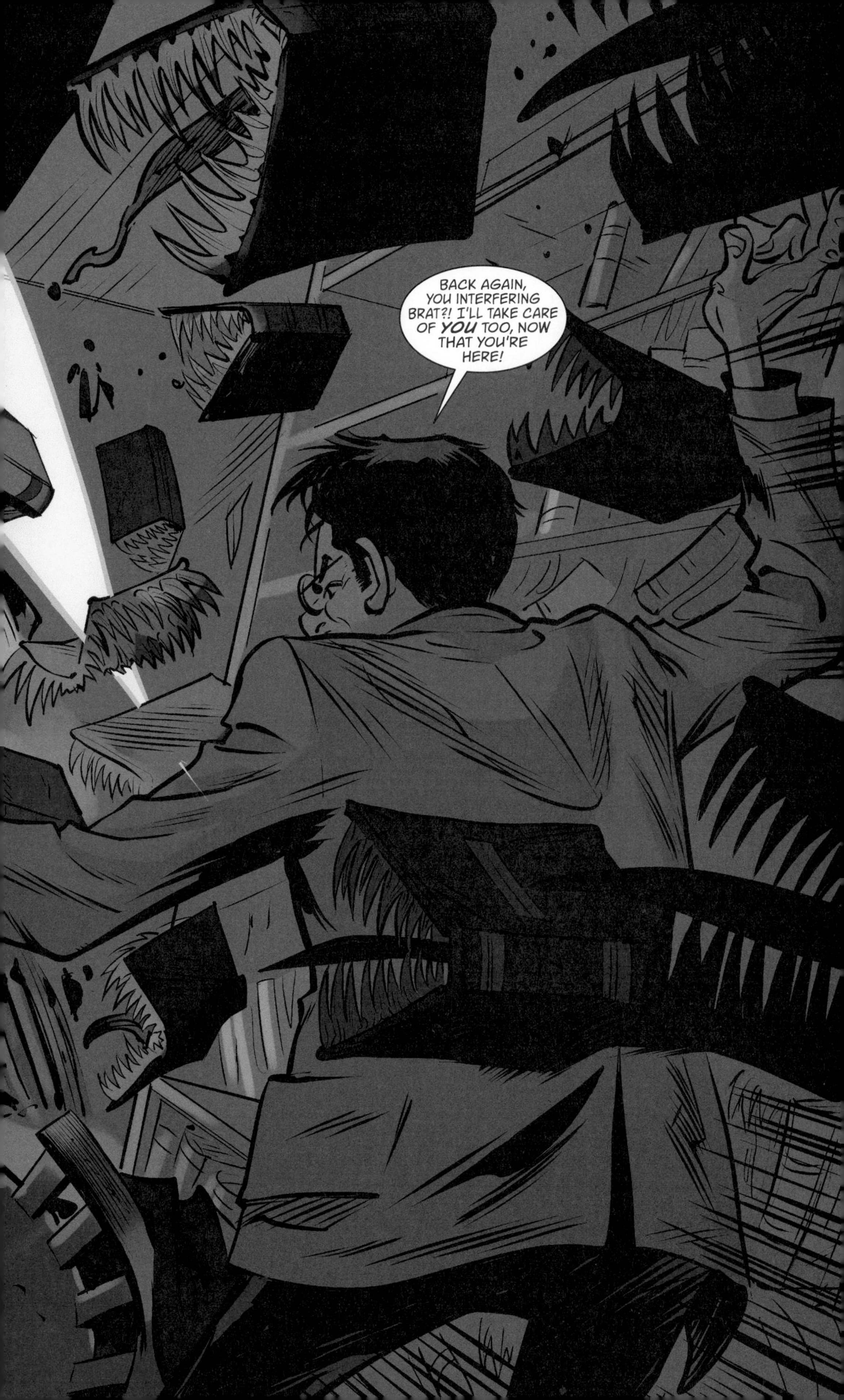
BACK AGAIN, YOU INTERFERING BRAT?! I'LL TAKE CARE OF YOU TOO, NOW THAT YOU'RE HERE!

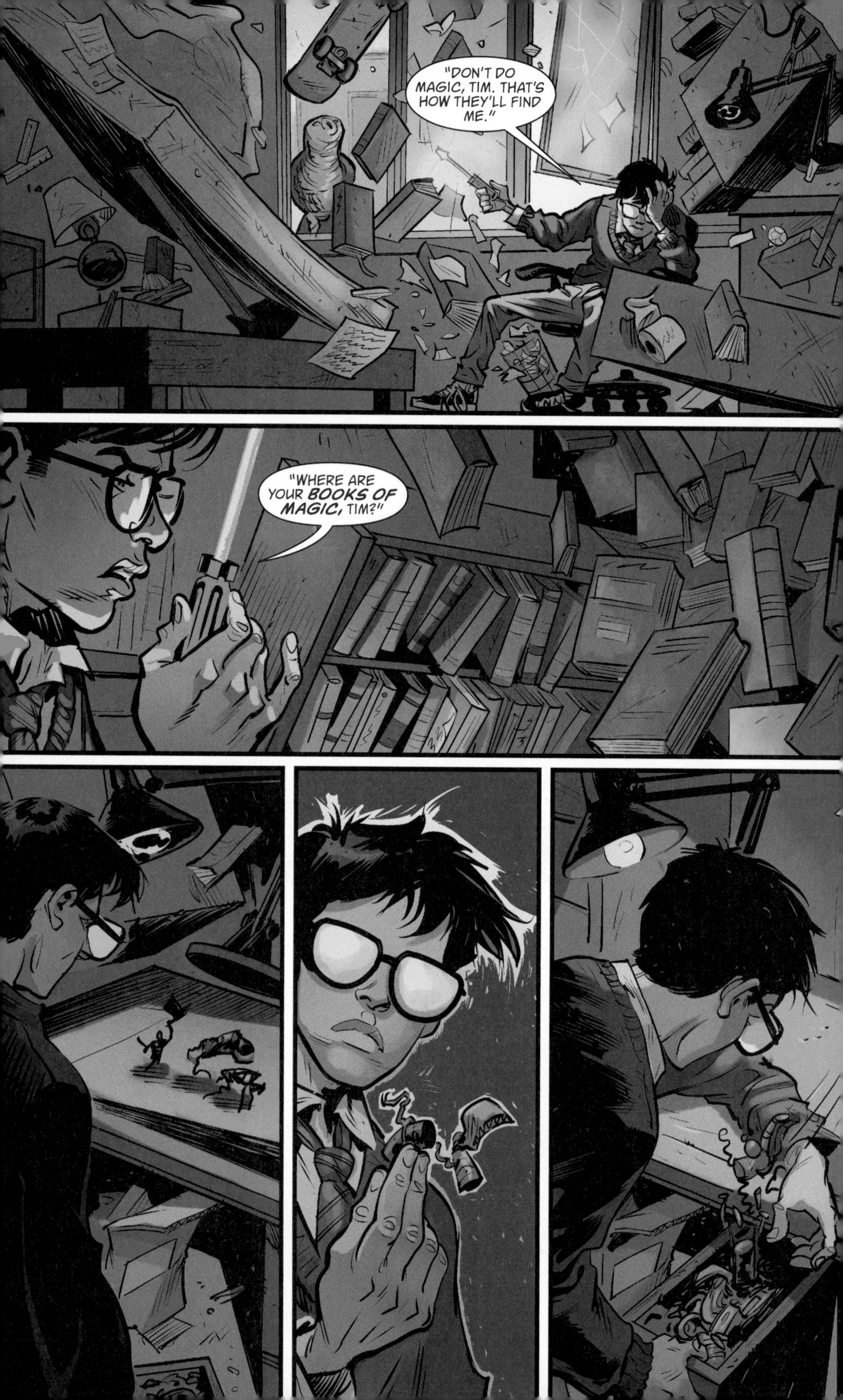
"DON'T DO MAGIC, TIM. THAT'S HOW THEY'LL FIND ME."
"WHERE ARE YOUR BOOKS OF MAGIC, TIM?"

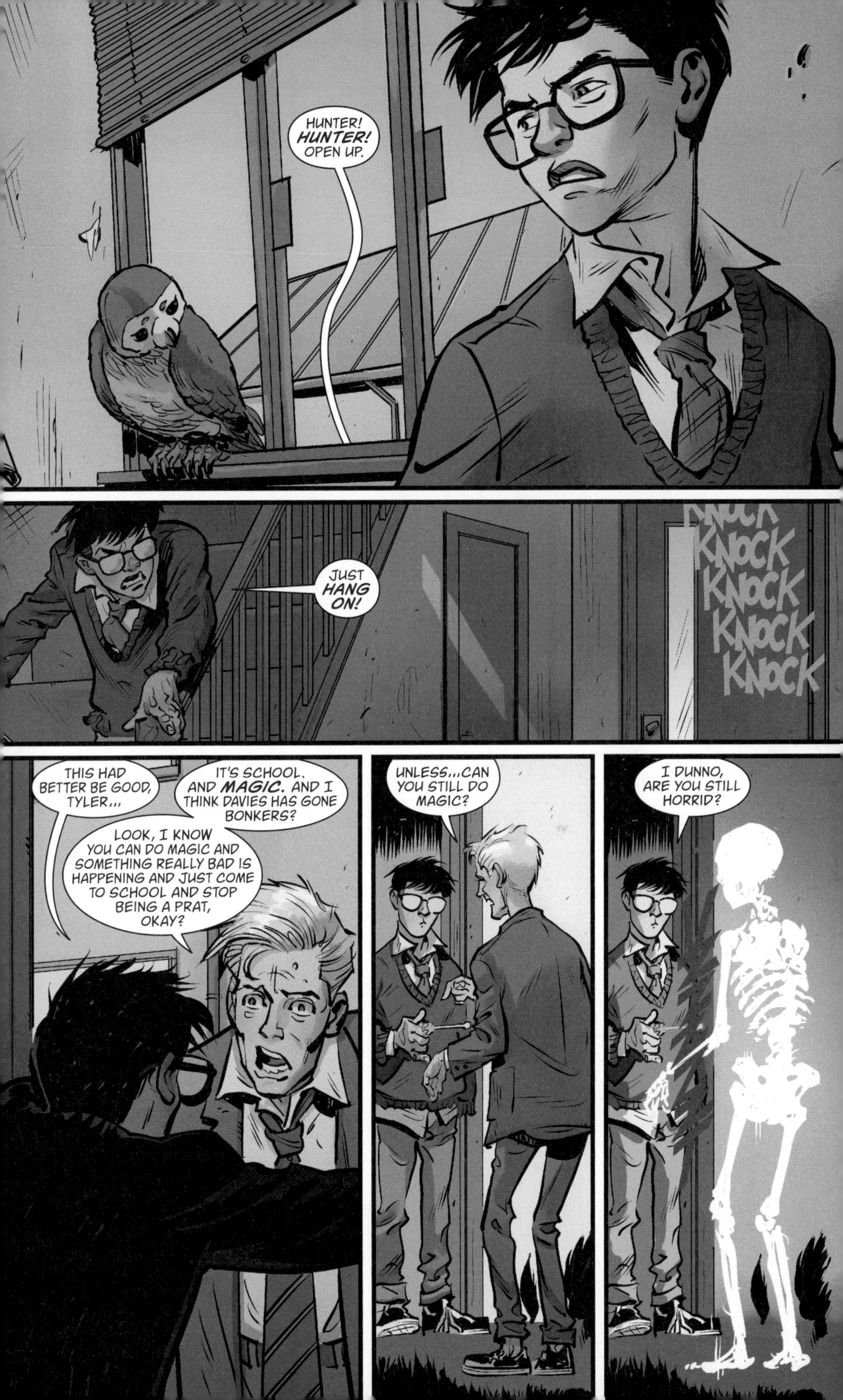
HUNTER! HUNTER! OPEN UP.
JUST HANG ON!
KNOCK KNOCK KNOCK KNOCK KNOCK
THIS HAD BETTER BE GOOD, TYLER...
IT'S SCHOOL. AND MAGIC. AND I THINK DAVIES HAS GONE BONKERS?
LOOK, I KNOW YOU CAN DO MAGIC AND SOMETHING REALLY BAD IS HAPPENING AND JUST COME TO SCHOOL AND STOP BEING A PRAT, OKAY?
UNLESS...CAN YOU STILL DO MAGIC?
I DUNNO, ARE YOU STILL HORRID?

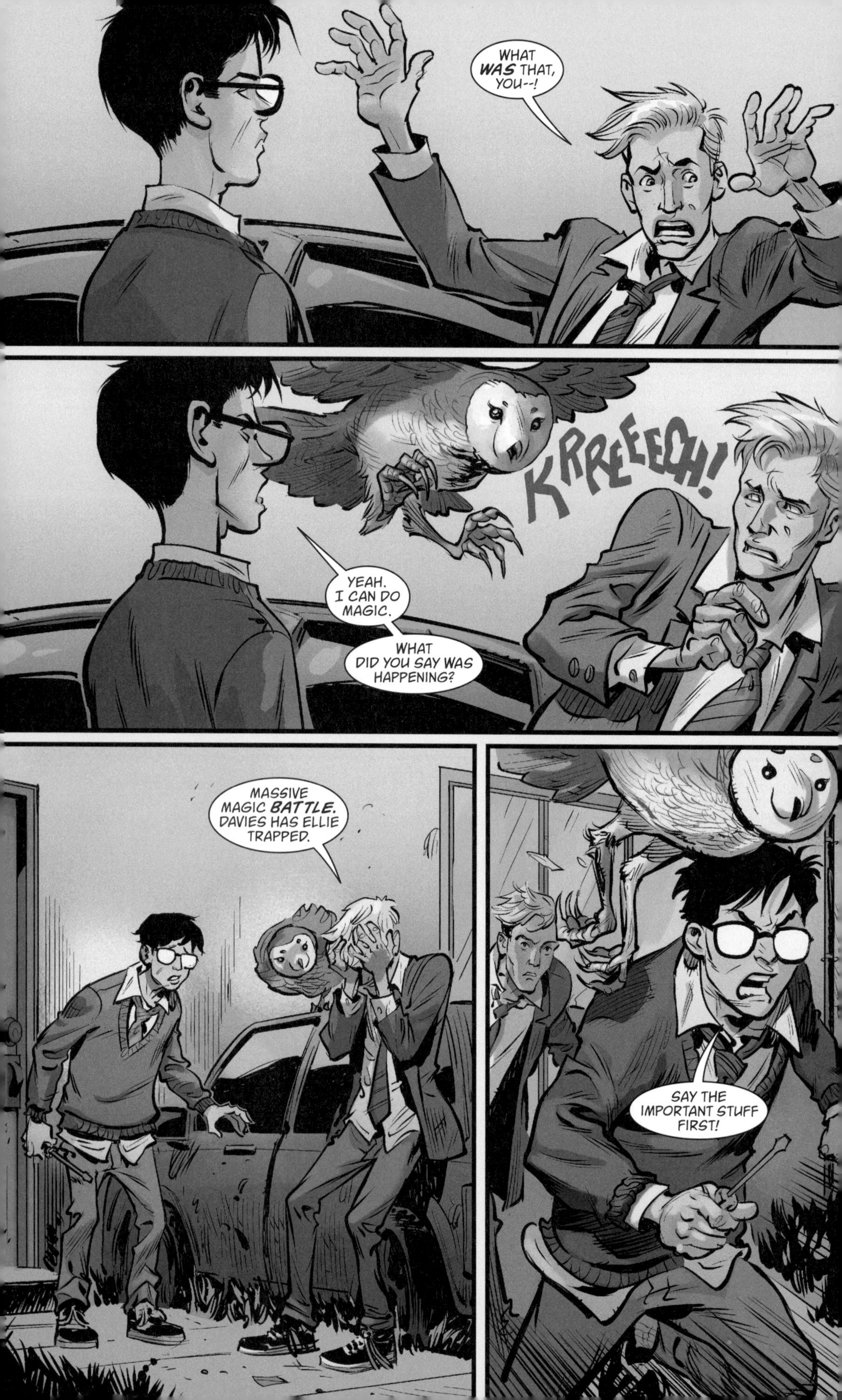
WHAT WAS THAT, YOU--!
KRREEEECH!
YEAH. I CAN DO MAGIC.
WHAT DID YOU SAY WAS HAPPENING?
MASSIVE MAGIC BATTLE. DAVIES HAS ELLIE TRAPPED.
SAY THE IMPORTANT STUFF FIRST!

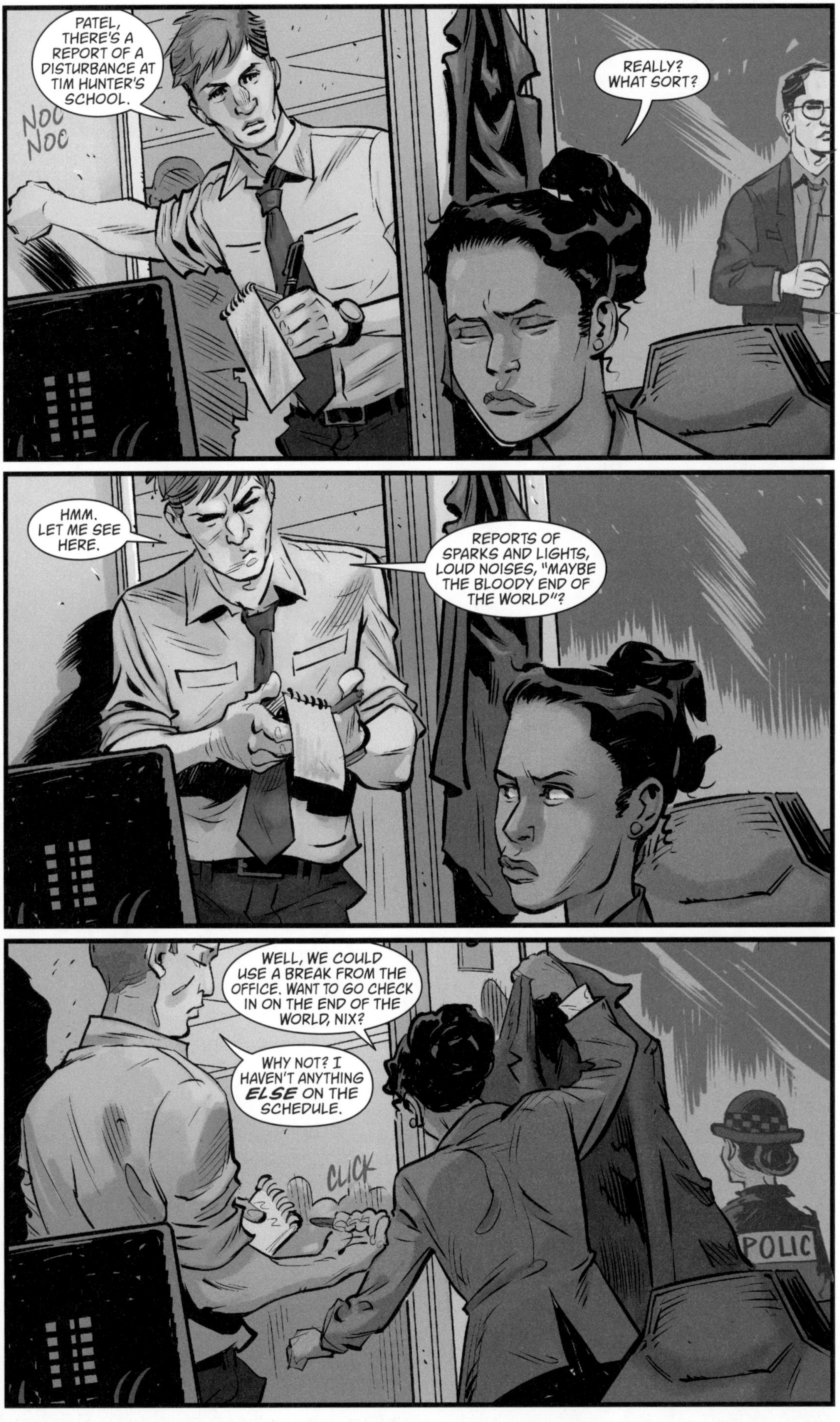

PATEL, THERE'S A REPORT OF A DISTURBANCE AT TIM HUNTER'S SCHOOL.
NOC NOC
REALLY? WHAT SORT?
HMM. LET ME SEE HERE.
REPORTS OF SPARKS AND LIGHTS, LOUD NOISES, "MAYBE THE BLOODY END OF THE WORLD"?
WELL, WE COULD USE A BREAK FROM THE OFFICE. WANT TO GO CHECK IN ON THE END OF THE WORLD, NIX?
WHY NOT? I HAVEN'T ANYTHING *ELSE* ON THE SCHEDULE.
CLICK
POLIC

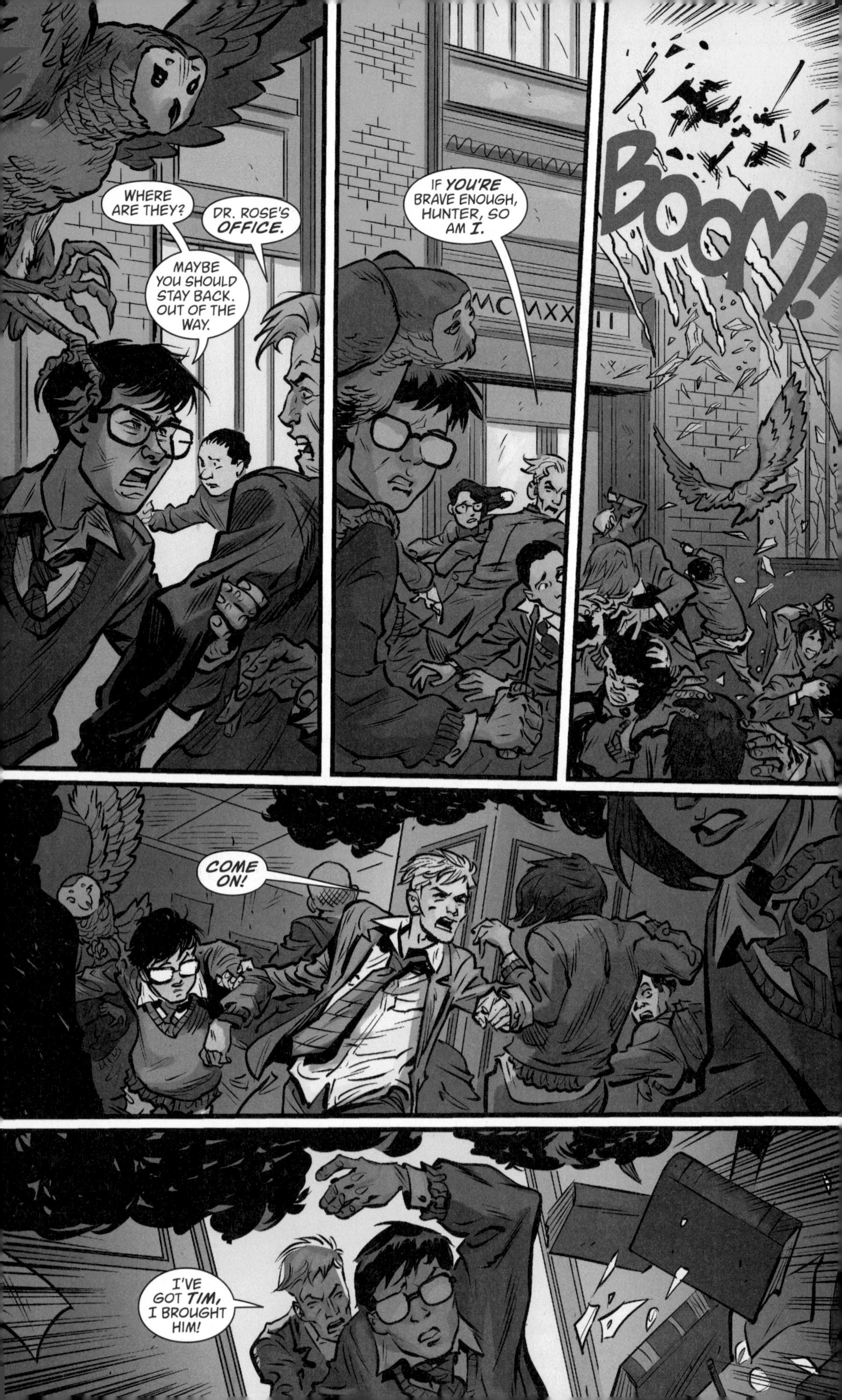

WHERE ARE THEY?
DR. ROSE'S *OFFICE.*
MAYBE YOU SHOULD STAY BACK. OUT OF THE WAY.
IF *YOU'RE* BRAVE ENOUGH, HUNTER, SO AM *I.*
MCMXXIII
BOOM!
COME ON!
I'VE GOT *TIM,* I BROUGHT HIM!

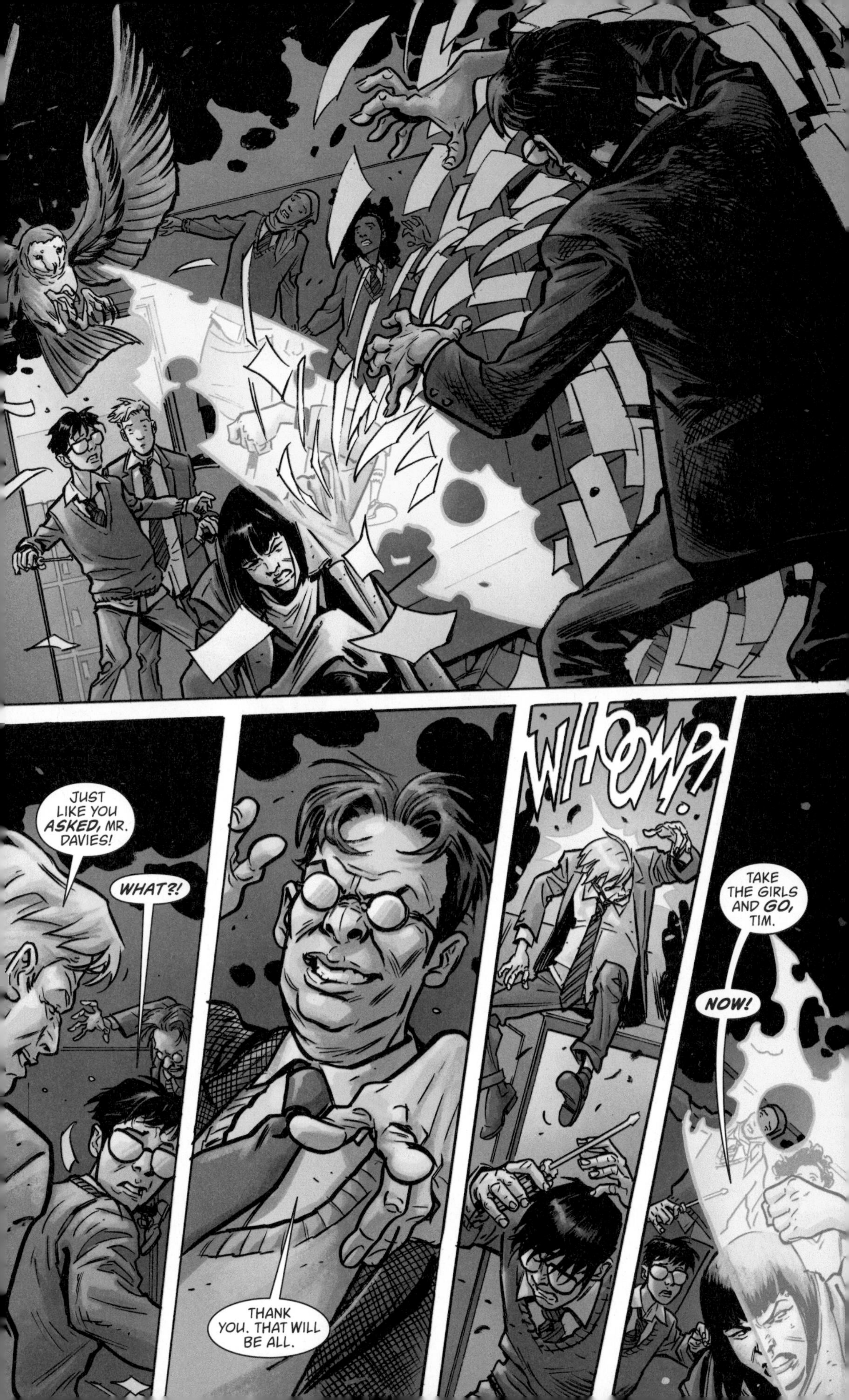
JUST LIKE YOU ASKED, MR. DAVIES!
WHAT?!
THANK YOU. THAT WILL BE ALL.
WHOMP!
TAKE THE GIRLS AND GO, TIM.
NOW!

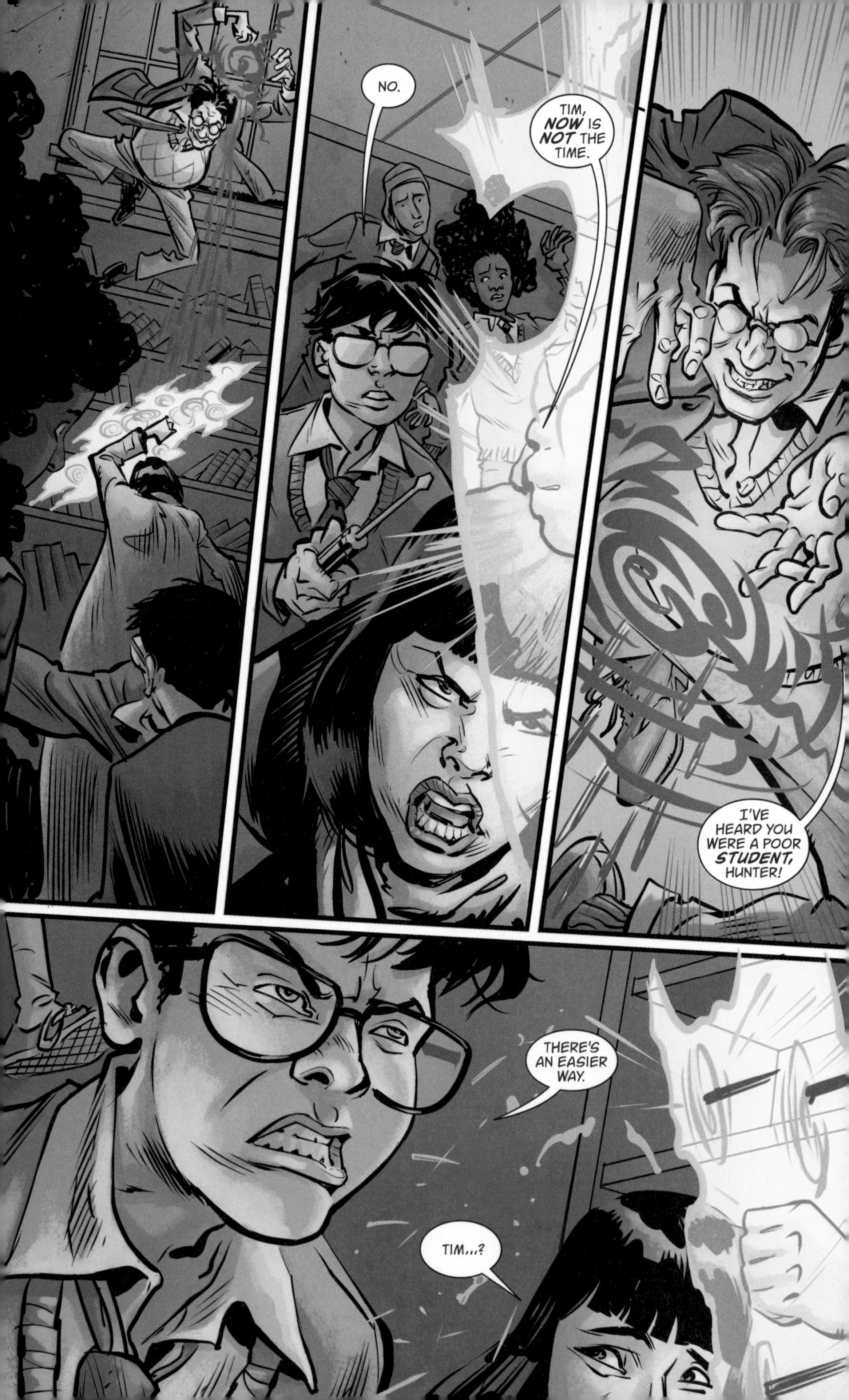
NO.
TIM, NOW IS NOT THE TIME.
I'VE HEARD YOU WERE A POOR STUDENT, HUNTER!
THERE'S AN EASIER WAY.
TIM...?

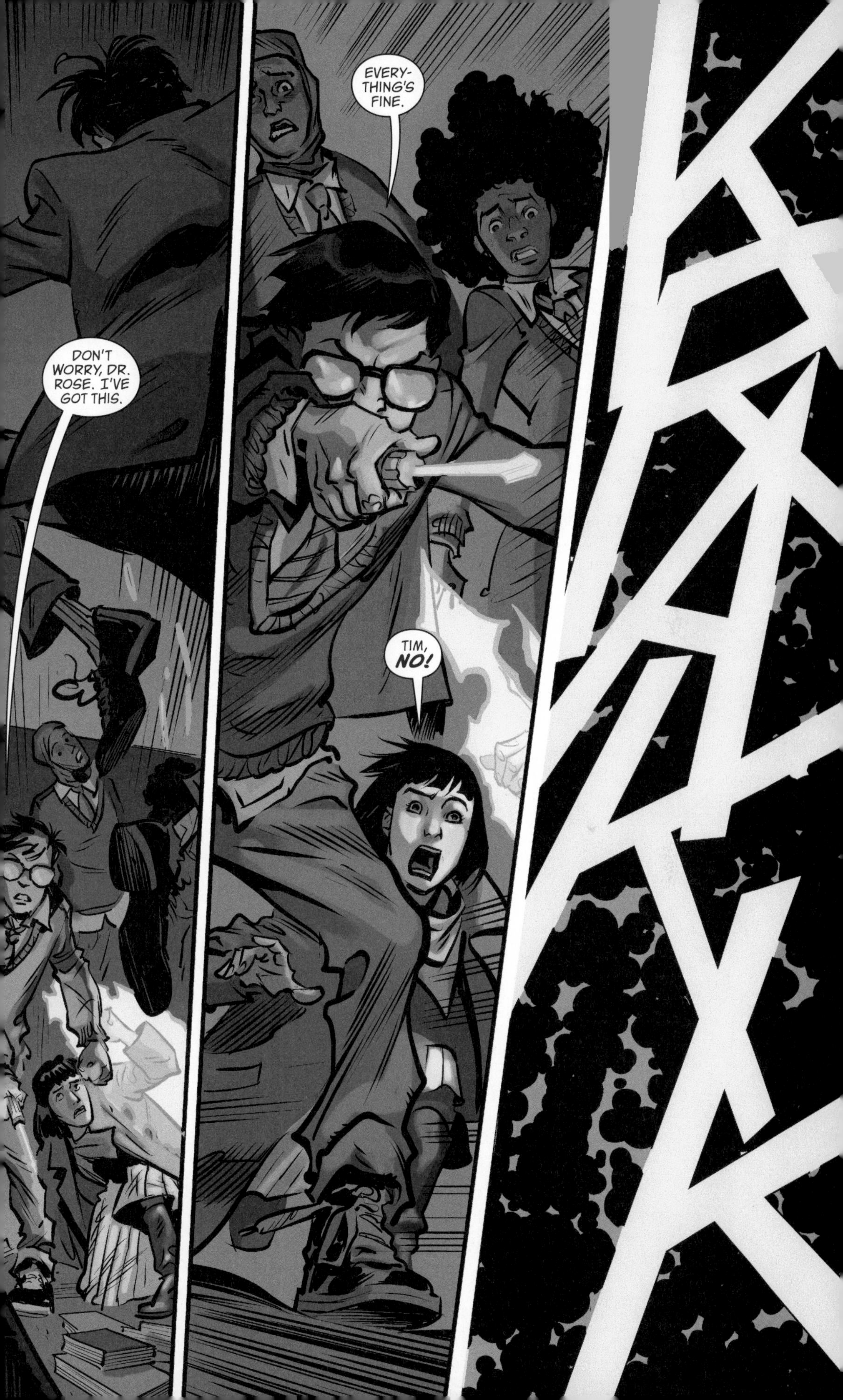

DON'T WORRY, DR. ROSE. I'VE GOT THIS.
EVERY-THING'S FINE.
TIM, **NO!**

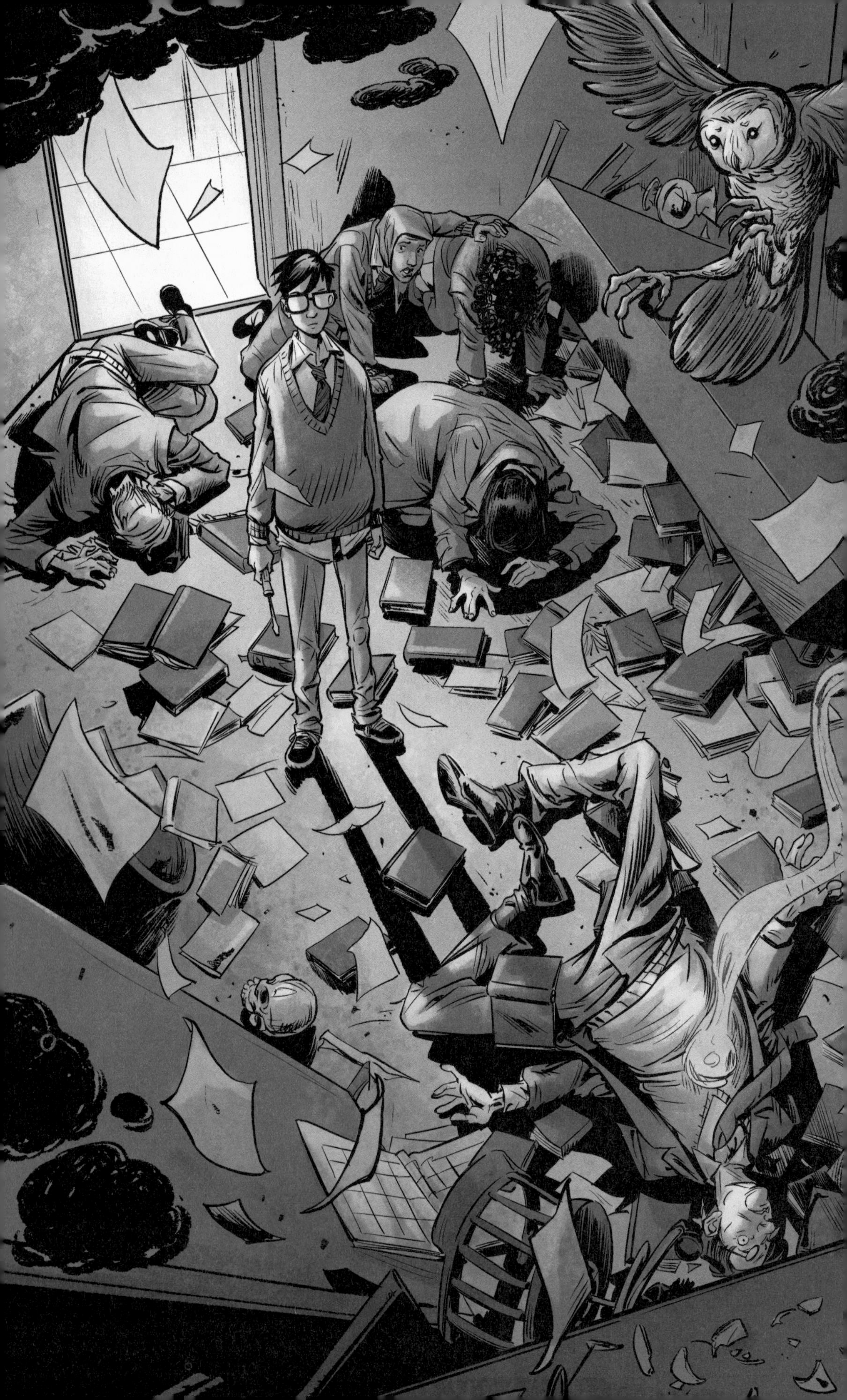

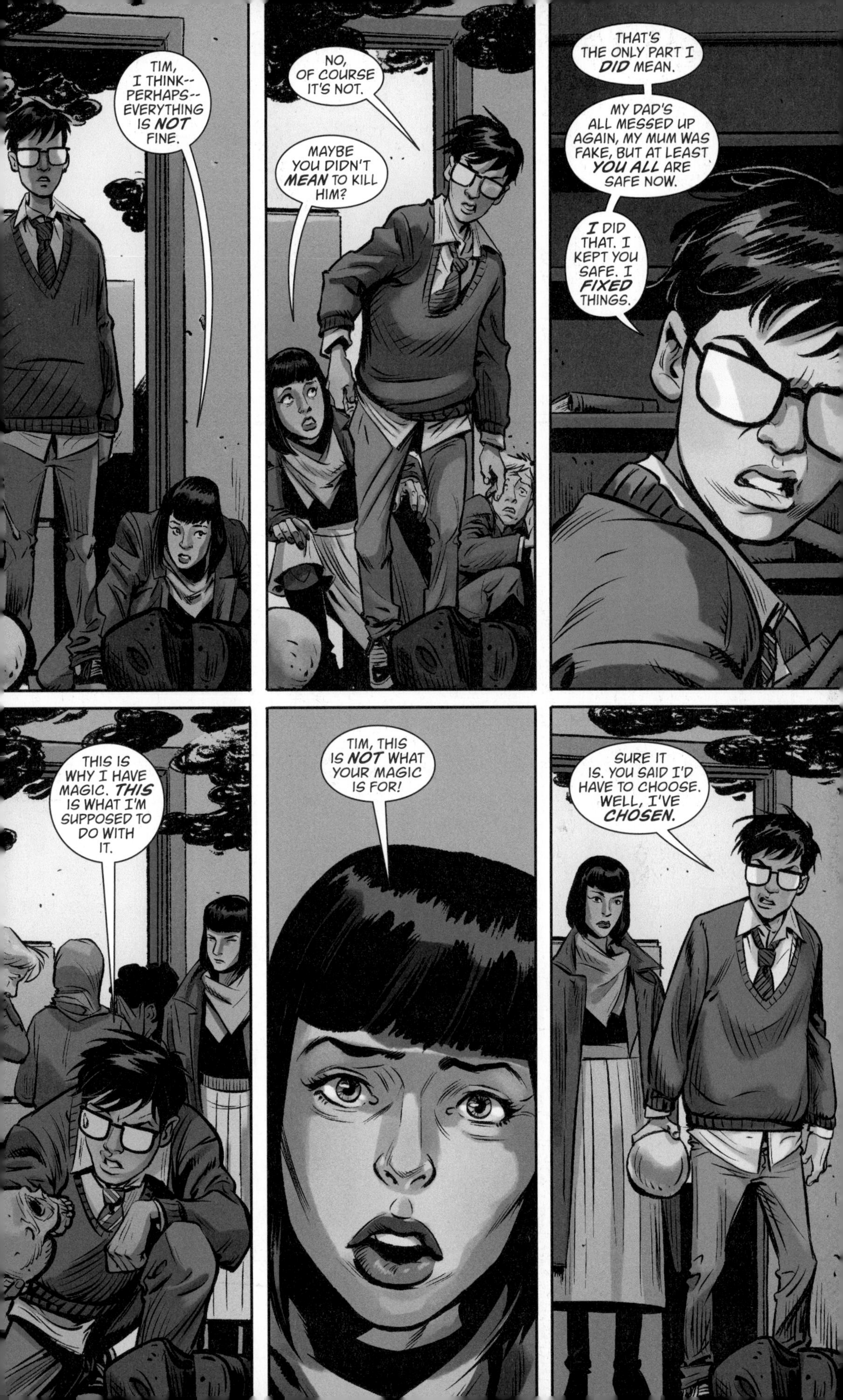
TIM, I THINK-- PERHAPS-- EVERYTHING IS NOT FINE.
NO, OF COURSE IT'S NOT.
MAYBE YOU DIDN'T MEAN TO KILL HIM?
THAT'S THE ONLY PART I DID MEAN.
MY DAD'S ALL MESSED UP AGAIN, MY MUM WAS FAKE, BUT AT LEAST YOU ALL ARE SAFE NOW.
I DID THAT. I KEPT YOU SAFE. I FIXED THINGS.
THIS IS WHY I HAVE MAGIC. THIS IS WHAT I'M SUPPOSED TO DO WITH IT.
TIM, THIS IS NOT WHAT YOUR MAGIC IS FOR!
SURE IT IS. YOU SAID I'D HAVE TO CHOOSE. WELL, I'VE CHOSEN.

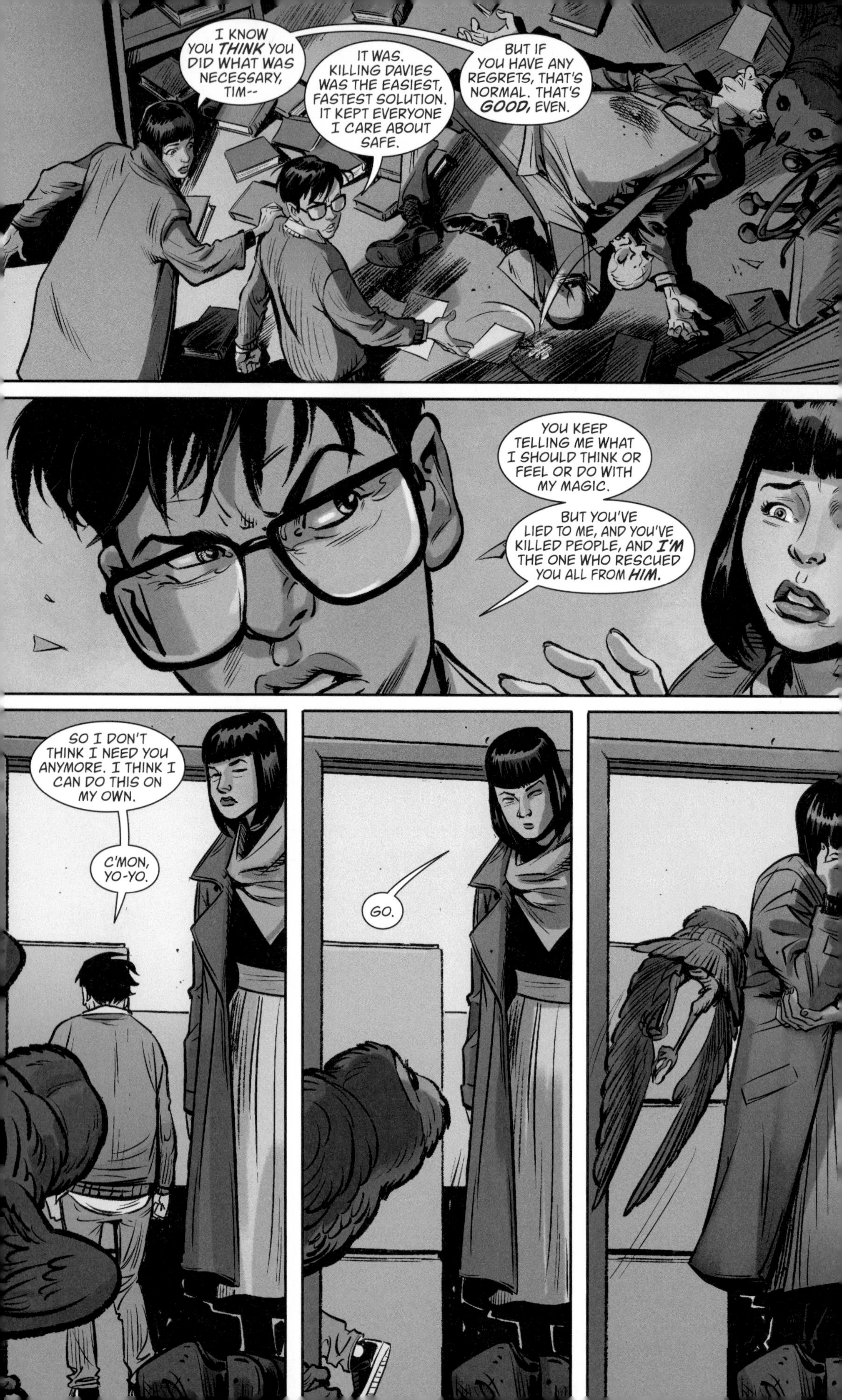
I KNOW YOU THINK YOU DID WHAT WAS NECESSARY, TIM--
IT WAS. KILLING DAVIES WAS THE EASIEST, FASTEST SOLUTION. IT KEPT EVERYONE I CARE ABOUT SAFE.
BUT IF YOU HAVE ANY REGRETS, THAT'S NORMAL. THAT'S GOOD, EVEN.
YOU KEEP TELLING ME WHAT I SHOULD THINK OR FEEL OR DO WITH MY MAGIC.
BUT YOU'VE LIED TO ME, AND YOU'VE KILLED PEOPLE, AND I'M THE ONE WHO RESCUED YOU ALL FROM HIM.
SO I DON'T THINK I NEED YOU ANYMORE. I THINK I CAN DO THIS ON MY OWN.
C'MON, YO-YO.
GO.

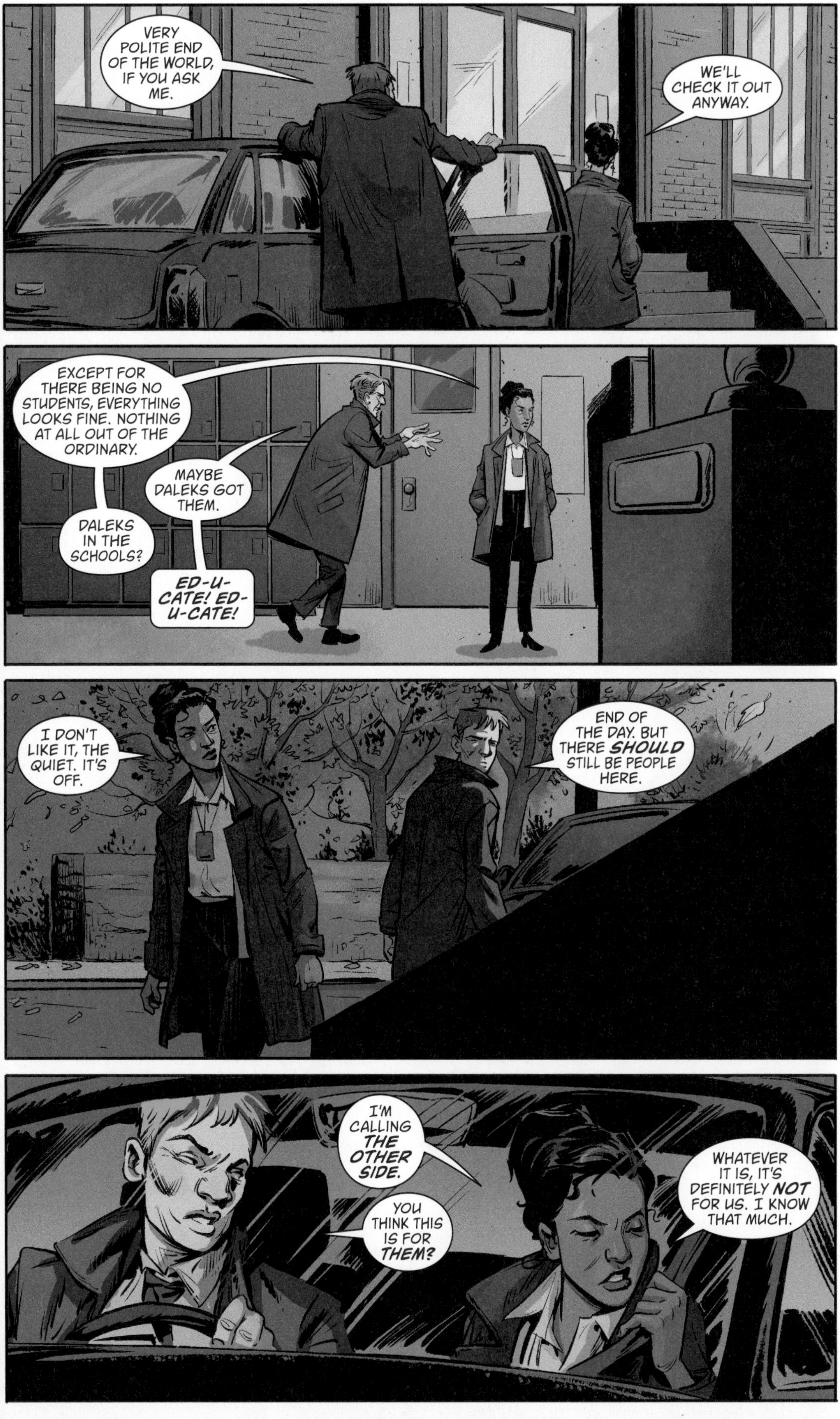
VERY POLITE END OF THE WORLD, IF YOU ASK ME.
WE'LL CHECK IT OUT ANYWAY.
EXCEPT FOR THERE BEING NO STUDENTS, EVERYTHING LOOKS FINE. NOTHING AT ALL OUT OF THE ORDINARY.
MAYBE DALEKS GOT THEM.
DALEKS IN THE SCHOOLS?
ED-U-CATE! ED-U-CATE!
I DON'T LIKE IT, THE QUIET. IT'S OFF.
END OF THE DAY. BUT THERE SHOULD STILL BE PEOPLE HERE.
I'M CALLING THE OTHER SIDE.
YOU THINK THIS IS FOR THEM?
WHATEVER IT IS, IT'S DEFINITELY NOT FOR US. I KNOW THAT MUCH.

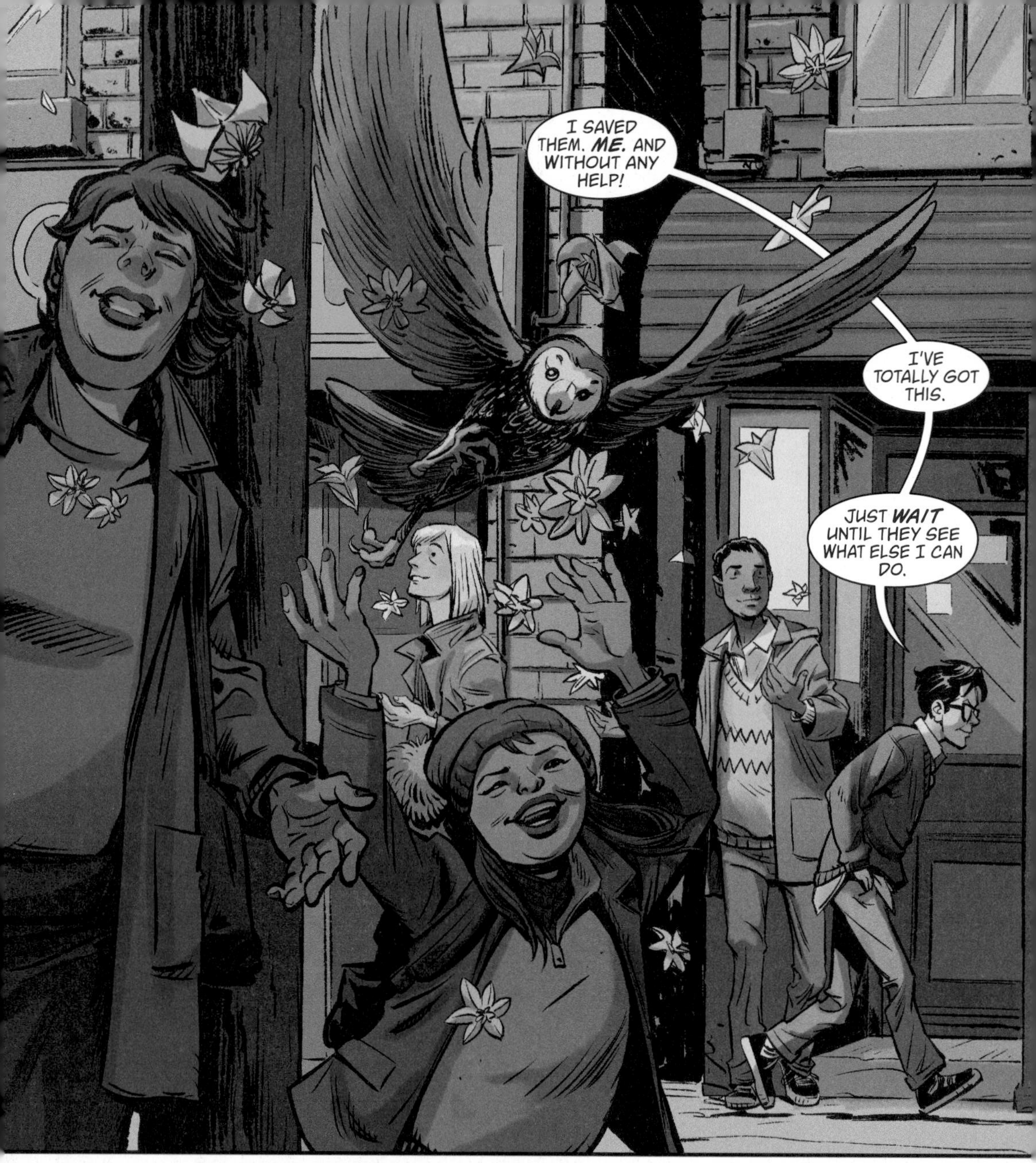
I SAVED THEM. ME. AND WITHOUT ANY HELP!
I'VE TOTALLY GOT THIS.
JUST WAIT UNTIL THEY SEE WHAT ELSE I CAN DO.

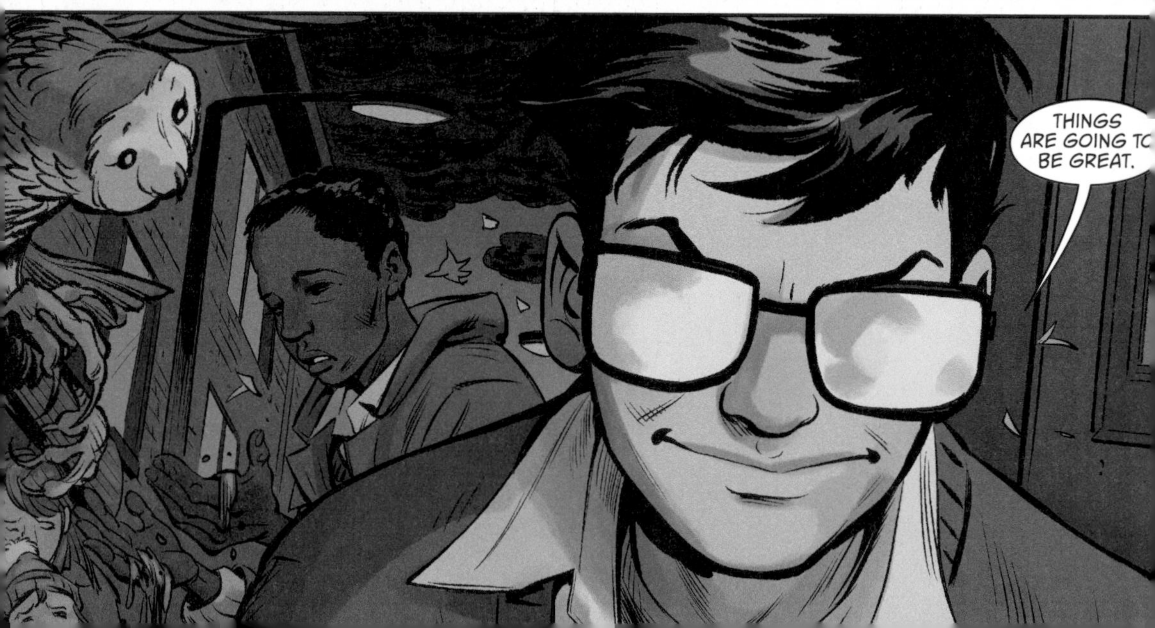
THINGS ARE GOING TO BE GREAT.

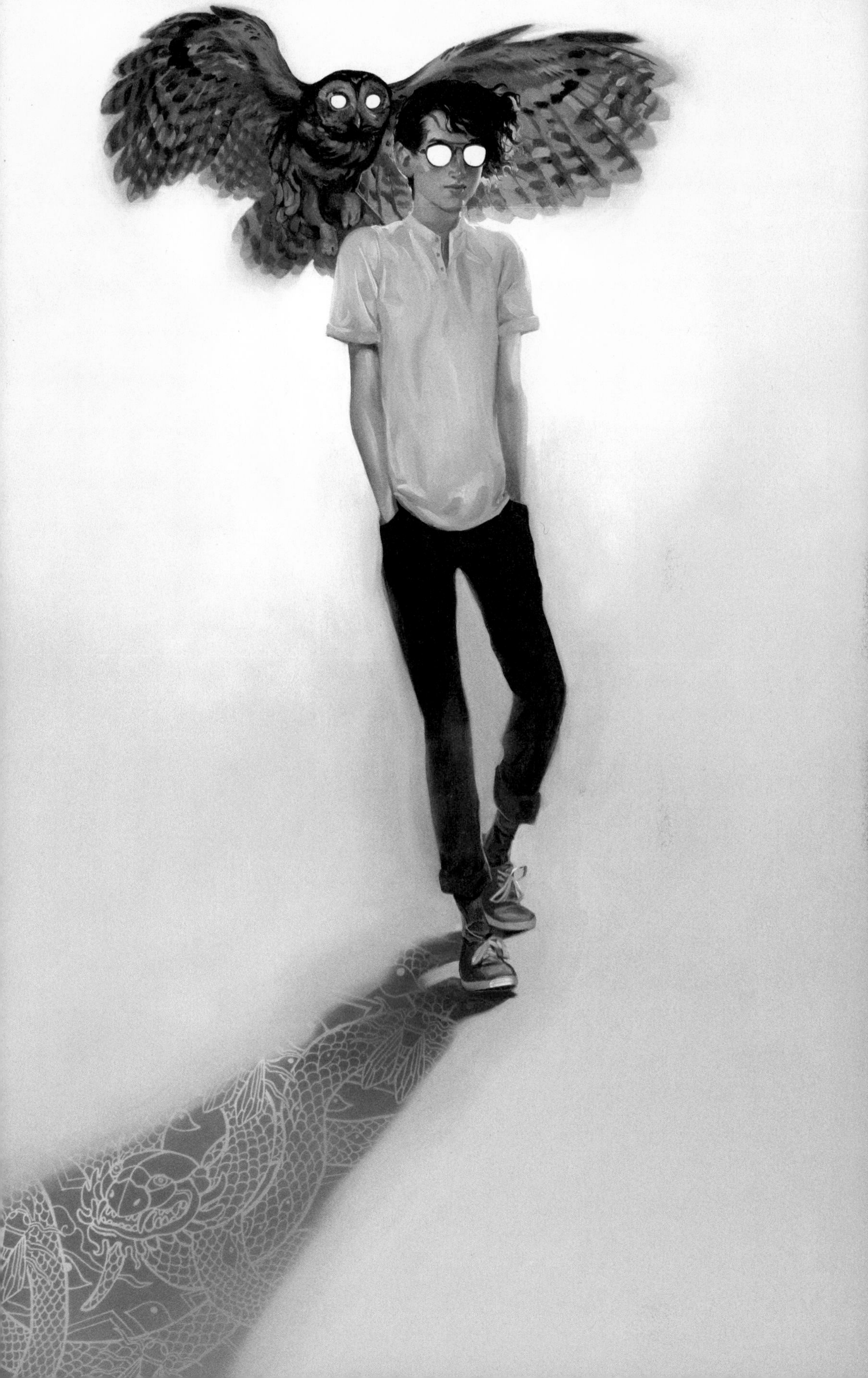

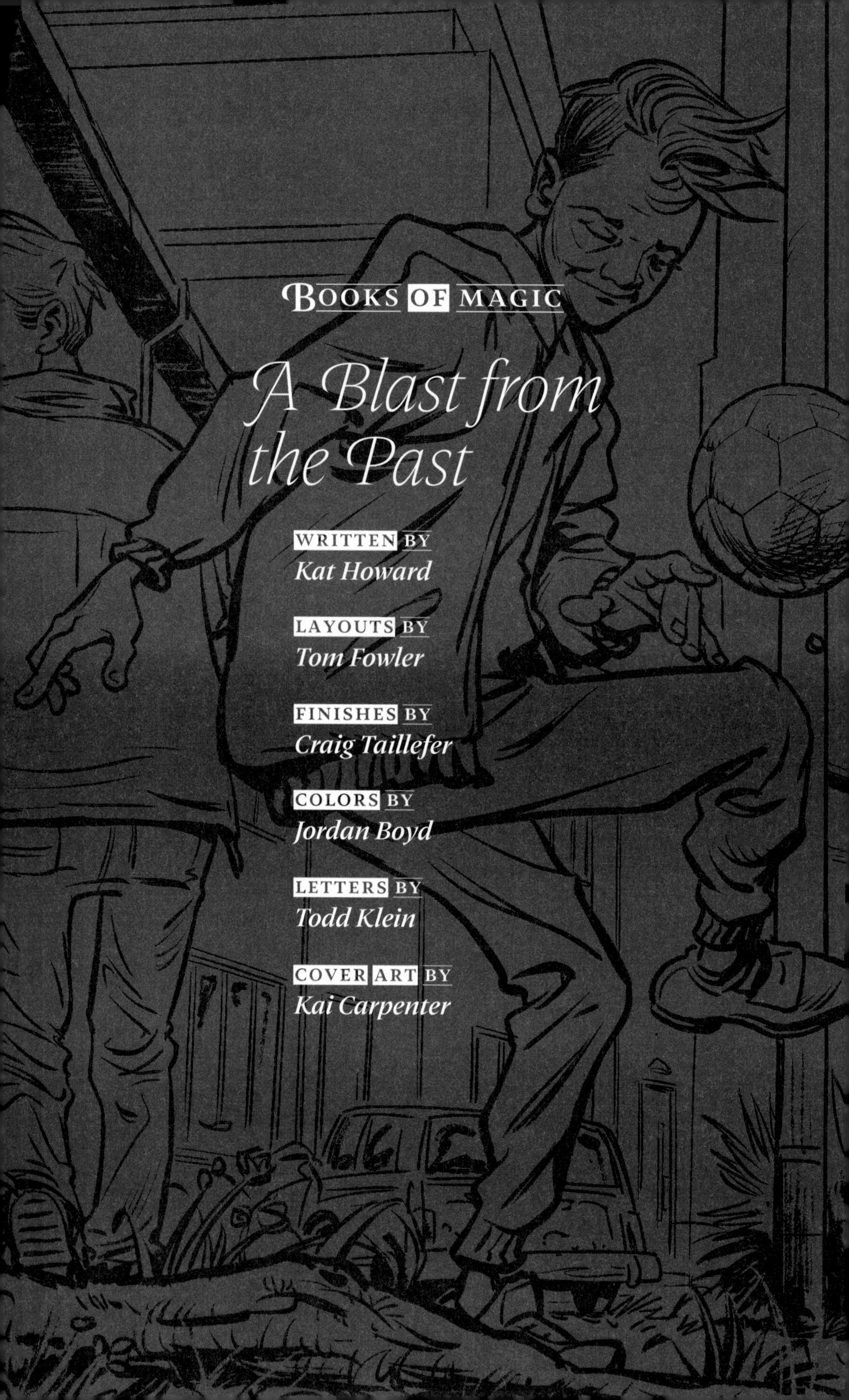

BOOKS OF MAGIC

A Blast from the Past

WRITTEN BY
Kat Howard

LAYOUTS BY
Tom Fowler

FINISHES BY
Craig Taillefer

COLORS BY
Jordan Boyd

LETTERS BY
Todd Klein

COVER ART BY
Kai Carpenter

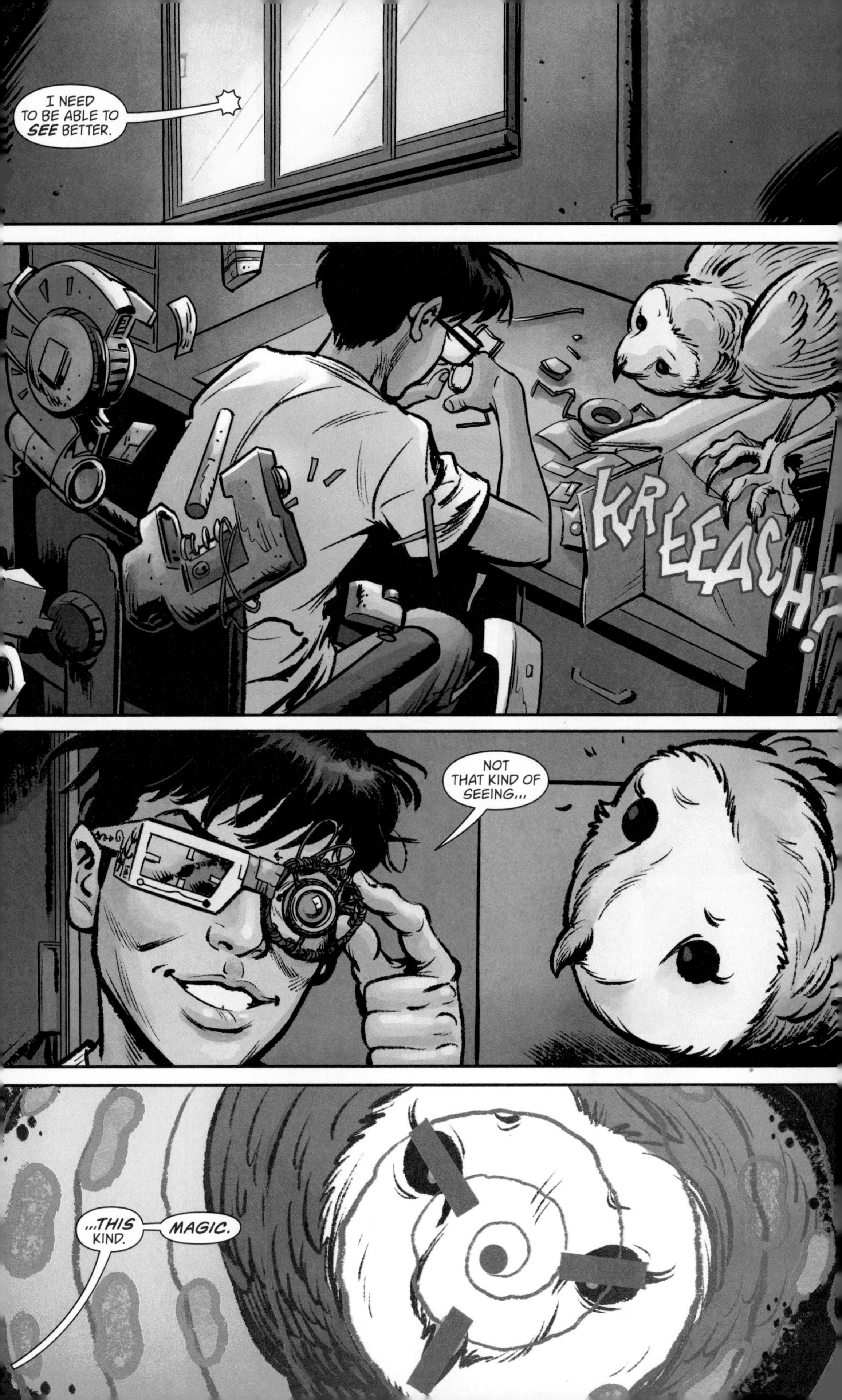
I NEED TO BE ABLE TO SEE BETTER.
KRREEACH?
NOT THAT KIND OF SEEING...
...THIS KIND.
MAGIC.

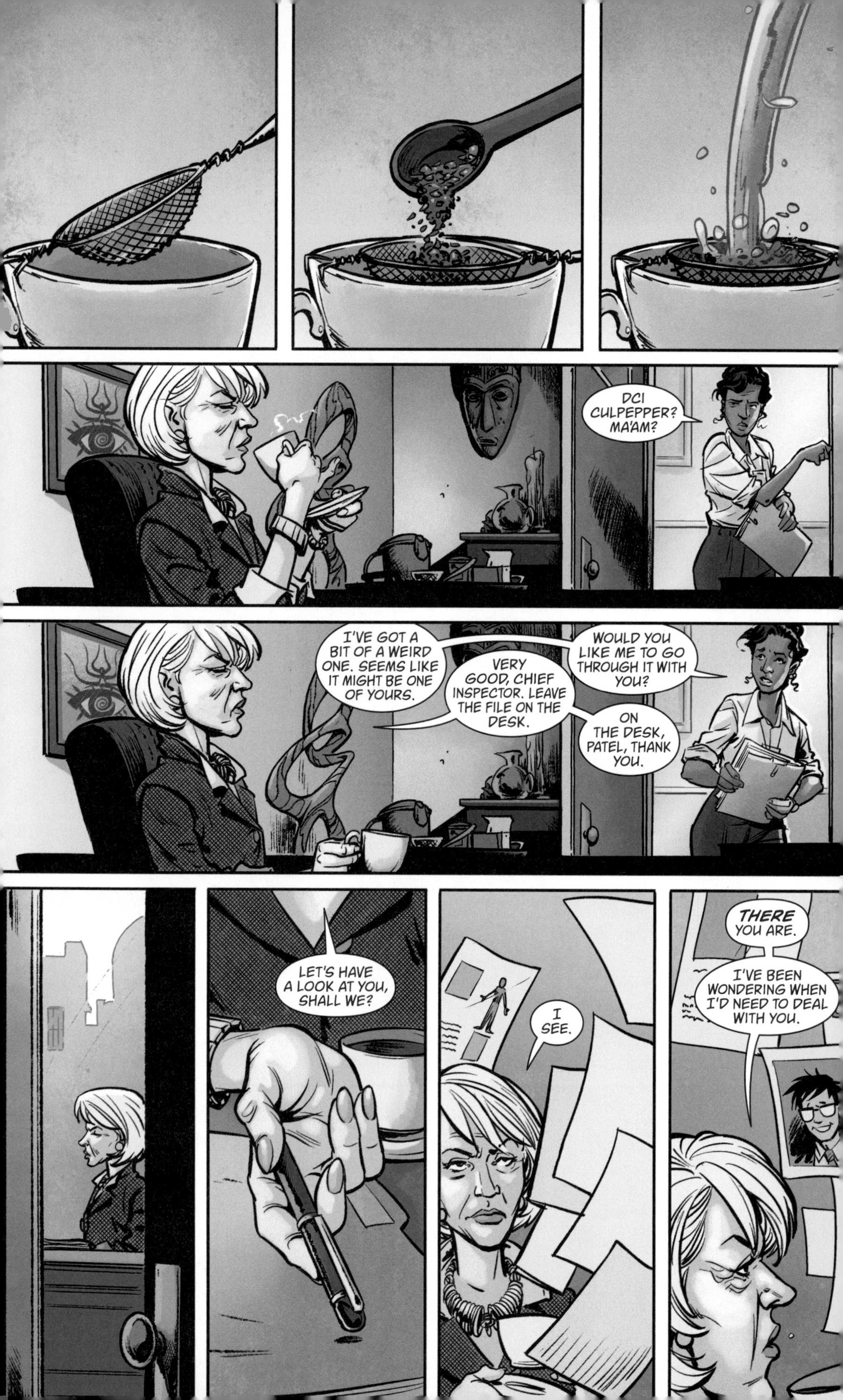
DCI CULPEPPER? MA'AM?
I'VE GOT A BIT OF A WEIRD ONE. SEEMS LIKE IT MIGHT BE ONE OF YOURS.
WOULD YOU LIKE ME TO GO THROUGH IT WITH YOU?
VERY GOOD, CHIEF INSPECTOR. LEAVE THE FILE ON THE DESK.
ON THE DESK, PATEL, THANK YOU.
LET'S HAVE A LOOK AT YOU, SHALL WE?
I SEE.
THERE YOU ARE.
I'VE BEEN WONDERING WHEN I'D NEED TO DEAL WITH YOU.

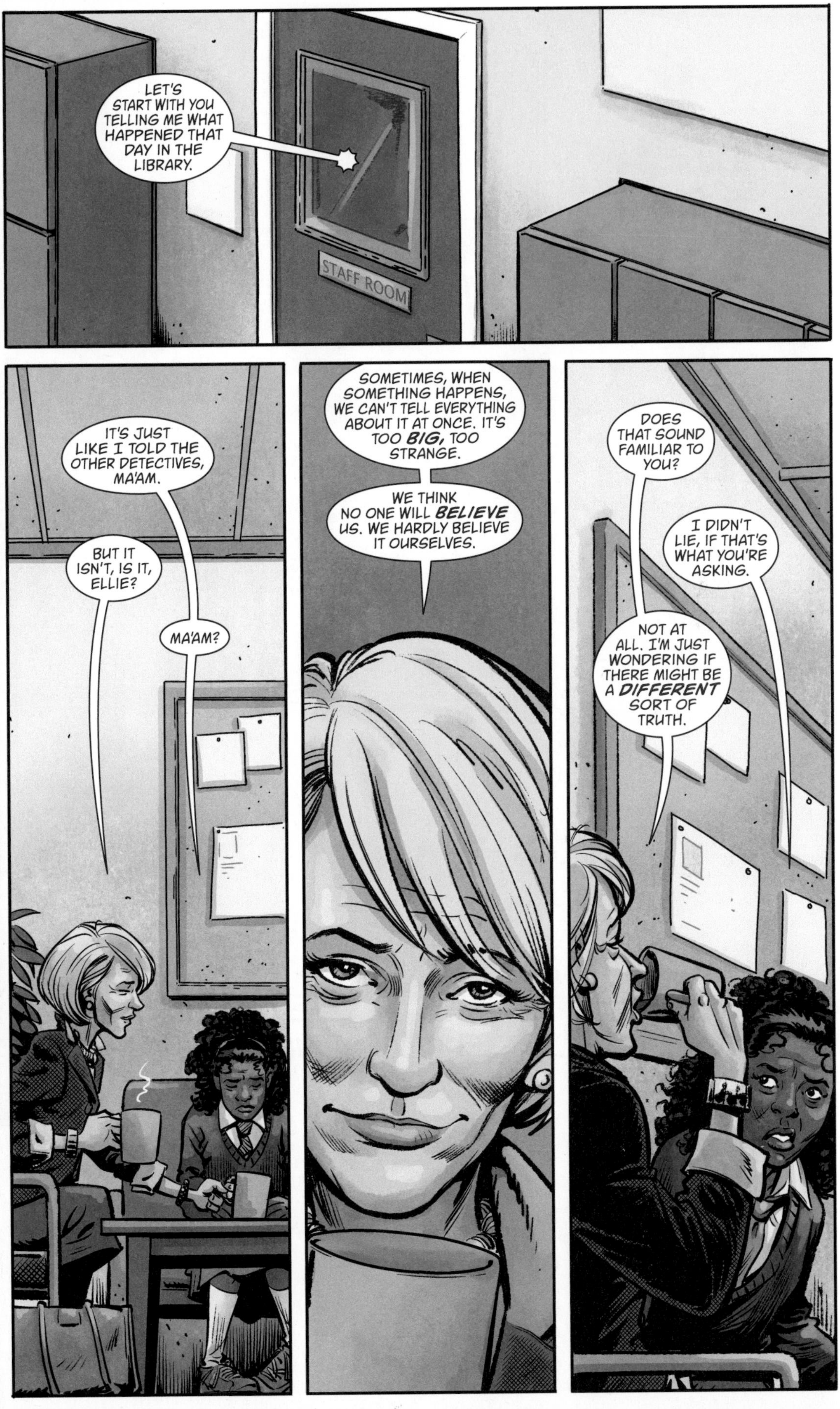
LET'S START WITH YOU TELLING ME WHAT HAPPENED THAT DAY IN THE LIBRARY.
STAFF ROOM
IT'S JUST LIKE I TOLD THE OTHER DETECTIVES, MA'AM.
BUT IT ISN'T, IS IT, ELLIE?
MA'AM?
SOMETIMES, WHEN SOMETHING HAPPENS, WE CAN'T TELL EVERYTHING ABOUT IT AT ONCE. IT'S TOO BIG, TOO STRANGE.
WE THINK NO ONE WILL BELIEVE US. WE HARDLY BELIEVE IT OURSELVES.
DOES THAT SOUND FAMILIAR TO YOU?
I DIDN'T LIE, IF THAT'S WHAT YOU'RE ASKING.
NOT AT ALL. I'M JUST WONDERING IF THERE MIGHT BE A DIFFERENT SORT OF TRUTH.

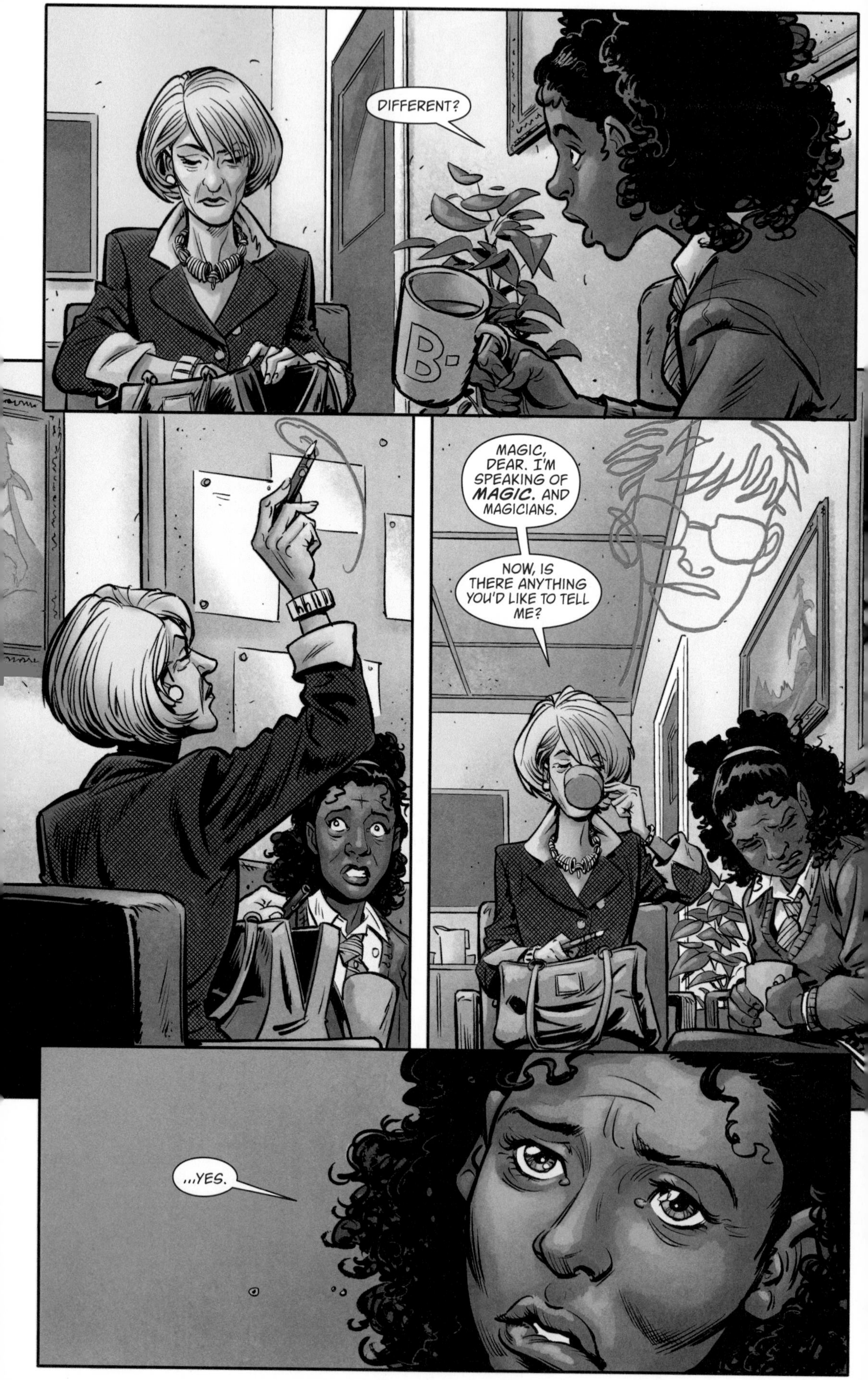
DIFFERENT?
MAGIC, DEAR. I'M SPEAKING OF MAGIC. AND MAGICIANS.
NOW, IS THERE ANYTHING YOU'D LIKE TO TELL ME?
...YES.

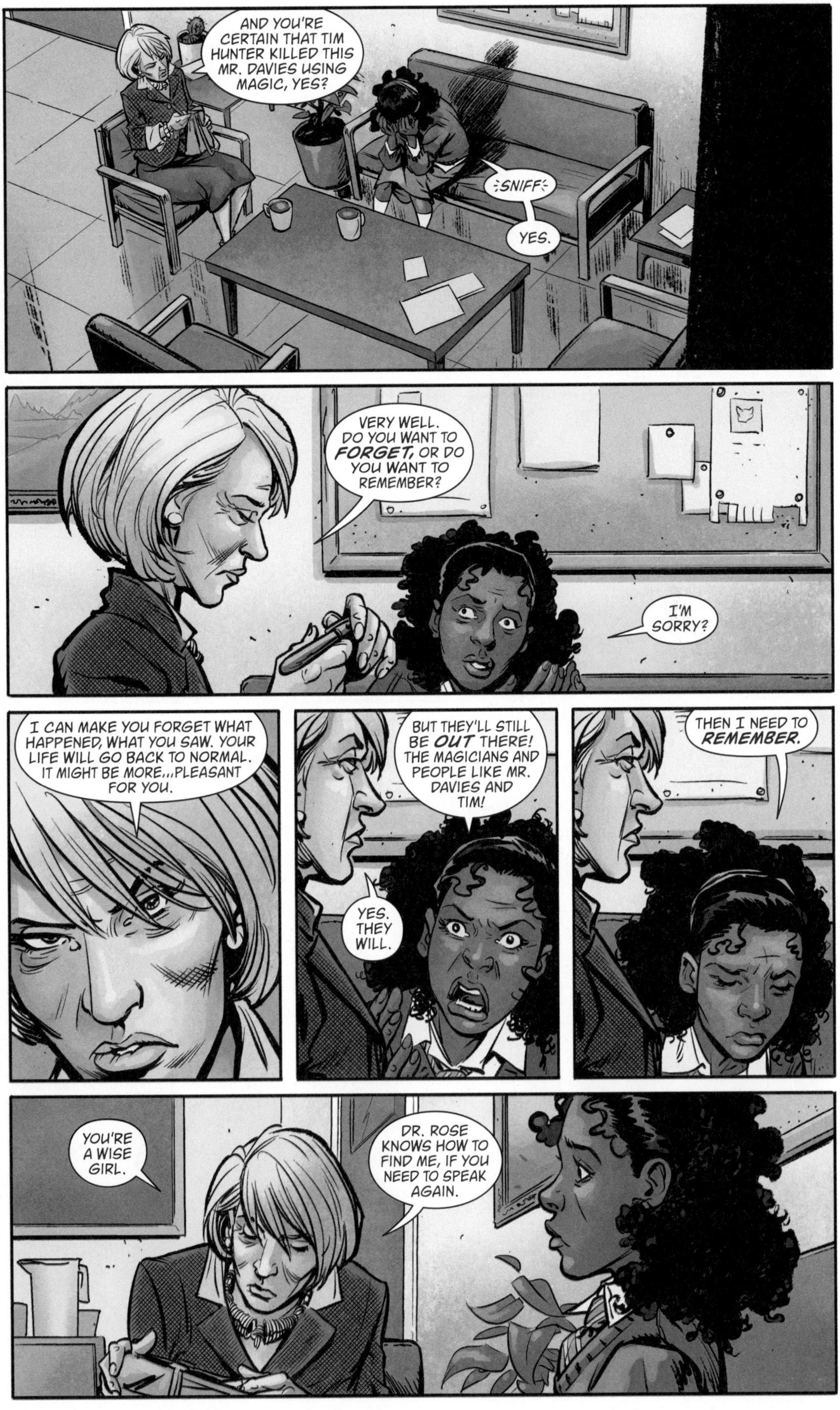
AND YOU'RE CERTAIN THAT TIM HUNTER KILLED THIS MR. DAVIES USING MAGIC, YES?
SNIFF
YES.
VERY WELL. DO YOU WANT TO FORGET, OR DO YOU WANT TO REMEMBER?
I'M SORRY?
I CAN MAKE YOU FORGET WHAT HAPPENED, WHAT YOU SAW. YOUR LIFE WILL GO BACK TO NORMAL. IT MIGHT BE MORE...PLEASANT FOR YOU.
BUT THEY'LL STILL BE OUT THERE! THE MAGICIANS AND PEOPLE LIKE MR. DAVIES AND TIM!
YES. THEY WILL.
THEN I NEED TO REMEMBER.
YOU'RE A WISE GIRL.
DR. ROSE KNOWS HOW TO FIND ME, IF YOU NEED TO SPEAK AGAIN.

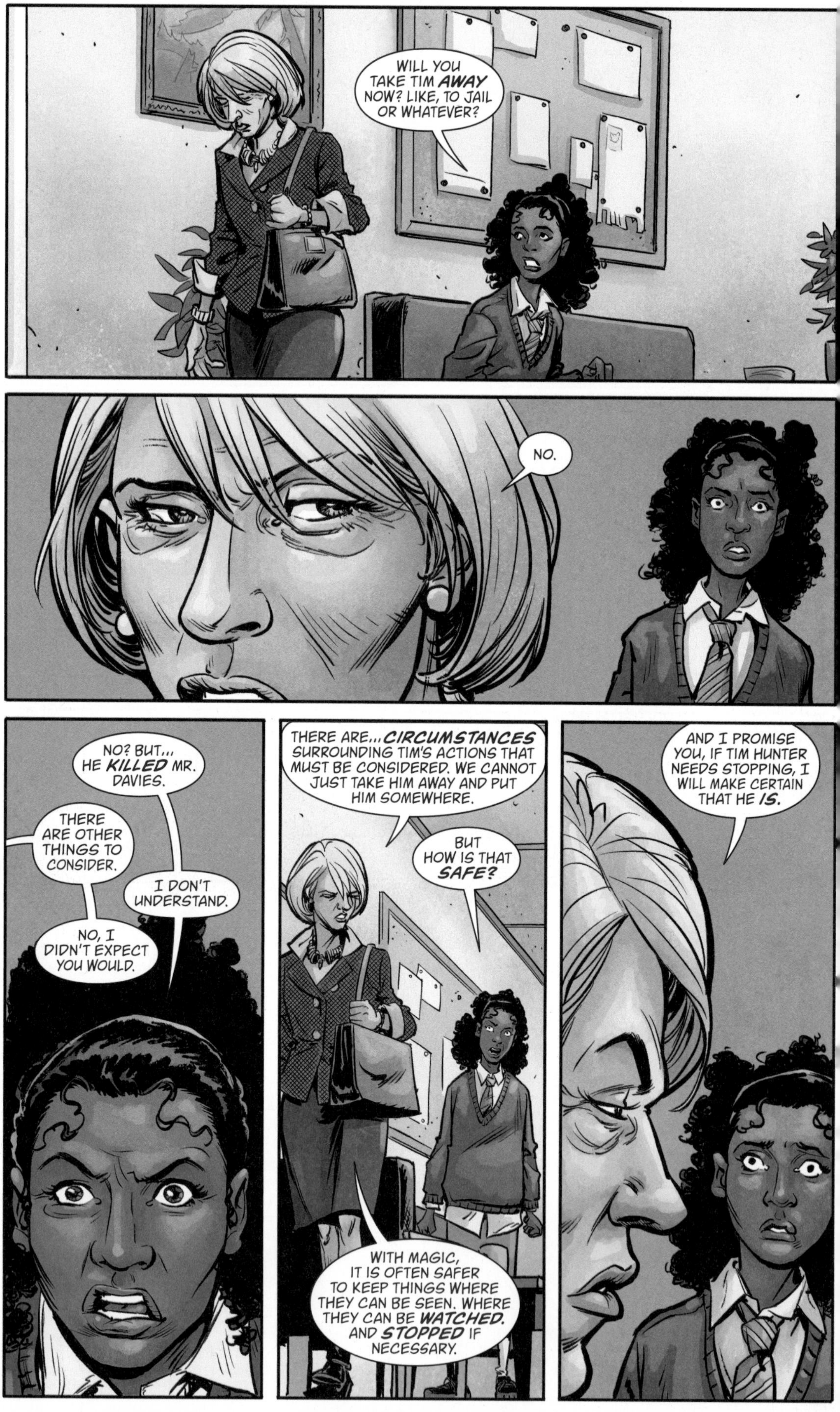
WILL YOU TAKE TIM AWAY NOW? LIKE, TO JAIL OR WHATEVER?
NO.
NO? BUT... HE KILLED MR. DAVIES.
THERE ARE OTHER THINGS TO CONSIDER.
I DON'T UNDERSTAND.
NO, I DIDN'T EXPECT YOU WOULD.
THERE ARE... CIRCUMSTANCES SURROUNDING TIM'S ACTIONS THAT MUST BE CONSIDERED. WE CANNOT JUST TAKE HIM AWAY AND PUT HIM SOMEWHERE.
BUT HOW IS THAT SAFE?
WITH MAGIC, IT IS OFTEN SAFER TO KEEP THINGS WHERE THEY CAN BE SEEN. WHERE THEY CAN BE WATCHED. AND STOPPED IF NECESSARY.
AND I PROMISE YOU, IF TIM HUNTER NEEDS STOPPING, I WILL MAKE CERTAIN THAT HE IS.

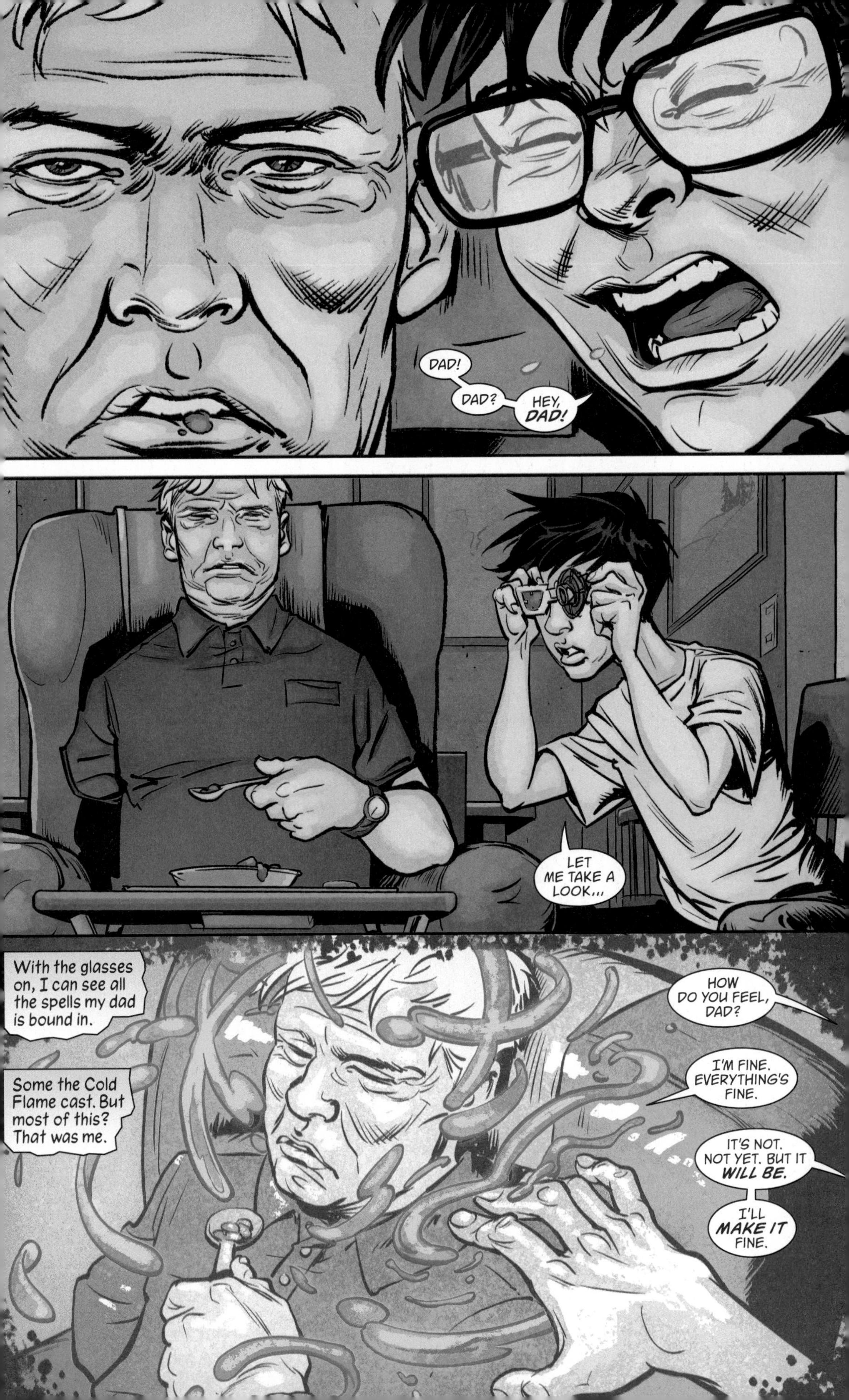
DAD!
DAD?
HEY, DAD!
LET ME TAKE A LOOK...
With the glasses on, I can see all the spells my dad is bound in.
HOW DO YOU FEEL, DAD?
Some the Cold Flame cast. But most of this? That was me.
I'M FINE. EVERYTHING'S FINE.
IT'S NOT. NOT YET. BUT IT WILL BE.
I'LL MAKE IT FINE.

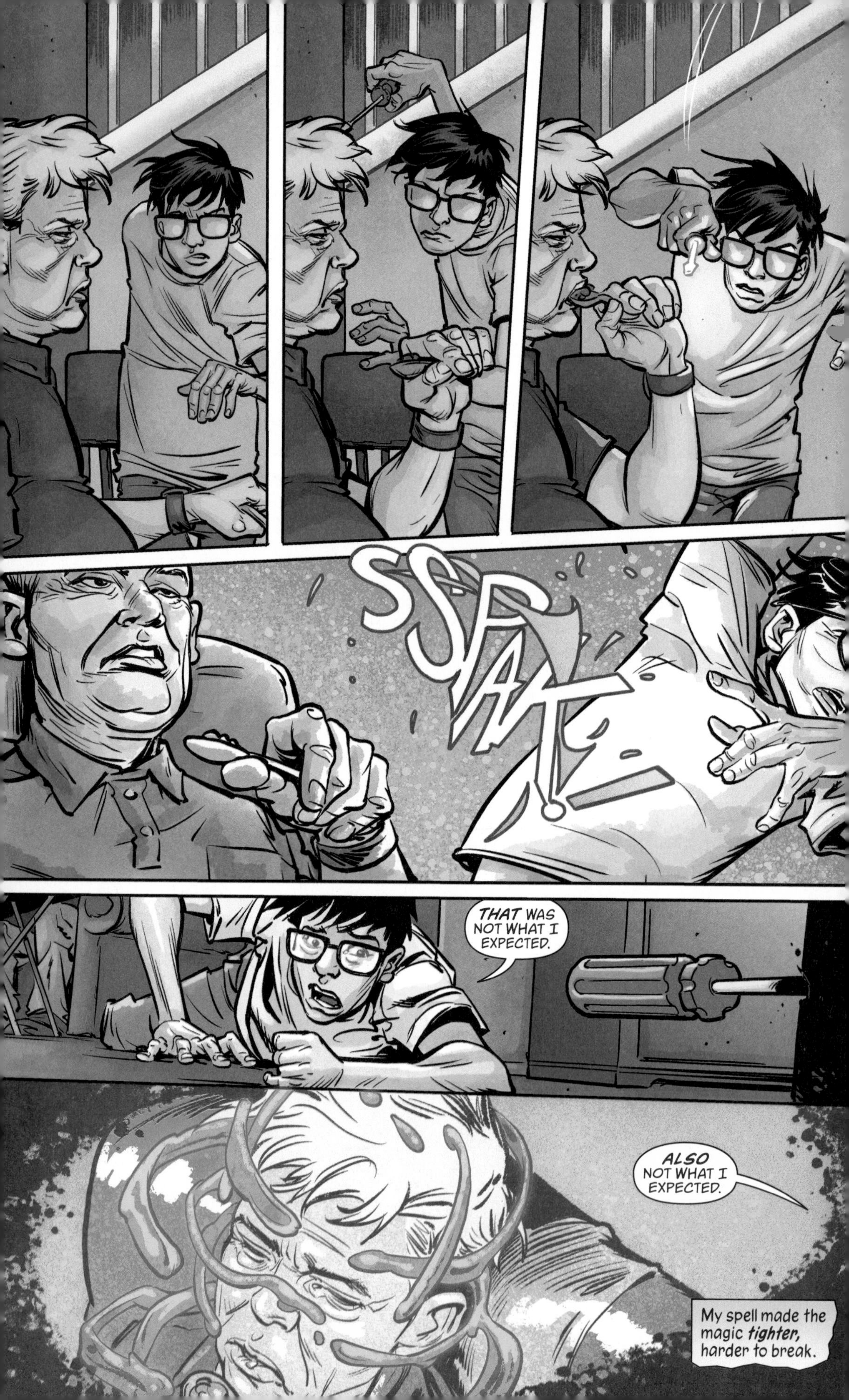
SSPAT
THAT WAS NOT WHAT I EXPECTED.
ALSO NOT WHAT I EXPECTED.
My spell made the magic tighter, harder to break.

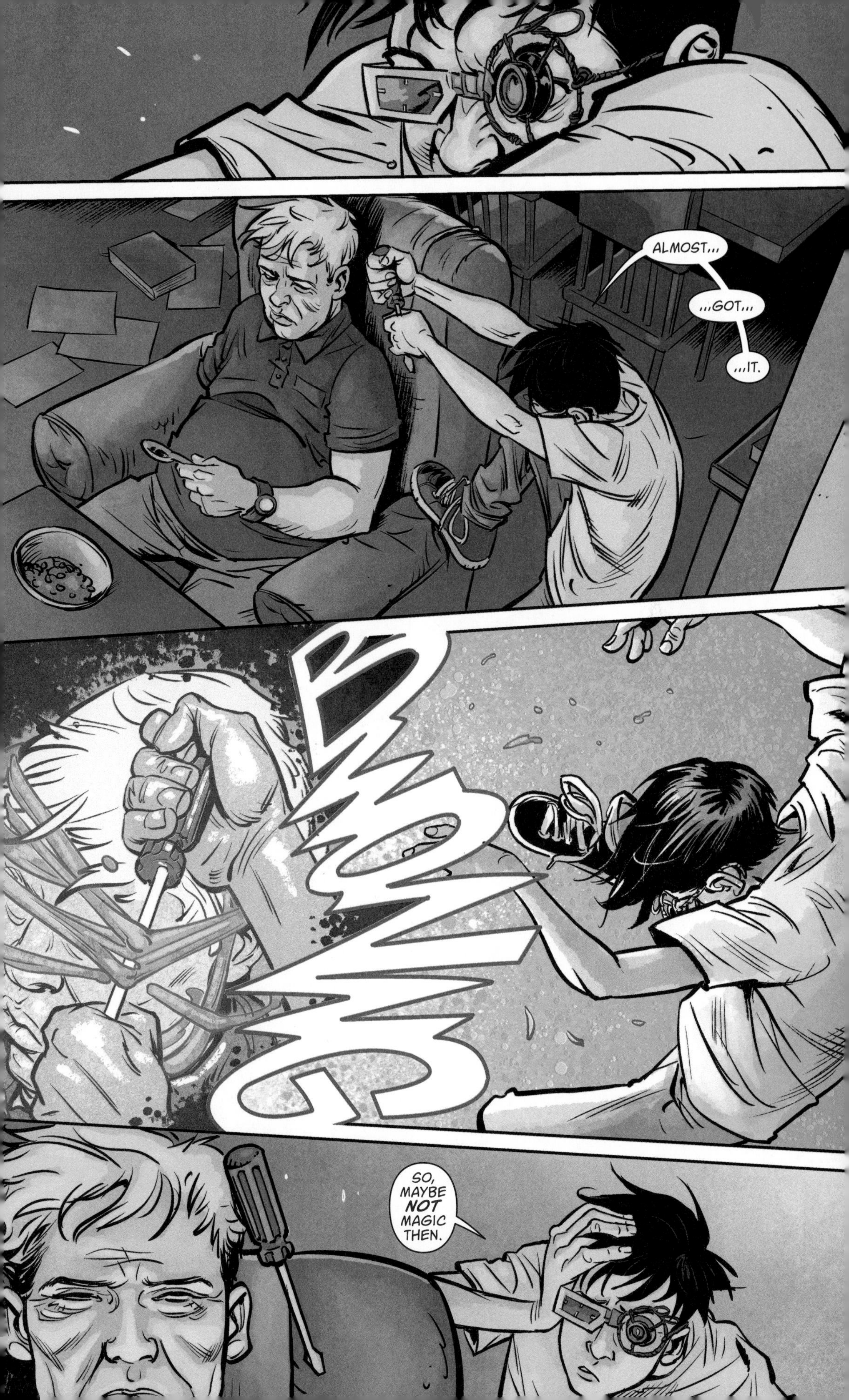
ALMOST...
...GOT...
...IT.
BWOWG
SO, MAYBE ***NOT*** MAGIC THEN.

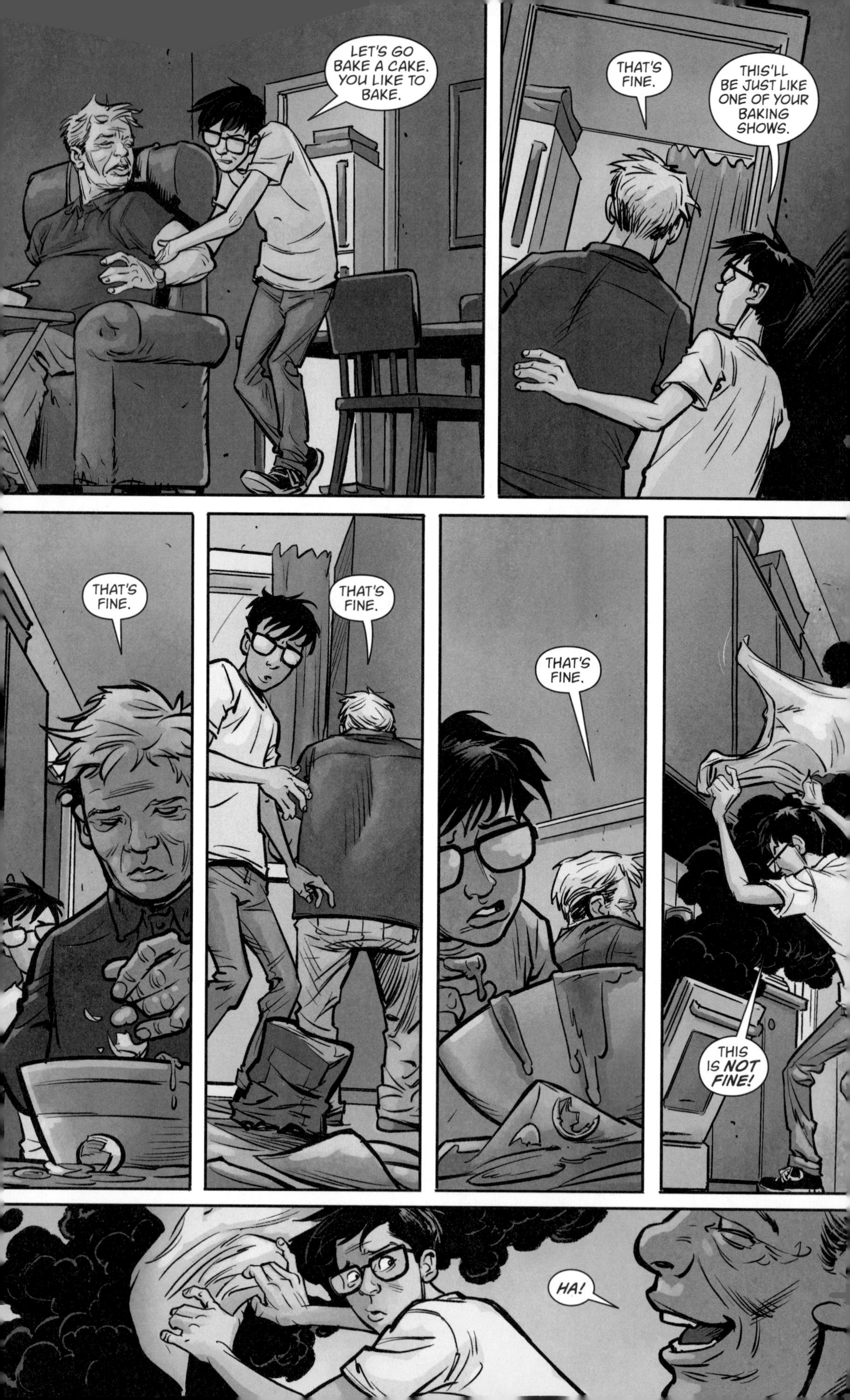
LET'S GO BAKE A CAKE. YOU LIKE TO BAKE.
THAT'S FINE.
THIS'LL BE JUST LIKE ONE OF YOUR BAKING SHOWS.
THAT'S FINE.
THAT'S FINE.
THAT'S FINE.
THIS IS NOT FINE!
HA!

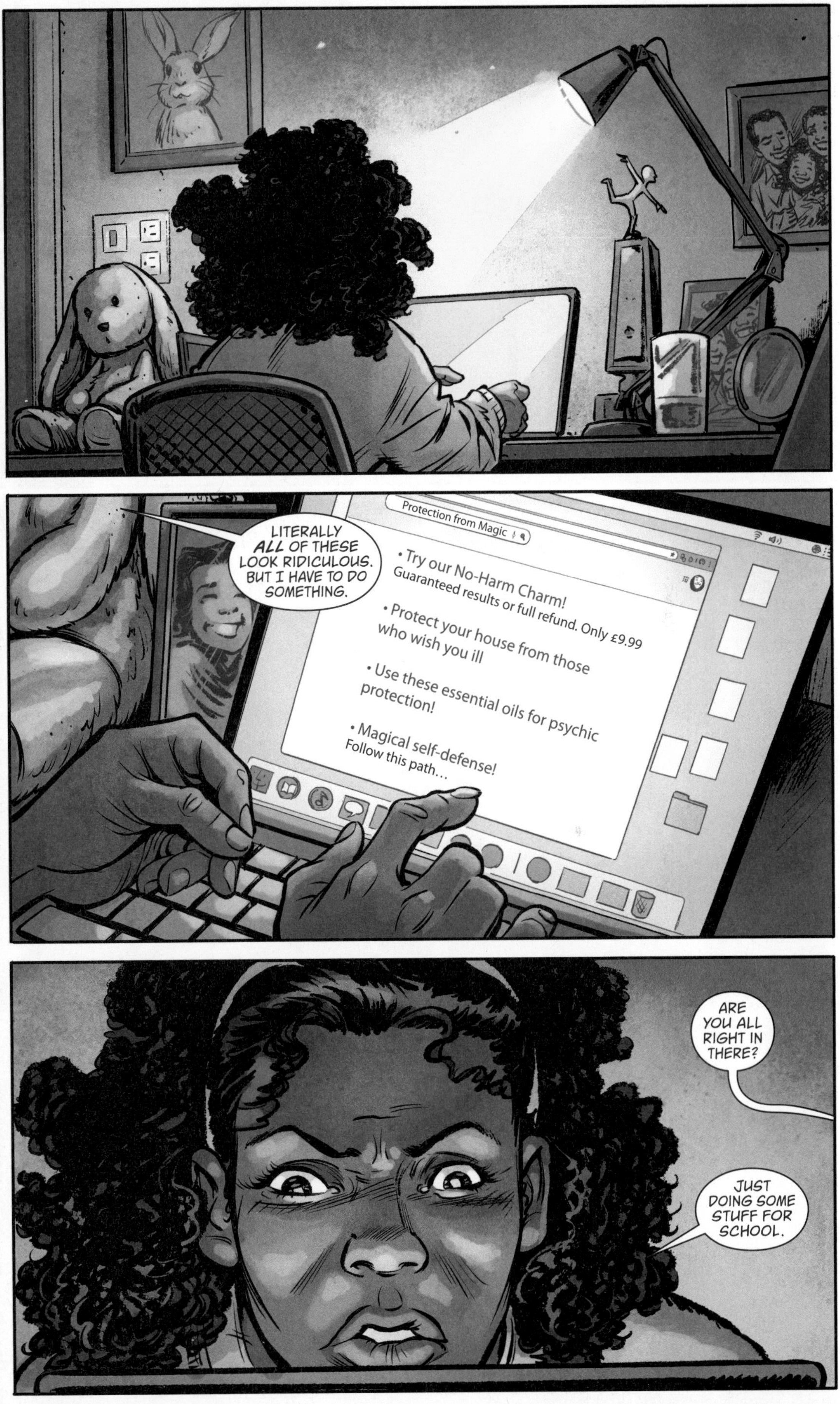
Protection from Magic
LITERALLY ALL OF THESE LOOK RIDICULOUS. BUT I HAVE TO DO SOMETHING.
• Try our No-Harm Charm! Guaranteed results or full refund. Only £9.99
• Protect your house from those who wish you ill
• Use these essential oils for psychic protection!
• Magical self-defense! Follow this path…
ARE YOU ALL RIGHT IN THERE?
JUST DOING SOME STUFF FOR SCHOOL.

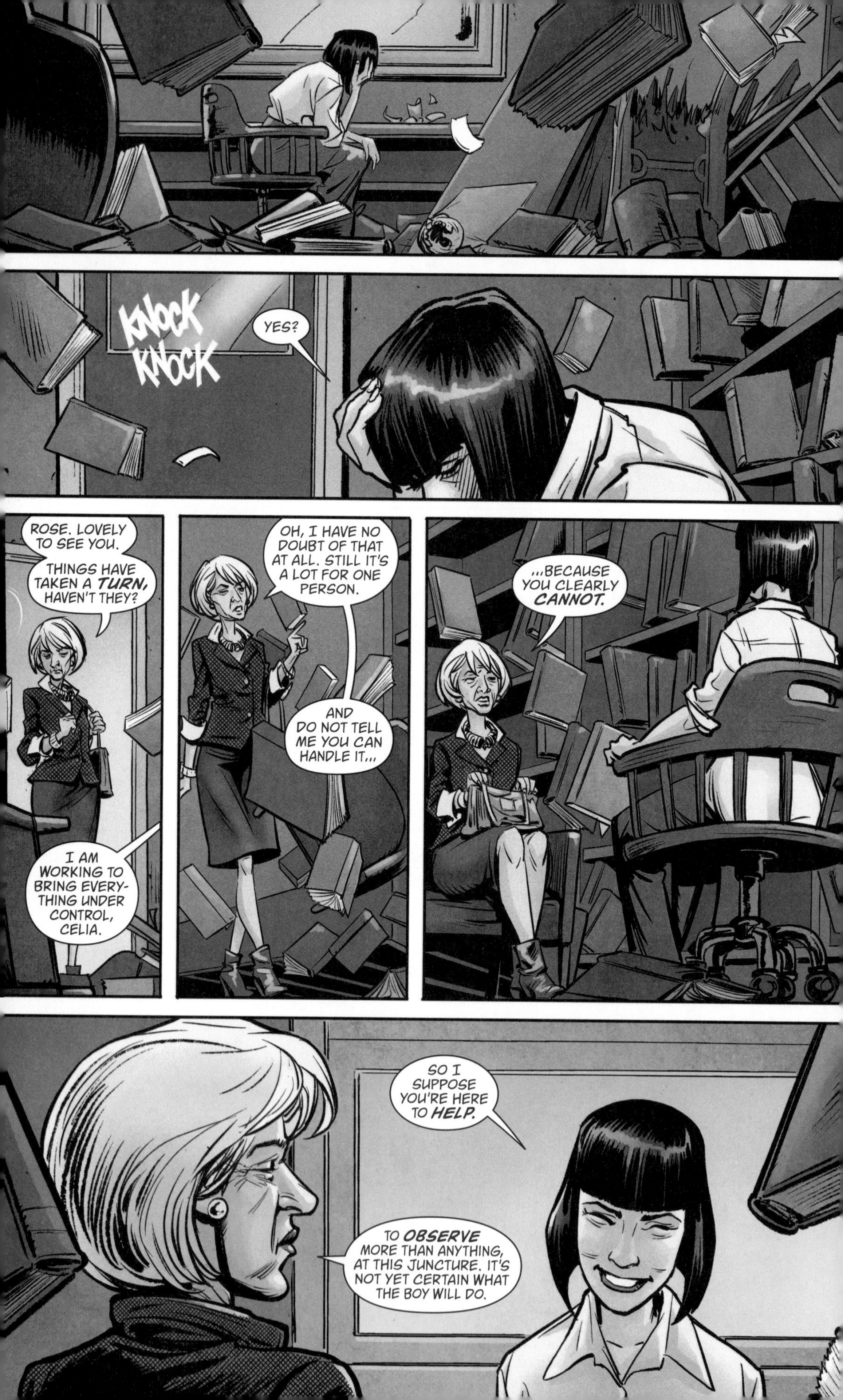
KNOCK KNOCK
YES?
ROSE. LOVELY TO SEE YOU.
THINGS HAVE TAKEN A TURN, HAVEN'T THEY?
I AM WORKING TO BRING EVERY-THING UNDER CONTROL, CELIA.
OH, I HAVE NO DOUBT OF THAT AT ALL. STILL IT'S A LOT FOR ONE PERSON.
AND DO NOT TELL ME YOU CAN HANDLE IT...
...BECAUSE YOU CLEARLY CANNOT.
SO I SUPPOSE YOU'RE HERE TO HELP.
TO OBSERVE MORE THAN ANYTHING, AT THIS JUNCTURE. IT'S NOT YET CERTAIN WHAT THE BOY WILL DO.

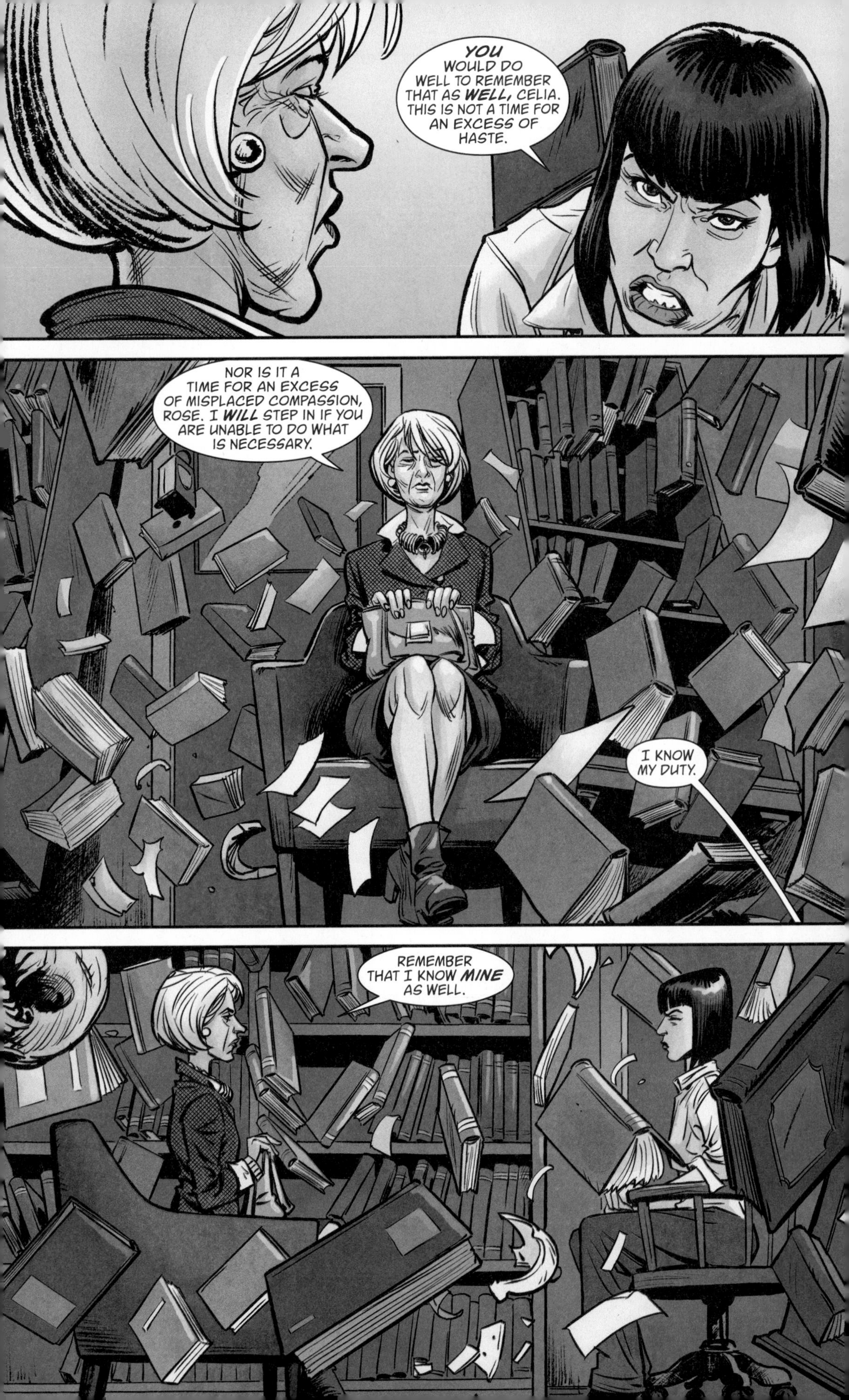
YOU WOULD DO WELL TO REMEMBER THAT AS WELL, CELIA. THIS IS NOT A TIME FOR AN EXCESS OF HASTE.
NOR IS IT A TIME FOR AN EXCESS OF MISPLACED COMPASSION, ROSE. I WILL STEP IN IF YOU ARE UNABLE TO DO WHAT IS NECESSARY.
I KNOW MY DUTY.
REMEMBER THAT I KNOW MINE AS WELL.

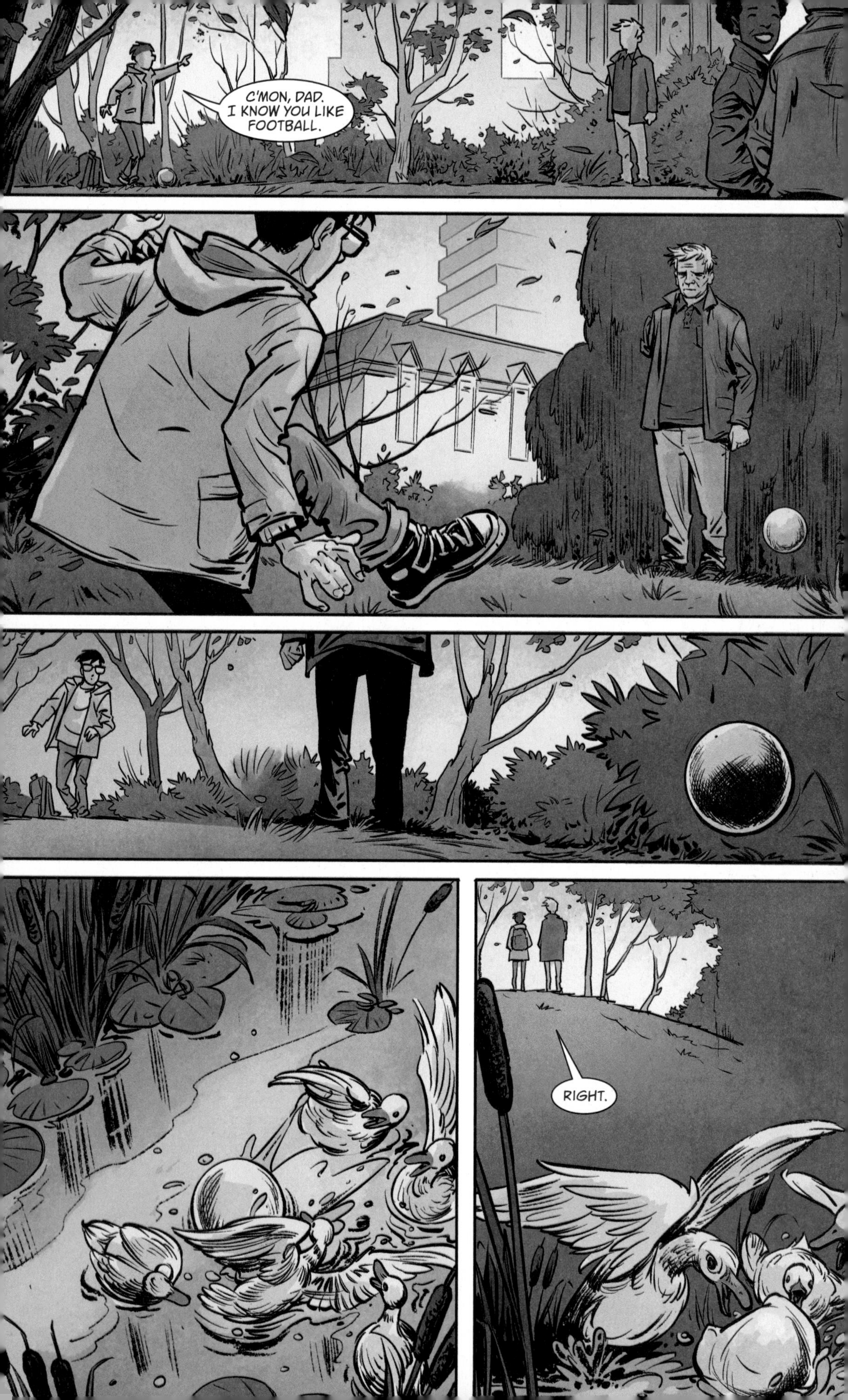
C'MON, DAD. I KNOW YOU LIKE FOOTBALL.
RIGHT.

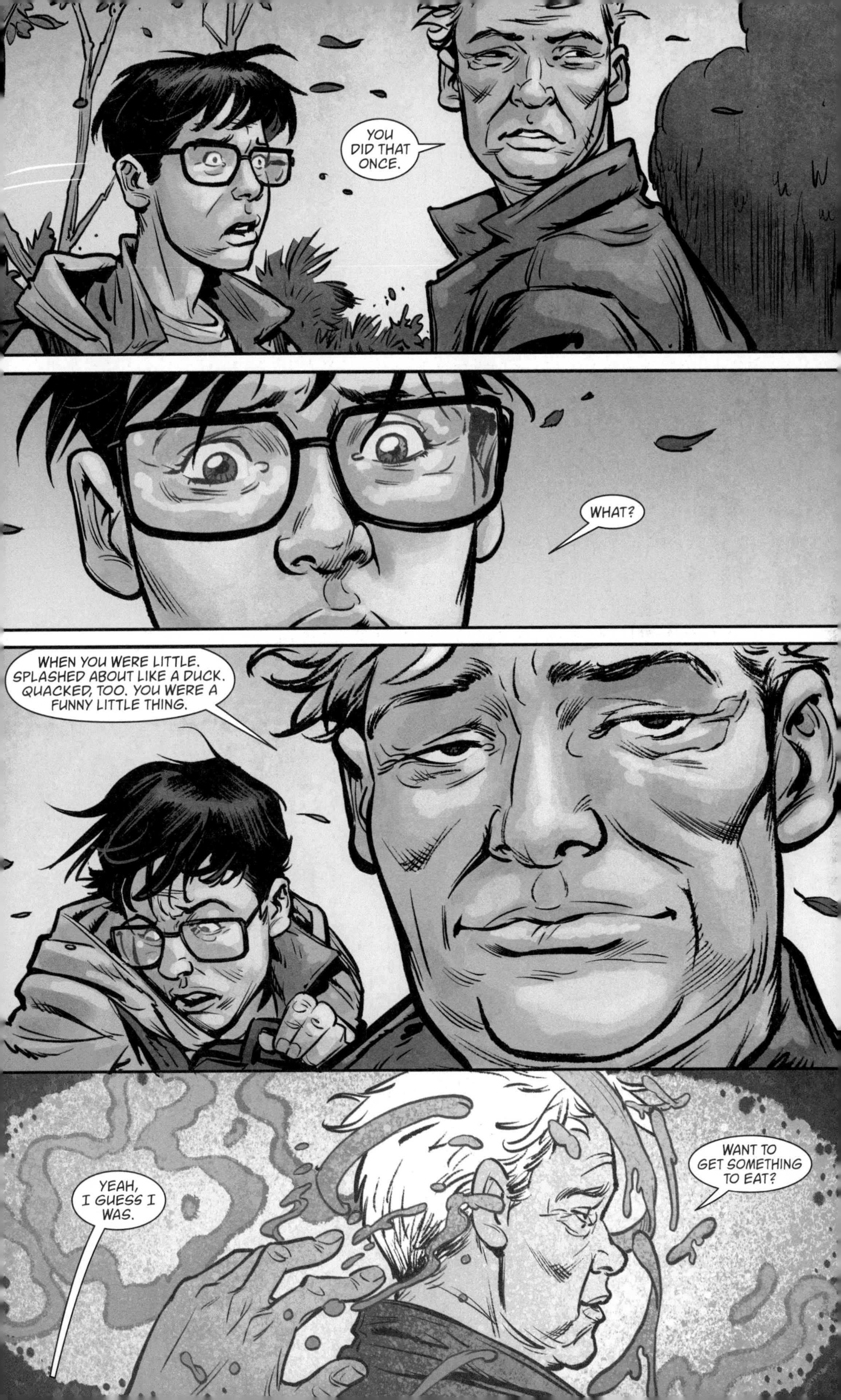
YOU DID THAT ONCE.
WHAT?
WHEN YOU WERE LITTLE. SPLASHED ABOUT LIKE A DUCK. QUACKED, TOO. YOU WERE A FUNNY LITTLE THING.
WANT TO GET SOMETHING TO EAT?
YEAH, I GUESS I WAS.

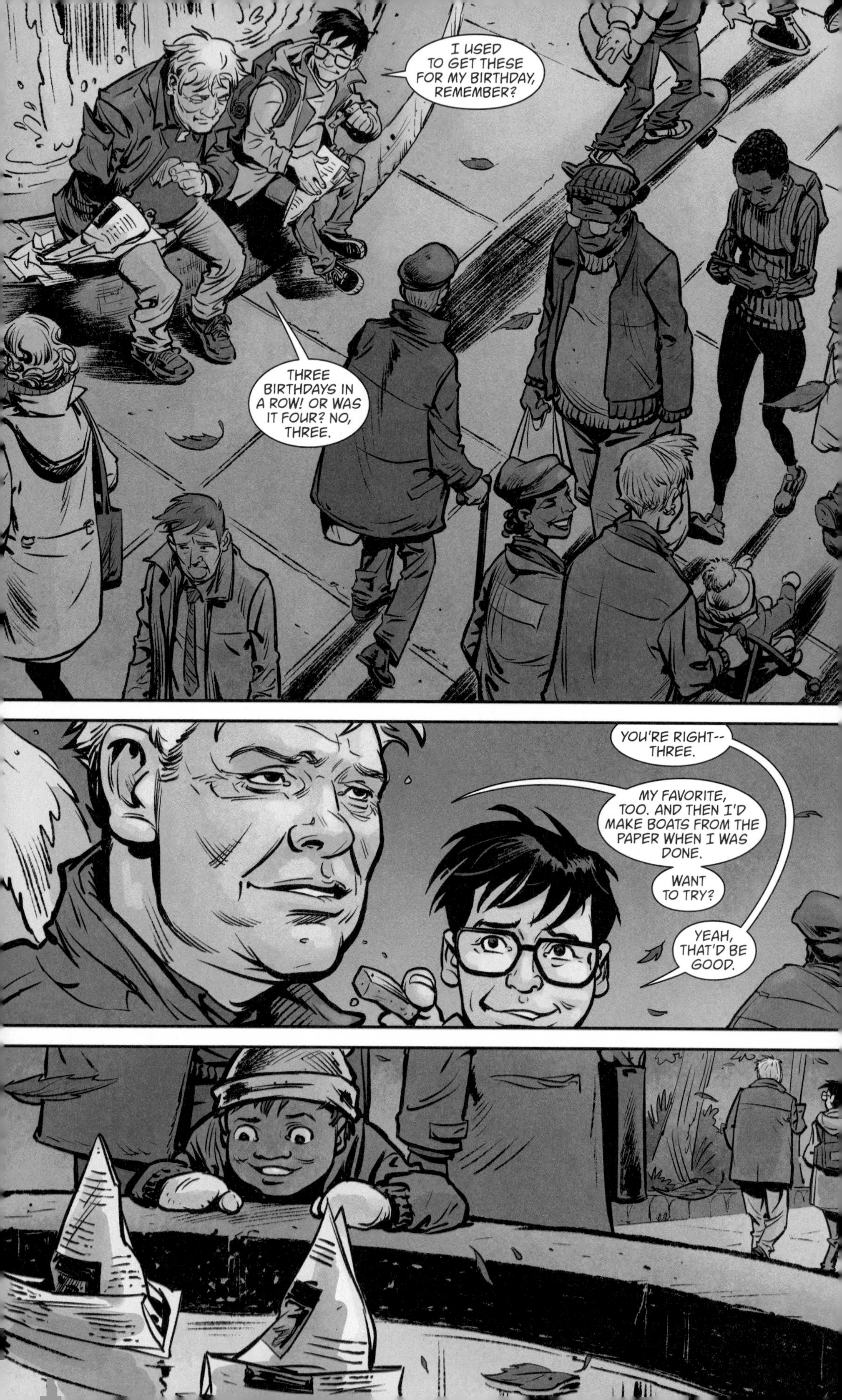
I USED TO GET THESE FOR MY BIRTHDAY, REMEMBER?
THREE BIRTHDAYS IN A ROW! OR WAS IT FOUR? NO, THREE.
YOU'RE RIGHT-- THREE.
MY FAVORITE, TOO. AND THEN I'D MAKE BOATS FROM THE PAPER WHEN I WAS DONE.
WANT TO TRY?
YEAH, THAT'D BE GOOD.

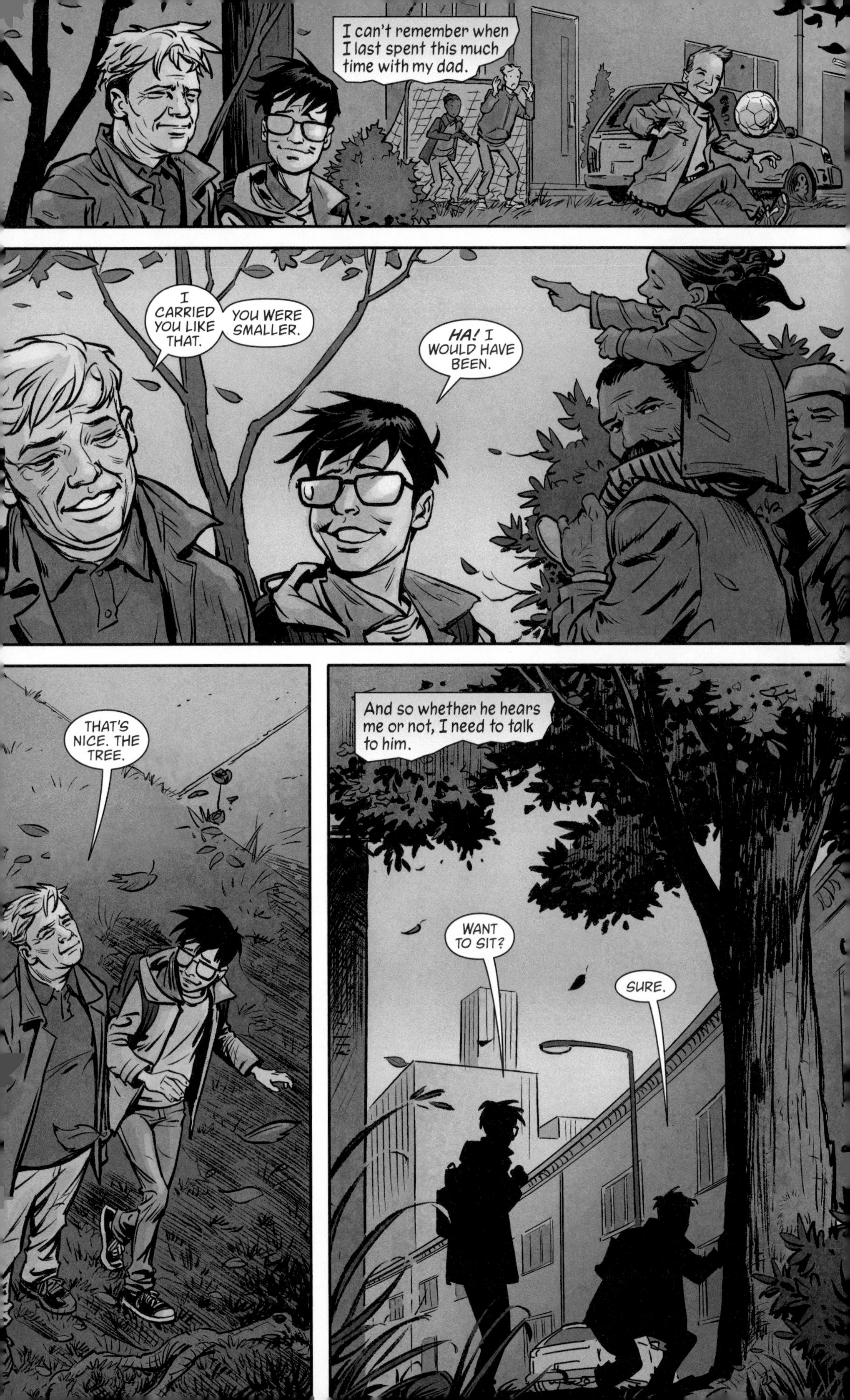
I can't remember when I last spent this much time with my dad.
I CARRIED YOU LIKE THAT.
YOU WERE SMALLER.
HA! I WOULD HAVE BEEN.
THAT'S NICE. THE TREE.
And so whether he hears me or not, I need to talk to him.
WANT TO SIT?
SURE.

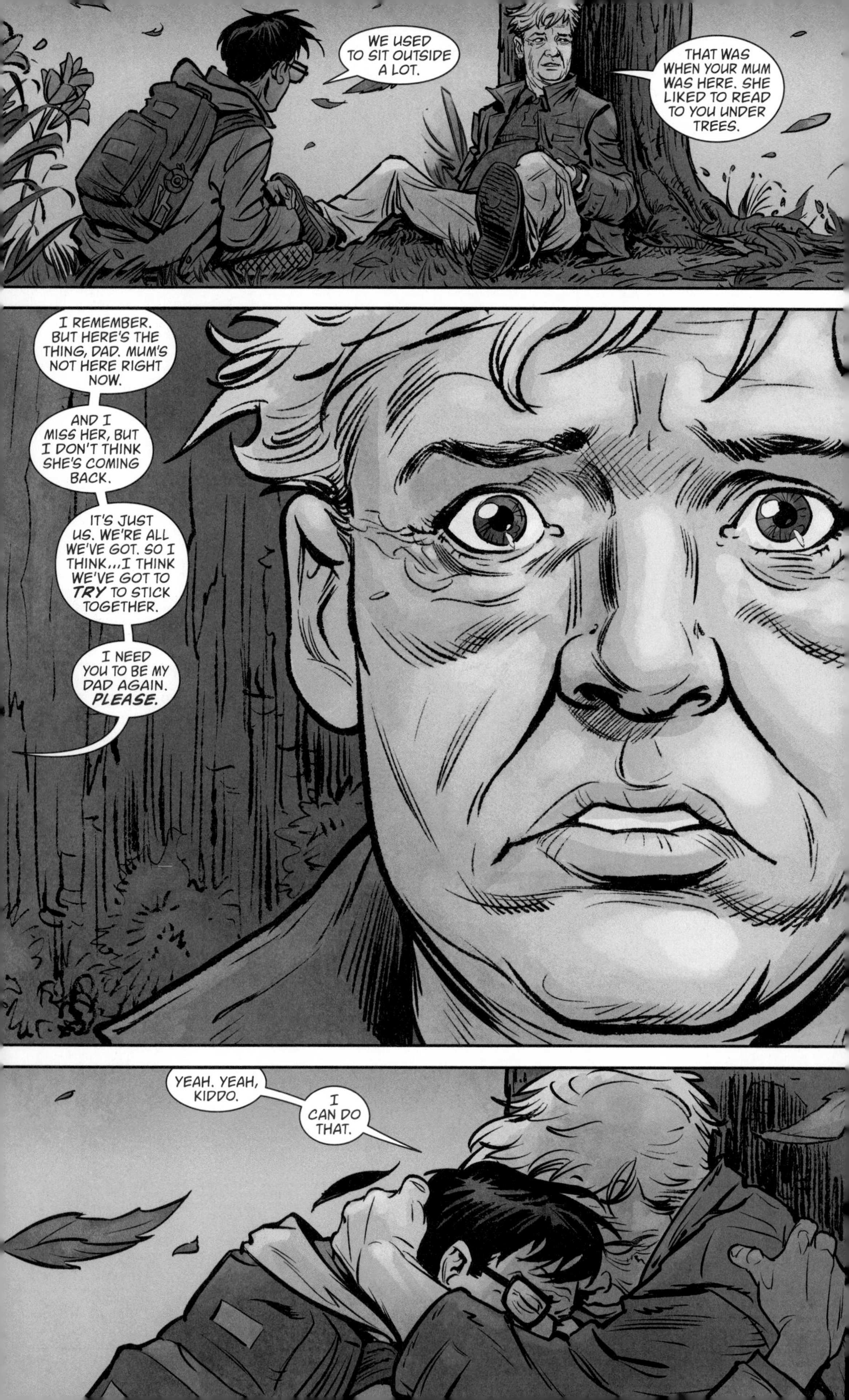
WE USED TO SIT OUTSIDE A LOT.
THAT WAS WHEN YOUR MUM WAS HERE. SHE LIKED TO READ TO YOU UNDER TREES.
I REMEMBER. BUT HERE'S THE THING, DAD. MUM'S NOT HERE RIGHT NOW.
AND I MISS HER, BUT I DON'T THINK SHE'S COMING BACK.
IT'S JUST US. WE'RE ALL WE'VE GOT. SO I THINK...I THINK WE'VE GOT TO *TRY* TO STICK TOGETHER.
I NEED YOU TO BE MY DAD AGAIN. ***PLEASE.***
YEAH. YEAH, KIDDO.
I CAN DO THAT.

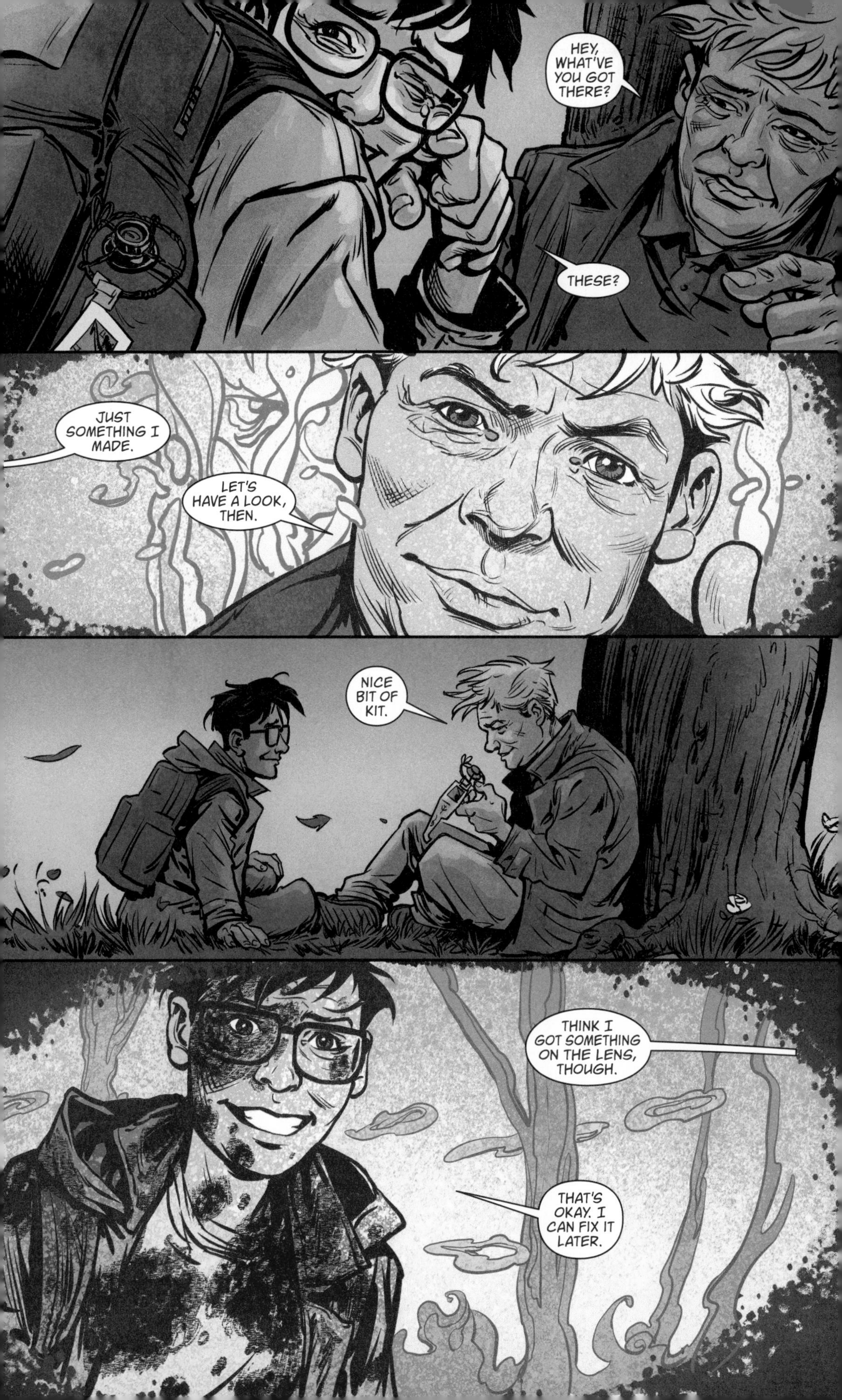

HEY, WHAT'VE YOU GOT THERE?
THESE?
JUST SOMETHING I MADE.
LET'S HAVE A LOOK, THEN.
NICE BIT OF KIT.
THINK I GOT SOMETHING ON THE LENS, THOUGH.
THAT'S OKAY. I CAN FIX IT LATER.

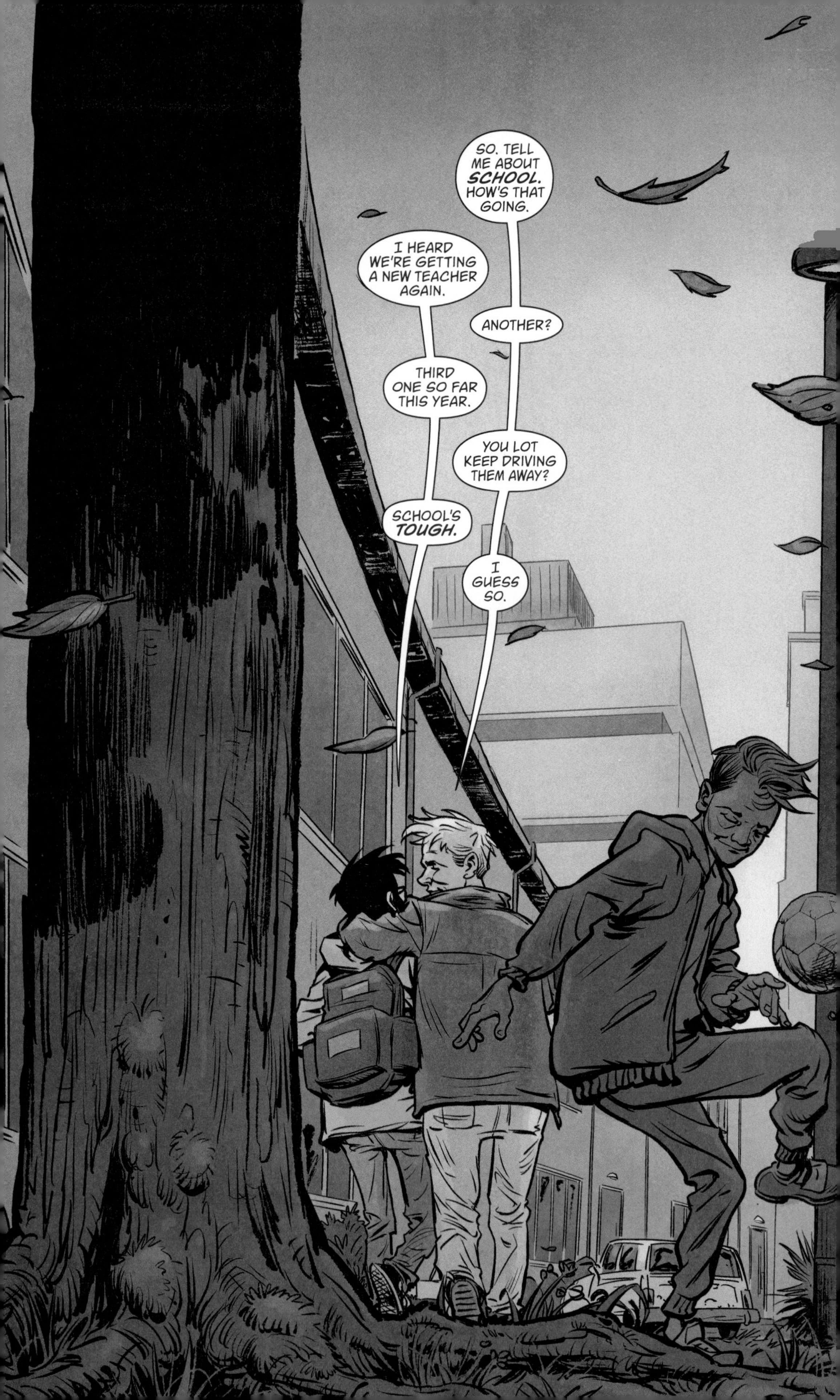
SO. TELL ME ABOUT SCHOOL. HOW'S THAT GOING.
I HEARD WE'RE GETTING A NEW TEACHER AGAIN.
ANOTHER?
THIRD ONE SO FAR THIS YEAR.
YOU LOT KEEP DRIVING THEM AWAY?
SCHOOL'S TOUGH.
I GUESS SO.

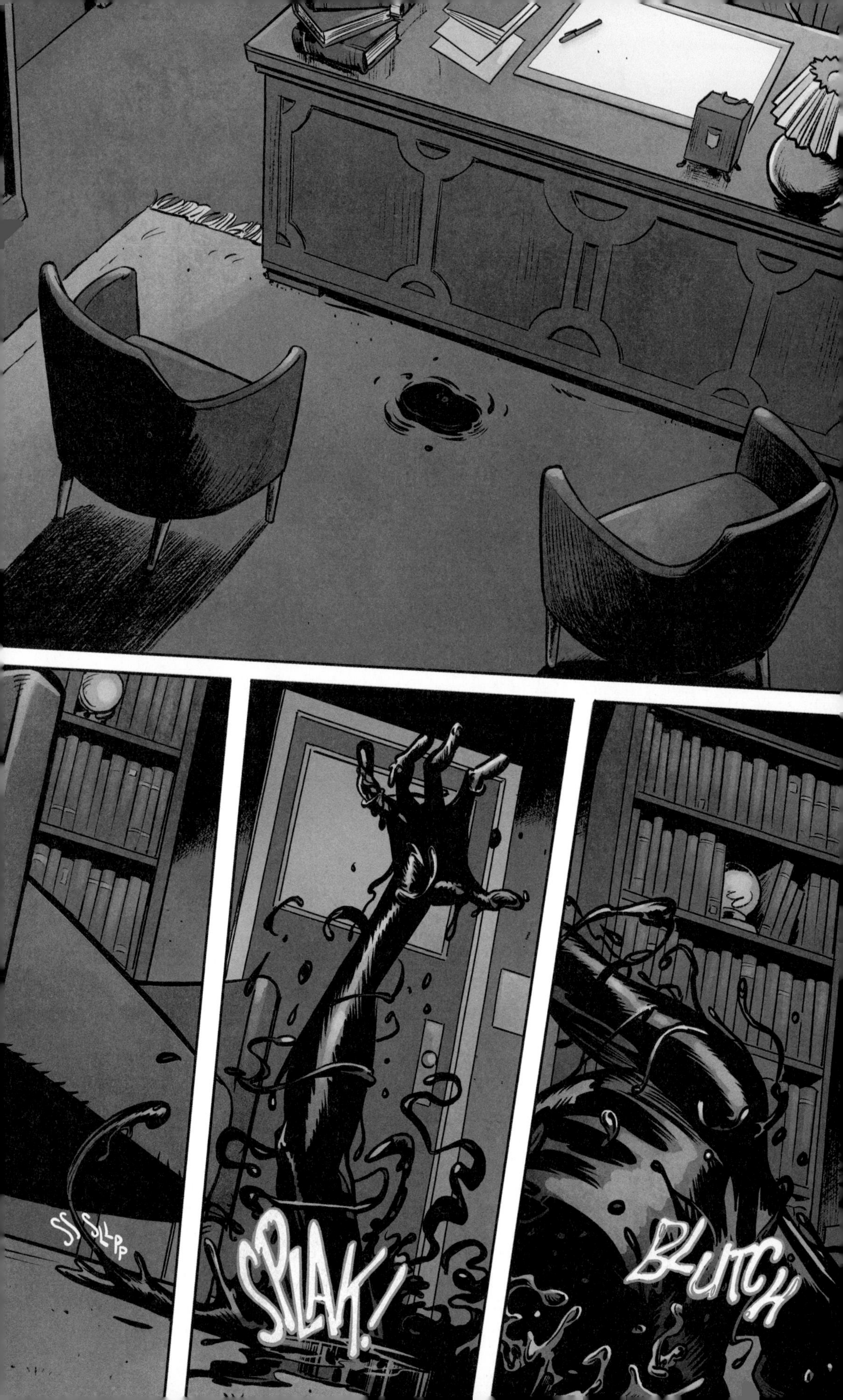
SSSLLPP
SPLAK!
BLUTCH

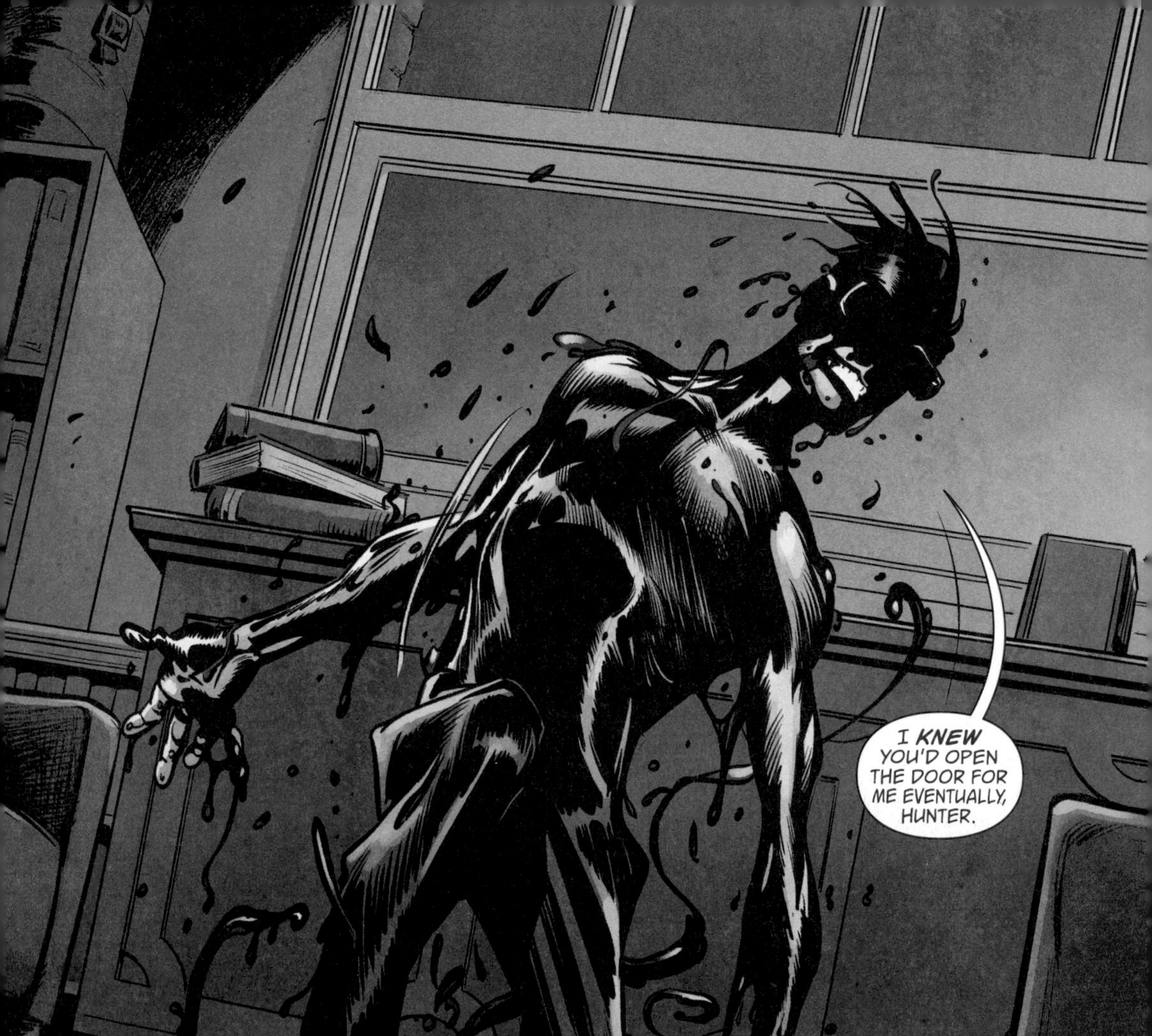
I KNEW YOU'D OPEN THE DOOR FOR ME EVENTUALLY, HUNTER.

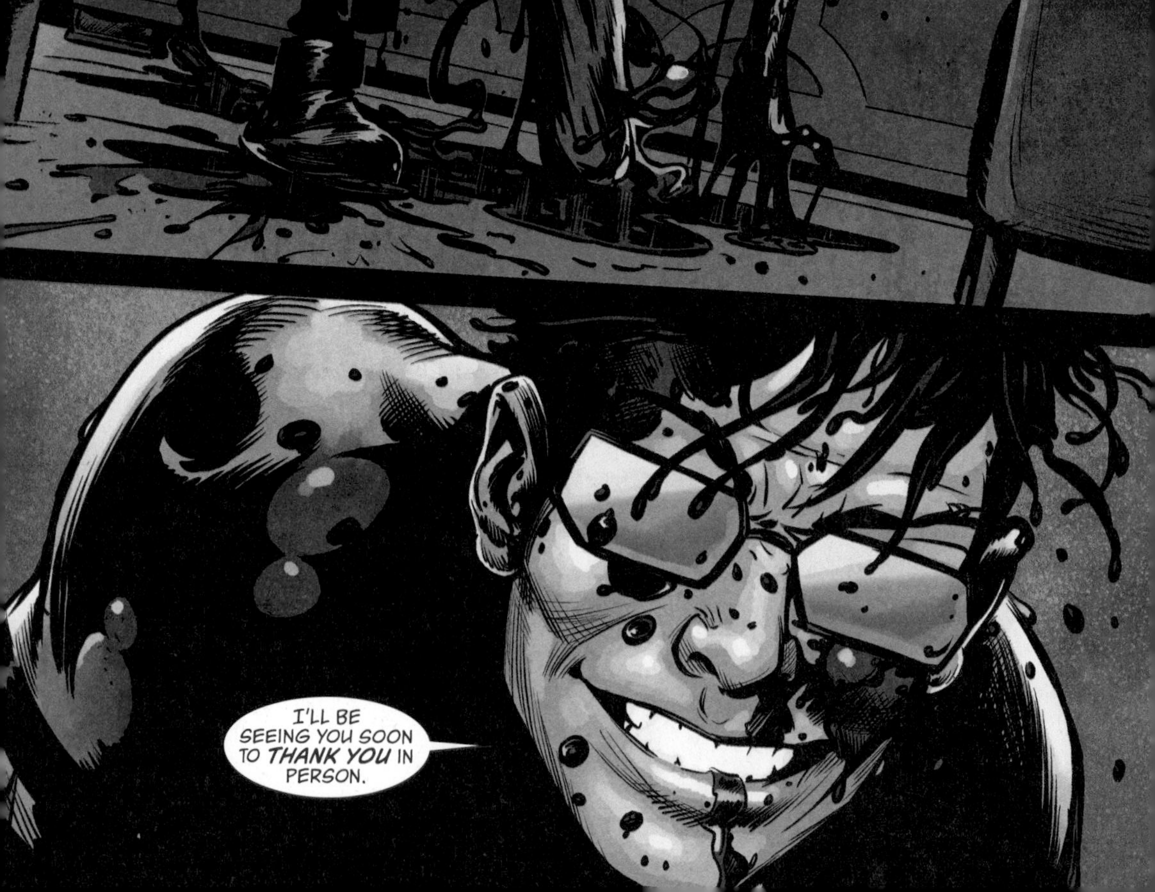
I'LL BE SEEING YOU SOON TO THANK YOU IN PERSON.

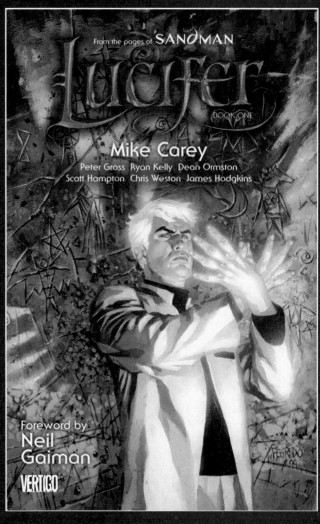
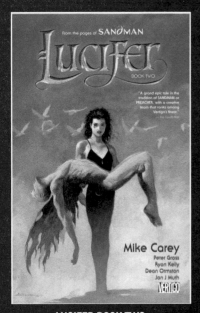
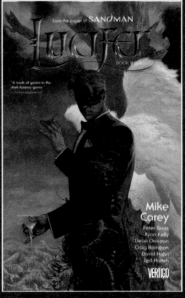

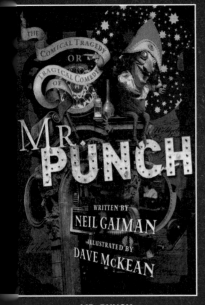

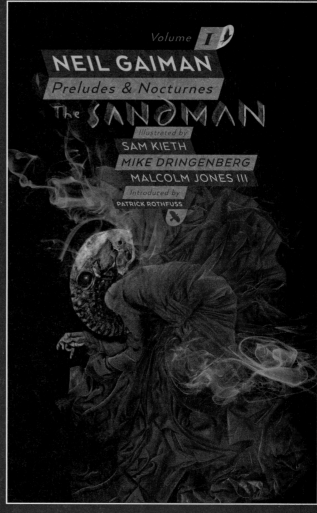

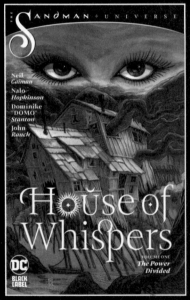